The Cinema of Ettore Scola

CONTEMPORARY APPROACHES TO FILM AND MEDIA SERIES
A complete listing of the books in this series can be found online at
wsupress.wayne.edu.

GENERAL EDITOR
Barry Keith Grant
Brock University

THE CINEMA OF ETTORE SCOLA

EDITED BY REMI LANZONI AND EDWARD BOWEN

WAYNE STATE UNIVERSITY PRESS
Detroit

© 2020 by Wayne State University Press, Detroit, Michigan 48201.
All rights reserved. No part of this book may be reproduced without formal permission.

ISBN 978-0-8143-4379-1 (paperback)
ISBN 978-0-8143-4747-8 (hardcover)
ISBN 978-0-8143-4380-7 (e-book)

Library of Congress Control Number: 2020931835

Wayne State University Press
Leonard N. Simons Building
4809 Woodward Avenue
Detroit, Michigan 48201–1309

Visit us online at wsupress.wayne.edu

Dedicated to Peter Bondanella

CONTENTS

Foreword   xi

Acknowledgments   xvii

Introduction   1
Edward Bowen and Rémi Lanzoni

PART 1. SCOLA AS SCREENWRITER AND DIRECTOR OF COMEDY ITALIAN STYLE

Thinking with His Hands: Ettore Scola's Narrative Intelligence as a Screenwriter and Compulsive Illustrator   23
   Mariapia Comand

Visual Transitions in Ettore Scola's Comedies   44
   Fabrizio Cilento

Premortem Identification of the *Commedia all'italiana*: The Grotesque in Scola's Comedy   67
   Rémi Lanzoni

PART 2. HISTORY, MEMORY, AND CRITIQUE OF THE PRESENT

Semo giudii: Cinema, Metacinema, and the Holocaust in Scola's Roman Jewish Trilogy (with a Special Focus on the Fictional Short *'43–'97*)   89
   Millicent Marcus

Ettore Scola and Digital Technology: History, Memory, and
Interpretation of the Present   102
   Christian Uva

The Three Figures of Nostalgia in Scola's Films   116
   Pierre Sorlin

La terrazza on the Circeo: Ettore Scola, Pasolini, and the
Critique of the Roman Intelligentsia in Late 1970s Italy   131
   Francesca Borrione

PART 3. SPACE AND PLACE

Italy Must Be Defended: Surveillance and Biopolitics in
Una giornata particolare   149
   Brian Tholl

Trevico-Torino: Viaggio nel Fiat-Nam: Metamorphoses of
Urban Space and the Multiplication of the Factory in the
Age of the Anthropocene   165
   Emiliano Guaraldo and Federica Colleoni

Gente di Roma under the Effect of Federico Fellini's Rome   186
   Marina Vargau

PART 4. SCOLA AND POLITICS

Sentenced to Death: The Proto-Berlusconi of
La più bella serata della mia vita   207
   Nicoletta Marini-Maio

Facing the Failure: Characters as Political Allegories in *La terrazza* 226
   Dario Marcucci and Luca Zamparini

Scola's Legacy: A Statesman for Italian Cinema   245
   Edward Bowen

CODA

Dancing and Drinking with the Muses: The Cinema of Ettore Scola   269
   Gian Piero Brunetta

Bibliography   289
Contributors   305
Index   309

FOREWORD

I AM HONORED TO have the privilege of opening this volume on one of the crucial authors of Italian cinema, Ettore Scola. Scola was a true intellectual, both politically involved and fully dedicated to aesthetic research in his work. With Scola, one could easily apply the formula of a "postmodern commitment," coined by Pierpaolo Antonello and Florian Mussgnug, a political commitment however commensurate with the new era, dominated by the crisis of ideologies.[1] One important point of the present volume is to underline how the analysis of Scola's cinema should be directed not only to its contents but also and above all to its form. Scola thus becomes—as this book recognizes—a laboratory case that allows for the application of all the tendencies of contemporary theory on cinema, from ideology to poststructuralism, from gender to genre, from the body to the mask, from the studies on perception and reception to film production.

This being said, it is difficult for me to talk about Ettore Scola from only a scholarly point of view. For me, Ettore was a mentor and an inspirational role model. At the beginning of the new millennium, I organized a retrospective on Scola for the Pesaro Film Festival, and Scola was also my guest at the Teatro Palladium in Rome in one of his last, if not last, public appearances for the Cinema and History conference, where I had the pleasure of speaking extensively with him and about him.[2] We spoke many times about politics and cultural policies, and he insisted that I should not abandon the National Association of Cinema Authors (ANAC) at a time of strong turmoil and scission. For a man of culture like him, political commitment and militant action were essential. He felt bound to that association, which gathered many authors of his generation, from Age and Furio Scarpelli to Leo Benvenuti and Piero De Bernardi (the founders of the *commedia all'italiana*), from Citto Maselli to Carlo Lizzani and Giuliano Montaldo (some of the fathers of post-neorealist auteur cinema).

Relevant to my thoughts on Scola, there is an expression that was coined by the Sicilian writer Gesualdo Bufalino: "la moviola della memoria" (the editing machine of memory). Memory, especially for a movie lover, works like a Moviola, the analog machine used for much of the history of cinema to edit films. Like film stock, memory unfolds in a serpentine fashion, sometimes making *insalate* (salads; in filmic jargon, a tangle of celluloid), and it can be moved forward and backward on a Moviola. It can be used for flashbacks and flash-forwards. That is what I am doing here, exercising my memory on a master filmmaker who also happens to be a familiar character. I would like to start from just a couple of flickering images of my encounters with Scola, which still move me today and in my opinion remain important finds, fragments of both archive and memory. First of all, I recall Scola's famous chat at the Pesaro Film Festival with his friend, exegete, and political companion Lino Miccichè,[3] which reappeared in the 2016 documentary on Scola, *Ridendo e scherzando* (*Laughing and Joking*, 2016) made by his daughters, Silvia and Paola Scola. There are many elements of interest in that visual testimony, including the role of directing versus screenwriting. "Directing is not what interests me the most," Scola affirms in his conversation with Miccichè. He explains that the things that impress him most of filmmaking are the story and good screenwriting. The rest comes by itself; it is a natural way of writing for images. In addition, he discusses his own formation as a screenwriter and director, his relationship with Antonio Pietrangeli, the *commedia all'italiana*, and of course his involvement with politics. It was exciting to see two men of this caliber, one of the greatest directors and one of the best-known critics and cultural operators of Italian cinema, conversing with each other. We experienced, I assure you (for me and the other cameraman who helped me film), a moving atmosphere and the feeling of living a historical moment, especially since the old critic was ill and the elder director had come to pay him homage at his home—a gesture that seemed to me of great nobility and generosity.

I will also never forget when Scola, his daughter Silvia, Christian Uva, and I met prior to the Cinema and History conference to prepare a video on the representation of history in his films. At the time, Scola's legs were bothering him, and he stated that "the legs go before one's mind"; his energy and irony were still intact. Scola's precious legacy still remains in me. It is as if Scola himself had accompanied me in this montage of sequences, even if he did not spare me some of his usual irony: "Ettore," I asked, "tell me which clips you want to choose for the audience." He simply replied: "I meet more and more people who want me to do the work that they have to do. So do your job and you choose the scenes!" Despite the good-natured rebuke, the indications were precise, starting from the initial frame in which Ornella Muti, in *Il viaggio di Capitan Fracassa* (*The Voyage of Captain Fracassa*, 1990), talks about the inexorable pace of time and the cyclic return of things. The theme of history, in fact, covers every possible discourse on Scola's cinema: the motif of nostalgia, the analysis of history and microhistory, the reflection on the relationship between history and film history, the reconstruction of the committed and militant filmmaker. In his films, *la Storia* (History) is found in the style of politics, but also in space, in the closed or open places that make the great scenography of History. History is a fundamental protagonist—History with a capital *H* and also history and histories (*storie*) with a lowercase *h*. Here, I am not only referring to the *histoire de longue durée* (history of long duration or the study of long-term historical structures), to use Marc Bloch and Lucien Febvre's phrase, and to the *histoire événementielle* (short-term history told by chroniclers), but also to the personal and private stories of many of his characters. Lastly, playing with the English language, Scola's cinema focuses on History, histories, and also "stories" in regard to the attention given to the subject, the plot, and the story.

I have investigated Scola as an architect of his narrative structure in a previous essay on the circular structure and the perfect geometry of the story in films like *C'eravamo tanto amati* (*We Loved Each Other So Much*, 1974), *La terrazza* (*The Terrace*, 1980) and *Una giornata particolare* (*A Special Day*, 1977).[4] In that article, I proposed these three case studies to exemplify the mastery of Scola the humanist, who inserts himself in a tradition inherited from the *commedia all'italiana* of high-level artisans, of a trade worthy of a Florentine workshop of the 1400s. These three texts are united by a common choice of "episodic circularity": in the first two cases, Scola and his co-screenwriters tend to fragment the plot into many separate episodes, and each one is played by a representative character of history; on the other hand, they recompose their segmentation into a harmonic circular-type scheme in which the end returns perfectly to the starting point. In the third case, the circularity is reiterated, even if the choice of characters leans in favor of star protagonists such as Sophia Loren and Marcello Mastroianni. The circularity, however, seems to be Scola's vision of the world: one can see it in *Ballando ballando*

(*Le bal*, 1983), which emphasizes the moments of "return," a type of History that always repeats itself, and the use of the long take to underline the circular aspect of the set (the claustrophobic location of the ballroom). More than Marxist determinism, based on the certainty of progress, Scola seems to be conjuring up Giambattista Vico's theory of course and recourse. From here, perhaps, one can notice a sort of pessimism, if not a disenchanted way of seeing things that verges on cynicism. It is a lucid disenchantment, however, that is not contradictory but rather enhances the pragmatic trust in the "subject-matter," which also explains the complexity of Scola as a character, always suspended between trust in man and mistrust in the world, between commitment to things and (self) ironical detachment.

Irony seems to me the most significant aspect of Scola's cinema, even during the period when Scola took on serious roles, like that of "shadow minister" of culture for the Partito Comunista Italiano (PCI, or Italian Communist Party). On this point, I would like to share a personal memory from 1974, when I was a student at the Centro Sperimentale di Cinematografia and involved in the student protests at that film school, overwhelmed like all other universities by the wave of post-1968 protests. At the time, the PCI opened its doors to host a group of film students. I had the honor of attending a couple of meetings of the party's Cultural Commission. Among the attendees were Mino Argentieri (film critic and university professor), Gianni Toti (poet, writer, filmmaker, and later video artist), Ansano Giannarelli, and many other filmmakers who then gravitated around the party. The leader was Aldo Tortorella, a true leftist intellectual. However, I remember the respect and the attention triggered by the intervention of Scola as a representative of cinematographic culture. He offered a comprehensive and charismatic speech that linked the battle of cinema to a more general societal battle.

Beyond the glimmering images that I have retrieved from my own *moviola della memoria*, I would like to say a few words about the compositions in Scola's films and his directing, that "not so important part," according to him, but which of course becomes a crucial point in his cinema. During the conference in Pesaro, I asked Scola to explain how he was able to shoot the extraordinary sequence of *Una giornata particolare* in which the camera shows the fascist condominium where the story unfolds and then enters the apartment of Antonietta (Sophia Loren) and moves through its rooms while the entire family wakes up. Even in that case, with a little reluctance, as if it were not so important, he revealed to me that he had a freight elevator built with a catwalk that allowed the camera to enter the house through the window (whose frame opened to let the camera in). This handicraft feat of skills, which today would be replaced by digital effects, still provokes in me a profound emotion and unavoidably conjures up a type of classical and analogic "old fashioned" cinema. Another instance that comes to mind is when I went to Luciano Ricceri's studio at Cinecittà (Ricceri was Scola's set designer): in that studio there was a world of drawings, sketches, and scenographies. Scola revealed himself—as Fellini—a great designer, always gifted with a capacity for observations and a scathing humor. I still have one of his drawings: it is a caricature of the Taviani brothers, which shows the affection and complicity—human and political—of that generation. In short, Ettore Scola was for me a crucial figure, a crossing point for many reasons and in many senses: politics, cinema, friendship, the political and cultural model of a master, the ethical heritage of a father—or of an uncle—which certainly influenced my life choices.

It is a great pleasure for me to see the addition of this volume, which features the work of different generations of scholars who apply a variety of approaches to film studies. Internationally known researchers, such as Millicent Marcus and Gian Piero Brunetta, along with younger theorists and historians, reflect on key stylistic and thematic features of Scola's work, including the seminal role of screenwriting (Mariapia Comand); the comedy genre (Fabrizio Cilento and Rémi Lanzoni); the concept of nostalgia (Pierre Sorlin); the Holocaust (Millicent Marcus), metacinema, urban space, and the cinematic city (Brian Tholl, Emiliano Guaraldo, Federica Colleoni, Marina Vargau); political allegories (Francesca Borrione, Nicoletta Marini-Maio, Dario Marcucci, Luca Zamparini); Scola's legacy for the younger generations of filmmakers and filmgoers (Edward Bowen); his use of new digital tools (Christian Uva); and finally the breadth of cultural references in his films (Gian Piero Brunetta). I am convinced that this book will stand as a turning point in the Anglo-American debate on Ettore Scola and hopefully an important step in film studies on both sides of the Atlantic, reinforcing the important bridge between two academic worlds. I wish a pleasant reading to the readers of this important volume.

Vito Zagarrio

Notes

1. Pierpaolo Antonello and Florian Mussgnug, eds., *Postmodern Impegno: Ethics and Commitment in Contemporary Italian Culture* (Oxford: Peter Lang, 2009).
2. Vito Zagarrio, ed., *Trevico-Cinecittà: L'avventuroso viaggio di Ettore Scola* (Venice: Marsilio, 2002).
3. This conversation is featured in the documentary *Permette? Ettore Scola: Una conversazione con Lino Miccichè*. A transcription of this interview is found in Lino Miccichè, "Il cinema non cambia il mondo, ma può farci riflettere: Una conversazione con Ettore Scola," in Zagarrio, *Trevico-Cinecittà*, 19–42.
4. Vito Zagarrio, "La sceneggiatura circolare: Strutture narrative in tre film di Ettore Scola," *Italianist* 29 (2009): 265–80.

ACKNOWLEDGMENTS

First and foremost, we would like to thank Peter Bondanella who worked with us in the early stages of this project and without whom gathering scholars for it would have been much more difficult. He immediately recognized the value of this project and shared it with Ettore Scola himself in Rome in November 2015. *The Cinema of Ettore Scola* also greatly benefited from the participation of Millicent Marcus. As scholar and mentor, she provided insightful feedback on the book proposal. We are indebted to the staff of Wayne State University Press who provided support and guidance throughout the entire process. In particular, we thank both Annie Martin, our acquisitions editor during the early stages of the process (now editor in chief of acquisitions), and Marie Sweetman, our acquisitions editor for the bulk of the review process. We are also extremely grateful for the editorial suggestions of our series editor, Barry Grant, the meticulous attention of copyeditor Jude Grant, and the assistance with design and formatting of Kristin Harpster and Andrew Katz.

The Cinema of Ettore Scola was greatly enhanced by the financial support of the Department of Romance Languages at Wake Forest University, the Office of the Dean, the Office of Global Affairs, and the Office of the Provost. In addition, Tony Marsh from the Office of the Dean provided generous grants for covering translation expenses. Moreover, we would like to thank Marguerite Shore for her translation of Gian Piero Brunetta's chapter. We would also like to express our sincere gratitude to the staff of Wake Forest University's libraries—Mary Reeves, Lauren Corbett, and Charles Bombeld—who diligently provided audiovisual materials, and to the staff of the Venice Campus at Casa Artom—Peter Kairoff, Laura Graziano, Roberta Cimarosti, and Shaul Bassi. Special thanks to Dr. Andrius Galisanka (Department of Political Science) who shared valuable information on his experience with edited volumes. Without this joint effort with administrators, professors, and staff members of Wake Forest University, our task would have undoubtedly been more difficult.

We are especially grateful to all our contributors for their professionalism, commitment to the project, and careful revisions of their chapters. In addition, all our reviewers deserve extensive praise for their contributions to this project. Before submitting the manuscript to the press, we created our own blind review process and received invaluable feedback that greatly enhanced the quality of each chapter. Each of the following reviewers provided detailed comments on a chapter or two. Their names appear in alphabetical order.

Nicholas Albanese (Texas Christian University)
Philip Balma (University of Connecticut)
Andrea Bini (American University of Rome)
Silvia Boero (Portland State University)
Ryan Calabretta-Sajder (University of Arkansas)
Daniele Fioretti (Miami University of Ohio)
Michele Guerra (Università degli Studi di Parma)
Daniel Grinberg (University of Pennsylvania)
Thomas Harrison (UCLA)
Alan José (Princeton University)
Stella Kim (Wake Forest University)
Irene Lottini (University of Iowa)
Sebastiano Lucci (Hobart and William Smith Colleges)
Nicola Di Nino (George Mason University)
Gloria Pastorino (Fairleigh Dickinson University)
Luca Peretti (Ohio State University)
Alan Singerman (Davidson College)
Veronica Vegna (University of Chicago)
Nathan Vetri (University of Massachusetts)
Antonio Vitti (Indiana University)
David Winkler (University of Delaware)

Beyond our group of readers, we are also extremely appreciative of the detailed and constructive feedback provided by the anonymous reviewers hired by Wayne State University Press.

In the final stages of this project, we sought copyediting assistance from several people. Among these, veteran editor Walter Michener appreciably improved the quality of several essays, and he also commented on our own contributions. Ellen Collier and Ross Gilmore each copyedited a chapter, and John Brewer proofread several essays.

Edward Bowen would like to thank the following people for granting him interviews for this volume: Ettore Scola's wife, Gigliola Scola; filmmaker Ugo Gregoretti; filmmaker and former mayor of Rome Walter Veltroni; director of the Centro Sperimentale di Cinematografia and the Bari International Film Festival Felice Laudadio; filmmaker and film critic Marco Spagnoli; filmmaker Daniele Vicari; president of the Association Piccolo Cinema America, Valerio Carocci, and secretary of the Giuseppe De Santis Association, Marco Grossi. Edward would also like to thank Alison Gabriele for her support and feedback as well as Marco Scola di Mambro for his collaboration, friendship, and assistance with finding and photocopying documents from Scola's private archive.

We would both like to thank Silvia Scola for permission to print some of Ettore Scola's illustrations in Mariapia Comand's chapter, and lastly we thank set photographer Roberto Biciocchi and his son, Franco Biciocchi, for the cover photo.

INTRODUCTION

Edward Bowen and Rémi Lanzoni

OMNIPRESENT IN THE COLLECTIVE imagination of Italian cinema for the past fifty years, Ettore Scola (1931–2016) is known as a master screenwriter, social satirist, and film auteur. In line with recent trends in film studies research, this volume dedicates considerable attention to Scola's screenwriting, to his contributions to Comedy Italian Style, and to the development of his prolific filmography as a director, as well as his commentaries on the history of Italy, Rome, and the film industry through his well-known metacinematic discourse. It also addresses representations of space and place in his films and focuses on different moments in his career, ranging from his early work as an illustrator and screenwriter to his political activism in the last years of his life.

While treating a wide variety of topics, the chapters in this volume offer a comprehensive vision of Scola's screenwriting and filmmaking by focusing on several of the themes and stylistic choices that prevail in his works. The book is not an exhaustive study of Scola's filmography, and it does not assume the burden of examining all the feature films that Scola directed.[1] Instead, it features in-depth chapters from a wide range of methodological approaches and theoretical perspectives that seek to make contributions to existing scholarship. Notably, it marks the first book-length study entirely dedicated to Scola in English. This may surprise some readers given that since the late 1970s Scola has been the subject of over a dozen monographs in Italian and several in French.[2] Indeed, scholarly discussions of Italian cinema in English have often given priority to a limited number of Italian auteurs, with an emphasis on the artistic genius of Federico Fellini, stylistic citation and representations of the sacred in Pier Paolo Pasolini, the operatic grandeur of Luchino Visconti's frescoes, and Michelangelo Antonioni's metaphysical questions, to name a few. By no means do we discount the important scholarship in English in articles and book chapters,³ many mentioned in this introduction, yet an in-depth and extensive approach in English to Scola's oeuvre is clearly missing. Collectively, the chapters in this volume make it possible to better understand the depth and coherence of his overall production as they contextualize and highlight the innovative qualities of his social and political commentary.

Before situating the chapters of this volume within existing scholarship on Scola, it is important to offer a few key biographical notes on his early career and to reflect on the essence of his cinematic style and legacy. The latter is not an easy task, considering that Scola collaborated on sixty screenplays—he received credit on approximately two-thirds of these—before his debut as a filmmaker in 1964, and in total he directed twenty-seven feature films of different genres (not counting documentaries, shorts, and episodes in other films), spanning five decades.

Scola was born in Trevico, a small mountain village in the Campania region, on May 10, 1931, but his family moved to Rome in 1936. As a child, Scola developed a passion for drawing comic vignettes, and he began to submit his work to magazines, including *Marc'Aurelio*, at the age of fifteen. His work was appreciated by the magazine's director, Vito De Bellis, and its regular contributors, who included Vittorio Metz, Marcello Marchesi, Ruggero Maccari, Federico Fellini, Steno (Stefano Vanzina), Furio Scarpelli, and others. Within a few years, Scola had his own column. The early connections he made at *Marc'Aurelio* helped open the doors for his work as a comic writer for radio programs and subsequently as an uncredited gagman for screenplays for films starring Totò in the late 1940s and early 1950s.⁴ Scola entered the world of cinema at a time when lighthearted episode films, written for stars of variety shows, were in vogue.⁵ One memorable film that he worked on in this period was Steno's *Un americano a Roma* (*An American in Rome*, 1954), and his meeting Antonio Pietrangeli in 1953 led to his collaboration on the latter's early film *Lo scapolo* (*The Bachelor*) in 1956.

From 1953 to 1964, Scola was officially credited with collaborating on the scripts of thirty-nine films, many of which were important in the history of postwar comic cinema, especially those written for Steno (*Un americano a Roma*), Dino Risi (*Il sorpasso*/*The Easy Life*, 1962; *I mostri*/*The Monsters*, 1963), and Antonio Pietrangeli (*Adua e le compagne*/*Adua and Her Friends*, 1960; *La visita*/*The Visit*, 1963).⁶ Scola cowrote eight of Pietrangeli's films, and this collaboration allowed him to mature as a screenwriter by focusing closely on the psychologies of characters, in particular women. Meanwhile, for Dino Risi, he also cowrote eight films, often teaming up with screenwriter Ruggero Maccari. The duo of Scola and Maccari wrote the script for Risi's *Il sorpasso*, a vibrant portrait of Italy's economic boom. According to Ennio Bíspuri, Scola added to Risi's films a dose of melancholy, disenchantment, and pessimism.[7] Scola thus had extensive training and contact with leading directors and actors before debuting as a filmmaker in 1964, with the episode film *Se permettete parliamo di donne* (*Let's Talk about Women*, 1964), featuring Vittorio Gassman. Scola's early comedies had success at the box office, but by the late 1960s he began to gain critical appreciation as a mature director, no longer viewed simply as a director of popular comedies. In the late 1960s, Scola also became more politically involved and joined the Italian Communist Party. As will be discussed below, his filmmaking evolved and embraced many different genres and styles over the course of five decades, and even his last film, *Che strano chiamarsi Federico* (*How Strange to be Named Federico*, 2013), featured cinematic innovations. Scola passed away on January 19, 2016. He was politically active, especially in advocating for improvements to film production and distribution, up until his last days.

One of Scola's close friends, Walter Veltroni, who served as both editor and film reviewer for the newspaper *L'Unità* before becoming the minister of culture and the mayor of Rome, provides us with a nice starting point in addressing Scola's artistic and political legacy:

> Scola had much success, but I believe his work will not only continue to speak to us in the decades to come, but that it will also have a cultural weight even more relevant than we perceive today. As a screenwriter and as a director, Scola knew, at the highest level, how to tell the story of his country. He did it with irony, with affection, and with a harsh gaze when necessary. He often told the story of Italy using the disorienting weapon of comedy, which in Italy is not the "sophisticated comedy" of the United States, but instead something rather different that has its roots in the Neorealist period but also draws from popular comedy. In Scola, the balance of different registers, between the profundity of the gaze and the lightness of the touch, is truly extraordinary. He had both the ability to make people laugh and the passion of a militant political thinker. And he trafficked in both of these dimensions, not as

alternatives but as a way of bringing strong, important, and high ideals to everyone, not only to elite intellectuals.[8]

Characteristic Features of Scola's Filmmaking

Many scholars have noted that categorizing Scola is complex, given that he was much more than just a director of Comedy Italian Style.[9] As with many other masters of the golden age of Italian comedy, in the 1960s, Scola's was a harsh and cynical representation of an Italy undergoing a hasty modernization. Then, in the early 1970s, his humor evolved as it featured a strong dose of the grotesque, even in representations of daily life. Ennio Bíspuri emphasizes that Scola brought new elements to Comedy Italian Style, such as "a strong civil engagement, a political sensibility, and a solidaristic component that is tied to an integral humanism," which directors such as Risi and Monicelli "had willingly overlooked or made ambiguous or relegated to a secondary plane."[10] Bíspuri further notes the evolution of Scola's "melancholic" and reflective style of comedy: "His films, marked by a soft and attenuated cadence, bring spectators less to laugh and more to reflect, bringing them inside the characters' soul and feelings and suffering with them."[11] It is precisely this type of distress that Scola chose to address via the lens of the grotesque, often using monstrous characters with extremely idiosyncratic flaws; their embodiment of social types was symptomatic of a tormented era. For Scola, the monstrosity was "a symptom of a social and cultural condition, when man loses his intelligence and dignity and becomes more like a monster or a child."[12] The grotesque was also a response to violence from domestic terrorism, a new type of social satire that took spectators inside an apocalyptic and dystopian world and served as a social barometer and a reflection on a nation exhausted by a decade of violence. *La più bella serata della mia vita* (*The Most Wonderful Evening of My Life*, 1972), *Brutti, sporchi e cattivi* (*Down and Dirty*, 1976), and episodes of *I nuovi mostri* (*Viva Italia!*, 1977) tackled difficult subjects through the apparatus of entertainment and humor. The aim of these comedies, overambitious for many viewers or too decadent for others, was to expose Italians' disregard for social evils. Some of Scola's later comedies are less searing in their social criticism, yet they still promote reflection on social issues, vices, relationships, and generational differences. In an interview, director Carlo Verdone remarked on the impact Scola had on other filmmakers: "He taught us to look at life with irony but also with a good dose of mercy. This means that he played on the weaknesses of men but he also respected their dignity. Many of us would not exist without the lesson of sensitive souls like Scola."[13]

Since it is commonplace among filmmakers and critics to praise Scola for his ability to "*raccontare l'Italia*," it is important to tease out his style of doing this. Millicent Marcus notes that there is not an easy short-form translation of the expression *raccontare l'Italia* into English, especially in relation to the works of engaged filmmakers, and she offers a more elaborate explanation: "*Raccontare l'Italia* means the invention of fictions which connect the plight of the individual to that of the larger social whole in an ideologically consequential way, so that imaginative identification with the former enables us to progressively analyze, and perhaps even intervene in, the latter."[14] Indeed, Scola was intent on showing how individuals, often marginalized figures, experienced key moments in history, remarking, "You cannot talk about history if you do not speak about the effects that it has on the individual."[15] Scola paid great attention to the effects of historical events on everyday life, in the context of such universal themes as the family, romantic relationships, friendships, and the plight of women and other marginalized figures. Both *Una giornata particolare* (*A Special Day*, 1977) and *Concorrenza sleale* (*Unfair Competition*, 2001) highlight the oppression felt by marginalized figures under fascism and they also feature Scola's trademark narrative technique of using single locations as microcosms for understanding history. The former, set entirely in the Palazzo Federici housing complex, features a chance encounter between an overburdened housewife and her antifascist, homosexual neighbor on a day when almost all residents have gone to celebrate Hitler's visit to Rome. Jacqueline Reich asserts that the film "efficiently implodes the gender mythologies through which the Fascist regime attempted to impose cultural and political conformity."[16] Meanwhile, the latter film, set in a fictional street near the Vatican, illustrates the brutal reality faced by a Jewish family (tailors by trade) during the time of the racial laws in Italy.

Almost all Scola's films are "characterized by a tension that is historical and political," yet Bíspuri emphasizes that Scola's style is neither to "directly show us history" nor to be didactic but instead to have the viewer infer the impact of history on the characters.[17] While many of his films are reflections on political issues, most of them are not as overtly militant as *Trevico-Torino: Viaggio nel Fiat-Nam* (*Trevico-Turin: Voyage in Fiatnam*, 1973), which strongly denounces the marginal living conditions of migrant workers from the south in Turin. For instance, in *Il mondo nuovo* (*That Night in Varennes*, 1982), set during the French Revolution, it is not the epic tale of the royal couple's flight from Paris that holds Scola's attention but rather the voyage of a disparate group of men and women who follow them by carriage and are forced to confront the changes that accompany liberation. Highly characteristic is Scola's interest in the passage of time and the delusions of his characters. *C'eravamo tanto amati* (*We All Loved Each Other So Much*, 1974), one of Scola's best-known films, is emblematic of this narrative strategy. It traces thirty years of Italian history—and Italian film history—from the end of World War II through the mid-1970s, telling the bittersweet story of three former antifascist partisans, all lovers of the same woman, who must face the disappointments and compromises of Italy's economic miracle. In pursuing his interest in social changes, the passage of time, and how characters' individual stories can represent periods of history, Scola also adopted the technique of using a single setting over a long time period, with segments set in different decades. For instance, *Ballando ballando* (*Le bal*, 1983), set in a Parisian dance hall, features sequences set in four different decades, and *La famiglia* (*The Family*, 1987), set entirely in a Roman apartment, tells the story of Carlo and his family over the course of eighty years with nine different segments. The weakening of Carlo's ideals and his delusions over the decades, in the midst of political strife, wars, and domestic terrorism "incarnate . . . and thus represent Italian history."[18] According to scholar Alberto Cattini, this type of narrative structure is "essentially a cycle of syntagms that metonymically refer to the defeats in each segment, such as personal disasters, and their relation to the metaphorical arc of history, understood each time as socialism, defeat, and a desire to try again."[19]

Scola's penchant for observing the unities of place, action, and time in his films (often using closed settings) allowed him to focus on the everyday conflicts and psychologies of his characters, and it required much skill in directing actors. For instance, *Una giornata particolare* and *Che ora è?* (*What Time Is It?*, 1989), with their restricted locations[20] and time (each takes place within a single day), showcase the bravura exchanges, glances, and movements of Scola's star actors—Marcello Mastroianni and Sophia Loren in the former and Mastroianni paired with Massimo Troisi in the latter. In *Che ora è?*, the father–son duo is often framed closely together in conversation, and their body language becomes almost as important as the dialogue in conveying their different personalities, anxieties, and difficulties in understanding each other. The emphasis on dialogue and scenic details in restricted spaces lent Scola's works a theatrical quality. Gianni Rondolino refers to this style as "filmed theater, or a theatrical cinema" and considers Scola at his best in this mode, as it placed all the focus "on the characters, on their words, on their actions, and on their reciprocal reactions."[21] For instance, the film set of *La cena* (*The Dinner*, 1998), which presents a night at a Roman restaurant with diners at fourteen tables, "is arranged as an actual stage," as Alessandra Fagioli points out.[22]

Scola found many innovative cinematic solutions to add commentary to his stories and avoid monotony in restricted settings: thus, it would be reductive and inaccurate to refer to them merely as "theatrical." Following the opening newsreel footage of Hitler's visit to Rome in *Una giornata particolare*, Scola presents the setting of the film through a series of panoramic shots of the Palazzo Federici courtyard and many of its apartments with the blinds open, before transporting the camera into Antonietta's apartment in a fluid long take: an early sequence that conveys the idea that everyone was watched by the fascist regime. Likewise, the slow and repetitive dolly shots down the hallway in Carlo's house in *La famiglia* serve as segues from one time period to another and also offer a melancholic commentary on the passage of time. Similarly, in order to interrupt and temper the constant and at times intense conversations of the diners in *La cena*, Scola inserts a peaceful harp and flute performance, which provides him an opportunity to frame everyone in the restaurant up close using a Steadicam—a three-minute "choral" long take of over fifty people in multiple rooms. Moments such as these vary the pace and add breathing room and time for reflection.

Scola excelled in creating *film corali*, ensemble films that offered portraits of Italian and French society. Many feature top actors, as in *La terrazza* (*The Terrace*, 1980), which includes some of the leading figures of Comedy Italian Style: Marcello Mastroianni, Vittorio Gassman, Ugo Tognazzi, Stefania Sandrelli, Jean-Louis Trintignant, and Stefano Satta-Flores. As Dario Marcucci and Luca Zamparini aptly point out in their chapter, Scola had a knack for utilizing emblematic characters to personify political persuasions, intellectuals, film history, and more. Several of his famous "choral" films feature circular narratives[23] (beginning and ending in the same place), perhaps none more touchingly than *La famiglia*, which features characters preparing for family portraits in a living room in 1906 and again in 1986. Scola's portrayals of families, couples in distress, and their obstacles to communication have inspired filmmakers today, such as Ivano De Matteo (*I nostri ragazzi*/*The Dinner*, 2014)[24] and Paolo Genovese (*Perfetti sconosciuti*/*Perfect Strangers*, 2016). The latter film pays homage to Scola's filming in closed spaces, use of theatrical sets, and representations of Italy's middle and upper-middle classes.

Rome and the daily life of its people provided rich material for Scola's choral cinema. Approximately half his films are set there, including several studio-shot films that explicitly or implicitly feature Roman locations.[25] Today in Rome, tourists can find markers on the streets and piazzas where scenes from *C'eravamo tanto amati* were shot. Franco Montini writes that beyond offering a portrait of a generation, the film "tells of the transformations of a city," noting the rapid boom of construction and urban sprawl.[26] Scola's Rome presents life on the street, in apartments, on terraces, in trattorias, and in shantytowns. His films focus on many aspects of Roman identity, and how Romans eat, speak, joke, argue, sing, and more. Scola's ultimate tribute to Rome, Roman identity, and the city's new multicultural reality is *Gente di Roma* (*People of Rome*, 2003), which features a patchwork of episodes of life in different parts of the city. The film is dedicated to Alberto Sordi, a symbol of Roman identity, and it includes tributes to screenwriter Cesare Zavattini and Roman dialect poet Giuseppe Gioachino Belli. In addition, *Gente di Roma* is in dialogue with Fellini's Roman poetics, as scholar Marina Vargau underscores in her chapter in this volume. Scola's commentary on Rome also includes a personal touch best evidenced in his last film, *Che strano chiamarsi Federico*, shot in Cinecittà, which narrates his friendship with Federico Fellini and their many encounters at cafés, in piazzas, and in other locations in the city.

Scola's taste for revisiting and commenting on Italian history through references to Italian film history is one of his signature qualities as a filmmaker, most memorably in *C'eravamo tanto amati*. Peter Bondanella asserts that "implicit in the film's structure resides the director's belief that Italian cinema comprises the best means of understanding postwar Italy."[27] In this film and others, Scola comments on different periods in history and social changes through citations, reenactments, debates, and parodies of famous films and moments in film history. The early scene of Gianni, Antonio, and Nicola as Resistance fighters is shot in a neorealist style that evokes the era's hopes of rebuilding Italy. According to Millicent Marcus, the character of Nicola, who remains obsessed with Vittorio De Sica's *Ladri di biciclette* (*Bicycle Thieves*,

1948) and neorealist cinema for most of his adult life, becomes representative of "the impact of an entire cinematic movement on the life of a national culture."[28] In his parallel survey of Italian history and Italian film history, Scola also parodies Antonioni's trilogy of alienation—*L'avventura* (1960), *La notte* (1961), and *L'eclisse* (1962)—to comment on the economic boom years, and he re-creates the shooting of Fellini's famous Trevi Fountain scene from *La dolce vita* (1960) complete with Fellini and Mastroianni playing themselves. Cinematic references help Scola enrich his melancholic portrait of the loss of values and hope over the course of the three decades following World War II. Scola's interest in parodying film critics and directors in his early years as a vignettist for *Marc'Aurelio* reappears in films such as *La terrazza*, which comments on the failure of Italian intellectuals, including filmmakers, to play a key role in society. Other reflections on the history of Italian cinema and the importance of theatrical exhibition can be found in *Splendor* (1988), the short film *'43–'97* (1997), and *Che strano chiamarsi Federico*.

As with any filmmaker, it is important to emphasize Scola's collaborations with screenwriters, actors, musicians, photographers, set designers, and others. For example, it would be difficult to reflect on Scola's work as a screenwriter without acknowledging his partnership with Ruggero Maccari, which spanned from the 1950s until Maccari's death in 1989. Together, they wrote some of the most important films of Comedy Italian Style, and Maccari collaborated on nineteen of the films that Scola directed. Mariapia Comand and Fabrizio Cilento emphasize the importance of this collaboration in the development of Scola's narrative style in the first two chapters of this volume.

The study of Scola's work with specific actors, especially male actors (given that most of the protagonists were male), provides a fertile ground for investigations of stardom and masculinity. Scholar Veronica Pravadelli states that it is difficult not to view Scola's cinema as a "cinema maschile" (masculine cinema), because the "feminine subject almost always has a secondary role."[29] Pravadelli adds that "even though there are numerous figures of courageous and transgressive women, who challenge implicit rules and taboos, and attempt emancipation, these [figures] remain marginal in relation to the principal narratives."[30] Scola cast stars Sophia Loren, Monica Vitti, and Stefania Sandrelli in important roles, though his main protagonists were males interpreted by Vittorio Gassman, Alberto Sordi, Marcello Mastroianni, and Massimo Troisi. Gassman starred in all nine episodes of Scola's debut,

Se permettete parliamo di donne, and subsequently in *La congiuntura* (*Hard Time for Princes*, 1964), *L'arcidiavolo* (*The Devil in Love*, 1966), *C'eravamo tanto amati*, and *La famiglia*, to name a few. Many of these roles capitalized on the actor's sarcastic, detached, and at times cruel humor. In *Stardom Italian Style*, Marcia Landy emphasizes that "among the many attributes of postwar-era male stardom possessed by Gassman, the most prominent is how he embodies the image of an anti-hero whose skill lies in living by his wits, manipulating and seducing others, and succeeding for a time."[31] While many of the characters in Scola's films interpreted by Gassman and Sordi can be labeled as chauvinist, it is also true that Scola used these roles to unveil the hypocrisies, anxieties, and immorality of the economic boom (e.g., Gianni Perego in *C'eravamo tanto amati* and Alfredo Rossi in *La più bella serata della mia vita*). Mastroianni had an equally important role in Scola's career, with virtuoso turns in *Dramma della gelosia—tutti i particolari in cronaca* (*The Pizza Triangle*, 1970), *Una giornata particolare*, *La terrazza*, *Il mondo nuovo*, and *Che ora è?*. The documentary *Ridendo e scherzando* (*Laughing and Joking*, 2016), by Scola's daughters, Silvia and Paola, emphasizes the novelty of Scola's decision to cast stars Mastroianni and Sophia Loren in *Una giornata particolare* against their star personas and their past of acting together in romantic comedies (fig. 1). Scholar Sergio Rigoletto's *Masculinity and Italian Cinema* explains that the film "draws in particular on the formula of the odd-couple plot that is typical of some romantic comedies," but he asserts that the film "dismantles one of the topoi of the classic romantic comedy—the meeting between an unhappy woman and an attractive man who will save her."[32] Several chapters in this volume address Scola's work with actors, though stardom and performance are not their main focal points. The subject of masculinity, however, is significantly treated in chapters by Brian Tholl and Francesca Borrione, as discussed below.

Beyond actors, other important collaborators who left significant stamps on Scola's cinema were composer Armando Trovajoli and set designer Luciano Ricceri. Trovajoli created scores for most of Scola's films, and Ricceri, with whom Scola opened a studio at Cinecittà, helped Scola create singular locations such as the long, multi-room apartment in *La famiglia* (built inside Teatro 5) and the street scenes in *Concorrenza sleale*, shot on Cinecittà's back lot. One of the greatest feats of the partnership between Ricceri and Scola was shooting *Il viaggio di Capitan Fracassa* (*The Voyage of Captain Fracassa*, 1990)

FIGURE 1. Sophia Loren and Marcello Mastroianni in *Una giornata particolare*

in Cinecittà's Teatro 5, with scenes in castles, forests, and towns, using over eighty different sets.[33]

This excursus through the noteworthy features of Scola's cinematic content and style is certainly not exhaustive. Much more could be said about the dream-like moments in his films, his use of flashbacks and voyages as narrative strategies, and his skill for creating comic types and vignettes. On a thematic level, his literary references as well as his commentaries on politics, gender roles, nostalgia, and cultural differences are all key to understanding his cinema.

The Chapters

Part 1 of this volume, "Scola as Screenwriter and Director of Comedy Italian Style" addresses Scola's role in the development of the genre. These chapters analyze Scola's use of satire in his portraits of how Italians experienced and adapted to the advent of modernity. They also evaluate how his narratives broke with the conventions of the postwar era comedies. Scola's interpretive approaches and innovations are also considered, along with his collaborations with other major Italian filmmakers, such as Mario Monicelli, Luigi Comencini, and Antonio Pietrangeli, as well as screenwriter Furio Scarpelli.

Mariapia Comand's "Thinking with His Hands: Ettore Scola's Narrative Intelligence as a Screenwriter and Compulsive Illustrator" explores the formation of Scola's narrative methods by examining his early work as an illustrator, ghostwriter, and screenwriter in the 1950s and 1960s. Comand analyzes his comic timing and rhythm, his use of silence, and his predilection for setting stories in closed fictional spaces to create tension. In addition, her chapter addresses his working relationship with Antonio Pietrangeli and its importance for Scola's growth as a screenwriter and director interested in creating character-based stories. Comand examines sketches, screenplays, and letters from two archives—the Antonio Pietrangeli library and Ettore Scola's private collection—to reveal the development of his narrative techniques and thought processes. In a final section, Comand probes Scola's lifelong compulsive drawing, and how his drawing influenced his interest in spatial metaphors and his pursuit of new meanings and concepts.

In "Visual Transitions in Ettore Scola's Comedies," Fabrizio Cilento traces stylistic and narrative continuities between Scola's early comedic works (as illustrator, screenwriter, and director) and his well-known later films, *C'eravamo tanto amati* and *La terrazza*, advocating a criticism of Scola's cinema that does not posit two distinct phases in his career. Cilento underscores the role that Scola's apprenticeship for the satirical magazine *Marc'Aurelio* played in the maturation of his grotesque style of comedy and the nonlinear structure of his films. In his analysis of visual transitions (such as wipes, dissolves, split screens, visual grids, and kaleidoscopic images) in Scola's early comedies, Cilento identifies the roots of the director's comedic polycentrism and narrative experimentation. The chapter also illustrates how Scola addressed the debate over comedy versus auteur cinema in his films *C'eravamo tanto amati* and *La terrazza*, in which he caricatured film critics.

Rémi Lanzoni's "Premortem Identification of the *Commedia all'italiana*: The Grotesque in Scola's Comedy" examines how in spite of commercial demands, Scola's inspired cynicism drove him even further toward the grotesque. It assesses the innovative use of the cinematographic grotesque for examining social evils, and it illustrates how Scola was able to explore the extremity of a nation in crisis, linked to rapid modernization, by going outside the boundaries of comedy. Lanzoni argues that Scola's utilization of death through the lens of the grotesque in his films of the 1970s offers a coherent metaphor of a nation's tribulations under the spell of violence, as well as premonition about the end of the *commedia all'italiana*.

Part 2 is titled "History, Memory, and Critique of the Present." Scola is known for his "intense, lively, and original relationship with history,"[34] as many of his films focus on the lives of individuals, especially marginalized figures, during periods of great social and political change. This section does not pretend to cover all of Scola's historical portraits. Its first two chapters place much emphasis on Scola's films about fascist anti-Semitism and the Nazi occupation of Rome, as experienced and remembered, while the third chapter offers a broad reading of the theme of nostalgia in Scola's films about postwar Italy. The last chapter here focuses on the social critique of intellectuals in *La terrazza*, one of Scola's contemporary portraits that can also be viewed as "historical," as it documents a pivotal moment of transition in Italian society.[35]

Millicent Marcus's "*Semo giudii*: Cinema, Metacinema, and the Holocaust in Scola's Roman Jewish Trilogy" examines three films in which Scola addresses the Italian Jewish experience of fascist persecution during the Nazi occupation: the fictional short *'43–'97*, the feature *Concorrenza sleale* (2001), and an episode in *Gente di Roma* (2003). Marcus reflects on the push by Scola and other directors during the late 1990s and early 2000s to address a topic that had previously been rather neglected by Italian filmmakers, including neorealist directors. She investigates the imbricated nature of metacinematic commentary in various sequences of the trilogy, including the presentation of movie houses as places of refuge in *'43–'97* and Scola's reflection on his own filming of the Holocaust in a vignette of *Gente di Roma*. Marcus argues that Scola links his discussion of the Holocaust with a contemplation of the importance of cinema for personal growth as a way to insist that more films address this repressed historical moment.

Christian Uva's "Ettore Scola and Digital Technology: History, Memory and Interpretation of the Present" analyzes Scola's feature films of the new millennium: *Concorrenza sleale*, *Gente di Roma*, and *Che strano chiamarsi Federico*. Uva discusses the innovative ways in which Scola utilized lightweight digital cameras, Luciano Ricceri's digitally created set designs, and computerized special effects to reinvent places and revisit commonplace themes in his cinema, including a reflection on neorealist filmmaking and the dialectic between major historical events and the experiences of common people. With its special focus on cinematic innovations, Uva's study of *Concorrenza sleale* and *Gente di Roma* complements the chapter by Millicent Marcus.

Meanwhile, Pierre Sorlin's "The Three Figures of Nostalgia in Scola's Films" illuminates how nostalgia in Scola's cinema is a "multifarious mood" ranging from mourning missed opportunities, to indifferent or detached reflections on the past, to a blissful recollection that helps characters to cheer up and endure hardships, even if they realize that certain experiences cannot be repeated. Sorlin argues that Scola's works, such as *C'eravamo tanto amati*, *La terrazza*, and *La famiglia*, can be analyzed as a series of reflections on why promises are not always fulfilled.

Francesca Borrione's "*La terrazza* on the Circeo: Ettore Scola, Pasolini, and the Critique of the Roman Intelligentsia in Late 1970s Italy" argues that the episodes featuring the characters Luigi and Mario in *La terrazza* reframe Pasolini's essayistic critique of Italian society, most notably of intellectuals and politicians, during the 1970s. Borrione first illustrates how *Brutti, sporchi e cattivi* confirms Pasolini's claims of a "cultural genocide" of the subproletarian classes, and then explains how *La terrazza* is in direct dialogue with newspaper articles that Pasolini wrote following the rape of two women from Rome's periphery by three neofascist men in 1975. Borrione's article contributes to scholarship on Scola not only in drawing these connections between Scola and Pasolini but also through its analysis—firmly aligned in the field of gender studies—of Scola's critique of the apathy, ineffectiveness, and sexism of male intellectuals in the late 1970s.

Part 3, "Space and Place," responds to a recent trend in film studies research that evaluates the importance of representations of space and place in cinema, applying ideas from the works of theorists such as Henri Lefebvre, Michel Foucault, Gilles Deleuze, and others. Recent studies on space and place in Italian cinema by Natalie Fullwood, Tiziana Ferrero-Regis, and Laura Di Bianco, as well as essays in the volume *Taking Place* by John David Rhodes and Elena Gorfinkel, have enriched scholarship on Italian film, analyzing the importance of representations of place for plot and character development and marking identity.[36]

Brian Tholl's "Italy Must Be Defended: Surveillance and Biopolitics in *Una giornata particolare*" approaches one of Scola's best known and most frequently studied films from a lesser explored perspective, namely its commentary on surveillance and internal exile, or *confino*, during the fascist period. Drawing from theories on panopticism by Jeremy Bentham and Michel Foucault, Tholl analyzes Scola's use of the Palazzo Federici and his representations of citizen-to-citizen surveillance. He also investigates the biopolitical nature of Mussolini's speeches, including his calls for a *chirurgia fascista* (fascist surgery), to justify the exile of political opponents and others whom the Duce viewed as weak and inferior.

Emiliano Guaraldo and Federica Colleoni's "*Trevico-Torino: Viaggio nel Fiat-Nam*: Metamorphoses of Urban Space and the Multiplication of the Factory in the Age of the Anthropocene" contemplates the hybrid nature of Scola's *Trevico-Torino*, between documentary and fiction, and it highlights the film's focus on the displacement and disorientation resulting from internal migration and life in the industrial city of Turin. In dialogue with theoretical works by Mario Tronti, Toni Negri, and Henri Lefebvre, the chapter analyzes the role of Turin as a factory city in Scola's film, in which everyday life is impacted by the productive forces and rhythms of the factory. The coauthors conduct a close analysis of the film's editing, mise-en-scène, and juxtapositions to illuminate how the film portrays the concept of the social factory and the negative impact of the industrial landscape on workers and city residents. Their detailed analysis of this film's themes, characters, and historical context, as well as of its representations of urban space, fills a major gap in scholarship on Scola's cinema.

In dialogue with Deleuzian concepts on philosophical work such as encounter, dialogue, and effect, Marina Vargau's "*Gente di Roma* under the Effect of Federico Fellini's Rome" offers a comparative study on cinematic representations of the eternal city in Scola's *Gente di Roma* and in numerous films by Fellini, including *Block-notes di un regista* (*Fellini: A Director's Notebook*, 1969) and *Roma* (1972). Vargau analyzes how Fellini's narrative strategies and his focus on flânerie, spectacle, and memory affected Scola's "portrait" of the city. She argues that Scola's appropriation and reworking of Felliniesque themes and sequences in *Gente di Roma* resulted in an original and personal view of Rome.

Part 4, "Scola and Politics," offers three very different studies on Scola's relationship to ideology on and off the screen. It should already be evident that other chapters in this volume, especially those on *Una giornata particolare* and *Trevico-Torino: Viaggio nel Fiat-Nam*, would easily fit in a chapter on politics as well. The analysis of Scola and politics is one of the unique points of this volume and adds a significant contribution to the extant scholarship on Italian political cinema.[37]

In "Sentenced to Death: The Proto-Berlusconi of Ettore Scola's *La più bella serata della mia vita*," Nicoletta Marini-Maio argues that the main character in Scola's 1972 film, Alfredo Rossi, played by Alberto Sordi, can be read as a proto-Berlusconi figure. Beyond being a newly rich man, the origin of whose wealth is unclear, Rossi also embodies the stereotypical *italiano medio* (a mixture of scrupulous, inept, and sex crazed), an image Berlusconi embraced in constructing his public persona. Marini-Maio views the trial scene, sentencing, and downfall of Rossi (who dies pursuing a woman) as foreshadowing Berlusconi's sex scandals and trials. Her chapter explains how *berlusconismo*, the political posturing utilized by Berlusconi, which included "unbridled individualism," had its roots in a period preceding Scola's film. *La più bella serata* condemns the behavior and mind-set of Rossi and anticipates Scola's later frustration with and aversion for the prime minister.

Dario Marcucci and Luca Zamparini's "Facing the Failure: Characters as Political Allegories in *La terrazza*" examines Scola's use of allegorical characters to comment on political and social issues in Italy in the late 1970s. Before analyzing the use of this figurative rhetorical device in *La terrazza*, the coauthors discuss how Scola relied on it in previous well-known films such as *C'eravamo tanto amati* and *Una giornata particolare*. They also explore how allegory allows for metacinematic commentary using characters tied to the film industry. They conclude that *La terrazza* represents the pessimism that many Italians felt at the end of the 1970s regarding the role that intellectuals, including filmmakers, would play in promoting social change.

Edward Bowen's "Scola's Legacy: A Statesman for Italian Cinema" investigates Scola's political activism off the screen and his status as a statesman and defender of Italian cinema. Drawing from documents in Scola's private archive, videoclips of his public appearances, and original interviews with his collaborators and family members, this chapter sheds light on the principles and tactics of his political and social engagement. Beyond addressing his role as shadow minister of culture (1989–92), it focuses primarily on his activism in the last five years of his life: most notably, his efforts to protect film production jobs at Cinecittà and the zoning permits of closed cinemas in Rome, and his promotion of a tuition-free film school in Rome (the Scuola Volonté) and the Museum of Neorealism in Fondi. At the core of Scola's advocacy stood his belief in the importance of cinema for the cultural formation of young people. Scola utilized his reputation, knowledge of cultural institutions and politics, and contacts to promote and preserve sites of film production, exhibition, and education for future generations.

At the close of the volume, in the coda, is a broad-sweeping tribute to and reflection on Scola's filmmaking by Gian Piero Brunetta, a leading historian of Italian cinema who developed a close relationship with Scola over the years. "Dancing and Drinking with the Muses: The Cinema of Ettore Scola" revisits the themes, influences, and signature patterns that pervade Scola's films. Brunetta asserts that the director's extensive cultural formation is under the influence of the nine Muses. Beyond identifying connections to literature, cinema, music, theater and all forms of popular entertainment, Brunetta offers a comprehensive analysis of the rituals of food and drink in Scola's films. Of interest to scholars of film studies, Italian studies, and food culture, this chapter reveals the varied narrative strategies linked to food that the director utilized for character development and social commentary.

Notes

1. Given that this volume consists of fourteen essays on Scola's cinema, it is worth mentioning that not all twenty-seven films receive equal attention. Furthermore, several of his films, including *L'arcidiavolo* (*The Devil in Love*, 1966), *La congiuntura* (*Hard Time for Princes*, 1964), and *Passione d'amore* (*Passion of Love*, 1981), are not analyzed in detail for reasons of length constraints and the focal points of the individual chapters.
2. Several highlights among books in Italian on Scola include Vito Zagarrio, ed., *Trevico-Cinecittà: L'avventuroso viaggio di Ettore Scola* (Venice: Marsilio, 2002); Stefano Masi, *Ettore Scola: Uno sguardo acuto e ironico sull'Italia e gli italiani* (Rome: Gremese, 2006); and Ennio Bíspuri, *Ettore Scola, un umanista nel cinema italiano* (Rome: Bulzoni, 2006). Among the leading works on Scola to appear in French are Jean Gili's *Une pensée graphique* (Centre des Arts: Enghien Les Bains, 2008) and Catherine Brunet's *Le monde d'Ettore Scola: La famille, la politique, l'histoire* (Paris: L'Harmattan, 2012).
3. Millicent Marcus and Giacomo Lichtner have published extensively on Scola's historical films on fascism, anti-Semitism, and postwar Italian society and politics. Among the contributions by Millicent Marcus, see "Scola's *We All Loved Each Other So Much*: An Epilogue" in her book *Italian Film in the Light*

of Neorealism (Princeton: Princeton University Press, 1986), 391–422; "Un'ora e mezzo particolare: Teaching Fascism with Ettore Scola," *Italica* 83, no. 1 (2006): 53–61; and "Ettore Scola's *Concorrenza sleale*: The Alter-Biography of the Other-in-Our-Midst," in *Incontri con il cinema italiano*, ed. Antonio Vitti (Caltanissetta: Salvatore Sciascia Editore, 2003), 79–94. Her chapter in this volume is an expanded version of an earlier study on Scola's short film '43–'97 from her book *Italian Film in the Shadow of Auschwitz* (Toronto: Toronto Italian Studies, 2007). Giacomo Lichtner's studies on Scola include *Fascism in Italian Cinema since 1945: The Politics and Aesthetics of Memory* (New York: Palgrave Macmillan, 2013); "Italian Cinema and the Fascist Past: Tracing Memory Amnesia," *Fascism: Journal of Comparative Fascist Studies* 4 (2015): 25–47; and "Allegory, Applicability or Alibi? Historicizing Intolerance in Ettore Scola's *Concorrenza sleale*," *Journal of Modern Italian Studies* (2012): 95–102. Manuela Gieri's *Contemporary Italian Filmmaking: Strategies of Subversion; Pirandello, Fellini, Scola and the Directors of the New Generation* (Toronto: University of Toronto Press, 1996) offers a sweeping study of Scola's cinema, citing the importance of Pirandello's influence, from his metalinguistic works to his theories on *umorismo*.

4. Bíspuri, *Ettore Scola*, 27. Bíspuri affirms that Scola collaborated on *Totò le Mokò* (1949) by Carlo Ludovico Bragaglia and *Totòtarzan* (*Totò Tarzan*, 1950) by Mario Mattoli and that he also wrote gags for many other films by Mattoli.
5. Masi, *Ettore Scola*, 12.
6. Bíspuri, *Ettore Scola*, 28.
7. Bíspuri, 58.
8. Walter Veltroni, interview by Edward Bowen, October 5, 2016. All translations of quotations in this introduction are by Edward Bowen and Rémi Lanzoni.
9. Roberto Ellero, *Ettore Scola* (Florence: Nuova Italia, 1988), 11.
10. Bíspuri, *Ettore Scola*, 88.
11. Bíspuri, 96.
12. Ettore Scola, quoted in Antonio Bertini, ed., *Ettore Scola: Il cinema e io. Conversazione con Antonio Bertini* (Rome: Officina Edizioni, 1996), 148.
13. Gloria Satta, "Carlo Verdone: 'Ettore Scola ha insegnato a tutti noi l'importanza della commedia,'" *Il Mattino*, January 21, 2016, https://www.ilmattino.it/spettacoli/cinema/carlo_verdone_ettore_scola_commedia-1495894.html.
14. Marcus, "Ettore Scola's *Concorrenza sleale*," 79–80.
15. Ettore Scola, quoted in Bíspuri, *Ettore Scola*, 100.
16. Jacqueline Reich, *Beyond the Latin Lover: Marcello Mastroianni, Masculinity, and Italian Cinema* (Bloomington: Indiana University Press, 2004), 133.
17. Bíspuri, *Ettore Scola*, 97.
18. Bíspuri, 101.

19. Alberto Cattini, "Le strutture narrative nei film di Scola," in *Ettore Scola: Il volto amaro della commedia all'italiana*, ed. Giulio Marlia (Viareggio: M. Baroni, 1999), 35.
20. While *Una giornata particolare* is set in a housing complex, the setting for *Che ora è?* is less restricted, though it was entirely set in the port town of Civitavecchia.
21. Gianni Rondolino, "Le giornate particolari di Ettore Scola: Un profilo critico," in Zagarrio, *Trevico-Cinecittà*, 49.
22. Alessandra Fagioli, "Tra Studio e *Kammerspiel*. Tracce di teatro," in Zagarrio, *Trevico-Cinecittà*, 228.
23. For a detailed study on Scola's circular narratives, see Vito Zagarrio, "La sceneggiatura circolare: Strutture narrative in tre film di Ettore Scola," *Italianist* 29 (2009): 265–80.
24. Michela Greco, "*I nostri ragazzi* di De Matteo, adolescenti pericolosi," *Cinecittà News*, November 12, 2013, http://news.cinecitta.com/IT/it-it/news/55/5410/i-nostri-ragazzi-di-de-matteo-adolescenti-pericolosi.aspx.
25. Franco Montini, "La Roma di Scola," in Zagarrio, *Trevico-Cinecittà*, 218.
26. Montini, 219.
27. Peter Bondanella, *A History of Italian Cinema* (New York: Continuum, 2009), 206.
28. Marcus, *Italian Film in the Light of Neorealism*, 391.
29. Veronica Pravadelli, "Voci del maschile, corpi del femminile," in Zagarrio, *Trevico-Cinecittà*, 157–64.
30. Pravadelli, 157.
31. Marcia Landy, *Stardom Italian Style* (Bloomington: Indiana University Press, 2008), 154.
32. Sergio Rigoletto, *Masculinity and Italian Cinema: Sexual Politics, Social Conflict, and Male Crisis in the 1970s* (Edinburgh: Edinburgh University Press, 2014), 97, 100.
33. Masi, *Ettore Scola*, 103.
34. Pasquale Iaccio, "'Non ti piace la fine del XX secolo?' La storia nei film di Scola," in Zagarrio, *Trevico-Cinecittà*, 133.
35. Iaccio, 142–44.
36. Natalie Fullwood, *Cinema, Gender and Everyday Space* (New York: Palgrave Macmillan, 2015); Tiziana Ferrero-Regis, *Recent Italian Cinema: Spaces, Contexts, Experiences* (Leicester: Troubador, 2009); Laura Di Bianco, "Women in the Deserted City: Urban Space in Marina Spada's Cinema," in *Italian Women Filmmakers and the Gendered Screen*, ed. Maristella Cantini (New York: Palgrave Macmillan, 2013), 124–48; and John David Rhodes and Elena Gorfinkel, eds., *Taking Place: Location and the Moving Image* (Minneapolis: University of Minnesota Press, 2011).

37. See Giancarlo Lombardi and Christian Uva, eds., *Italian Political Cinema: Public Life, Imaginary, and Identity in Contemporary Italian Film* (Oxford: Peter Lang, 2016); Carlo Testa, ed., *Poet of Civic Courage: The Films of Francesco Rosi* (Westport, CT: Praeger, 1996); and Andrea Minuz, *Political Fellini: Journey to the End of Italy*, trans. Marcus Perryman (New York: Berghahn, 2015).

PART 1

SCOLA AS SCREENWRITER AND DIRECTOR OF COMEDY ITALIAN STYLE

THINKING WITH HIS HANDS

Ettore Scola's Narrative Intelligence as a
Screenwriter and Compulsive Illustrator

Mariapia Comand

THIS CHAPTER EXPLORES THE screenwriting activity of Ettore Scola during the 1950s and 1960s (in particular for Antonio Pietrangeli), with the hypothesis that this experience could have molded or may reveal the formation of his narrative thought, artistic method, or poetic world. The study is based on original materials (subjects, screenplays, treatments, notes and correspondence) kept in the Antonio Pietrangeli Archive at the Centro Cinema Città in Cesena and on documents from Ettore Scola's personal archive (currently being assembled at the Centro Sperimentale di Cinematografia in Rome). The analysis takes into consideration the sketches that Scola compulsively drew not just on his scripts but on paper napkins, scraps of papers, or the edges of notebooks. Following a neuroscientific, neuroaesthetic, and empirical aesthetic approach, these sketches are interpreted as indicating and resulting from his mental and creative process. The structuring idea of this chapter is that screenwriting—which requires a series of specific skills that Ettore Scola himself singles out—calls into play exactly the same cognitive abilities that neuroscience and cognitive science have identified as the building blocks on which we base our understanding of the world and how we interact with it.

Between the 1950s and 1960s:
Cartoonist, Gagman, and Lastly Screenwriter

In his piece "Qualche parentesi sul disporre in scene," Ettore Scola describes—as if it were the scene in a script—the reaction of his parents to the news that their second-born child, Ettore, had become a screenwriter. Naturally, he does so through an image, that of his father who, not knowing what a *sceneggiatore* (screenwriter) is, looks for the meaning of this mysterious word in the dictionary but cannot find it. Scola ironically comments:

> The fact that I was devoting myself to an activity ignored—or rather faintly contemplated—by the greatest dictionaries of the Italian language, for many years left my parents suspended in a limbo of uncertainty and alarm for the future of their second-born child. . . . I must also add that the apprehensions entertained by my parents were confirmed by the fact that for a couple of years my name did not appear in the opening credits of the films I claimed I was working on. Indeed, that day . . . when my father consulted his Petrocchi, I had in part lied. I wasn't embarking on being a screenwriter but a ghostwriter: a profession usually reserved for young writers and covered by anonymity, which consisted of providing jokes, gags, and comic situations to established screenwriters who would then include them in their scripts.[1]

As Scola himself recounts in the documentary film *Che strano chiamarsi Federico* (*How Strange to Be Named Federico*, 2013), he entered the culture industry thanks to his work as an illustrator for the humoristic magazine *Marc'Aurelio*,[2] for which Steno, Ruggero Maccari, Vittorio Metz, Marcello Marchesi, Mario Monicelli, Federico Fellini, and many others set for future glory already worked. The transition from cartoon strips to screenplays happened thanks to the two famous humorists, Metz and Marchesi, who enrolled the young Scola as a "workshop assistant" (the two had their headquarters in a Roman hotel, Hotel Moderno, where they had set up a sort of writers' room, distributing blocks of scripts to their collaborators to develop). In their first meeting, in 1950, Marchesi looked through the many scripts spread on the bed for one that was not ready for delivery. In the end, he chose *Totòtarzan* (*Totò Tarzan*; directed by Mario Mattoli and released in the same year). As Scola leafed through the first pages, he shyly made a joke. Marchesi liked it, so he offered him a down payment and an appointment for the next day. The words with which the director concludes the tale—"The wretched boy replied. And he became a screenwriter forever"[3]—deserve some attention because they are a perfect example of Scola's favorite form of linguistic pastiche, combining irony and wisdom in a literary and lexical mixture that blends japery with a cultured quotation (in this case, drawing from Alessandro Manzoni's *The Betrothed*). Moreover, these words are also an example of Scola's tendency to look at reality from a fresh angle by twisting the first and most expected meaning and to transform drama into comedy through "mode shifting."[4] Finally, these words suggest a research hypothesis that I intend to verify here, namely that screenwriting can be seen as a key to accessing and understanding all of Scola's cinema.[5] As a consequence, the 1950s and 1960s would be the conceptual and technical embryo in the formation of his narrative intelligence (meaning a particular cognitive ability employed to illuminate the human, cultural and symbolic world).[6]

A first reason for my assertion that screenwriting is the master and matrix of Scola's cinema is this: while these days the screenwriting profession may be sidelined in Italian cinema, this was even more so the case in the 1950s. It could be said this situation has always been the plight of screenwriters in Italy and even more so in Hollywood, so it would be helpful to have an explanation (beyond the quotes from Villa and Moravia) for why it was special in Italy in this time period. According to Federica Villa, "At no other time had Italian screenwriting felt its transience to be a value"; indeed at this point "it was having to deal with a cinema undergoing profound transformations . . . in search of its own identity."[7] It was in this same period that Alberto Moravia defined screenwriting as "rape of the intelligence."[8] For Scola, this marginalized working condition became an ideological stance and poetic choice, which gave him a view of things outside the mainstream. The characters penned by Scola in this period would indeed be misfits, eccentrics, belonging "outside the social and political field": women in the case of Pietrangeli's films—*Nata di marzo* (*March's Child*, 1958); *Adua e le compagne* (*Adua and Her Friends*, 1960); *La parmigiana* (*The Girl from Parma*, 1963); *La visita* (*The Visit*, 1963)—and outcasts as lead characters in the case of films scripted for Risi, such as *Il mattatore* (*Love and Larceny*, 1960), *Il sorpasso* (*The Easy Life*, 1962), *La marcia su Roma* (*March on Rome*, 1962), and *Il gaucho* (*The Gaucho*, 1964). In the works bearing his name as director, the stories would concern the anonymous, uncomfortable or secondary figures of official history: the repressed homosexual and the frustrated housewife in *Una giornata particolare* (*A Special Day*, 1977); the anonymous professor and dithering patriarch in *La famiglia* (*The Family*, 1987); the marginalized poor of Rome's periphery in *Brutti, sporchi e cattivi* (*Down and Dirty*, 1976); the builder Oreste and the florist Adelaide in *Dramma della gelosia—tutti i particolari in cronaca* (*The Pizza Triangle*, 1970), to mention just some of Scola's most memorable characters. Therefore, women, losers, and screenwriters were in a certain sense on the same level: forgotten by History (*la Storia*) or the forgotten creators of stories (*le storie*).

In Scola's professional and artistic career, the 1950s were therefore a fundamental period of growth. He was constantly in touch with the big screen, thanks to attending the *Circoli del Cinema* (cinematographic societies which were becoming popular in Italy at this time) and Pro-Deo, the Catholic university directed by Dominican film essayist Padre Morlion.[9] Scola's love for the cinema, expressed in the 1950s in the "Potito, il cinepatito" column of *Marc'Aurelio*, would be a distinct feature of his films. Dotted with various types of quotations, they demonstrated his encyclopedic and eclectic film culture which ranged, for example, from Marcel L'Herbier's *Histoire de rire* (*Foolish Husbands*, 1941), which is mentioned in Pietrangeli's *Lo scapolo* (*The Bachelor*, 1955), to Robert Wise's *The Day the Earth Stood Still* (1951), which is remembered in *Nata di marzo*. This passion for cinema would find full expression in the metacinematographic offerings of his older years, such as *Splendor* (1988) or the short '43–'97 (1997), praising cinema as a saving grace. Screenwriting was the common thread linking together the early years of his career and the decades of his maturity as a director. His snooty and pretentious screenwriter in Risi's *Il gaucho* and his neurotic character who writes laughs for money in *La terrazza* (*The Terrace*, 1980) are self-ironic portraits that nevertheless set out to cast attention on this key figure in cinema.[10]

Going back to the beginning of his career, when cinema formed the center of his passions, Scola was nevertheless busily engaged in various other media as well. In 1950, he entered Radio Rai and worked on the texts of radio comedian Tino Scotti. Thanks to Scotti, Scola wrote the screenplay for *Fermi tutti arrivo io!* (Sergio Grieco 1953),[11] an important script because it marked the debut of the Scola and Maccari scriptwriting pair, indestructible right up to the death of Maccari in 1989. Also fundamental for the future development of his career was his meeting Alberto Sordi, whom he accompanied first of all in writing the radio program *Il teatrino di Alberto Sordi* (on air as of 1952) and then as author of the screenplays for *Canzoni, canzoni, canzoni* (Domenico Paolella, 1953), *Accadde al commissariato* (*A Day at the Police Station*, Giorgio

Simonelli, 1954), *Un americano a Roma* (*An American in Rome*, Steno, 1954) and *Accadde al penitenziario* (Giorgio Bianchi, 1955).[12]

When looking at this phase, we can say that his role as cartoonist and *battutista* (writer of short comical exchanges) was complementary to that of screenwriter. While Scola's experience at *Marc'Aurelio* was decisive in refining his technical skills in quick comic timing, his screenwriting activity forced him to deal with the horizontal narrative structure of longer episodes. In this phase, his scriptwriting took two main directions. First of all, he worked on rhythm. Necessary for writing song movies (*Canzoni, canzoni, canzoni*), it was an activity that required him to practice harmonization—that is, connecting parts and identifying how to fit them together. Second, he tested out noncanonical narrative structures (different from the classic three-act structure[13]) with narrative segments that radiated from a central core, as in the *Accadde* films (namely, *Accadde al commissariato*, *Un americano a Roma*, and *Accadde al penitenziario*).

His exploration of possible storytelling methods went hand in hand with his reasoning on diegetic time, as seen in his liberal use of flashbacks in this period. Reflection on storytelling methods and time would be a constant in Scola's scriptwriting with Maccari for Pietrangeli, as can be seen in *La parmigiana* and *La visita*, for example, as well as in his films as director, above all *C'eravamo tanto amati* (*We All Loved Each Other So Much*, 1974), which stood out not because of the circularity of its production but because of its meditation.[14]

A third consideration stemming from an analysis of the early films Scola wrote concerns his dramaturgical use of space. One of Scola's topoi was his propensity for closed fictional places, where it is easier for the narrative energy to rise and generate tension: comic in the case of the *Accadde* trilogy and dramatic in the films for Pietrangeli, such as *La visita* and *Adua e le compagne*. This internal dynamic of restraining narrative energy within closed environments to make it grow can be seen at work again in such Scola films as *La famiglia*, *La più bella serata della mia vita* (*The Most Wonderful Evening of My Life*, 1972), *Ballando ballando* (*Le bal*, 1983), *Una giornata particolare*, and *La cena* (*The Dinner*, 1998), to name just a few.

The experimentation with nonlinear narration (in which it is the timeline that vitalizes the story) and noncanonical narrative structures constitute the core of Scola's world. At this point, it is essential to analyze his collaboration with Pietrangeli in order to understand the definitive evolution of Scola's artistic personality and his work method.

Screenwriter for Antonio Pietrangeli

In the early 1950s, Italian cinematic production was in full ferment. It was a flowing environment that fostered exchanges, meetings, and passages between one field of the industry and another. There were noninstitutional places, such as the "workshop"[15] of Marchesi and Metz but also the famous Roman *salotti* or the trattorias like Otello alla Concordia frequented by directors and screenwriters—where "craftsmen" doled out popular products at a great rate. These hotbeds of creation generated relations, connections, and projects and in the meantime also performed a formative function. The heart and soul of one of these places was producer Carlo Infascelli. In his office, writers worked on musical films and episodic feature films inspired by light theater: Scola figured in the writing team of various productions of this genre, such as *Canzoni di mezzo secolo* (Domenico Paolella, 1952), *Amori di mezzo secolo* (*Mid-century Loves*, Glauco Pellegrini, Antonio Pietrangeli, Pietro Germi, Mario Chiari, and Roberto Rossellini, made in 1952 but released in 1954), *Canzoni, canzoni, canzoni*, *Gran varietà* (*Great Vaudeville*, Domenico Paolella, 1953–54) and *Ridere! Ridere! Ridere!* (Edoardo Anton, 1954). Here, he met many personalities from the cinema field and more, including Rossellini and Pietrangeli, the latter of whom was drafting the screenplay for *Amori di mezzo secolo* following his debut as director with *Il sole negli occhi* (*Empty Eyes*, 1953). Pietrangeli involved Scola in the preparation of the screenplay for *Lo scapolo*, a film that required a humoristic talent that Pietrangeli did not possess.[16] From that moment on, Scola (along with Maccari), wrote all of Pietrangeli's films (except for the last): *Souvenir d'Italie* (*It Happened in Rome*, 1957), *Nata di marzo*, *Adua e le compagne*, *Fantasmi a Roma* (*Phantom Lovers*, 1961), *La parmigiana*, *La visita*, *Il magnifico cornuto* (*The Magnificent Cuckold*, 1964), and *Io la conoscevo bene* (*I Knew Her Well*, 1965). Reading through these titles, his interest in the female universe is clear, as is underlined by Scola himself:

> When working with him, I first of all discovered a new theme. In years when there was no talk whatsoever of feminism . . . Pietrangeli above all wanted to tell stories of women. He had started with *Il sole negli occhi*,

the story of a waitress in Rome, then he continued with *Nata di marzo*, the story of a middle-class teenage bride, and again with *Adua e le compagne, La visita, La parmigiana*. . . . It was quite a rare preference. At that time cinema was 100 percent male, stories of men, with Totò or Sordi or Mastroianni in the leading roles; actresses were chosen for their physical appeal or for roles as mothers, sisters, and so on. Instead Pietrangeli placed his attention on female issues, they were the core of his poetics.[17]

While it was without doubt a new topic from a sociological point of view, in literary terms it was not: both Pietrangeli and Scola were indebted to the lessons of the nineteenth-century novel and fascinated by the heroines of European literature, from *Anna Karenina* to *Emma Bovary*, figures whom we find in the unresolved restlessness of Dora in *La parmigiana* or in the splendid fatuous vitality of Adriana in *Io la conoscevo bene*. Moreover, we find literary influence in the motif of female suicide (or attempted suicide), with the dark thread linking Karenina and Bovary to Adriana in *Io la conoscevo bene*, Celestina in *Il sole negli occhi* (who, Karenina style, threw herself under a tram), and Luciana in *C'eravamo tanto amati*. It must also be considered that the literary matrix (and in particular the modern European novel) connects an important part of Scola's production, as both a young and a mature author. Clotilde Bertoni and Massimo Fusillo assert, "In a dynamic note of neat reflection, but of reformulation of its problems, the main input for the plots' exuberant inventiveness and their alternation of registers remained the consolidation of modern society, and its oscillation between dynamism and restlessness, energy and discontent."[18] Intimately connected to this topic is another element common to Scola and Pietrangeli—their attention to contemporary society—which in Pietrangeli came from his neorealistic formation and in Scola from his experience at *Marc'Aurelio*. In this light, their interest in women helps us understand the social and cultural changes in postwar Italy, especially if we consider Stephen Gundle's assertion that female figures were at the forefront of negotiations between levels of power and desires.[19] Pietrangeli was fully aware of this. In an interview from 1967, Pietrangeli explicitly claimed that the entry into modernity had a female stride: "In the process of social transformation . . . women indisputably have a leading role . . . and it is not just a fact of habit, but of radical . . . interior revolution: a process that . . . is perhaps in anticipation of the evolution of Italian society."[20] The centrality of the topic of women in Pietrangeli's cinema is confirmed by studying materials in his archive. For example, studies emerge for secondary female figures in *Io la conoscevo bene*, such as the portrait of Eva Rossetti, a young escort who was part of the Roman film underworld; or Adelaide Franchetti, a nurse during the war, an occasional model and steadfast friend of a fashionable actor, with her ne'er-do-well father; or Esterina Libassi, from a modest Umbrian family, whose brother was a pottery designer. While not decisive in the plot's development (they sporadically appear in the story, not going unnoticed, however), these figures constitute lesser yet "round" narrative subjects, to use the definition given by Forster.[21] In other words, they are capable of dynamism despite the few occasions in which they appear. Another characteristic that relates these women to those of Scola's future films is that they are victims of male arrogance: just think of Elide Catenacci in *C'eravamo tanto amati*, a touching portrait of "female solitude."[22] It certainly comes as no surprise that after this apprenticeship Scola's directorial debut, *Se permettete parliamo di donne* (*Let's Talk about Women*, 1964), would feature a marked female component.

In terms of method, the lesson learned from Pietrangeli was decisive in pointing Scola toward a scientific approach to artistic production: while the humoristic movies were written at breakneck speed (obliging him to temporarily juggle several roles at the same time), Pietrangeli's comedies required absolute concentration and full immersion for their preparation. They demanded a long gestation period, with the consequent intensive exploitation of the preproduction phase, so that on-set mishaps and requirements could be reduced to a minimum. Scola claimed that these meticulous and precise studies alongside Pietrangeli had saved him from having to train as an assistant director.[23] Writing screenplays could take a year or even more and involved in-depth research and a long phase dedicated to discussion. The scriptwriting process followed a complex routine of devising and drawing up the subject, drafting the film treatment, and finally completing the script outline. Having clarified the movements and fundamental points in the plot, the scriptwriters divided the parts and each one began to write independently. The whole script was then entirely rewritten by Pietrangeli before the final, slow revision process.[24]

In terms of narrative substance, it can undeniably be said that the characters took priority over the story in Pietrangeli's cinema. The subjects generally consisted of the presentation of the characters' emotional and psychological stories. For example, this is how the subject for *Io la conoscevo bene* began:

> Today, it makes almost no more sense to say "a girl" and that's it—there are so many different types, characters and ways of living among the young women we meet in the news, in "serious" literature, in our own experience. . . . There are girls like Adriana Bucelli who do not fall into any . . . category. . . . It's difficult to give her a label that defines her whole, what she's like, in a word. Adriana is a calm girl, serene, happy, "carefree," as those who know her say and as we're authorized to believe too, from that smile that never leaves her lips. She's a "restful" girl. Wherever she's put, she stays. Wherever she's taken, she goes. She's naive, submissive, spontaneous, she says what she thinks: perhaps that's why she speaks so little. She has the same capacity of immobility as a stone: on the beach, baking in the sun for hours and hours, with her eyes closed, only moving a finger every so often to change the channel on the transistor radio and look for other music if someone has started to talk or read the news (one of the things that bores her most in the world); and on her bed at home, looking at the ceiling, with the record player next to her, a black dog, a goldfish in a bowl and all around her an absolute mess. . . . This is what we want to say about Adriana. It's not really a story, because it doesn't have—just like all of Adriana's character—a precise beginning or a reasoned and consequent development.[25]

From the beginning of the subject, the story's modernity is clear: it is programmatically released from the links of cause and effect, centered on an undecided and nonprogressive narrative course, on the one hand, and a definite focus on the character's temperament, above all marked by its elusiveness, on the other. In the same way, the premise of another subject written by Scola and never realized is significant. Titled "Il cameriere" (The Waiter), it meekly announces, in parentheses, the ideological heart of Scola's cinema: "(This film proposes the description of a character instead of telling a story. Therefore, I have deliberately set out a simple, free, unexceptional plot, so that we can follow the protagonist's daily life while examining its funny, human, comical, and pathetic aspects)."[26]

With Pietrangeli, Scola embarked on the road of character-based cinema. Already then, and even more thereafter, he forewent flat and monotonous, edifying and comforting, human portraits to take instead an interest in figures shining in their obscurity, intense in their uncertainty and actions, and substantial in their apparent lack of consistency. He always placed himself empathetically on the character's side, no matter what,[27] in the conviction that "the awful thing about life is this: Everybody has their reasons," as Jean Renoir reminds us in *La règle du jeu* (*The Rules of the Game*, 1939). A rule that Scola always observed.

Ettore Scola, Compulsive Drawer

The documents in the Pietrangeli archive overflow with tangible signs of Scola's personality. His drawings are everywhere as they peep out from the margins of screenplays and cover his pages of notes (fig. 2). They blossom between the points in a script outline: sketches, little figures, geometrical shapes, female bodies, faces, improvised fantasies, and inventive flourishes. Ettore Scola's personal archive holds similar surprises for us. There are various types of drawings: the originals of cartoons published in magazines; the preparatory sketches for sets; the visualization of some scenes from the screenplays (fig. 3).

Since Scola was an illustrator (as is also seen in various publications), it is natural that many pages of his archive concern this ability.[28] In all the above cases, they are functional drawings that refer to intentional, controlled, and conscious processes of elaboration. However, what attracts the attention more than anything else and arouses one's curiosity are the sketches that the director compulsively dotted around practically everywhere. As Scola himself explained, he was following a peremptory instinct: "I've always had this habit of dirtying paper, ever since I was little. At home I still have books whose margins are full of drawn comments, little characters, scribbles. Still now, when I speak, when I write, I always draw. They aren't logical drawings connected to a reasoning, but they help me to think. It's a tic, it's automatic."[29] This need to process thoughts manually, to think with one's hands, links Scola to different artists, including Federico Fellini, who was also a compulsive doodler. Fellini stated:

> I always scribbled making caricatures of friends. I always had this uncontrollable tic to draw faces with a pen. . . . This almost unconscious,

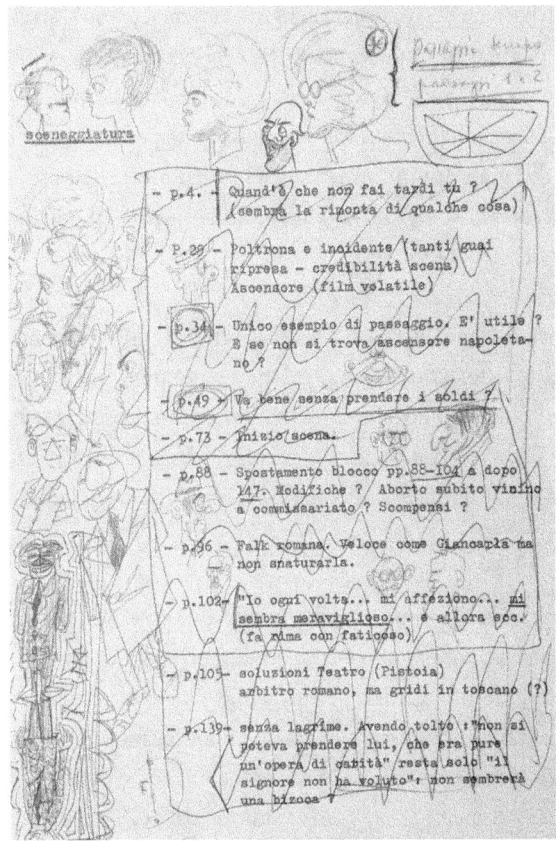

FIGURE 2. Centro Cinema Città di Cesena, Antonio Pietrangeli, sketches

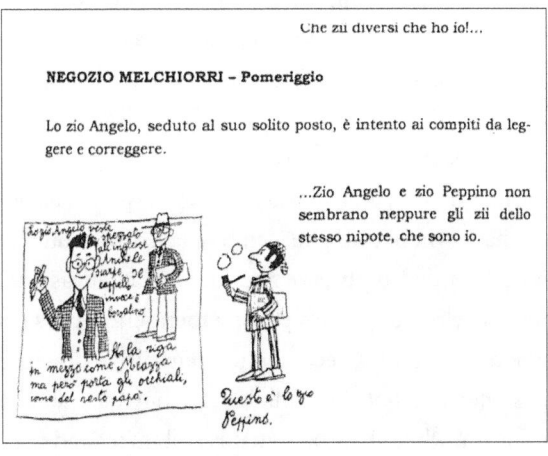

FIGURE 3. Archivio Scola, *Concorrenza sleale*

involuntary tracing of doodles, hanging caricature notes, making inexhaustible puppets that stare at me from every corner of the sheet . . . and endless other sketches, hieroglyphics, dotted with telephone numbers, addresses, delusional verses, tax calculations, appointment schedules, in short, all this graphic junk, rampant, inexhaustible . . . perhaps it is a kind of trace, a thread, at the end of which I find myself with the lights on, on stage, the first day of shooting.[30]

Art historian David Rosand calls this kind of quick and swift sketch that seems to want to externalize thoughts "the seeing pen,"[31] and he connects it to the theory and practice of drawing in the Italian Renaissance, when artists like Leonardo da Vinci used drawings to explore the natural world and produce new knowledge. Scola also interprets this aptitude as a mental rather than artistic process:

Mine aren't real drawings sketched with artistic ends. Instead, they're mental doodles, almost never with an aim or imposed by precise goals. . . . In my work, although distractedly, I make sketches to clarify the initial ideas for a scene, a costume, a character, both for me and my colleagues. In a certain sense, it's a "prior vision" of the images in a film that is still in the making. Let me be clear, it isn't a storyboard. . . . They are work notes, a way of thinking out loud and immediately transferring onto paper the images and indications that appear in my mind. That's what drawing is for me, a way to mentally unload: I've always drawn, on whatever and wherever I could, also outside my work. It's another way of concentrating better on certain ideas or of keeping your distance from others.[32]

From a cognitivist and neuroscientific perspective, this activity—apparently bizarre, random, and accessory—is interpreted as helping create a physical-visual space where thoughts can be played with outside the boundaries of the mind in order to observe and manipulate ideas and perceptions; it allows them to develop fully, since putting them into words could interrupt the flow of reasoning.[33] So his recourse to compulsive drawing tells of how he follows the somersaults of thoughts before they take on a definitive and communicative form, when their potential is still intact and they have not yet taken on their end form.[34] For this reason, studying these quirks can be useful

FIGURE 4. Archivio Scola, cartoon

from different points of view. First, it visualizes the "Scola method": the using of his hands to fulfill the potential of his thought[35] is the method he chooses to embrace his screenwriting. By doing this, he reactivates the relationship both between hand and mind, and between image and concept, and the awareness—well known to screenwriters—that knowledge has to pass through the funnel of the senses.[36] How this mental process reflects on Scola's cinema can be seen both in its long silences and its touches of semantic nervousness. Scola's cinema often celebrates silence as a status of watchful waiting, a moment for processing sense, and the opening of thought, as evidenced, for example, with the virtuoso initial sequences of *La famiglia* or *Una giornata particolare* or in the final scene of *Splendor*. These are powerful images precisely because they are silent, because "the word is a key, but silence is a picklock."[37] All the same, at times Scola's cinema is recognizable thanks to a certain nervous syntax, typified by the suppression of middle steps, as happens, for example, in *C'eravamo tanto amati*. This is a type of sequence that we find at work in a multitude of cartoons, whose effect on the reader derives from compressing meanings and jumping to conclusions and from putting together the consequences of the facts rather than showing the events themselves—like a cartoon that Scola drew in which the secretary puts pistols next to the board of directors' files, considering the terrible profit trends hanging on the wall (fig. 4).[38] In other

THINKING WITH HIS HANDS - 35

words, the cartoon anticipates the outcome of the reasoning, just like Scola's sketches taught him to do.

The small figures filling Scola's documents highlight at least two tendencies. First, identical forms return in different contexts. On one drawing in Ettore Scola's private archive, a triangle creates a Christmas tree with some decorations and a star on the top, which also recalls the triangular roadside signal that signifies caution. Scola jokes with this double meaning, and Santa Claus is forced to stop to repair the sleigh drawn by the reindeer (fig. 5). His reasoning on the functions of shapes, and the different possible functions for the same shapes, returns in a more structured way in a figure titled "Il trionfo della geometria" (The Triumph of Geometry, fig. 6).[39] Scola can be seen playing with the polysemous meanings of the same shape in a cartoon of a

FIGURE 5. Archivio Scola, drawing

36 – MARIAPIA COMAND

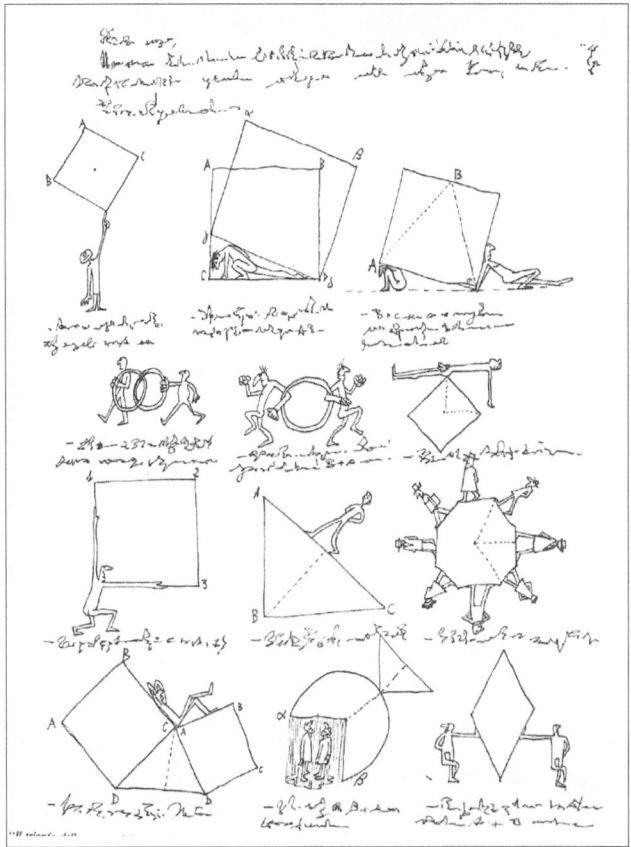

FIGURE 6. Drawing, *The Triumph of Geometry*

footballer kicking a ball: the ball hits someone on the head, the head falls off and goes into the goal, while the football remains on the person's neck (fig. 7).

These sketches help us reconstruct the thought processes of Scola. Through Scola's drawings we can also reflect on the thought processes that we all have, such as how we try to understand the figurative and narrative schemes under the surface of meanings and how our minds tend to function under a logic of association. According to neuroscientist Vinod Goel, the indeterminacy of sketching reflects the procedural, creative nature of thought: it accustoms us to considering recurrences in an elastic manner; that is, by expanding the range of possible configurations of the same form, it trains us for the unexpected.[40] In other words, one could say that the ambiguity of sketches keeps our attention aroused, questions it, and is a fertilizer for new

FIGURE 7. Archivio Scola, cartoon

ideas because the imprecision (of the mark, meant as the signifier) prevents the ossification of meaning. This is why Scola's sketches can be read as maps of the relations explored by the imagination. They are useful for transmitting spatial concepts or metaphorically spatial concepts, or complete or incomplete objects. His sketches are also useful when we are considering many alternatives and weighing up (unconsciously, mentally) the general configurations before being bound by particular connections and specific forms. This metacognitive training allows us to discover secret affinities and unusual possibilities while paving the way for invention and new ideas.[41] Scola showed this inventive skill, this ability to produce new relations of meanings, through his decisions in casting and direction of actors. He often came up with unusual expressive and dramaturgical ideas for Italian stars: thanks to Scola, Mastroianni—until then the quintessential on-screen Latin lover—became a convincing, listless homosexual capable of enchanting with his fine manners in Una giornata particolare. In the same film, Sophia Loren, until then a commanding physical presence and sex symbol, becomes an unappealing, dull, frustrated housewife. Meanwhile in La famiglia, Vittorio Gassman—the first actor capable of dominating any stage—becomes an unresolved, irresolute man, incapable of leading his own life.

Inventing new relations is very much a screenwriters' skill. Screenwriters are required to capture the relations between images and concepts, to conjure up the abstract by mastering the figurative, to possess deductive ability and narrative imagination. Scola himself was convinced of this and expressed (more poetically) this conviction in his piece "Qualche parentesi sul disporre in scene," which I quoted at the beginning:

> Perhaps the difficulty of saying what screenwriting is, and the resulting contrasts, is precisely because we are trying to nail down an activity that has always been a part of the human brain as something specific and recent: when we put our behavior in love, in groups, or in social conflict into scenes; when we assess and vary the manifestations of reality according to our mind-set and feelings; when we leaf through our personal history and remember what we did yesterday or predict what we will do tomorrow. Until the words THE END.[42]

As Scola acutely perceives, the activity of screenwriting follows a narrative mode of thought, narrative intelligence: in thought and in script, experiences are codified through symbolic models and a subjective time, which are emotional and psychological. In Scola's creative experience and artistic routine as a scriptwriter and compulsive drawer, we see some universal cognitive processes at work and at the same time the formation of his expressive and discursive modalities. One can also note in this activity a constant reflection on the meanings and perceptions of human time, on the constriction of space, and on the limits of the body. There is also an incessant questioning, between the hands and the thoughts, with the schemes and the forms, in a fascinating wandering among the meanings in search of an unprecedented mix of meaning. The outcome of this wandering of thought and hands (or thoughts through hands) produces unexpected artistic combinations on the narrative, figurative, and representative levels as evidenced in his creation of original women characters for Italian cinema.

Notes

1. Originally published in Vittorio Spinazzola, ed., *Pubblico 1981: Produzione letteraria e mercato culturale* (Milan: Milano Libri, 1981), the speech was then republished in Antonio Maraldi, ed., *I film e le sceneggiature di Ettore Scola* (Cesena: Quaderni del Centro Cinema, 1982), 19–20. Translations throughout the chapter are my own unless otherwise noted. Petrocchi was one of the most

renowned Italian dictionaries of the time. Policarpo Petrocchi, *Novo dizionario universale della lingua italiana* (Milan: Treves Editore, 1912).

2. The satirical magazine, founded in 1931 by Oberdan Cotone and Vito De Bellis, was directed by De Bellis from 1931 to 1945 and from 1948 to 1954. Scola started to work for the magazine at age fifteen. Angelo Olivieri, *L'imperatore in platea: I grandi del cinema dal Marc'Aurelio allo schermo* (Bari: Dedalo, 1986); on *Marc'Aurelio* as a magazine spanning different media, see Alessandro Faccioli, *Leggeri come in una gabbia. L'idea comica nel cinema italiano (1930–1944)* (Turin: Kaplan, 2011).

3. Ettore Scola, "Qualche parentesi sul disporre in scene," in Maraldi, *I film e le sceneggiature di Ettore Scola*, 21. The reference is to the episode of Monaca of Monza in Alessandro Manzoni, *I Promessi Sposi* (Milan: Vincenzo Ferrario, 1827).

4. "The 'mode shifting' consists of adopting a grotesque tone in a dramatic situation in order to convert it to comedy. This is the case for Ettore Scola's *Brutti, sporchi e cattivi (Down and Dirty*, 1976)." Rémi Fournier Lanzoni, *Comedy Italian Style: The Golden Age of Italian Film Comedies* (New York: Continuum, 2009), 166.

5. On Scola as a screenwriter: Giuliana Muscio, "Un mestiere come un altro: Scola sceneggiatore," in *Trevico-Cinecittà: L'avventuroso viaggio di Ettore Scola*, ed. Vito Zagarrio (Venice: Marsilio, 2002), 51–58; Ivelise Perniola, "Il mestiere di scrittore: Dalla sceneggiatura presunta alla sceneggiatura desunta," in Zagarrio, *Trevico-Cinecittà*, 244–54; Ennio Bíspuri, *Ettore Scola: Un umanista nel cinema italiano* (Rome: Bulzoni, 2006), in particular the chapter "Le sceneggiature," 37–86; and Ennio Bíspuri, "Ettore Scola: Uno scrittore di cinema," in *Nero su Bianco: Sceneggiatura e sceneggiatori in Italia*, ed. Paolo Russo (Barcelona: Quaderni del CSCI, 2014), 143–48. Here, Bíspuri singles out three figures of particular influence in Scola's formation as a screenwriter: Antonio Pietrangeli, Dino Risi, and Sergio Amidei. Scola recognized the role of mentor and educator played by Sergio Amidei, his scrupulousness in gathering information in the documentation phase prior to writing, his ability to inject cultural substance into comic material, and his skill in observing timing and characters. In this connection, I refer to Ilaria Borghese, Mariapia Comand, and Maria Rita Fedrizzi, *Sergio Amidei, sceneggiatore* (Gorizia: Grafiche Goriziane, 2004).

6. Under the term *narrative intelligence*, we can include observations and research from different fields, such as cognitive psychology (see, for example, Jerome Bruner, *Actual Minds, Possible Worlds* [Cambridge, MA: Harvard University Press, 1986]), linguisitics (Mark Turner, *The Literary Mind: The Origins of Thought and Language*, Oxford University Press, 1996]), and artificial intelligence (Roger Schank, *Tell Me a Story: Narrative and Intelligence*

[Evanston, IL: Northwestern University Press, 1990]). At the center of this vast scientific area are the processes of categorization (typical of narrative activity as in everyday life) and of subjectification (e.g., in the description of time in narrative experiences), in the framework of attention to context and common sense.

7. Federica Villa, "Cordoglio ed euforia: La sceneggiatura negli anni '50," in *Sulla carta: Storia e storie della sceneggiatura in Italia*, ed. Mariapia Comand (Turin: Lindau, 2004), 143–62, 144.

8. Alberto Moravia, *Contempt*, introduction by Tim Parks, trans. Angus Davidson (New York: New York Review Books, 1999; first published as *Il disprezzo*, 1957), 41.

9. Ettore Scola, quoted in Antoni Bertini, ed., *Ettore Scola: Il cinema e io. Conversazione con Antonio Bertini* (Rome: Officina Edizioni, 1996), 40–41.

10. In *Il gaucho*, the character of the screenwriter (Marco Ravecchio) has a subordinate role, both from a narrative point of view (he is a secondary figure in the plot) and figurative point of view (he always appears at the margins of the groups he interacts with). The film offers a nonedifying representation of the writer who is inept, asocial, and closed off by an intellectual way of speaking. Not even in *La terrazza* is the writer a positive character, as he is always crushed by the expectations of the producer, a lack of ideas, and by neurosis.

11. According to Bíspuri: "Starting in 1952, the presence of Scola as a screenwriter for popular films of the so-called comic genre, often of poor quality and either disengaged or openly indifferent, intensified to an almost exponential level. . . . The first film definitely scripted by Scola alongside Giuseppe Patroni Griffi, Oreste Biancoli, Dino Falconi, and Vinicio Marinucci, and produced by Carlo Infascelli, was *Canzoni di mezzo secolo* by Domenico Paolella, which was incredibly successful among the public and opened the floodgates to a series of dozens and dozens of films with more or less the same theme" (*Ettore Scola: Un umanista nel cinema italiano*, 38). Scola, however, declared that his first screenplay was *Fermi tutti arrivo io!* (script written in 1951, film released in 1953): "Maccari was supposed to write the script by himself: he knew that I was working for Metz and Marchesi, and he proposed that I write the script with him, while this time including me in the credits." Ettore Scola, quoted in Bertini, *Ettore Scola*, 46.

12. According to Scola, the meeting with Sordi took place in 1948, on the radio, when Scola was writing radio features with Nino Meloni and Riccardo Mantoni. Giancarlo Governi, *Alberto Sordi, l'italiano* (Rome: Armando Curcio, 2010), 93–105.

13. The structure canonized by Syd Field: *The Screenwriter's Workbook: A Workshop Approach* (New York: Dell, 1984). Also useful as a historical framework: Steven Price, *A History of the Screenplay* (New York: Palgrave Macmillan, 2013).

14. On the circular structure of *We All Loved Each Other So Much*: Vito Zagarrio, "La sceneggiatura circolare: strutture narrative in tre film di Scola," *Italianist* 29 (2009): 265–80; on the short circuit between time, memory, and storytelling, I refer to my analysis: "Mentre è già: Tempo, memoria e ricordo in *C'eravamo tanto amati*," in *Commedia all'italiana*, ed. Mariapia Comand (Milan: Castoro, 2010), 126–35.
15. On the concept of "writing workshop," a sort of twentieth-century renewal of the Renaissance workshop for writing in images, see Federica Villa, *Botteghe di scrittura per il cinema italiano: Intorno a 'Il bandito' di Alberto Lattuada*, Bianco e Nero (Venice: Marsilio, 2002).
16. On Pietrangeli: Guglielmina Morelli, Giulio Martini, Giancarlo Zappoli, *Un'invisibile presenza: Il cinema di Antonio Pietrangeli* (Milan: Il Castoro, 1998); Piera Detassis, Emiliano Morreale, Mario Sesti, eds., *Antonio Pietrangeli: Il regista che amava le donne* (Rome: Edizione Sabinae, 2015).
17. Ettore Scola, quoted in Bertini, *Ettore Scola*, 49.
18. Clotilde Bertoni and Massimo Fusillo, "Tematica romanzesca o topoi letterari di lunga durata?" in *Il romanzo*, ed. Franco Moretti, vol. 4, *Temi, luoghi, eroi* (Turin: Einaudi, 2003), 47. See also Franco Moretti, ed., *The Novel*, vol. 1, *History, Geography and Culture* (Princeton, NJ: Princeton University Press, 2006).
19. Stephen Gundle, *Bellissima: Feminine Beauty and the Idea of Italy* (New Haven, CT: Yale University Press, 2007).
20. Antonio Pietrangeli, "Ritratti cinematografici della donna italiana," *Bianco e Nero* 28, no. 5 (1967): 36.
21. For Forster "flat characters" are the most recognizable characters, whom we remember because they fundamentally never change throughout the story: "Flat characters are very useful . . . since they never need reintroducing, never run away, have not to be watched for development, and provide their own atmosphere—little luminous disks of a pre-arranged size, pushed hither and thither like counters across the void or between the stars." On the contrary, "round characters" are complex, with a certain emotional and psychological breadth, and therefore with a personal history marked by change, choice, and transformation. Edward Morgan Forster, *Aspects of the Novel* (New York: RosettaBooks, 2010; first published 1927), 105.
22. Marcia Landy, *Italian Film* (Cambridge: Cambridge University Press, 2000), 362.
23. Mario Sesti, "Conversazione con Ettore Scola," in Detassis, Morreale, and Sesti, *Antonio Pietrangeli*, 49–56.
24. According to what emerged from examining the documents housed in the Antonio Pietrangeli Archive at the Centro Cinema Città in Cesena.
25. The subject is kept in the Antonio Pietrangeli Archive at the Centro Cinema Città in Cesena.

26. The subject is part of the private archive of Ettore Scola. My thanks go to Silvia Scola, Gigliola Scola, and Marco Scola di Mambro for their helpfulness and for making the material available and to Giovanni Grasso for his support.
27. For example, Scola places himself on Adriana's (intepreted by Stefania Sandrelli) side in *Io la conoscevo bene* (Antonio Pietrangeli, 1965). Chiara Tognolotti underlines the indecipherable and unconventional aspect of her character and the complicity with which she is described in the screenplay and by the camera. See Chiara Tognolotti, "Io la conoscevo bene (Antonio Pietrangeli, 1965)," in *La donna visibile: Il cinema di Stefania Sandrelli*, ed. Daniela Brogi (Pisa: ETS, 2016), 59–66.
28. Pier Marco De Santi, ed., *Ettore Scola: Immagini per un mondo nuovo* (Pisa: Giardini editori, 1989).
29. Ettore Scola, quoted in Bertini, *Ettore Scola*, 31.
30. Federico Fellini, *Fare un film* (Turin: Einaudi 1980), 68.
31. David Rosand, *Drawing Acts: Studies in Graphic Expression and Representation* (Cambridge: Cambridge University Press, 2002).
32. De Santi, *Ettore Scola*, 4.
33. Jonathan W. Schooler and Tonya Y. Engstler-Schooler, "Verbal Overshadowing of Visual Memories: Some Things Are Better Left Unsaid," *Cognitive Psychology* 22, no. 1 (1990): 36–71. Andrea Kantrowitz adds a neuroaesthetic and empirical aesthetic slant. See her "The Man behind the Curtain: What Cognitive Science Reveals about Drawing," *Journal of Aesthetic Education* 46, no. 1 (2012): 1–14.
34. Marco Iacoboni, *Mirroring People* (New York: Farrar, Straus, & Giroux, 2008).
35. Maria Konnikova, "What's Lost as Handwriting Fades," *New York Times*, June 3, 2014. I would like to thank Millicent Marcus for pointing out this article to me.
36. See the section "The Senses" in David Corbett, *Art of Character* (New York: Penguin Books, 2013), 127–28.
37. Gesualdo Bufalino, *Il malpensante: Lunario dell'anno che fu* (Milan: Bompiani, 1987), 17.
38. Ettore Scola's private archive, courtesy of the family.
39. Pier Marco De Santi and Rossano Vittori, "'Il trionfo della geometria,' divertimento con nonsenso di Scola, 1977," *I film di Ettore Scola* (Rome: Gremese, 1987), 25.
40. Vinod Goel, *Sketches of Thought* (Cambridge, MA: MIT Press, 1995).
41. Barbara Tversky and Masaki Suwa, "Thinking with Sketches," in *Tools for Innovation*, ed. Arthur Markman and Kristin Wood (Oxford: Oxford University Press, 2009), 75–85.
42. Scola, "Qualche parentesi sul disporre in scene," 26.

VISUAL TRANSITIONS IN ETTORE SCOLA'S COMEDIES

Fabrizio Cilento

> *My departure point always pertains to the solution of a narrative problem.*[1]
> Ettore Scola

THIS CHAPTER EXPLORES THE continuities and ruptures within Ettore Scola's apprenticeship, screenwriting, and directorial style over several decades. In their reviews, academics and popular critics such as Lino Miccichè and Tullio Kezich juxtapose the erotic eclecticism, histrionic acting, and vignettes that inform the early screenplays and films directed by Scola against the post-1968 sociopolitical awareness that manifests itself in *C'eravamo tanto amati* (*We All Loved Each Other So Much*, 1974) and *La terrazza* (*The Terrace*, 1980).[2] Blending a close textual analysis with film history, however, I engage with the shifting critical perception of Scola's work to demonstrate how these alleged "two phases" are not to be conceived as compartmentalized boxes but are strongly interrelated. Scola's apprenticeship at the *Marc'Aurelio* satirical magazine, where he encountered screenwriters Vittorio Metz and Marcello Marchesi, was crucial for the development of his signature use of the grotesque and nonlinear narratives. Such continuity also emerges in the screenplays of Antonio Pietrangeli's *La parmigiana* (*The Girl from Parma*, 1963) and *Io la conoscevo bene* (*I Knew Her Well*, 1965), which Scola coauthored; the metatextual transitions between the various episodes of *Se permettete parliamo di donne* (*Let's Talk about Women*, 1964); the visual grids that connect the various characters of *Il commissario Pepe* (*Police Chief Pepe*, 1969); and the ending of *Riusciranno i nostri eroi a ritrovare l'amico misteriosamente scomparso in*

Africa? (*Will Our Heroes Be Able to Find Their Friend Who Has Mysteriously Disappeared in Africa?*, 1968). Significantly, these works present a critique of Italian sexual mores and at times of the cinematic industry itself, along with innovative narrative solutions and visual patterns that the more mature movies clearly echo. In sum, a generous read of Scola's early career will uncover the roots of his comedic polycentrism and more complex story line experimentations of the 1970s and early 1980s.

On the innovative side, *C'eravamo tanto amati* involves multiple character types and predictable identities without limiting them to the conventional episodic structure of the comedy genre. Instead, the film presents a new degree of self-reflexivity and challenges the potential of the medium through the inclusion of a variety of intertextual and multimedia references. The patterns of this storytelling mode suggest a range of reasons for their emergence in the mid-1970s, when Scola overturns the usual characters and identities by embracing nonlinearity. At the same time, *C'eravamo tanto amati* melds the traditionally disjointed nature of Comedy Italian Style into a coherent discourse, by displaying its multiple narratives in a series of fluid and permeable time loops that overlap into each other.

The film's experimentation with form begins with the opening sequence, when Gianni (Vittorio Gassman) exits through the same door multiple times and programmatically breaks the fourth wall until the image freezes (an homage to Frank Capra's *It's a Wonderful Life*, 1946) in an eloquent close-up that shows his middle-aged disillusionment. While the voice-over continues, the second sequence switches to black and white and is set in 1943. Through a long flashback (and a series of flashbacks within the flashback), we learn about the relationship between the three protagonists over a period that spans from World War II to the affluent years of the economic miracle. These three segments intersect when the protagonists fall in love with Luciana (Stefania Sandrelli), when they watch or participate in television programs, or when they engage with the political events of their time. The final sequence frames the film and provides some visual symmetry by returning to the freeze frame of Gianni diving into the pool; now we see the completion of his dive into the water. In this sense, *C'eravamo tanto amati* circles back to the time and place where it began—to the present tense in which it was shot.

While Scola's narrative technique reaches a new level of complexity, *C'eravamo tanto amati* also presents continuity with the past. Although the characters are psychologically more sophisticated than the previous ones (drifters motivated by transgressive sexual instincts or monetary greediness), some stereotyping persists, and these obvious traits are representative of different social categories. Furthermore, the use of sketches endures, and the trivial jokes that characterize Scola's early comedies are not absent. These emerge especially if one looks at the minor characters, particularly the corrupted tycoon Romolo Catenacci (Aldo Fabrizi), in whom one can recognize the comedy type of the enriched boor. Gianni first meets Romolo in a steam room, with only a towel covering the overweight body of his future father-in-law. Catenacci tells him that the loneliest creature in the world is the rich man, because he is rare, while poor people are always ready to befriend each other. If it were not for the rich fooling the poor, the poor would not exist, and Jesus, who said, "Blessed are the poor, because they will be seated on my right hand," would be condemned to sit alone. This monologue, which subverts Christian pauperism, anticipates Gianni's destiny. The display of wealth reemerges a few minutes later when a crane brings a roasted pig resting on an Italian flag to a celebratory banquet. This is followed by a close-up of people involved in the construction business and their family members eating pork sandwiches. "And what about the crap in the sewers?" somebody asks Romolo. "The sewers? What's the Tiber for? . . . When we receive the approval from the mayor in Rome, everything is set," the tycoon answers. Immediately after this exchange, Gianni warns his pretty but unrefined wife, Elide, about eating too many carbohydrates, and a moment later she tells her mother not to eat too many hydrocarbons. In these farcical moments, the linguistic jokes, the ignorant manners of the characters, and the subversion of the traditional moral values recall the most familiar aspects of Comedy Italian Style.

One indication that Scola never disavowed his origins despite his innovations to the genre is the fact that many key collaborators who contributed to the success of *C'eravamo tanto amati* are the same who worked with Scola in his previous films. These include actors Vittorio Gassman, Nino Manfredi, Aldo Fabrizi, Giovanna Ralli, and Stefania Sandrelli, screenwriters Age and Furio Scarpelli, composer Armando Trovajoli, and cinematographer Claudio Cirillo.[3] In addition, Scola directed seven episodes of *I nuovi mostri* (*Viva Italia!*, 1977), a sequel of Dino Risi's hugely successful 1963 film *I mostri*. In *Che strano chiamarsi Federico* (*How Strange to Be Named Federico*, 2013), Scola's memory goes back to the years of *Marc'Aurelio*, whose vignettes did not follow a unified structure but were the result of the composition of various gags typical of comic strips. The film thus offers Scola a chance to portray his apprenticeship in the postwar years, which led to his activity as a ghostwriter for screenplays starring comedians such as Totò, Macario, Walter Chiari, Croccolo, Billi, and Riva. In turn, this formed the roots of his rigorous work and the creation of the screenplays for Antonio Pietrangeli (in collaboration with Ruggero Maccari) in the early 1960s.

Che strano chiamarsi Federico is paralleled by Scola's last published article, "The Passport for Cinema," in which he comments: "I believe that there is a sense of [the] grotesque in my movies and that this derives from the comical farce of Vittorio Metz and Marcello Marchesi."[4] The exploitative situation in which Scola worked with the well-established duo resembled that of an assembly line.[5] While Metz was a prolific writer, Marchesi engaged in the difficult task of organizing the numerous screenplays that they produced simultaneously (even twelve at a time). Marchesi merged the different parts and administered his screenplays as if they were a deck of cards, transferring scenes from one story to another and exchanging characters between the various scripts. He focused so much on the narrative structure of his comedies that Scola jokingly calls him "a structuralist," alluding to the dominant semantic and syntactic theories of the 1960s.[6] On an oxymoronic note, I would add that Marchesi was a chaotic structuralist. "But let's proceed with disorder. Disorder provides some hope, order none. Nothing is more ordered than emptiness," Marchesi quipped in *Il malloppo*.[7] His logic of screenplay production had little in common with the abstract methods of inquiry practiced by theorists such as Christian Metz, Roland Barthes, Gérard Genette, and Tzvetan Todorov, who sought to understand the proliferation of various genres by examining their different forms, the abstract meaning of narratives, and the general principles that make them comprehensible.[8] Nevertheless, despite the evident lack of scientific methodology, Marchesi pragmatically stresses the possibilities of the comedy genre in self-reflexive ways through a seemingly endless permutation game. For example, at a certain point in *Biancaneve e i sette ladri* (*Snow White and the Seven Thieves*, Giacomo Gentilomo, 1949), written by Marchesi, the police chief exclaims, "This story is too complicated for my taste," and in effect the screenplay presents unlikely adventures and exchanged identities between a Neapolitan accountant (Peppino De Filippo), a rich jeweler, and a Moldovan thief in a deserted mid-August Milan cityscape.[9]

Marchesi's screenwriting puts into play various combinations and compounds and achieves its power through exchanges and reversals. His narrative competence serves both as a tool for contextualizing Metz's heterogeneous micronarratives and for delimiting their otherwise erratic meanings. In this sense, *Che strano chiamarsi Federico* and its companion article emphasize two key aspects of Scola's approach to the genre that persist throughout his career: the chaotic structuralism and the vitriolic grotesque that derive from the influence of Marchesi, whose screenplays are inspired by the *Marc'Aurelio* vignettes.

The subversion of physical laws and realistic temporalities that distinguishes the first and other sequences of *C'eravamo tanto amati*, in which time stops (e.g., the reenactment of *Strange Interlude* by Eugene O'Neill) and ghosts appear (Elide's presence), are somewhat similar to those in *Il monello della strada* (Carlo Borghesio, 1951), cowritten by Marchesi. In this earlier film, the American adventures of Macario are displayed through comic techniques such as onomatopoeic freeze frames. Toward the end of the film, there is also an angelic figure who freezes time, allowing Macario to work for the common good while the rest of the world is on standby. In *Maciste contro Ercole nella valle dei guai* (*Hercules in the Valley of Woe*, Mario Mattoli, 1961), characters engage in time traveling thanks to a time machine. Even *Totò, Vittorio e la dottoressa* (*The Lady Doctor*, Camillo Mastrocinque, 1957), with the use of an old-fashioned car in which the protagonists move, and *Io Piaccio* (Giorgio Bianchi, 1955), with the chameleon-like transformations of Professor Roberto Maldi (Walter Chiari), present strong similarities with the *Marc'Aurelio* aesthetic.[10]

Vignettes, windows, and metatextual transitions immediately emerge in Scola's directorial debut as well. *Se permettete parliamo di donne* is composed of nine short episodes in which women are seduced by Vittorio Gassman, who plays roles such as a Sicilian *picciotto* (young man), a parasitic employee, an impatient lover, and a concerned brother. Film critic Tullio Kezich remarked that the episodes are repetitive, not every vignette has the consistency to stand alone, and that the film is permeated by moral ambiguity: "Many of us left [the movie theater] with a sense of shame. Spectacles in which humor has lost every aggressive charge and everything is resolved in a licentious dimension bring to mind Freud's distinction: not costume satire but complacent obscenity."[11] However, to date, little if any attention has been paid to how the metatextual

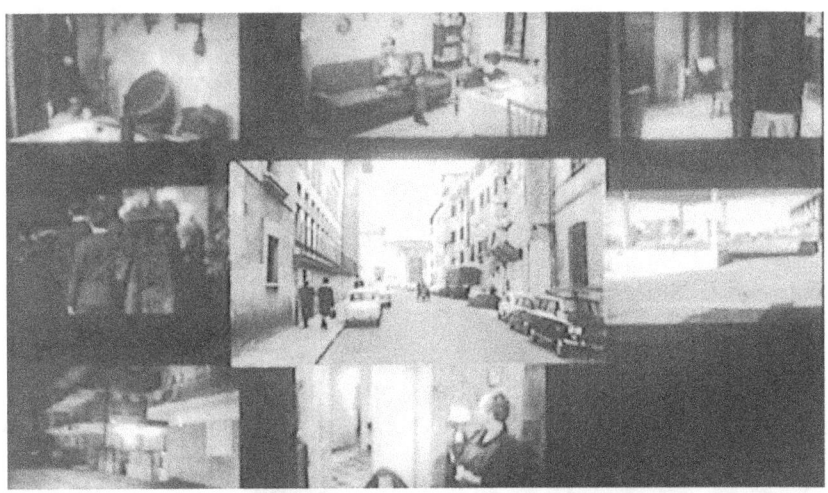

FIGURES 8 & 9. Metatextual transitions between a sequence and another in *Se permettete parliamo di donne*

transitions consciously reveal the overall structure of the film. These pop out between one episode and another, displayed in rectangles that change size, reduce and enlarge, leading us toward the next episode while creating suggestive movement and depth (figs. 8 and 9). Even the English and French versions of the movie's poster display several windows in which actresses Sylvia Koscina, Antonella Lualdi, and Giovanna Ralli appear (figs. 10 and 11). They suggest the idea of spying through multiple windows, or a catalog of the Latin lover's conquests.[12]

FIGURES 10 & 11. English and French movie posters of *Se permettete parliamo di donne*

As Natalie Fullwood asserts, "Comedy Italian Style is undeniably extremely masculinist in tone and structure, and predominantly (although not exclusively) heterosexist; the vast majority of films focus on straight, male protagonists. The representation of women largely posits them as sexual objects, and attention to women for reasons other than their sex appeal is relatively rare."[13] Antonio Pietrangeli's *La parmigiana* and *Io la conoscevo bene*, whose screenplays Scola coauthored while shooting his Gassman exploitation trilogy, which includes *Se permettete parliamo di donne*, *La congiuntura* (*Hard Times for Princes*, 1964) and *L'arcidiavolo* (*The Devil in Love*, 1966), belong to such infrequent terrain. In these movies, coming-of-age starlets who are obsessed with their own appearance are victimized by the misogyny that permeates the underbelly of the national media industry, leading them to prostitution or suicide. The narrative is based on the apparently random fluctuation of memories charged with emotional meaning. As Luca Barattoni explains in an interview for the Criterion Collection DVD of *Io la conoscevo bene*, the film "consists of nineteen microsequences each with its own climax. We feel the presence of Scola in the way Pietrangeli shifts seamlessly from the realistic to the grotesque to the horrific and to the sublime."[14] The *Io* in the title implies a multiplicity of subjects, the male predators whom Adriana (Stefania Sandrelli) encounters, as well as the complicit gaze of the audience.

Even the sequences of *La parmigiana* are neither displayed in chronological order nor linked to each other through the traditional use of the wipe or dissolve. Instead, the camera pans around and gets close to an object until the image goes out of focus. This is usually followed by a graphic match constructed around one of the movie's key themes, the contrast between nature and civilization, which bring us into a different scenario each time. For example, the informal reflection on the water of the Po river suddenly turns into a cityscape, and the crumbling wall of a condo becomes tree bark in a forest. In some of these transitions, even the female body is fetishized through a series of symbolic associations. For instance, the young orphan Dora (Catherine Spaak) is portrayed as a lifeless object among items to consume or to be exchanged in return for something, consistent with the materialist attitudes brought by the economic miracle. Such commodification takes place with the involvement of the image industry: the "occult persuaders" (as Dora calls them) of fashion magazines, television advertisements, and cinema itself. There is an evident tension between the representation of women in *Se permettete*, on the one hand, and in *La parmigiana* and *Io la conoscevo bene*, on the other. While the chaotic structuralism and the use of the grotesque remain the common denominator of all the films Scola authored and directed up to this point, the oscillations between male chauvinism and protofeminism reflect the moral ambivalence that accompanied the boom and lead us to a more refined understanding of Comedy Italian Style as a multifaceted genre.

The critique of Italy's sexual politics, in which characters from different backgrounds converge in public and private spaces, creating a crucible of social dynamics, returns a few years later in Scola's *Il commissario Pepe*. In the opening credits, we see a police car patrolling the streets of Vicenza. The screen splits in four quadrants (a representational strategy similar to that of *Se permettete*), implying that only a prismatic approach to everyday life can lead to the solution of an intrigue related to an underground prostitution network.

In the end, the reluctant police chief Pepe (Ugo Tognazzi) finds out that the whole town is involved. His list of perpetrators with a double identity includes his lover, the sister of his vice police chief, and various institutional figures. As Roberto Ellero writes, "The spirit of the *Marc'Aurelio* lives in the delightful sketch of the conformists, in the moralistic pomposity, but it is a *bozzettismo* that does not harm the events."[15] Aware that justice will not be equal for everyone, Pepe destroys the incriminating materials and submits his resignation. Toward the end of the film, the dossier of his investigation becomes an animated structural grid in which the numerous characters that we have seen so far move and talk (fig. 12). Those who will not pay because of

FIGURE 12. The visual grid that connects the various characters at the end of *Il commissario Pepe*

FIGURE 13. The kaleidoscopic ending of *Riusciranno i nostri eroi*

their political and religious connections are crossed out one by one by Pepe, who proceeds by elimination. Then the frustrated chief walks from his desk to the fireplace, which suddenly turns into a television screen that shows images of powerful First World politicians juxtaposed on those of starving African children. The latter is a reference to the movie Scola had shot a year earlier, *Riusciranno i nostri eroi a ritrovare l'amico misteriosamente scomparso in Africa?* On the one hand, this is a moralistic moment in which Scola emphasizes the economic asynchronies that separate the two hemispheres; on the other, it anticipates the intertextuality that characterizes his later comedies. *Riusciranno i nostri eroi* ends with kaleidoscopic images (fig. 13) until Fausto's (Alberto Sordi) head spins when he faces the dilemma of whether to return to his oppressive family life in Rome or embrace an adventurous but uncertain future in Angola. In a centrifugal montage, he sees again all the minor characters and micronarratives of the film. As in many of Scola's comedies, the minor characters are used to convey meaning, but everything in the end is a psychological representation of the perceptual disintegration that Sordi's character is experiencing, divided as he is between two diametrically opposed existences.

These two films are often dismissed as transitional, but they are actually pivotal, because for the first time Scola experiments with high "vernacular modernism"[16] to introduce and wrap up the episodes that his chaotic screenplays present, overcoming the apparent randomness of his early directions. Thus, if one wants to read Scola's early career generously, here we find the roots of his comedic polycentrism and narrative experimentation of the 1970s. In the metatextual transitions, visual grids, and kaleidoscopic endings, there is the suggestion of potentially infinite humorous plots through brilliant compositional arrangements. One story extends into another, one character into the other, the spectator into the spectacle and the spectacle into the spectator—a dynamic that fully flourishes in the collective movies of the 1970s.

To the equation traced so far (a chaotic structuralism that combines a series of vitriolic vignettes), *C'eravamo tanto amati* adds a renewed level of civil commitment and a stylized approach to the genre. The first manifests itself through a nostalgic return to the pivotal moment of liberation, which allowed everyday life ethics and neorealist cinematic aesthetics to embrace each other. The latter is expressed by an increasing intertextuality: characters attend theatrical plays, pursue acting careers and engage in film criticism, appear on television, read sociological inquests, and find echoes of the historical present in novels by Alexandre Dumas and Hermann Hesse. In this sense, the majority of the characters present a shift from neorealist poetics in that they are highly educated (or at least in the process of being educated, as Elide). When their initial Resistance ideals are defeated, Gianni ascertains that "the future passed us by and we didn't even realize it;" this sentiment is echoed by Nicola who claims later in the film, "We thought we could change the world but the world has changed us," while listening to a speech by Vittorio De Sica. These two key sentences set the tone for the comedy, which is permeated by a melodramatic feeling of "too late" and is a form of social criticism. Toward the end there is a sense that the passage of time has not produced progress, and even those characters who do not regress in a downward spiral fall into an ideological stagnation or are left alone to wither inside. For example, as alluded to earlier, Gianni loses his depressed wife and is condemned to remain alone with his physically impaired father-in-law. In addition, the exclusive villa in which he lives becomes a sort of golden prison. Despite his affluent lifestyle, he appears as to be the least fortunate of the three protagonists. Nicola (Stefano Satta Flores) abandons his family and career as an educator in the high school of Nocera Inferiore, only to become a minor Marxist film critic. Antonio marries Luciana and keeps embracing Resistance ideals but remains a hospital aide. There is a clear sense that Antonio's economic struggle is due to both his good-hearted inclinations and his lack of political conformism.

While Scola's narrative technique in *C'eravamo tanto amati* is more sophisticated than in *Se permettete, Riusciranno i nostri eroi*, or *Il commissario Pepe*, it is rarely mentioned that the film also presents continuity with his earlier work. Scola rearranges the sense of the grotesque typical of the *Marc'Aurelio* magazine and of his earlier films to create *C'eravamo tanto amati*. Scola's 1974 film represents a chance for an all-star Comedy Italian Style ensemble to retrace its own history from a generational point of view, while providing a metacommentary on the current status of Italian culture. Taking the passage of time as a subject, the movie observes without indulgence the simultaneous betrayal of postwar political ideals (the Resistance) and cinematic aesthetics (neorealism). Scola, Age, and Scarpelli, along with their actors and collaborators, stare at their own ghosts and romanticized past, asking questions about the clichés they have become. However, only the act of portraying these incongruities allows them to remain somehow faithful to their younger selves. This bittersweet comedy maintains the old rhythms and style of delivery, but it is also unusually serious, functioning as a natural transition (rather than a rupture) toward the melancholic tones typical of Scola's later movies.

After numerous years of work within the genre, the "collective" of artists interrogates itself on its role within the film industry and on the necessity to adapt its humor to a society in turmoil, haunted by irrational signs.[17] Some of the first Comedies Italian Style that dealt with political violence are Mario Monicelli's *Vogliamo i colonnelli* (*We Want the Colonels*, 1973) and Dino Risi's *Mordi e fuggi* (*The Dirty Weekend*, 1973), which refer to the *golpismo* (tendency toward military coups) and the growing sense of social disjunction throughout the 1970s.[18] Differently from other founding fathers of the genre, though, Scola fully integrated his fame into the pervasive flux of protests. He embraced artistic antagonism and experimented with alternative forms of production and distribution outside the mainstream commercial system. In 1968, he joined the Communist Party and shot the militant documentaries *Lotta Continua a Napoli* (*Continuous Struggle in Naples*, 1971) and *Trevico-Torino: Viaggio nel Fiat-Nam* (*Trevico-Turin: Voyage in Fiatnam*, 1973), which respectively portray the extraparliamentary groups and the alienation of immigrant factory workers within the automobile industry. Thanks to these experiences, in the 1970s Scola found a unique niche between the tradition of

Comedy Italian Style, auteur cinema, and the cinema of civil engagement. In this context, the *Marc'Aurelio* vignettes encounter modernist cinema's existential malaise. In *C'eravamo tanto amati*, grainy black-and-white footage is used to narrate the partisans' accomplishments that coexist with charged colors in the fashion of Michelangelo Antonioni's *Deserto rosso* (*Red Desert*, 1964). The postwar ethical impulse turns the nation into consumerist euphoria and politically driven real estate speculations. The egotism of the male characters leads to depression rather than satisfaction. Finally, the issues of auteurism and prestige (represented by Federico Fellini) intersect with genre cinema and militant cinema. The latter emerges not only in the sentimental memory of the anti-fascist ideals but also in the depiction of a final bonfire demonstration in front of a public school to which Antonio participates by singing a Resistance song. Other examples are the portrait of Nicola as a struggling revolutionary Marxist who reenacts *Battleship Potemkin* (Sergei Eisenstein, 1925) on the Spanish Steps in Rome and the explicit denunciation of the corrupted system in which Gianni is compromised. It is significant that within the progressive desertification of ideals and feelings, the only residual hopes are linked to the character of Antonio, who prevails on his sentimental rivals and continues to engage in political activism.

In *C'eravamo tanto amati*, the love stories of the characters overlap with the sunset of leftist utopias and their normalization. Scola reveals only partial sympathy for his characters and at times adopts an entomological gaze through the use of high-angle shots. These happen when Gianni and Luciana reveal their love affair to Antonio, who grabs an oxygen mask to overcome the emotional shock of the news, and when the ghost of Elide looks at Gianni from above, nailing him to his moral responsibilities regarding her suicide. In such circumstances, the camera operates as if it were a surveillance tool, as a pure and impersonal but cinematic force filming in an automatic mode. Such techniques show how the protagonists are smashed and defeated by history and remorse, slapped by their own mistakes and the process of aging.

With *C'eravamo tanto amati*, Scola develops some auteurist ambitions that academics and popular critics are not always able to second. Rather than confronting the vital tensions that animate Scola's career, critics generally delineate between the histrionic acting and episodic nature of the early comedies (in the fashion of the previously mentioned review by Kezich of *Se permettete*) and the spatial and temporal narrative ambition that Scola manifests in his more recent productions. The most interesting case study is that of Lino Miccichè, who argues:

> The debuts were not particularly praiseworthy. As a director, from *Se permettete parliamo di donne* to *Riusciranno i nostri eroi a ritrovare l'amico misteriosamente scomparso in Africa?* Scola has been between the proponents and the perpetrators of the culturally degraded and politically regressive current (even if for this precise reason sociologically relevant) called "Comedy Italian Style," the cinematic place where the obscenely disengaged games of that dangerous anthropoid that is the "average Italian" are often celebrated.[19]

In several articles, Miccichè reiterates a Manichean vision of Scola's career, which separates the grain (the masterful comedies that present a degree of sociopolitical engagement) from the husks (the 'morally deviant' early ones), taking 1968 as a watershed.[20] The passage quoted above belongs to the enthusiastic review of *C'eravamo tanto amati* in which, despite the initial concerns about the comedy genre, Miccichè appreciates the mobile relationships between the group of characters and the attention that the director dedicates to the historical environment that produces them.[21] However, the narrative strategy of posing characters against the background of major historical events is more a heritage of the *Marc'Aurelio* vignettes than the fruit of Scola's newly acquired sociopolitical militancy. Since World War II, the magazine provided commentary on actual events, portraying various trending social types, celebrities, and politicians such as Winston Churchill, Joseph Stalin, and Franklin Roosevelt in almost every issue. Scola's sociopolitical engagement is most effective when the director replaces such powerful figures to give voice to characters who would only appear in a footnote of a huge history book and characters who are ultimately exploited by the neocapitalist machinery even when they acquire a wealthy status. The continuity between the old and more recent comedies is often dismissed, as well as the long-lasting influence of *Marc'Aurelio*. There is no doubt that Scola's movies are very diverse from each other in quality, purpose, and the contingent circumstances in which they were produced. Nevertheless, it is possible to problematize the dual-track career pathway traced by Miccichè to establish a symbiotic relationship between Scola's early apprenticeship and his mature masterpieces.

The sociopolitical awareness acquired after 1968 does not generate a Copernican revolution in Scola's cinema, but it adds yet another element to the already rich texture of his early comedies. To demonstrate this thesis, I have touched on the *Marc'Aurelio* years and the influence of Metz and Marchesi, the visual transitions between various sequences in the comedies shot in the 1960s, and Scola's seminal collaboration with Pietrangeli as a screenwriter. Furthermore, in *I nuovi mostri*, Scola (together with Risi and Monicelli) pushes the prototypes of the original film *I mostri* to an extreme level of characterization, and the use of the grotesque results in "a hyperbolical vision of Italian society."[22] The tragicomic episode "Elogio funebre" reveals how even at the funeral of a *capocomico* (leader of a theater company) comedians can hardly contain their desire to laugh, sing, and above all to perform.

The careers of the other two directors involved in the collaborative project follow opposite trajectories: at the peak of Scola's critical appreciation, when he reconciles with most of the leftist critics, Risi and Monicelli were in decline, while in the 1960s Scola was considered one of their numerous epigones. This is due to the fact that in the 1970s Scola admirably reconciles the either/or dilemma of choosing between the modernist films of Antonioni, Pier Paolo Pasolini, and Bernardo Bertolucci and the "guilty pleasure" and physical energy of genre and subgenre comedies. Not only does he deliberately refuse to choose between these two tendencies, but he also calls for a narrative of national (critical and cinematic) pacification. *C'eravamo tanto amati* is dedicated to the memory of De Sica, and it also pays homage to Cesare Zavattini, Luchino Visconti, Sergio Amidei, Luigi Zampa, Roberto Rossellini, Fellini, and Antonioni.[23]

A key to understanding where Scola stands in relation to the critical debate that juxtaposes auteur cinema with comedy can be found in the affectionate but also caustic caricatures of the intransigent critic that Stefano Satta Flores plays in both *C'eravamo tanto amati* and *La terrazza*. In the first, Nicola aspires to go "beyond the beyond" but at the same time is so stuck in the militant paradigms of the magazine he founded, *Cinema e cultura*, that he physically and allegorically sinks into his own chair. In the second, Tizzo engages in a verbal and physical fight with comedy screenwriter Enrico (Jean-Louis Trintignant), who struggles to maintain his edge, until a film producer intervenes to separate them.

TIZZO: You draw caricatures without depth.

ENRICO: Well no, this is cultural provincialism. I want to make caricatures and satire, and not some problematic petty portraits.

TIZZO: Because you don't know how to do them.

ENRICO: Not even Molière intended to do them. The truth is this: the critic's cruel intolerance is the proof that you don't love cinema.

TIZZO: I don't love cinema? It's you who doesn't love cinema. But what is this satire? It's impairment with the power. If you want to learn something more about irony go read Nietzsche, *Beyond Tragedy*, great master of humor.

ENRICO: And you should read Wittgenstein. The cage of the language can be destroyed even with comedy. Look at Totò. Even comedy of manners contributed to form a democratic conscience.

TIZZO: Nice democratic conscience. Ah, it was you guys. Let's thank Enrico for the shitty country that we have become. Thank you, *merci*.

Not only do Nicola and Tizzo reveal a contempt for popular genres, but they are also unable to share their expertise with a generalist audience or to adapt their understanding of cinema to new forms of communication, which are crucial in Scola's comedies of this period, moving toward multimediality and intertextuality.

C'eravamo tanto amati challenges the potential of the comedy genre and analyzes cultural shifts that took place over several decades through the inclusion of a rich grid of theatrical, cinematic, and televisual references. The film maps the flow of content and the connections between multiple media industries, along with the erratic habits of 1970s audiences. Characters are not only eager to consume the sort of entertainment they want, but they also aim to integrate into the society of spectacle. In this sense Luciana Zanon (Stefania Sandrelli) is emblematic, since she engages the already mentioned reenactments of O'Neill's *Strange Interlude* and of *Battleship Potemkin* and appears on the set of Fellini's *La dolce vita* (1960), for which she is an extra. Her struggles as an aspiring actress are linked to those of Adriana in *Io la conoscevo bene*. Both characters are physically attractive, come from small towns (Luciana is "from Trasaghis near, Peonis," in the province of Udine), and attempt to break into the movie business but in the end obtain only limited visibility. As a result, both end up working as movie ushers. After a series of exploitative love affairs, they become delusional and suicidal (while in *Io la conoscevo bene* death for Adriana represents a liberation and probably her only "successful attempt," in *C'eravamo tanto amati* Antonio manages to save Luciana's life).

On the contrary, the unattractive Nicola in *C'eravamo tanto amati* is the one who is granted fifteen minutes of fame, to use Andy Warhol's expression. Nicola appears on the show *Lascia o raddoppia*, which is recorded live from the Fiera di Milano (Milan Fair Theatre), as an expert in Italian cinema. This is a chance for Nicola to advocate for cinema to become part of the education curriculum and to endorse an alternative to the cultural dominion of TV programs. Nicola starts with great success and trusts he will pursue his dreams and publish a monograph on the topic. As a consequence, he chooses to double the wager. In the meanwhile, the protagonists of *C'eravamo tanto amati* gather around the television sets in bars, squares, or houses to witness the fate of their friend. Gianni is in Rome having dinner with his in-laws. While they avidly eat some spaghetti, he discloses to them (who both remain indifferent) that he spent some days with Nicola fighting the fascists in the mountains during the Resistance. Not by chance, Gianni only remembers his friend in the moment in which he is becoming wealthy and famous against all expectations. Even in Nocera Inferiore, everybody celebrates Nicola's success. Those who had violently criticized him in the past, such as the mayor of the hometown and the school superintendent (who fired him for advocating in favor of neorealist aesthetics), have now become fans and eagerly invite him to come back.

However, Nicola's apparently irresistible ascent only continues for a few weeks, until he must answer questions about his favorite movie, *Ladri di biciclette* (*Bicycle Thieves*, Vittorio De Sica, 1948). He wastes time with the last question, trying to explain the trick De Sica used to make the young actor Enzo Staiola (Bruno) cry in the shoot, until the time is up and the answer is considered wrong. When he loses everything, audiences shift from unconditional love to resentful hate toward him, who just wasted a chance to change his life, symptomatic of the ephemerality of television-generated fame and the volubility of Italian audiences.

An uncredited character in *C'eravamo tanto amati* is the television set. Scola shows how *Lascia o raddoppia* was the first broadcasting event that aroused interest nationally, with its race against time, its potentially life-changing prize money, its competitors armed with knowledge, and the compassion of the moderator, who shares in the emotions of the participants. In *C'eravamo tanto amati*, images of television replace the grids, windows, and quadrants typical of the visual transitions of *Se permettete* and *Il commissario Pepe* and the kaleidoscopic montage in the finale of *Riusciranno i nostri eroi* that connect the various characters. In *C'eravamo tanto amati*, the simultaneity of RAI (Radiotelevisione italiana, or Italian National Broadcasting Company) broadcasting from north to south becomes for Scola an expedient to move to a less experimental narrative structure.

The choice to display social criticism through the incorporation of various media becomes more virtuoso in the subsequent *La terrazza*. This time Scola challenges himself by mostly limiting the field of action to a luxurious Roman penthouse, where a group of aging leftists who work in the media industry occasionally converge. Thanks to the emphasis on different forms of communication that emerge in many sequences, the limitation of the set does not become a constriction. On the contrary, Scola's freedom appears much greater and more meaningful the more he circumscribes his characters to a few square meters. The multiple episodes are not isolated but intersect with one another thanks to a series of nonlinear narrative knots.

The argument between Tizzo and Enrico in *La terrazza*, mentioned above, is replayed several times, each time framed from a different angle. It is from this scene that the major concentric narratives depart. These involve Luigi (Marcello Mastroianni), a journalist who is undergoing both a professional and personal crisis, and the two are strongly interrelated. While he experiences a generational disconnect from his readers, he watches his wife successfully espouse her feminist principles via the small screen. Other episodes involve Amedeo (Ugo Tognazzi), a producer of comedies who is convinced to finance an avant-garde film; Sergio, an unappreciated RAI executive who literally sees his office space shrinking in front of his eyes and then lets himself die on the set of one of his most expensive productions, *Capitan Fracassa*; Mario (Vittorio Gassman), a marginalized member of the Italian Communist Party who falls in love with a younger woman (Stefania Sandrelli) but whose love story is ruined when she is photographed by the tabloid press; and, finally, Enrico, the above-mentioned screenwriter of Comedies Italian Style, who experiences writer's block due to the exploitative environment that surrounds him. These brief character sketches show that Scola is bringing the narrative multiplicity of *Se permettete* and *C'eravamo tanto amati* to its extreme consequences. Also, in many sequences, we see the protagonists of *La terrazza* melancholically staring at the glimpses of the small screen or reading a newspaper alone in their living rooms. They do not look at the world directly anymore, but they look at it as it appears after being filtered through the same media to which they contribute and by which in turn they are also heavily impacted.

La terrazza was one of the first Italian comedies to pay close attention to the relationship between sound and dialogue, with the goal of replicating environmental conversational sound. The film involves an ensemble cast of almost thirty people who talk simultaneously, à la Robert Altman. The polyphonic soundtrack created in postproduction mixes the volumes of the voices of the single characters, allowing us to hear multiple scraps of conversations at the same time. However, the internal audio editing suggests who to listen to in a specific moment, which dialogues are crucial and which are secondary. Since the immersive sound of *La terrazza* allows us to hear the ideas, desires, and the fantasies of the protagonists in detail, upon multiple viewings we may choose to listen to secondary characters, creating our own connections. If André Bazin talked about the optical democracy of the deep-focus long take,[24] *La terrazza* can be likened to sonic democracy—the ability of a viewer to focus on various sounds and bits of dialogue. The director delivers social criticism by capturing the insignificant murmur of Roman intellectuals and deliberately juxtaposes all the voices coming from the terrace to make them sound as a cacophonic background of cicadas.

La terrazza remains one of the most pessimistic films of Scola's career, unsanitized by any bittersweet or consolatory tone. Manuela Gieri affirms:

> No hope is left to either contemporary human beings or characters: they are all ridiculous individuals caught in the cage of language, trapped in an endless game of signification and interpretation. Humor seems to be the only alternative, the only tool that will allow the transgression and eventually the subversion of a given order of things. The five characters are ridiculous, and yet their audiences—the audience in the film and the audience outside the movie—are also ridiculous. As we watch *The Terrace* approach its choral ending, we are also forced to face a frozen image, a distorted reflection of ourselves.[25]

The conscientious hall of mirrors that Gieri evokes is made possible by the audiovisual triangulations that Scola establishes among life itself, cinema, and media other than cinema. The frozen image she mentions is obviously allegorical but in the end is very much mindful of Gianni's dive at the beginning of C'eravamo tanto amati, which remains Scola's best representation of a generational paralysis.

In conclusion, this chapter has suggested a framework for studying Scola that is liberated from the polemics between those who praise genre and those who praise auteur cinema. This methodology allowed me to establish connections between the chaotic structuralism that organizes the vignettes of his early comedies with the stylized sociopolitical sophistication of his maturity. It is not by chance that in his last movies, articles, and filmed interviews Scola champions the impact that the *Marc'Aurelio* years and the productions of the 1960s played in his growth as a filmmaker, taking position against the traditional critical reception of his work. One is free to reject the director's last words, but I am inclined to read them as a call for new approaches that link the comedies that we consider secondary to those that we consider essential.[26] Of course, this does not mean obsessively looking for coherence in a career that is objectively heterogeneous and spans almost seven decades, but it does mean recognizing that the convenient label of Comedy Italian Style is reductive and does not give full justice to the narrative and audiovisual complexity so eloquently displayed in many of Scola's screenplays and movies.

Notes

1. Ettore Scola, quoted in Roberto Ellero, *Ettore Scola* (Florence: La Nuova Italia, 1996), 1. Translations throughout the chapter are my own unless otherwise noted.
2. Tullio Kezich, *Il filmsessanta: Il cinema degli anni 1962–1966.* (Milan: Il Formichiere, 1969), especially "*Se permettete parliamo di donne* di Ettore Scola," 216–17, and "*La congiuntura* di Ettore Scola," 67–68; Lino Miccichè, *Cinema italiano degli anni '70* (Venice: Marsilio, 1980), especially "Il commissario Pepe di Ettore Scola," 41–42, "*C'eravamo tanto amati* di Ettore Scola," 215–19, and "*Il dramma della gelosia* di Ettore Scola," 71–72.
3. For instance, Vittorio Gassman starred in many of films that Scola cowrote, including *Il mattatore* (*Love and Larceny*, Dino Risi, 1960), *Il sorpasso* (*The Easy Life*, Risi, 1961), and *La parmigiana* (*The Girl from Parma*, Antonio

Pietrangeli, 1963). He also starred in some of Scola's earliest films: *Se permettete parliamo di donne* (*Let's Talk about Women*, 1964), *La congiuntura* (*Hard Time for Princes*, 1964), *L'arcidiavolo* (*The Devil in Love*, 1966). Aldo Fabrizi starred in films that Scola cowrote, including *Accadde al penitenziario* (*A Day at the Police Station*, Giorgio Bianchi, 1955); *I pappagalli* (Bruno Paolinelli, 1955) and *Mi permettete babbo!* (Mario Bonnard, 1956). Stefania Sandrelli and Nino Manfredi starred in *Io la conoscevo bene* (*I Knew Her Well*, Pietrangeli, 1965), written by Scola. Manfredi also acted in *Riusciranno i nostri eroi a ritrovare l'amico misteriosamente scomparso in Africa?* (*Will Our Heroes Be Able to Find Their Friend Who Has Mysteriously Disappeared in Africa?*, 1968). Marcello Mastroianni was a protagonist in *Dramma della gelosia—tutti i particolari in cronaca* (*The Pizza Triangle*, 1970). Giovanni Ralli was also a longtime collaborator of Scola's, as she appeared in *Se permettete parliamo di donne* and in films that Scola cowrote, such as *Nel blu dipinto di blu* (Piero Tellini,1959). Armando Trovajoli wrote most of the soundtracks for Scola's early films, with the exception of *La congiuntura* and *Trevico-Torino: Viaggio nel Fiat-Nam* (*Trevico-Turin: Voyage in Fiatnam*). Claudio Cirillo began to consistently work as a director of photography for Scola on *Riusciranno i nostri eroi*.

4. Ettore Scola, "Il passaporto per il cinema," *Panta Agenda Marchesi* 32 (2015). Kindle ed.
5. Scola was paid according to the number of jokes, gags, and comic situations that were approved by Metz and Marchesi, and he was promoted to the role of screenwriter only in 1952, with *Canzoni di mezzo secolo* (Domenico Paolella) and *Fermi tutti, arrivo io!* (Sergio Grieco). Marco Dionisi and Nevio De Pascalis, "'Negro' con Metz e Marchesi,'" in *Piacere, Ettore Scola*, ed. Marco Dionisi and Nevio De Pascalis (Rome: Edizioni Sabinae, 2016), 68–73.
6. Scola,"Il passaporto per il cinema."
7. Marcello Marchesi, *Il malloppo* (Milan: Bompiani, 1971), 73.
8. For a survey on the rise and fall of structural approaches to cinematic narratives, see Dudley Andrew, *Concepts in Film Theory* (New York: Oxford University Press, 1984), 75–95.
9. *Susanna tutta panna* (Steno, 1957) is another example of the capacity of Marchesi to create a connective texture, with the numerous male characters who dream of seducing Susanna (Marisa Allasio). One may also consider the visions and hallucinations that characterize the hell sequence in *Totò al Giro d'Italia* (*Toto Tours Italy*, Mario Mattoli, 1948) or the ghostly presence that permeates *La paura fa 90* (Vittorio Metz and Giorgio Simonelli, 1951).
10. Rinaldo Vignati, "Marcello Marchesi, autore di sceneggiature," *L'avventura* 2 (July–December 2016): 231–54; 236, 248–50.
11. Tullio Kezich quoted in Ellero, *Ettore Scola*, 20.

12. While in Italy, the sexy comedy subgenre, which accentuates some of the moods of Scola's early comedies, would be in full swing a decade later than *Se permettete*, posters with sexual innuendos permeated the European market since Roger Vadim's *God Created Woman* (1954).
13. Natalie Fullwood, *Cinema, Gender, and Everyday Space: Comedy, Italian Style* (New York: Palgrave Macmillan, 2015), 11.
14. For a discussion of the impact of Pietrangeli as a director, see Luca Barattoni, *Italian Post-neorealist Cinema* (Edinburgh: Edinburgh University Press, 2012), 133–42.
15. Ellero, *Ettore Scola*, 35.
16. "I take the study of modernist aesthetics to encompass cultural practices that both articulated and mediated the experience of modernity, such as the mass-produced and mass-consumed phenomena of fashion, design, advertising, architecture and urban environment, of photography, radio, and cinema. I am referring to this kind of modernism as 'vernacular' (and avoiding the ideologically overdetermined term 'popular') because the term vernacular combines the dimension of the quotidian, of everyday usage, with connotations of discourse, idiom, and dialect, with circulation, promiscuity, and translatability." Miriam Hansen, "The Mass Production of the Senses: Classical Cinema as Vernacular Modernism," *Modernism/Modernity* 6, no. 2 (1999): 59–77, 60.
17. On December 12, 1969, a bomb exploded in Milan's Piazza Fontana, killing sixteen people. An anarchist, Giuseppe Pinelli, was arrested. During the interrogation, he fell to his death from the fourth floor of the police headquarters. Years later, the Italian justice concluded that Pinelli was innocent and that it was the neofascists in contact with the Italian Secret Service who were responsible for the bombing. As a response to this so-called strategy of tension adopted by neofascist terrorists, the Brigate rosse killed police official Luigi Calabresi, launching a series of political assassinations that lasted over a decade and culminating in a crescendo that marked the assassination of the Christian Democrat prime minister Aldo Moro in 1978.
18. Alan O'Leary, *Tragedia all'italiana: Italian Cinema and Italian Terrorism, 1970–2010* (Oxford: Peter Lang, 2011), 19. For an in-depth discussion on the relationship between terrorism and Italian-style comedies by Risi, Monicelli, and Scola, and also by Luigi Comencini, Luigi Zampa, Lina Wertmüller, and Marco Ferreri, see Rémi Fournier Lanzoni, *Rire de plomb: La comédie à l'italienne des années 70* (Paris: Editions L'Harmattan, 2017).
19. Miccichè, *Cinema italiano degli anni '70*, 215–16.
20. Similar remarks about the first phase of Scola's career appear in the reviews of *Il commissario Pepe*, 41–42, and *Il dramma della gelosia*, 71, in Miccichè, *Cinema italiano degli anni '70*.

21. Cf. Lino Miccichè, "Il cinema non cambia il mondo ma può farci riflettere: Una conversazione con Ettore Scola," in *Trevico-Cinecittà: L'avventuroso viaggio di Ettore Scola*, ed. Vito Zagarrio (Venice: Marsilio, 2002), 27.
22. Rémi Fournier Lanzoni, *Comedy Italian Style: The Golden Age of Italian Film Comedies* (New York: Continuum, 2008), 165.
23. Millicent Marcus, *Italian Film in the Light of Neorealism* (Princeton: Princeton University Press, 1986), 413.
24. Dudley Andrew, *André Bazin* (New York: Columbia University Press, 1990), 128.
25. Manuela Gieri, *Contemporary Italian Filmmaking: Strategies of Subversions; Pirandello, Fellini, Scola, and the Directors of the New Generation* (Toronto: University of Toronto Press, 1995), 195.
26. The volume on the director's career, *Trevico-Cinecittà*, published in the new millennium is an encouraging step in this sense. "Great artisan or author? . . . The question appears again in the moment in which we set about to analyze a polyhedral man like Ettore Scola. . . . The authoriality of this director of multiple and multiform activity lays in the narrative turns, in the inventions of the mise-en-scène, in the common threads of his texts (including the screenplays he wrote for others), in the traces of style derivable from his filmography. And thus, Scola's cinema . . . deserves a new vision." Vito Zagarrio, "Se permettete, parliamo di Scola," in Zagarrio, *Trevico-Cinecittà*, 10–11.

PREMORTEM IDENTIFICATION OF THE *COMMEDIA ALL'ITALIANA*

The Grotesque in Scola's Comedy

Rémi Lanzoni

AT THE DAWN OF the 1970s, during a time of social and political turmoil, terrorism, and increasing skepticism of the country's economic situation, Ettore Scola and other Italian directors felt a pressing need to rejuvenate Italian comedy. Many screenwriters realized that the grotesque vein within the genre offered great promise and could provide an ideal transition from the effervescent comedies of the economic miracle, often portraying the euphoria of happy days in a resurgent nation, toward a more adventurous and even more cynical type of realism. In Italian comedy, the exultation of the economic miracle dissipated and was substituted with a more contemptuous humor during a decade of violence (the so-called *anni di piombo*, or years of lead). Moreover, the usual actors (Ugo Tognazzi, Nino Manfredi, Alberto Sordi, and Vittorio Gassman) already exhibited a noticeable predisposition for the grotesque vein in their respective repertoires, and all made easy transitions to this new type of comedy. Following the individualist humor of the 1960s came the advent of a comedy based on collective perspectives, with an inherent capacity to indict Italian society. The aim of these new cynical and confrontational narratives was to desacralize Italian institutions: bureaucracy, corruption, religion, the nuclear family—in a few words, the fossilized traditional social order.

The following analysis draws on traditional interpretations of Italian film comedies but also focuses on the theme of death, which critics of Scola's comedies have rarely addressed. Scola's style of comedy was often complex, and despite its ability to make Italians laugh through technical expertise, it also aimed at communicating a very personal symbolic vision of life and death. One of the goals of the present work is also to conceptualize the comedic incongruity and irreverence toward social customs in Scola's films.[1] Incongruity can be best described as a variance between the spectators' expectations of how an action will likely unfold or a protagonist will likely behave and a particular moment in a scene that negates these expectations. However, this theory does not focus on the incongruous action or speech but rather the consequences and resolution that its juxtaposition triggers. For Schopenhauer, the more unexpected the incongruity is, the more violent the triggered laughter.[2] Later during the twentieth century, a new notion (called the incongruity-resolution theory)[3] held that laughter arises because the audience realizes that the incongruity can be resolved eventually. In the case of Scola's grotesque comedies, neither theory applies, as no contrast and no resolution are proposed. By moving away from the master narrative, Scola takes his stories in a new direction, one that thrusts spectators into a grotesque and outrageous sphere, disconnected from any type of normalcy, such as the dreadful microcosm in *Brutti, sporchi e cattivi* (*Down and Dirty*, 1976), depicting the claustrophobic slum inhabited by the overcrowded Mazzatella family on the slopes of Monte Ciocci overlooking St. Peter's Basilica. Scola's comedies reveal that humor grows with the refinement of perception: as Italian society evolves from the boom years of the economic miracle to the disillusion of the following decades, both the writers of comedies and the viewing public become more sophisticated and demanding in the content of humor. There is no longer lenience for the simple reparatory conclusions of pink neorealism[4] or the cynical gags from the comedies of the boom years: these forms of comedy no longer satisfy the innovative taste of the 1970s. While nonsensical humor seems spontaneous and playful in the work of many comedy filmmakers, in the case of Scola it is a reflection, though not always a blatant one, of a nation marred by violence and chaos. Stefano Masi describes this type of chaos as a "regression to primal bestiality, in which animalistic impulses and aspirations in a consumer society are curiously mixed."[5] Finally, the ultimate intent of this chapter is to argue that Scola stages the burial of the *commedia all'italiana* as a premonitory sign and carefully planned exit strategy in his films of the 1970s. These signs of mortality function as a premortem identification for the *commedia*, as they identify the symptoms of its impending finale.

Ever since the *commedia dell'arte* of the Renaissance period, Italian comedies have consistently included a great dose of inherent tragedy in their master narratives. It is essential to differentiate the *commedia all'italiana* from the *commedia dell'arte*. The latter is a genre in Italian theater from the Renaissance up to the 1700s, and the former is a specific genre within modern-day film comedy (1958–80). Both scrutinize society through a satirical lens while simultaneously presenting a desacralizing vision of the world. The grotesque film comedies of the 1970s offer comic patterns inspired by the recurrent violence taking place in Italy. Susan Snyder argues that comedy and tragedy are opposing visions to comprehend the real world and ultimately "project their own opposing worlds."[6] Snyder also points out that in narratives tragedy is often governed by a dimension of *inevitability* and contrasts it to comedy, in which a notion of *evitability* is assumed. She concludes that "instead of heroic or obstinate adherence to a single course, comedy endorses opportunistic shifts and realistic accommodations."[7] Therefore, according to this concept of evitability, humor can spark strong emotional responses because it often reevaluates preconceived ideas and principles like modernity, coherence, and rational systems. This chapter revisits some of Scola's grotesque comedies, such as *La più bella serata della mia vita* (*The Most Wonderful Evening of My Life*, 1972) and episodes of *I nuovi mostri* (*Viva Italia!*, 1977) and allows us to understand and expose his strategy as a departure from traditional incongruity theory.

The pervasive presence of tragedy in comedies invites a reflection on its origins: where does this inherent tragic component in master narratives come from? William Thompson states that Italian comedies have always had an innate sense of detachment, which is a guarantee of intellectual independence—a fundamental form of freedom—as he also wonders, "Should we begin to speak about tragedy when comedy is our concern? Say that the opposite of freedom is evil; then both tragedy and comedy concern the problem of evil. Or put it this way: comedy offers a way out, a rebirth; tragedy also offers a way out, but it is a way out through evil, through death. Comedy avoids evil; tragedy confronts it."[8] Despite his logic, which is applicable to the vast majority of conventional comedies, Thompson's position on the role of tragic versus comic may arguably find itself extraneous when confronted with the master narratives of the grotesque comedies written by Scola. While Scola's satires and the cynicism in them regularly challenged the conceptualization of comedy throughout the 1960s, the implementation of the grotesque at the turn of the new decade perpetuated the challenge while presenting a new concept clearly in tune with the aesthetics of evil and its representation. In the case of Scola, comedies such as *I nuovi mostri* promoted a humor mainly focused on evil without the tradition angle of incongruity and its potential resolution. In denouncing the corruption of the church, sexual abuses, *omertà* (code of silence), the Italian health care system, ongoing domestic terrorism, and antiquated family hypocrisies, Scola took the spectators of the 1970s into a captive and violent world, similar to the real world at the time.

Grotesque Humor as a Response to Violence

By the early 1970s, despite commercial demands, Scola began to push his social satire even further, toward the grotesque, adding an incongruous dimension that explored the harsh reality of Italian life. The scope of these comedies was to uncover the complacency of Italians to social evils, driven by uncontrollable addictions. The two reigning theories of humor (incongruity and incongruity-resolution theories) do not fit Scola's films from this period. Scola's incongruity is a disorder of the mind, to be understood as a diagnosis of a pathology, "the chance to have a new outlook on the world, to realize the relative nature of all that exists, and to enter a completely new order of things," as Bakhtin defines it.[9] There seems to be a fundamental paradox in trying to understand the source of humor when that humor arises from the very disruption of sense: a society caught in a spiral of death, dominated by destruction and self-destruction and epitomized in the suicidal drive of the protagonists on the screen.

Therefore, grotesque humor breaks the conventional pattern of comedy altogether,[10] and as Kirby Olson argues, is "based on the transgression of categorical and conceptual boundaries and norms."[11] In such an extreme environment for comedy, the unthinkable can be said, and the undoable done. During the previous decades, humor had protected and structured the individual psyche by keeping its comedic devices within socially acceptable boundaries. The grotesque comedies were artistically mature films that employed a double-edged comedy with a potentially destructive power. One of the major proponents of grotesque comedy, Dino Risi, once stated: "Spectators must form their own opinion.... Morality is only a behavior. One cannot identify it *a priori* out of necessity: neither categorically nor hypothetically."[12] In other words, for the new comedy filmmakers, morality and its cinematographic rhetoric were never a part of humor, and the new satires, with their open-ended questions, represented a substantial development when compared to the comedies of the economic boom era (1959–64). As Roberto De Gaetano explains: "Grotesque is the only means of approaching reality without turning it into chronicle."[13] Cynical comedies affirmed the wisdom of societal authority as opposed to the barbaric folly of primitive, antisocial behavior, whereas grotesque comedies affirmed the vitality of human activity free from any restraint.

In this respect, one may ask how De Gaetano's assertion is relevant to the motivations and goals of this unmatched artistic movement: Was the grotesque simply a bittersweet distortion of existence through a "monstrous" lens, or was it there to investigate the extremity of reality? According to theorist Mikhail Bakhtin and his work on the functions of the grotesque, "exaggeration, hyperbolism, excess and superabundance" are among the characteristics of satire.[14] The grotesque in comedy, whether in theater or in cinema, has always been an effective microscope through which to examine reality, as Bakhtin describes it in his study on Rabelais.[15] The Italian comedies of the 1970s brought the comic genre to a new level of intensity (or outrage, for its detractors) thanks to the great attention paid to human mannerism and unprecedented mental perversion as well as the more demanding expectations from the public. Alan O'Leary takes this theory a step further by arguing that Bakhtin grants the grotesque "an anarchic aesthetic that employs and celebrates the body-based and chaotic elements of popular culture ... and that refuses all authority."[16] For O'Leary, the representation of "carnivalization" of the body is also a "social" body, representing the cyclical character of life in society, where mortality does not fit the conventional tragedy but appears as necessary for regeneration.

With the increase in such events as the tragedies of Piazza Fontana in Milan (1969) and of Piazza della Loggia in Brescia (1974),[17] among others, topics like terrorism and social unrest abruptly became too challenging for most comedy screenwriters to engage with. Along with Risi (*Mordi and fuggi / The Dirty Weekend*, 1973) and Mario Monicelli (*Vogliamo i colonnelli / We Want the Colonels*, 1973), Scola was one of the first to realize that the grotesque mode could succeed not only as a critical approach but also as an alternative way to increase the reflection of popular audiences on the gravity of Italy's predicaments. The moment had come to evolve toward a more daring style of skepticism.[18] Without respect for any preestablished modus operandi, grotesque comedy no longer relied solely on cynicism but rather on dark humor, using psychological distortion as its weapon to expose the dark side of the human psyche, society's ultimate evil. Scola's *Brutti, sporchi e cattivi*, Marco Ferreri's *La grande abbuffata* (*The Big Feast*, 1973),[19] Fausto Tozzi's *Trastevere* (1971), Monicelli's *Un borghese piccolo piccolo* (*An Average Little Man*, 1977), and Risi's *Sessomatto* (*How Funny Can Sex Be?*, 1973) did not only offer commentaries on current affairs from a sardonic point of view but were now firmly establishing a new comedy style, with the acerbic force of the grotesque.

For Scola, an important aspect of these new comedies was that they shared a new controlled cinematographic tone. Their common denominator was not exclusively ironic sarcasm but also certain nuances of phrasing, socially unacceptable behaviors, and unrestrained collective movements. Devoid of all conventional logic, and in a resolute break from past comedies, grotesque humor was based more on black comedy, psychological provocation, and incongruous caricature. In the early years of the 1970s, the popular trend of grotesque humor became the expression of subjectivity par excellence. De Gaetano asserts that the grotesque "was not a genre or a style. It was above all a vision of the world."[20] Indeed, *Travolti da un insolito destino nell'azzurro mare d'agosto* (*Swept Away*, 1974) by Lina Wertmüller and *Amici miei* (*My Dear Friends*, 1975) by Monicelli were provocative attempts to address contemporary issues through a satirical lens, now strengthened by the caustic vigor of the grotesque. But to fully understand the reasons for the genre's progressive expansion, one must take a critical step back and realize that the fundamental nature of the phenomenon was nothing new. In classical literature, grotesque elements generally are used to differentiate between two opposing feelings: splendor and desolation, empathy and disgust. The *commedia dell'arte* had frequent recourse to this burlesque approach by creating a visible change among the comic, the lyrical, and the pathetic. Consequently, the grotesque in Italian film comedies established a most convincing link between hysterical laughter and the worst pathologies. Many of Scola's comedies feature narratives in which evil and tragic events are not completely mastered on a narrative

FIGURE 14. Giacinto Mazzatella (Nino Manfredi) displaying the proof of adultery to his wife, Matilde (Linda Moretti), in *Brutti, sporchi e cattivi* (1976).

level. In *Brutti, sporchi e cattivi*, the line separating humor and grotesque is progressively blurred as the narratives unfold. An example of this blurring can be found in the scene in which Giacinto aggressively interrogates his wife, Matilde, after finding a new toilet brush in the house and forces her to confess that it was offered by Cesare, a neighbor and potential suitor (fig. 14). The visual focus of the brush serves here as an incongruous delineator between what appears as a harmless (also unromantic) domestic utensil and an object of immediate violence, a kitchen knife, which Giacinto uses to stab Matilde in the arm in punishment.

Scola's humor, like postmodernity (if we consider the advent of postmodernity following the economic boom), had the function of disrupting the master narrative (often in comedy serving as a device to juxtapose incongruity) by leaving spectators immersed in an unrelenting scenario of chaos and no longer confronted between their perceptions and their rational knowledge. According to Olsen, "Postmodernity is a matter of avoiding getting narrated," whereas "postmodernity and comedy are aligned in that they function by overturning master narratives and ridding metaphysics of transcendence and closure."[21] With Scola's narratives, and in particular during the burial scene in "Elogio funebre" (an episode of *I nuovi mostri*), humor, embodied by Alberto Sordi, was evidently a strategy for avoiding dependence on any master narrative. The spectator witnesses the burial of Formichella, once a famous stand-up comedian. Around the grave stand all the members of an *avanspettacolo* troupe (variety show), weeping in sorrow behind one of the prominent members (Alberto Sordi), who begins what appears to be the usual homage to the departed. However, Scola, in part as a tribute to Italy's *avanspettacolo* heritage, mixes the macabre with the comedic, employing the symbol of death in a purely grotesque way. The end result was something new and a clear sign of the times: through the lens of the grotesque, he was able to challenge any idealization of mortality. The hyperboles of death, the derision of rites, the burlesque logic, mixing farce and carnival with solemn eulogy, were the ultimate escape from a dominating logic (funerary traditions), which until then was the main reference point, with the usual expectation of familiar outcomes.

For Scola and his generation of comedy filmmakers (Monicelli, Risi, Ferreri, and Luigi Comencini, among others), moral concerns were typically secondary, thereby explaining the absence of proposed resolutions (incongruity-resolution theory). The emphasis was instead on the grotesque present, often on the influence of psychopathologies, in complex personalities in order to trigger the spectators' response, challenge their expectations, and secure new momentum within comedy spectatorship (not seeking laughter in the Hollywoodian sense of the term but rather an emotion and/or awareness). As amoral as Scola's narratives may be, they all manage to capture a raw vision of modern social decadence. His films remind spectators of the extremely narrow line between order and chaos, tragedy and laughter, all closely interrelated in comedy. Scola does not juxtapose incongruity, nor does he try to solve it; his main intention is to immerse spectators in a visual turmoil. Regarding the cruelty in his own films, Monicelli defended grotesque humor, stating: "The lack of compassion is a sign of intelligence: it is the one that sharpens the mind. This is how, between laughter and tragedy, I chose, and continue to choose, laughter."[22] Similarly, Scola's humor immerses spectators in laughter with the same lack of compassion, but he does this through chaos, with no juxtaposition of what qualifies as incongruous and what qualifies as socially acceptable. For example, in its depiction of disarray, the microcosm of the *baraccopoli* (shantytown) in *Brutti, sporchi e cattivi* seems detached from Italian society, from civility, and irrelevant for any juxtaposition spectators may be tempted to draw. Masi's notion of "bestiality" is illustrated in the scene in which a young teenage girl rounds up the children of the shantytown in the

FIGURE 15. Child in "day care" cage in *Brutti, sporchi e cattivi*

FIGURE 16. "Day care" cage at the edge of the shantytown (*Brutti, sporchi e cattivi*)

morning for "day care" and locks them in a secluded and squalid cage like chicken or cattle.

Scola uses recurrent close-ups of the children's faces (fig. 15), from inside and outside the cage—made of old mattress springs, posts, and other scraps of wood and metal by scenographer Luciano Ricceri—to emphasize this imprisonment. The cage (fig. 16) visually reinforces how, for the poor, marginalization and restricted space begin at an early stage of life and remain present as a quotidian reality until the end. As mentioned earlier, it is once more the transgression of the norms, combined with the incongruous nature of grotesque humor, that serves Scola's point as a response to social violence.

Death in Comedy: A Critical Observatory

The thematic innovation of using death as a plot function was much more than an ephemeral infatuation. Death as a topic in comedy had come a long way, argues film historian Enrico Giacovelli, and since the time of Risi's *Il sorpasso*, it was no longer "an intrusion, a premonition, but now was in vogue."[23] During the *anni di piombo*, death, even in its most macabre aspects (e.g., the ghastly visit Sordi makes to the cemetery in *Un borghese piccolo piccolo*) was no longer a collateral device but rather a mature topic. In addition to the *commedia dell'arte* of the Renaissance, remembered for its ability to address taboos via a corrosive use of facial expressions and masks,[24] grotesque discourse also manifested itself in modern variety shows very popular in postwar Italy, a tradition known for improvisation, spontaneity, and energy. Reinforced by some forerunners in the sixties, such as Antonio Pietrangeli's *Il magnifico cornuto* (*The Magnificent Cuckold*, 1964) and Franco Giraldi's *La bambolona* (*Baby Doll*, 1968), grotesque comedies of the 1970s avoided the rules of traditional narrative by presenting a succession of autonomous gags linked together to form a global narrative strategy.[25] Filmmakers identified society itself as the ultimate architect of social monstrosities like the ones in *I nuovi mostri*, which focused on an element of the grotesque, and these hyperbolic visions of Italian society are remembered as the most flamboyant film experiences of the decade. Scola's narratives, which predominantly dealt with the social behavior of the *homo italicus* (average Italian male), developed a strategy of incendiary depictions of Italians' evil conduct while keeping a convincing component of social satire. In *I nuovi mostri*, the grotesque consists of a compelling search for the boundary beyond which popular audiences no longer respond only with laughter, the intended humoristic response now entering the realm of discomfort.

The episodes of *I nuovi mostri* that Scola directed point out the flaws of a nation without real configuration, left unattended by the surrounding violence of the time. The most compelling use of the grotesque takes place in the episode "Come una regina," following the self-inflicted torment Franchino (Alberto Sordi) must go through in order to install his elderly mother in an assisted-living community under the pretext of offering her a short vacation to a countryside hotel. The son is ultimately forced to tell his mother the truth after she raises concerns about certain details of the guesthouse (the disproportionate number of old "vacationers") but eventually resigns herself to her own fate. At the crucial moment of the story, the son must depart, and pointing his finger, he shouts to the personnel a now famous quote in Italian popular culture: "E trattatela come una regina!" (And treat her like a queen!).

Franchino's decision to abandon his mother can be understood as a short allegory of life and death, a common theme in Scola's universe, as it offers a description of mortality transferred to a highly symbolic level. In his persuasive criticism of Italian society and family values, Scola (along with Risi and Monicelli) successfully exposed different authenticities of violence on-screen through the use of short episodes. Much more than Risi's flirting attempt made a decade before with *I mostri* (*The Monsters*, 1963), this new vision of Italian society is much more apocalyptic, and it serves as a warning to prevent any aspirations of self-destruction and the marginalization of Italians in their own society. Marshaling laughter, irony, and cynicism to exorcise death and rob it of its solemnity was the main objective of two episodes in *I nuovi mostri*, in which Ornella Muti's characters experience violent and absurd deaths. In the episode by Monicelli, "Autostop," Muti plays a young hitchhiker who is shot by a man who wrongfully suspects her of being a terrorist. Meanwhile, in the episode "Senza Parole" by Risi, Muti interprets an airline stewardess, who is offered a gift by her lover moments before boarding the plane: the package reveals to be a time bomb, which eventually explodes in flight at the conclusion of the episode. In this collaborative film, the directors dragged their protagonists toward the only truth: death. Every scene creates a claustrophobic sensation, enough to evoke the feeling of being trapped in a universe where death was literally the only escape.

In his premortem identification, a gaze at the bleak future of Italian comedy, Scola, alongside several other authors of comedy, took a courageous stance when depicting death and funerals. And it is precisely this last element that characterizes his idiosyncratic vision of comedy: the image of memorials, funerary rites, as one of the focuses of the *commedia all'italiana*. Due to its grotesque and even macabre features, this may leave the spectator a bit perplexed. However, the central question is whether the *commedia all'italiana* took death and funerals seriously. According to Gianni Canova, it is because

FIGURE 17. Final scene of "Elogio funebre" in *I nuovi mostri*

"Italian comedy wishes to take death seriously . . . that it almost never takes the funeral seriously."[26] The answer can be found again, in the "Elogio funebre" episode mentioned above, in which Scola immerses the spectators in an utterly macabre vision of death, with no juxtaposition nor resolution.

While death was essentially contemplated acerbically, the narrative strategy was, however, never contemptuous in its content or form. The aspiration to momentarily defy death was a simple device to reduce its overpowering aspect. As the eulogy reveals the rich personality of the defunct comedian, the anecdotes of Sordi's character gradually transform the weeping crowd into a rejuvenated and hysterically tittering *avanspettacolo* troupe (fig. 17). According to film scholar Jean Gili, "The eulogy for the deceased comic actor turns again into a show in which hedonism and the pleasure of living prevail once more."[27] In medieval popular culture, the rejuvenating merriment generated by collective hysteria, a temporary challenge to death's authority, can be also understood in terms of comedy versus tragedy, according to Snyder's theory of evitability. As in the cynical farce (*beffa* Tuscan style), Scola's use of a "liberatory" grotesque effectively functioned as a tool to desacralize death. Gili, in fact, argues that Scola, like a few other comedy authors of the time, not only avoided conventional portrayal of funerals in his comedies—too often restricted to the private domain of society—but, more important, deliberately confronted audiences with death so as to mitigate its power. Consequently, it is no surprise to see the funeral procession arrive at the graveyard, here a metaphor for Italy's nightmare of violence and death, conjured up in one well-delineated public area. Unlike conventional comedies, mortality is defined through a strategy of abstraction where protagonists are represented by their symbolic presence. Similarly, Scola makes the members of the troupe struggle to fit in contemporary Italian society, which no longer favors the *avanspettacolo*. It is no surprise to see them represented in a frantic final parade as a metaphor of a confused society without an exit plan, as Canova states: "Cinema highlights and stigmatizes the significant a-sociality of its characters, integrating them precisely the way in which the act of mourning is removed (dismissed as a solemn rite, as a gesture of heartache or as a failed act). Its strongest criticism is against the social immaturity of contemporary Italy."[28] Canova insists that the choral nature of the ceremony combined with the histrionic mourning was not only the *commedia*'s trademark but also its very strategy. Italian society, immature indeed, was moving closer to political chaos (as in *I nuovi mostri*, released a few months before Aldo Moro's assassination),[29] and grotesque comedy was just as anarchical as the violent world around it. With *I nuovi mostri*, Scola's narrative, which included a rather unforeseen outcome emphasizing the precariousness of a humanity without real perspective, stood light years away from the Italian comedies of the 1950s, with their iconic happy endings.

Before the critical and commercial success of *I nuovi mostri*, Ettore Scola had already employed grotesque humor in his 1972 film *La più bella serata della mia vita* (taken from a well-known novel by Friedrich Dürrenmatt, *Die panne*).[30] It tells the story of an unscrupulous businessman Alfredo Rossi (Alberto Sordi) who seeks assistance after his Maserati breaks down in Switzerland nearby what looks like a Transylvanian castle. There he meets several retired magistrates who occasionally gather to practice their former profession in private. The exuberant Italian is charmed by the them and accepts their invitation to stay for the night. He finds himself subject to a mock trial led by his hosts and during the prosecutor's cross examination, Rossi's entire life is examined, and his small defects are eventually transformed into serious crimes. Drawing on the performances of exceptional actors, Scola used the resources of the *commedia all'italiana*, this time with a more psychological register. Both the prosecutor Zorn (Michel Simon) and the accused Rossi (Sordi) use alternatively tense dramatic visual expressions and diabolical laughter in order to express dismay or anger, revealing both men to be potential predators with ill intent. The involuntary visit allows the protagonist to fall into the meshes of fiction and leads him into a destructive spiral.[31] Sordi's character is one of those nouveaux riches whose lack of scruples have made it possible to make the most of the economic boom. The first interview between Rossi and his judges, in the castle transformed into a courthouse, comically portrays their antagonistic relationship through their language. The prosecutor is above all a fine speaker whose logorrhea is nothing but pedantic, while the accused's language tends toward seduction and falsehood. From the first scenes, Rossi's pride is obvious, and the hosts do not fail to point this out:

> PROSECUTOR: You say, *dottore*, that you only did elementary school. But then how did you get your degree and become a doctor?
> ROSSI: I'm not a doctor. Everybody calls me a *dottore*. It is an Italian habit, especially Roman. With us, Signor Rossi, it does not sound good, but Dr. Rossi . . .
> PROSECUTOR: It sounds better maybe, but title usurpation is a crime.
> ROSSI: Oh yeah? So half of Italy should go to jail. Hey . . . sorry!

Faithful to the *commedia all'italiana* and its favorite targets, Ettore Scola argues that in matters of corruption Italians have often found themselves in the position of accomplices, just as Rossi tries to coax the judge by using rhetorical detours (partially replacing the words of the witnesses). Rossi's verbose exaggerations use metaphor for the purpose of swindling and dissimulation. The use of *dottore*, in this verbal frame, was a weapon of defense, substituting an embellished image for trivial reality. He is the target of choice for these magistrates. Yet, if Rossi is afflicted with many vices, he is not as monstrous as the film implies throughout the investigation. Conversely, the judges, despite their obsession with integrity and moral rigor, finally discover themselves to be as cowardly and manipulative as their opponent/victim. Nonetheless, they are still suspicious as to the true purpose of the game. Rossi's amorality is attenuated by his status as an ideal victim, when the prosecutor Zorn says to him: "See, you also have a corpse in your closet!" As Scola reveals the fragility of Rossi who is sometimes touching and pathetic, he reinforces the blindness of Zorn, who thus becomes a cold and inhuman incarnation of power. This progressive reversal of the forces at play, in which the status of predator and victim is much more ambiguous than one would like to believe, suggests a third voice in the film: that of the filmmaker himself, who sends each character back to their loneliness and refuses to arbitrate this duel. The film can be seen as a satire of unscrupulous counterjustice in which the integrity of all can be disputed: an attorney shaping nonexistent or falsified facts; a lawyer who, by manipulative and elaborate remarks, manages to make his client appear innocent; a judge with partial decisions who asks only to punish. One can also see in this comedy a ferocious criticism of Italians driven by *arrivismo* (a strong desire to advance), vengeance, lies, and deceit: the line between good and evil becomes blurred as both accused and accuser incarnate evil.

If Ettore Scola assumed the role of political filmmaker, it was because comedy, his genre of predilection, had never ceased to be a place from which to observe Italian society in the midst of reconstruction in the decades following World War II. He refused to rely solely on ideology, which was often at the heart of left-wing Italian political cinema. Though the film preceded the Berlusconi years, Scola's critique of the unscrupulous businessman (unintentionally) heralded a future Berlusconi as Marino-Maio argues in this volume.[32] Scola pushed the character of the pre-Berlusconian businessman to the worst avowal of failure: his dubious rise to power. The filmmaker's work consists, therefore, not only in inventing images but also intercepting and/or anticipating moments of reality. The death sentence at the end of *La più bella serata* is thus an amusing metaphor of the decadence of the elites to come. The political chaos of the *anni di piombo* was a rich source for the farcical allegories that give political satire its firepower.

A Strategy of Degeneration, Outrage and Absurdity

Through his comedies Scola revealed his own perplexity about human nature. His effort was, therefore, to upset the submissiveness of Italian spectators and to make them confront the "strangeness" of modern society, as well as the enigmatic character of their existence. Scola's cynical narrative invective remains today his main trademark. While the dominant aspect of Italian comedies in the 1960s had been the radical assimilation of its main characters (the main comic trajectory of the protagonists being to integrate themselves into society, primarily through work and/or marriage), a decade later this approach appeared rather superseded. Certainly, Scola's new films no longer featured protagonists fitting into society but instead marginals, self-sufficient characters, and even extremely cynical protagonists who circumvented Italian institutions, such as Giacinto and the Mazzatella family in *Brutti, sporchi e cattivi*. His comic heroes in some ways were no longer indebted to society nor did they adapt to Italian institutions but rather visibly experienced a process of degeneration and outrage.

The strategy of degeneration and outrage making a link between absurdity and death can be demonstrated by Monicelli's *Pronto soccorso* from the episode film *I nuovi mostri*[33] in which nobleman Giovan Maria Catalan Belmonte (Alberto Sordi) comes across a wounded man lying on the street. After some moments of reluctance, he takes him aboard his white Rolls Royce to a neighboring hospital. This hospital is already overcrowded, and he is told to take the dying man to the Misericordia hospital. There, the Mother Superior tells him that they do not accept patients after midnight and advises him to seek help at the military hospital. Finally, at the gate of the third hospital, he is told civilian patients are not allowed. After failing to secure help, the nobleman leaves the wounded, now lifeless, man where he had found him earlier, on the steps of the same monument.[34] This new type of grotesque comedy visibly targeted a certain type of scapegoat or social monster that seldom corresponded to actual individuals (as they typically had in the 1960s), but now Italian society itself, as the ultimate representation of a destructive labyrinth.

Many of Scola's comedies of the 1970s, such as *Dramma della gelosia—tutti i particolari in cronaca* (*The Pizza Triangle*, 1970), *Permette? Rocco Papaleo* (*My Name Is Rocco Papaleo*, 1971), *Signore e signori, buonanotte* (*Goodnight, Ladies and Gentlemen*, 1976), *Brutti, sporchi e cattivi* and *La terrazza* (*The Terrace*, 1980), have an uncompromisingly existential tone that reveals the mood of the time and also suggests that the experience of the absurd is evidence of man's individuality and freedom. Out of this also comes the absurd hero, whose fundamental ambiguity is here defined by Thompson:

> The hero of the farce demands that the universe be changed; the hero of the comedy demands that society accommodate itself to his will; the absurd hero makes no demands: the universe is beyond mere belief and society is incorrigibly a hoax. The absurd hero withdraws into himself, or rather he makes a gesture of his self: the infinite expressions of the human face gain the exact freedom of an immovable, absurd mask. Half

the audience will see the mask as tragic; half the audience will see the mask as comic.³⁵

In Scola's comedies, the concept of heroic absurdity is often linked to the idea of a potential death, a death in suspension or in progress. Death is almost always intensely present along with the theme of the absurd and the grotesque (e.g., Dr. Rossi's death at the end of *La più bella serata della mia vita* or Sergio's suicide in *La terrazza*). As paradoxical as it may appear, it can be interpreted as a powerful representation of man's victory over his too often monotonous existence.

But death is far from being a victory over the absurd. Promising and deceptive, innovative and repetitive, rushed and measured, it always becomes an illusory vision before turning into derision. In addition, absurdity and the grotesque give Scola's protagonists a fatal ending but also, strangely enough, inscribe them into an eternity that in due course will save them. Scola's hero has only one modest recourse to escape his fatal and final destiny: he must ignore his destiny and instead shape the final stage of existence (e.g., Franchino's decision to abandon his elderly mother in the episode "Come una regina" in *I nuovi mostri*). Scola's comedies deal with "existential" anguish and its implications in quotidian life. Whether contemplating death or a long existence, the Scola hero remains in an eternal state of anguish: the fear of life during youth and the apprehension of death during adulthood.

In conclusion, revisiting some of Scola's narratives during that decade reveals that the grotesque, combined with a rhetoric of death, was much more than a coherent metaphor for the collapse of the Italian social order; it was also a premonition about the end of the *commedia all'italiana* (eventually taking place just a few years later with his very own pseudo-testament *La terrazza*).³⁶ In the grand season finale of a glorious journey, the *commedia all'italiana* was able to look into the darkest corners of the Italian psyche while never neglecting the original objective: that of reproving a nation lost in the torments of domestic terrorism and violence. Scola's inherent goal was to propose a cinema of disclosure and disconnection not only to take spectators inside an apocalyptic world but also to serve as a social barometer and to reflect on a nation exhausted by a decade of violence. In the present context, should film historians consider the end of the *commedia all'italiana* the result of a natural degeneration of a no longer popular genre? What remains evident from the critical perspective of forty years is that Scola's comedies were able to impose a tangible cultural shift. Along with such films as Ferreri's *La grande abbuffata*, Comencini's *Lo scopone scientifico* (*The Scientific Cardplayer*, 1972), or Monicelli's *Un borghese piccolo piccolo*, Scola left his imprint on the collective imagination and cinematographic memory of a country, tackling difficult subjects through the power of entertainment and humor. While deploring the daily horrors of terrorism, the lost dreams of the economic miracle, the *incomunicabilità* between Italians, and their acquiescence to social evils, Scola, more than any other comedy author, succeeded in imposing his feelings on society without focusing on the survival of the genre.

Notes

1. Without having to go back to Plato, for modern thinkers such as Arthur Schopenhauer incongruity is one of the most important of the many theories of humor (e.g., relief theory, superiority theory, and incongruous juxtaposition theory, as later exposed in the works of other theorists such as Henri Bergson).
2. "The greater and more glaring their incongruity with it, from another point of view, the greater is the ludicrous effect which is produced by this contrast. All laughter is occasioned by a paradox and therefore by unexpected subsumption, whether this is expressed in words or in actions." Arthur Schopenhauer, *The World as Will and Idea*, trans. Richard Haldane and John Kemp, 6th ed., vol. 1, sec. 13 (London: Routledge & Kegan Paul, 1966), 95.
3. See Graeme Ritchie, "Developing the Incongruity-Resolution Theory," in *Proceedings of the AISB 99 Symposium on Creative Language, Humour and Stories* (Edinburgh: University of Edinburgh, 1999), 78–85.
4. In many romantic comedies from the period of pink neorealism, happy endings were a common denominator for many of these films. In Luigi Comencini's *Pane amore e fantasia* (*Bread, Love and Dreams*, 1953), Maresciallo Carotenuto (Vittorio De Sica) begins a new romantic life with Anna (Marisa Merlini), and in Alessandro Blasetti's *Peccato che sia una canaglia* (*Too Bad She's Bad*, 1954) the final shot zooms on a reparatory kiss between Paolo (Marcello Mastroianni) and Lina (Sophia Loren).
5. Stefano Masi, *Ettore Scola: Uno sguardo acuto e ironico sull'Italia e gli italiani degli ultimi quarant'anni* (Rome: Gremese, 2006), 58. Translations throughout the chapter are my own unless otherwise noted.
6. Susan Snyder, "Romeo and Juliet: Comedy into Tragedy," *Essays in Criticism: A Quarterly Journal of Literary Criticism* 20, no. 4 (1970): 391–402, 391.

7. Snyder, 391.
8. William I. Thompson, "Freedom and Comedy," *The Tulane Drama Review* 9, no. 3 (1965): 216–30.
9. Mikhail Bakhtin, *Rabelais and His World* (Bloomington: Indiana University Press, 1984), 34.
10. Notably, it is not the concept of grotesque that takes on new shape and content; it is only its use that is a novelty and consequently breaks with the usual comedy style (i.e., from the boom years). Grotesque has always appeared incongruous before and after modernity. What is in discussion here is that grotesque is now used in the 1970s within a conservative genre (comedy) resulting precisely in a groundbreaking transformation.
11. Kirby Olson, *Comedy after Postmodernism: Rereading Comedy from Edward Lear to Charles Willeford* (Lubbock: Texas Tech University Press, 2001), 14.
12. Dino Risi quoted in Valerio Caprara, *Mordi e fuggi: La commedia secondo Dino Risi* (Venice: Marsilio, 1993), 8.
13. Roberto De Gaetano, *Il corpo e la maschera: Il grottesco nel cinema italiano* (Rome: Bulzoni, 1999), 61.
14. Mikhail Bakhtin, *L'opera di Rabelais e la cultura popolare* (Turin: Einaudi, 1995), 332.
15. Bakhtin insists on the peremptory essence of the grotesque as a mode to produce laughter through a satirical lens: "Therefore, the grotesque is always satire. Where there is no satirical orientation there is no grotesque." Bakhtin, *Rabelais and His World*, 306.
16. Alan O'Leary, "Of Shite and Time," *Italianist* 35, no. 2 (2015): 294–99, 294.
17. These two tragedies, caused by bombs placed by neofascist groups, were symptomatic of the ongoing urban violence raging during the decade in Italy and illustrated the so-called strategy of tension.
18. In addition, the usual recognizable actors (Ugo Tognazzi, Nino Manfredi, Alberto Sordi, and Vittorio Gassman) had already disclosed a visible propensity for the grotesque vein in their respective repertoire, so it was no surprise to see them able to make an easy transition to this new type of comedy.
19. In Marco Ferreri's *La grande abbuffata* (1973), Marcello Mastroianni, Ugo Tognazzi, Michel Piccoli, and Philippe Noiret meet in a Parisian villa for a gastronomical feast (gradually revealing itself as a collective enterprise of planned suicide). With the sudden urge for female presence, they also invite three prostitutes along with a schoolteacher and begin their euphoric orgy.
20. De Gaetano, *Il corpo e la maschera*, 7.
21. Olson, *Comedy after Postmodernism*, 6.
22. Mario Monicelli, *Autoritratto* (Florence: Polistampa, 2002), 21.
23. Enrico Giacovelli, *Non ci resta che ridere: Una storia del cinema comico italiano* (Turin: Lindau, 1999), 111.

24. For a discussion on the notion of grotesque in the *commedia dell'arte*, see Domenico Pietropaolo's article "Commedia dell'arte as Grotesque Dance: Decline or Evolution?," in *The Routledge Companion to Commedia dell'arte*, ed. Judith Chaffee and Oliver Cric (New York: Routledge, 2015), 338–45.
25. This type of grotesque comedy, also defined as "grottesco gioioso" by De Gaetano as a subgenre of the *commedia dell'arte* (*Il corpo e la maschera*, 22), with the renewed Greek tradition of masks, was also promoted beyond its field of performance in modern carnivals (*mascherate*).
26. Gianni Canova, "Figure di un ordine cannibale," in *Lo sguardo eclettico: Il cinema di Mario Monicelli*, ed. Leonardo De Franceschi (Venice: Marsilio, 2001), 176–88.
27. Jean Gili, *Arrivano i mostri: I volti della commedia italiana* (Bologna: Cappelli, 1980), 188.
28. Canova, "Figure di un ordine cannibale," 181.
29. *I nuovi mostri* was released in Italy on December 15, 1977.
30. As it was often the case in Scola's work, the script was written by Sergio Amidei, who was for a long time Rossellini's screenwriter and whose neorealistic contribution was fundamental.
31. Insolent, cynical, rogue, infidel, Sordi is a man ready for anything to succeed, but whose apparent flamboyance conceals a great solitude. Scola does not make this duel a simple Manichaean struggle between good and evil: behind their social mask, Simon and Sordi remain uniformly pathetic characters.
32. Nicoletta Marini-Maio, "Sentenced to Death: The Proto-Berlusconi of Ettore Scola's *La più bella serata della mia vita*," this volume.
33. *I nuovi mostri*, written by Agenore Incrocci, Ruggero Maccari, Giuseppe Moccia, and Bernardino Zapponi and codirected by Dino Risi, Mario Monicelli, and Ettore Scola, was nominated for Best Foreign Film Award at the 1978 Academy Awards.
34. Interestingly enough, among the many representations of death in Monicelli's comedies, none occurred in a hospital. Death takes its toll on the street (*I soliti ignoti: Un Borghese piccolo piccolo*), inside homes (*Amici miei*), and at war (*La grande guerra*); ironically, in the only instance where a character is supposed to die in a hospital, he/she ends up dying on the street (*I nuovi mostri*).
35. Thompson, "Freedom and Comedy," 230.
36. Scola's vision of Italian bourgeoisie at the turn of the new decade and its disillusions from years of violence can also be compared with the end of the glorious season of comedy.

PART 2

HISTORY, MEMORY, AND CRITIQUE OF THE PRESENT

SEMO GIUDII

Cinema, Metacinema, and the Holocaust in Scola's Roman Jewish Trilogy (with a Special Focus on the Fictional Short *'43–'97*)

Millicent Marcus

DURING THE FINAL PHASE of his career, well after the events of World War II, Ettore Scola displayed a marked concern for the plight of Italian Jews in the throes of fascist anti-Semitism and the Nazi occupation. The result was a trilogy of works, ranging from the short fiction film *'43–'97* (1997) to the full-length feature *Concorrenza sleale* (*Unfair Competition*, 2001), to a brief episode in *Gente di Roma* (*People of Rome*, 2003). In his desire to revisit a painful and relatively neglected chapter of Italian history,[1] Scola shared in the recent cultural trend toward confronting his country's anti-Semitic past by contributing to the wave of films on the subject to have emerged since the 1990s (exemplified most spectacularly by Roberto Benigni's *La vita è bella / Life Is Beautiful*, 1997). Such an openness to the Jewish plight was occasioned by the radical shift in Italian culture that followed the fall of the First Republic and the collapse of the ideological polarization that monopolized national political life throughout the postwar years. Dominated by World War II historiographies favored by the Left and the Right, both of which skirted the Shoah for reasons of political expedience,[2] Italian culture demonstrated a distinct reluctance to confront a historical chapter that threatened the basis

---

This chapter is an expanded version of the epilogue of *Italian Film in the Shadow of Auschwitz* (Toronto: University of Toronto Press, 2007), 161–67.

of the postwar order. This relative blind spot regarding the subject of the Holocaust was especially surprising with respect to Italian cinema, whose neorealist tradition had always been characterized by unswerving courage in facing instances of social injustice past and present. With the fall of the First Republic, and the loosening of the Left–Right stranglehold on World War II historiography, the cinematic mandate to address fascist anti-Semitism and the Final Solution could finally be given free rein.[3]

Concorrenza sleale is Scola's most celebrated contribution to this welcome trend. In hailing the film's release, Paolo Finn noted that "in fifty years of Italian cinema there has been a decidedly limited production of works" on the topic of fascist anti-Semitism and the fate of the Jews under the Nazi occupation. He added that it was "a theme absolutely unpleasant to mass audiences [because] it would have raised unresolved questions about our embarrassing recent past, one of the most despicable and dramatic pages in our history."[4]

Though *Concorrenza sleale* limits itself to the period of the fascist anti-Semitism from 1938 to 1939, its ending anticipates the dire fate of Roman Jews during the 1943–44 Nazi occupation. The story of a rivalry between two shopkeepers, Umberto Melchiorri and Leone Della Rocca, whose competition becomes "unfair" with the intervention of the racial laws (1938–43), concludes with the wrenching scene of the Jewish family's exile (the Della Rocca family) from the cozy confines of Via Ottaviano on their way to the ghetto, the site of the Nazi roundup to take place some years later. The final frames of the film are devoid of dialogue—the solemn gazes between individual members of the Della Rocca family and their counterparts among the Melchiorris tell us all we need to know about the characters' painful understanding of this historically fraught relocation.

'43–'97 takes up where *Concorrenza sleale* left off, chronicling the next chapter in the plight of the Jews under Nazi-fascist rule: the roundup of ghetto dwellers and their deportation to Auschwitz (the destination of the great majority of Italian Holocaust victims). The ghetto of Rome had become the foremost symbol of Italian Judaism—the Semitic synecdoche, the concrete location that had come to signify the whole of the Italian Jewish experience. The assault on this space constituted an unprecedented outrage, the violation of the protective cocoon that enveloped Roman Jewish life for centuries.[5]

Those famous walls were infamously breached on October 16, 1943. It is with this primal wound that Ettore Scola's short film begins. By now, no expository captions are needed to identify the day, month, and location of this nefarious event. It is enough to show the license plate of a waiting truck featuring the stylized double S of the *Schutzstaffel*, or the careening motorcycles, or the lines of guards, or the solemn parade of people meekly advancing with their suitcases and satchels, to know what is taking place. Scola's black-and-white camerawork is restrained in its documenting of this relentless roundup, showing tenements emptying out in sad processions under assorted arches, down staircases, across walkways, alternating group shots with close-ups of beautifully sculpted faces and, in one instance, of a white-bearded, black-scarfed old man who could come right out of an art-historical engraving. There is one particular little boy who recurs throughout the sequence and who we expect to become the focalizer of this event—the set of eyes through which we will experience the narration. With his jaunty cap and his calf-length pants, he recalls the heartbreaking and well-known image of the boy in the Warsaw ghetto with the yellow star immortalized in a photograph that has entered into the archive of collective memory as a prime signifier of Holocaust atrocity.

Now the film cuts to an interior scene of a woman draping a blanket over a folded-up cot. After brutally ushering her out, the SS recede down the steps and Scola's camera closes in on the cot to reveal a boy peaking his head out, putting on his glasses, and emerging from hiding once the coast is clear. It bears noting that the boy who escapes and survives wears glasses—a detail that I, in my wishful thinking, see as a link between this child and the bespectacled and lovable Lele, son of Leone Della Rocca, in *Concorrenza sleale*. (Of course, the glasses in '43–'97 signify the surviving child's ability to *look*, an interpretive key of great significance to the rest of Scola's short film.) Escaping from a back doorway and leaping to the ground, the boy catches the eye of an SS man who takes off after him at breakneck speed. Using parallel montage to great effect, Scola intercuts between the frantic chase through the curved and cobblestone streets of the ghetto and the grim, slow roundup of passive deportees. Acoustically, this contrast takes the form of a musical counterpoint: the escape is accompanied by an animated and anxious piano score, while the roundup takes place against the backdrop of a mournful violin piece, resembling a Hebraic lament. The Italian characters in this sequence remain in utter silence, and the only words that we hear are the German orders "Raus, Schnell." Significantly, the last shot of the Nazi sweep features the little boy with the cap who climbs onto the truck and vanishes from the film. He is the boy who does not make it, and his image remains etched in our memory, even as we cheer on the other boy in his successful efforts to evade Nazi capture.

It is the marquee of the neighborhood "Cine" that beckons our protagonist toward safety. As he ducks into the theater, the woman in the ticket booth feigns indifference, and his Nazi pursuer continues down the street. Within the theater, a newsreel announcer boasts of the "crushing victories" of German forces and touts the complete agreement of the axis countries "in the political and military sphere." Documentary footage of Hitler-Mussolini camaraderie is succeeded by a clip of the Führer's deranged and incendiary speechmaking. This then modulates into its satiric reenactment in the frenzied oratorical gibberish of Charlie Chaplin's *The Great Dictator* (1940), followed by a montage of Italian film clips that traverse the period from 1945 to 1997. (For a list of film clips inserted into '43–'97, see this chapter's appendix.)

Guiding Scola's selection of clips is a variety of factors, including the most obvious one of personal taste. Among the scenes are a number from groundbreaking films within the history of postwar Italian cinema, as well as those that represent an array of genres—neorealism, *commedia all'italiana*, *cinema politico*—and auteurs, including Roberto Rossellini, Vittorio De Sica, Federico Fellini, Michelangelo Antonioni, Nanni Moretti, Giuseppe Tornatore, Gianni Amelio, Paolo and Vittorio Taviani, Francesco Rosi, and needless to say, Scola himself. (I think it was a sign of great generosity and humility to include a snippet of *Nuovo Cinema Paradiso/Cinema Paradiso* [1988], in the light of Scola's own failure in *Splendor* [1988] to do what Tornatore so brilliantly achieved in his Oscar-winning film). Many of the clips include child protagonists, and most foreground both their own spectacular nature and internalized responses to the power of cinematic spectacle.

At the end of the montage, the lights of the theater go up to reveal that in place of the boy escapee of 1943, there sits a white-haired gentleman who cleans his glasses. We have transitioned now to color,[6] but there is an acoustic throwback to the 1940s segment in the sound of footsteps echoing on the cobblestones, and we hear the return of the hurried piano music that had accompanied the Nazi chase. At this point, an adolescent of African descent runs panting into the theater and sits one row behind our aged protagonist. Recognizing his younger self in this desperate fugitive, the Jewish gentleman bestows on him a knowing smile—one of understanding and consolation.

Now both of them sink down into their seats as the lights go off and the credits for Scola's film scroll down the screen within the screen.

At its most obvious, '43–'97 is about the link between the past and the present of racial intolerance, about the urgent need to revisit Holocaust history now, lest the logic of persecution visit itself on the new Italian "other" of Third World immigration. As Scola will write in the preface to the screenplay of *Concorrenza sleale*, his film is about what it means "to discover being considered 'different' for [one's] birth or for [one's] race. It happened in the past to Jews and to blacks, it happens today to immigrants and to undocumented non-Europeans."[7] On the metacinematic level, the film is a complex study of the relationship between off-screen historical context and on-screen cinematic representation—in other words, the film self-reflexively asks us what it means to seek sanctuary in a movie theater. Cynically understood, such a turning away from the cobblestone streets suggests that cinema is a place of denial, escape, or withdrawal from the arena of necessary historical action. But the relationship that Scola posits between the montage on the screen within the screen and the frame story of the two minority fugitives from persecution is far more complex and nuanced. By embedding a panorama of Italian film chronicle within a narrative of searing historical allusiveness, Scola confronts one of the largest and most abstract of theoretical issues: the connection between the film medium and its referent in the life of the country, or, in specifically semiotic terms, the writer-director investigates the link between cinematic signifier and historic signified. In the Italian case, Scola has always been a proponent of the particularly close ties between film and national history. "The specificity of Italian cinema," he claimed in a recent interview, "as opposed to the cinemas of France or Germany, is that of being so intertwined with reality that it scans *la vicenda Italia* [the Italian case]. Our cinema has always been social chronicle."[8]

For one thing, '43–'97 represents in remarkably distilled form, a tendency that we can see throughout Scola's career—the ambition to telescope into a single full-length film, the history of an entire generation. *C'eravamo tanto amati* (*We All Loved Each Other So Much*, 1974), *La famiglia* (*The Family*, 1987), *Splendor*, and *Ballando ballando* (*Le bal*, 1983)—immediately come to mind in this regard. These films are straightforward chronicles that filter historical events through the personal stories of individuals or small groups of closely knit characters. What Scola does in '43–'97, instead, is to entrust the entire historical sweep of time to the *films* that came out during that period and that shaped the imaginary of its spectators, so that it is enough to see a few representative frames for viewers to be transported back to the time when they first beheld them on screen. In other words, these films have come to stand for the zeitgeist into which they emerged.

Scola's montage of clips from 1943 to 1997 forms a kind of parahistory—one that at every point asks us to question the way in which what is happening outside the theater is mirrored, critiqued, transformed, transcended, overlooked, sanitized, and so forth on the screen. Perhaps more than a parahistory, the montage creates a simulacrum of history—each clip has the power to conjure up and signify the moment of its making—*Roma città aperta* (*Rome, Open City*, Rossellini, 1945) is equated with the struggles of the Roman Resistance, *Il sorpasso* (*The Easy Life*, Risi, 1962) is the Italy of "Il boom" (the economic miracle), *Palombella rossa* (*Red Wood Pigeon*, Moretti, 1989) heralds the waning of the Italian Left, and so on. In his choice of clips, then, Scola has selected cinematic signifiers that not only represent but also have actually come to replace in the public mind the historical and cultural signified that produced them. This blurring of the distinction between the cinematic medium and its external referents is made explicit in the confusion of levels between Scola's "outer film"—the story of the Jewish escapee from the ghetto roundup—and the montage we see on the screen within the screen. Such a collapsing of levels occurs when the closing credits for Scola's outer film are projected on the inner screen, so that the boundaries between outside and inside, container and contained, break down. The implications for us in the viewing audience are not far to seek. When the elderly Jewish gentleman turns around to acknowledge the fugitive within the audience of which he himself is a part, it is as if the film were turning to us and asking us to confront the social injustices in our midst. In this scene, the old man's gaze is focused on the young immigrant. The cross-cutting of tight close-ups between the two indicates that this is an intense *exchange* of gazes, communicating the old man's profound understanding of the boy's plight and serving to calm and reassure this young fugitive that he is safe, at least for the moment. If the old man were to look directly into the camera, it would break this exclusive and intimate bond. We are not the object of the old man's gaze. And yet, as witnesses to this exchange, we are nonetheless called to accountability. Here, we become acutely aware of what it means to be spectators—of the montage on the screen within the screen (and the history it traverses) and of this final act of profound human solidarity across zones of difference. That message of connection—between on-screen representation and audience members' lived experience—finds in us, the viewers of Scola's film, the next link in this chain of ethical accountability.

In this way, the cinema's status as sanctuary can be defended from charges of escapist withdrawal from the cobblestone streets of the historical arena. It is the cinema's commitment to monitor, critique, and engage in the progress of *"la vicenda Italia"* that can provide the impetus to corrective action. The refuge offered by the movie theater points to the ultimate power of the cinema to intervene in the off-screen world, to bring about a condition of enlightenment and social desire that will obviate the need for the kind of sanctuary that our film's minority protagonists had to seek in the first place.

It is significant that Scola's plea for the utopian potential of cinema should pivot on the issue of Holocaust representation. By bracketing his short film with an allusion to the roundup of Roman Jewry on October 16, 1943, and Francesco Rosi's cinematic treatment of the Holocaust in his 1997 film *La tregua (The Truce)*,[9] Scola foregrounds the process by which this repressed history has belatedly become the subject of cinematic representation. In his decision to frame the film within a Holocaust narrative but to embed within it a microhistory of Italian cinema, Scola constructs a "representational parable"—an instructive tale about the media's need to take on this repressed chapter of the past. Such a strategy vindicates both the specificity and the greater applicability of the Italian Holocaust case. While '43–'97 asserts the uniqueness of this particular "recovered memory," it also insists on the cinema's responsibility to challenge all such instances of public unwillingness to face disquieting truths, past or present.

Concorrenza sleale and '43–'97 did not exhaust Scola's need to revisit the Italian Jewish plight. He continued to be haunted by this woeful history. He could not let it go. In his penultimate film, *Gente di Roma*, Scola would dedicate one of his vignettes to the ordeal of an elderly Auschwitz survivor.

By now, Scola's film language has reached maximum compression—he can relate a complex incident in simple and effective shorthand. The ghetto location is fleetingly established by a set of easily recognizable landmarks—the synagogue and Portico d'Ottavia—while the main character's Jewish identity is conveyed through a series of briefly glimpsed images—a menorah, a star of David necklace, a page of a book portraying two candlesticks illustrating the text of a Hebrew prayer.[10] But such a distilled cinematic language is hardly reductive. Scola enriches this portrait by adding details that complicate her minority status—she is also a generic *casalinga* (housewife) whose television watching includes infomercials for vacuum cleaners and whose defining activity (for the purposes of this vignette) is to go grocery shopping, as signaled by the "trolley" characteristic of so many Italian matrons on their trips to the market.

The entire vignette lasts only two minutes and thirty-five seconds (from 56:44 to 59:19) and it begins as the camera enters the protagonist's home with neorealist curiosity, surveying the objects that define her orderly and ritualistic domestic routine. A split screen, featuring on the left a television tuned to a housekeeping ad and on the right an open window giving out to a picturesque scene of roofs and ivy-covered buildings across the way, introduces us to the protagonist's living space. An old woman clad in a black coat and hat enters the frame to close her window and prepare for an outing. As the camera pulls back, it reveals a scenario of modest, impeccably ordered domesticity: an ironing board with a neatly stacked pile of newly pressed clothes, a stately cupboard, sideboards adorned with knickknacks, a wall decorated with tastefully arranged paintings or prints, a table protected by an oilcloth covering. The old woman moves purposefully through this dining room/living room suite to fetch her "trolley" and exit the apartment. The camera cuts to an outdoor shot of the ancient archway over Portico d'Ottavia before descending to ground level and panning left to record the protagonist's slow progress along a series of ramps and a short pedestrian bridge. The blocking of this scene, with its insistence on the woman's movement along an elaborate elevated walkway, serves a double purpose—it both reveals the archaeology of the ghetto, perched on ancient ruins excavated beneath the surface of contemporary life, and it lengthens the amount of time that the camera can focus on the woman's enactment of her daily routine. Like her, we too are lulled into the state of peaceful complacency, which is soon to be disrupted by the hum of a motor revving up on the soundtrack. Now the camera cuts to a slow parade of people carrying suitcases toward a truck guarded by soldiers, before returning us to an extreme close-up of the old woman showing her eyes wide with terror as she relives the infamous Nazi roundup of October 16, 1943.

While the action up to this point has been filmed by an "objective camera," Scola now locates us within the subjectivity of the protagonist. Fragmented close-ups of young SS guards alternate with swish pans of crowd activity: an elderly woman is shown hoisted onto a truck; images of helmets emblazoned with Nazi symbols flash by; the face of a doll is framed by converging rifle barrels; a girl is herded onto the vehicle clutching another doll. Camera movements seem random and disjointed; unmotivated zooms and sudden changes in focus abound. Acoustically, this frantic montage is accompanied by a musical score of the utmost urgency and angst, ending with the piercing scream of the protagonist as she loses consciousness. At this point, we hear a voice call out "Stop!" and Scola's camera pulls back to reveal that this is a film shoot, that the Nazi roundup of ghetto dwellers has been staged by a troupe of actors and extras for cinematic consumption. "Che succede?" ("What's going on?"), asks the director within Scola's film, getting up from his seat to investigate the cause of the commotion. "Signora, mi sente?" ("Do you hear me, ma'am?"), he inquires, as he grasps her wrist and uncovers the tattooed numbers inscribed on her forearm in the last frames of the vignette.

It is through the aged survivor's traumatic brush with the past that Scola seeks closure for his own attempts to come to terms with this historical trauma, what Primo Levi called "the central fact ... the stain, of our century."[11] The term *trauma* is derived from the Greek word for wound, and in Freudian theory it signifies a psychic shock that has never been worked through therapeutically—a wound that has healed imperfectly, if at all. For the aged survivor, whose damaged psyche has been tenuously held together by the balm of daily routine and the peaceful passage of time, this sudden recall obliterates the distance between then and now, plunging her into what Lawrence Langer has labeled "deep memory," precipitating a temporary loss of consciousness.[12]

What we realize at the metalevel of the film's reflection on its own mechanisms is that the survivor is performing her own editing job on the raw material of the action unfolding before the camera of the filmmaker within the film. She experiences not the smooth procession of deportees, squired by orderly SS guards, as the filmmaker records them on camera, but instead a hectic and disjointed collage of assorted faces, random details, blurry movements, changes in focus—an incoherent perceptual field, unreadable and unassimilable.

For us, as the privileged viewers of '43–'97, the awareness that Scola is explicitly alluding to his own filming of an earlier work (complete with a few strains of its mournful musical sound track) gives this vignette a dizzying specularity. In the *Gente di Roma* episode, we get simulation at two removes—Scola's reenactments of his own filming of '43–'97, which is itself a reenactment of the actual historic event. Of the utmost significance is the fact that the vignette of the woman's traumatized witness is based on a true story—that an elderly Auschwitz survivor had actually stumbled on Scola's filming of the roundup scene in '43–'97 and that Scola was accused of behaving with insensitivity in her regard. I cannot help but think that Scola made this vignette as a form of atonement in an attempt to find a cinematic language adequate to the experience of trauma, to the reopening of the wound that he inadvertently triggered in this deeply damaged psyche. By inhabiting the survivor's subjectivity, by seeking an emotional identification with her traumatic vision and translating it into the language of film, Scola is fulfilling a solemn ethical imperative—to enter into the condition of the aggrieved "other" and to invite us to imaginatively share that condition. In so doing, he is exploiting cinema's medium-specific powers to elicit compassion in the etymological sense (to suffer with), prompting us to engage in the kind of activism that would alleviate such suffering in the world of lived experience.

As a result, Scola's Roman Jewish trilogy enacts, in highly condensed form, two of the broadest and most consequential trends within his filmography—the transfiguration of the *commedia all'italiana* into a vehicle of *impegno* and the elaboration of a metacinematic consciousness to reflect on the power of film as social intervention. These threads come together with particular poignancy in the *Gente di Roma* vignette, in which the phrase *semo giudii* could be seen to characterize Scola's empathic, highly self-conscious filmmaking—an approach that ushers us into the subjectivity of the other and asks us to ponder the unique capacity of cinema to bring us to this ethically charged pass. In the Holocaust context of his Roman trilogy, Scola's cinema gives new urgency and meaning to that age-old, but never obsolete, admonition: *mai più* (never again).

Appendix: List of Film Scenes Anthologized in '43–'97

1. *Roma città aperta* (*Rome, Open City*, Roberto Rossellini, 1945). Pina (Anna Magnani) runs after the Nazi truck that carries off her fiancé, Francesco (Francesco Grandjacquet). She is shot down before the eyes of her son, Marcello (Vito Annicchiarico); the priest, Don Pietro (Aldo Fabrizi); and the entire community of which she has been so important a part.

2. *Ladri di biciclette* (*Bicycle Thieves*, Vittorio De Sica, 1948). Antonio (Lamberto Maggiorani) races off on a stolen bike to the shock and horror of his son, Bruno (Enzo Staiola).

3. *I soliti ignoti* (*Big Deal on Madonna Street*, Mario Monicelli, 1958). Dante Cruciani (Totò) demonstrates his safe-cracking system for the benefit of his incompetent cohorts.

4. *Il sorpasso* (*The Easy Life*, Dino Risi, 1962). Roberto Mariani (Jean-Louis Trintignant) and Bruno Cortona (Vittorio Gassman) careen around the curve in their sports car and are met by an oncoming truck.

5. *Il gattopardo* (*The Leopard*, Luchino Visconti, 1963). Don Fabrizio, Prince of Salina (Burt Lancaster), dances a waltz with Angelica (Claudia Cardinale) that signals the debut of his nephew's wealthy bourgeois bride in the upper reaches of Sicilian aristocracy.

6. *Amarcord* (Federico Fellini, 1973). The oceanliner *Rex*, symbol of fascist pretentions to world power, appears to the waiting populace, and the blind accordion player asks insistently, "What's it like?"

7. *Una giornata particolare* (*A Special Day*, Ettore Scola, 1977). The fascist housewife Antonietta (Sophia Loren) confesses her infatuation with the gay, politically subversive Gabriele (Marcello Mastroianni), admitting, "Ever since this morning I've been watching you," as they fold the laundry on their apartment rooftop.

8. *Ricomincio da tre* (*I'm Starting from Three*, Massimo Troisi, 1981). Marta (Fiorenza Marchegiani) announces to her boyfriend, Gaetano (Massimo Troisi), that she is pregnant, and they discuss what to name the child.

9. *Nuovo Cinema Paradiso* (*Cinema Paradiso*, Giuseppe Tornatore, 1988). The child Totò (Salvatore Cascio) manipulates Alfredo (Philippe Noiret) into giving him a ride home on his bicycle.

10. *Palombella rossa* (*Red Wood Pigeon*, Nanni Moretti, 1989). Michele Apicella (Moretti) inveighs against a journalist (Mariella Valentini) for her use of trendy jargon.

11. *Il ladro di bambini* (*Stolen Children*, Gianni Amelio, 1992). In a train compartment, Antonio (Enrico Lo Verso) looks at the two hapless children, Rosetta (Valentina Scalici) and Luciano (Giuseppe Ieracitano), whom he must escort to an orphanage.

12. *La tregua* (*The Truce*, Francesco Rosi, 1997). A throng of survivors rushes toward freedom as the gate of Auschwitz is torn down.

Notes

1. There are several superb studies on the issue of Holocaust historiography and memory. Among them are Robert S. C. Gordon's *The Holocaust in Italian Culture, 1944–2010* (Stanford: Stanford University Press, 2012), and Emiliano Perra, *Conflicts of Memory: The Reception of Holocaust Films and TV Programmes in Italy, 1945 to the Present* (Oxford: Peter Lang, 2010).
2. The Right, in particular the Alleanza Nazionale Party, which sought to distance itself from its fascist forebears, had obvious reasons to shun reminders of Italy's anti-Semitic past. The Left had more complex reasons for sidestepping this history. As heir to the Resistance, the Left was reluctant to revisit a past that highlighted the movement's failure with regard to this persecuted minority. In addition, the Left's discomfort with the State of Israel played into its reticence on the subject of the Shoah.
3. While a series of films regarding the Italian Jewish plight were made prior to the 1990s (most notably Vittorio De Sica's 1970 *Il giardino dei Finzi Contini / Garden of the Finzi-Continis*), these works were relatively few in number, and they failed to coalesce into a coherent cinematic lineage that could be accessed by subsequent Italian filmmakers willing to approach this difficult subject matter. For a more in-depth treatment of the issue, see my *Italian Film in the Shadow of Auschwitz*, 29.
4. For Paolo Finn's review of *Concorrenza sleale*, see his "Concorrenza sleale," *Cinemasessanta* 42 (March–April 2001), 21–22. Translations throughout the chapter are my own unless otherwise noted.
5. Despite the privations that beset the Jews confined to this restricted space, ghettoization is now being "re-evaluated," according to historian Anna Foa. The ghetto, she claims, represents "the concrete realization of those invisible walls that the Law had constructed around the identity of the Jewish people, to protect it and conserve it." See Anna Foa, *Ebrei in Europa: Dalla Peste Nera all'emancipazione* (Milan: Mondadori, 2001), 160.
6. This transition in the outer film had already been anticipated in Scola's montage of clips on the screen within the screen, which had traced the evolution of Italian film technique as well as content.
7. Ettore Scola, *Concorrenza sleale* (Turin: Lindau, 2001), 5.
8. See the interview with Maria Pia Fusco, "Scola: uno specchio per i giovani," *La Repubblica*, July 16, 2004, 45.
9. Rosi's *La tregua* is an adaptation of Primo Levi's second Holocaust memoir, which documents his liberation from Auschwitz and the ensuing nine-month odyssey back to his home in Turin. Scola privileges Rosi's adaptation by granting it the climactic position in his montage, thereby countering the film's uncharitable reception by Italian and French reviewers. See Cosetta Veronese,

"Paying the Price of Perpetuating Memory: Francesco Rosi's Interpretation of Primo Levi's *The Truce*," *Studies in European Cinema* 5 (January 2008): 55–66.

10. For a superb study of Italian cinematic signs of Jewish identity, see Virginia Picchietti, "A Semiotics of Judaism: Representations of Judaism and the Jewish Experience in Italian Cinema 1992–2004," *Italica* 83, nos. 3–4 (2006): 563–82. See also Guido Fink's seminal study, "Semo tutti cristiani? Ebrei visibili e invisibili nel cinema italiano," in *In nome del cinema*, ed. Vito Zagarrio (Milan: Il Ponte, 1999), 83–102.

11. Primo Levi, *I sommersi e i salvati* (Turin: Einaudi, 1991), 10.

12. See Langer's canonical study, *Holocaust Testimonies: The Ruins of Memory* (New Haven, CT: Yale University Press, 1991), especially the chapter "Deep Memory," 1–38.

ETTORE SCOLA AND DIGITAL TECHNOLOGY

History, Memory, and Interpretation of the Present

Christian Uva

THIS CHAPTER FOCUSES ON Ettore Scola's methods of using digital technology during the last stages of his career. It explores the ways in which this technology accentuated the porosity and dialectical tension that is commonplace in Scola's cinematic style between the Great History, the official one, and the history of the common people (microhistory) that is configured at various levels in his films: for example, in the dialectic between the dimensions of *presenza* (presence) and *assenza* (absence), *fuori* (outside) and *dentro* (inside), *interno* (interior) and *esterno* (exterior) in regard to the anthropological and social microcosms staged by the director. This chapter examines the feature films that Scola made in the new millennium in which the use of the new digital medium was, in certain aspects, a pioneering development. In fact, Scola was one of a few "old masters" to adopt digital technology in its early hours, not only for reasons tied to production, but above all because he was interested in making it an object of reflection, which ended up implicating the ontology of cinema and, at the same time, that of history itself.

From this point of view, the final shot of a film made by Scola at the end of the last century, *La cena* (*The Dinner*, 1998), could prove to be emblematic and illuminating. Evoking the famous scene of Vittorio De Sica's *Miracolo a Milano* (*Miracle in Milan*, 1951), in which the young Totò and his homeless friends fly over Milan on a broomstick in search of a friendlier land "where good morning means good morning," Scola here uses the 8-bit animation of a Nintendo video game (typical of the mid-1990s) to represent a young Japanese boy's imagination when looking up at the sky over Rome upon leaving a chaotic trattoria. The boy imagines a magician and his sidekick (two of the diners in the restaurant that night) on a broomstick flying over the rooftops of Rome and by St. Peter's Dome, when they are shot down by a UFO, letting us know that the film is over, like a video game—a lighthearted way of suggesting that fifty years after World War II it is difficult to find a friendlier place.

Yet the use of digital in this scene has further significance. Vito Zagarrio asserts that this scene offers "an image of pure utopia, a desire for an empowered imagination . . . that combines the brooms of *Miracolo a Milano* with digital technologies [and] neorealism with the PlayStation. It is an image that combines tradition and (Post)modernity, which travels *back to the future* wisely mixing sharp social observation with a touch of poetry."[1] This first incursion into the digital by Scola was interpreted by film historian Gianni Canova to be an acknowledgment by the director of an "already obsolete historical function of cinema" and hence of the need to find "other glances and other media, more capable of giving form to History and also of representing spectres [*fantasmi*] and needs of the soul."[2]

It is precisely this blending of social and historical inquiry with a constant poetic annotation, sealed by the new technology, that characterizes the works analyzed below—namely, *Gente di Roma* (*People of Rome*, 2003) and *Che strano chiamarsi Federico* (*How Strange to Be Named Federico*, 2013), which were entirely made with digital technology, and also *Concorrenza sleale* (*Unfair Competition*, 2001), albeit filmed with traditional film stock, which contemplates some computer-related interventions relevant to the issues addressed in this chapter. Respecting chronological order, this chapter begins with an examination of *Concorrenza sleale* in order to highlight important questions of Scola's use of digital technology that merit reflection.

The Refuge from History: Digital Images and Plaster Board Sets

Concorrenza sleale is a story entirely set in the "shadow" of St. Peter's dome, during the sixteenth year of the fascist era (1938), when racial laws were first promulgated in Italy. The film's treatment by Furio Scarpelli opens with a creative and original cue: the competition of two adjoining stores—a traditional tailor's shop in crisis, run by Umberto (Diego Abatantuono) and an emerging sewing store under the management of the Jewish merchant Leone (Sergio Castellitto)—which transforms into a relationship of solidarity during a tragic moment in Italian history. This is the context in which the director brings back to life the social climate and characters of the era through a dialectic that in more than one moment engages *Concorrenza sleale* in a dialogue with the setting and the historical framework of another "classic," *Una giornata particolare* (*A Special Day*, 1977), implicitly recalled in the scene of Hitler's visit to Rome.

The Rome of *Concorrenza sleale*, as in *Una giornata particolare*, appears to be enclosed in a microcosm pervaded by a centripetal energy in which the exterior—namely, history—is swallowed up and represented by the most minute scenic details of an interior. Beyond the protagonists' individual homes in *Concorrenza sleale*, the story primarily unfolds in the neighborhood microcosm: the street where the workshops of Umberto and Leone are located, their respective apartments, the police station, and the wine cellar. In particular, this unity of place finds an ideal fulfillment in the street, which set designer Luciano Ricceri entirely rebuilt at Cinecittà in order to represent Scola's topographic fantasy. The "Via Settimiano" of the film alludes in a somewhat apparent manner to the real Via Ottaviano (a street near San Pietro characterized by the presence of many traditional Jewish shops), but it does not have a direct and faithful correspondence to the urban reality of Rome. It is an invention derived from the condensation of urban fragments drawn from the Prati district, the area of Castel Sant'Angelo, and the Vatican.

In short, we are dealing with a "mixed place." To use computer terminology, we are in the presence of a true image of synthesis or, if one prefers psychoanalytic terms, a Freudian *condensation*.[3] The Rome of Scola is a mix of areas that in reality are distinct and separate, but cinema has the power to reunite and synthesize these, also with the assistance of computer technology. In this case, digital technology intervenes to complete the dome of the Vatican Basilica, rebuilt in the studio by set designer Ricceri. In the film, the actual base of the Basilica is shown but not the true cupola. The visual effects created by Proxima rebuild virtually one of the most famous emblems of *romanità*, the "cupolone," as it is popularly called, meaning "big dome," that reigns over everything. Thus, according to Scola, the dome in *Concorrenza sleale* becomes a symbol of the "absolute indifference of Pius XII toward Jews and their tragic fate."[4]

The function of this symbol of *romanità* is ultimately that of an icon of a presence–absence that evokes the role it had already carried out in Scola's earlier film *Brutti, sporchi e cattivi* (*Down and Dirty*, 1976), in which St. Peter's dome in its majesty towers over the horizon of the film's main location, a shantytown, and also in the finale of *Roma città aperta* (Roberto Rossellini, *Rome Open City*, 1945), where the dome, according to Adriano Aprà, is "the backdrop for an 'open' journey that takes into consideration our [Italy's] cultural heritage, which for Rossellini is above all a Catholic one."[5]

In the mise-en-scène of *Concorrenza sleale*, an explicit and frontal theatrical look dominates. This look is aimed at creating a historical set design with a decorative character that is explicitly fictional. The digital image—through a *compositing* process—virtually integrates what scenographers created with plasterboard in the theaters of Cinecittà, as is seen with the dome of the Vatican and in the scene of the fascist parade, in which combat jets cross the sky in a computer-generated image. As Roberto Silvestri notes, there is a "flavor of Universal studios"[6] in that theatrical set whose perspective framework, deliberately stereotyped, signals a sort of return to certain panoramic views dear to early cinema and, even before, to the optical devices from the *precinema* era, such as those illustrated by Scola in *Il mondo nuovo* (*That Night in Varennes*, 1982). The Rome of *Concorrenza sleale* is, in fact, intentionally one-dimensional, flat, anti-immersive: in a nutshell, it is a theatrical backdrop, that of a perfect and abstract "Roman exterior."

Thanks to this integration of "real" and "virtual," what is being established in this work is a new variation of Scola's dialectic between presence and absence, between what is outside and what is inside the set, functional again for a reflection on History. History with a capital *H* is deliberately left out of the frame, in a space seemingly nonrepresentable, to which the director presupposes, in this as in many of his other films, a multiplicity of histories with lowercase *h*'s, the histories of the "little people who did not get to participate in any historical decisions,"[7] whose space of action is the explicitly fictional set. This confirms that the concrete experiences of the characters are always the ones that express, according to Millicent Marcus, "the movements and conflicts of the great historical processes that condition their lives."[8]

From this point of view, *Concorrenza sleale* is ideally connected to the aforementioned *Il mondo nuovo*, which, according to Ennio Bíspuri, is equally interested in "recording the imperceptible movements of the seismograph of History at the beginning of great revolutions and transformations."[9] Bíspuri also identifies this connection in *C'eravamo tanto amati* (*We All Loved Each Other So Much*, 1974), "which maintains a profound desire and attempt to reflect on the evolution of History in its relentless impact on minute human events, devastating feelings and impoverishing the dignity of existence."[10] It is as if that virtual microcosm, that ideal synthesis of the Roman district of Prati at the end of the 1930s, ended up echoing the function performed by the Palazzo Federici of *Una giornata particolare*. As Stefania Carpiceci notes, in fact, the closed and seemingly isolated locations of the world in *Una giornata particolare* and *Concorrenza sleale* resemble isolation cells "where the protagonists are forced to live alone and in slavery: ashamed of their own identity, performing tasks and duties imposed by social roles, threatened in their physical and moral integrity, hindered from having freedom of movement, action and expression, and, we could add, even of observation and participation."[11] At the same time, however, that microcosm is set up as a shelter from the "storms" of History, whose wind can, at most, hiss, even if in a threatening manner, in the interstices of the scenic construction but without ever totally harming those who live there. The problem arises when, from that set, that theatrical stage, that fictitious microcosm—protected and definable in terms of *hortus conclusus*[12]—one is forced to exit from History with the capital *H* when it decides to devour the histories with the lowercase *h*.

As it happens, and not by chance, in the conclusions of both films (the physical limits of fiction), marginalized characters are removed from the scene and taken elsewhere: Gabriele, the homosexual protagonist in *Una giornata particolare*, is escorted out of the Palazzo Federici by two fascist officials and taken into exile; in a similar way, the *condanna* (sentence) of Leone's Jewish family in *Concorrenza sleale* is deportation to the Roman ghetto. In the latter film, Leone and his family are excluded from that unrealistic dimension in which Jews and Aryans are "unfair competitors" but ready "to shake hands, to live on the same hallway, to laugh for not knowing what to talk about."[13] Their exit from the set thus literally becomes a marginalization coinciding with an expulsion "from this haven of *italianità* into the segregated recesses of the ghetto."[14] Millicent Marcus explains that this scene "foreshadows the

Final Solution for over one thousand of Rome's Jewish population,"[15] thereby making reference to what happened on October 16, 1943, the "black Saturday" of the ghetto of Rome when, at 5:15 a.m., the SS invaded the streets of Portico d'Ottavia and gathered up 1,024 people, including over two hundred children.

The Digital Flânerie between Past and Present

In an ideal film edit, one could accomplish a *simbolica ellissi temporale* (symbolic temporal ellipsis) by connecting the final scene of the carriage taking away the Della Rocca family of *Concorrenza sleale* toward its tragic destiny with a scene from *Gente di Roma* set in the Jewish Quarter. In the latter scene, set in the early 2000s, an old Jewish resident of the ghetto in Rome, upon leaving her home to go grocery shopping, suddenly finds herself in front of a group of Nazi soldiers and faints; however, one finds out seconds later, in that place filled with painful memory, that a film is being shot on the deportation of the Roman Jews on October 16, 1943. According to a real game of mirrors, Scola is actually quoting himself. In fact, six years before, when shooting the short film *'43–'97* (1997), which depicts the deportation of Roman Jews, Scola had disseminated a multitude of extras dressed as Nazi soldiers throughout the area of the Portico d'Ottavia, in the heart of the ghetto. In this circumstance, he involuntarily caused an analogous incident, immediately accompanied by a controversy within the Jewish community of Rome that had led some of its members to speak of an "overly philological re-enactment" and to accuse Scola of a "lack of sensitivity."[16]

Cinema, in the *immaginario* (imagination) of the director from Trevico, seems to assume, with respect to the never-healed wounds of history, the value of a pre-eminent and redemptive device. If in the aforementioned episode of *Gente di Roma*, inspired by a true story, a cinematic apparatus proves capable of causing real traumas from its ontological realistic vocation, its role is quite opposite in the short film *'43–'97*, which tells the story of a Jewish child who succeeds in escaping the dramatic roundup of October 1943, taking refuge in a movie theater which has a salvific function. Fifty years later, as an adult, the Jewish protagonist exits from the same movie theater after having witnessed masterpieces of the history of world cinema which are suggested as being important for one's intellectual growth and freedom, including *The Great Dictator* (Charlie Chaplin, 1940), Scola's own *Una giornata particolare*, and

Tornatore's *Nuovo Cinema Paradiso* (*Cinema Paradiso*, 1988). The latter film is not mentioned randomly given that we also find in Tornatore's work the very idea of a cinematographic device as a shelter from real life.

As in *Splendor* (1988) and partly in *C'eravamo tanto amati*, History in the short film of 1997 seems to substantiate itself using images from the history of cinema. On the other hand, as Scola asserted, "in Italy cinema has had a greater importance than it has had in other countries. Films like *Ladri di biciclette* (*Bicycle Thieves*, Vittorio De Sica, 1948) or *La dolce vita* (Federico Fellini, 1960) have not only marked their cinematic ages, but they also function as a mirror reflecting the moments of transition in Italian society."[17] This function of cinema as a device for remembrance, as well as for narration, reappears in *Gente di Roma*. Here Scola creates a personal album of brief and piercing annotations on the Eternal City from which a sum of sketches emerges that help shape the image of a place that absorbs and assimilates everything, and where the changing colors of the present coexist with the never healed wounds of History.

It is the immersive and richly perceptive vision of a contemporary Rome whose topography is reframed and reinvented by a cinema that fully exploits the versatility of digital technology (here in the form of camerawork). This digital cinematography gives birth to an immense postmodern flânerie that plays a prominent role as a real leitmotif that stitches the various episodes together: a city bus. Scola fully exploits the extraordinary metacinematographic potential of this form of public transportation as a *medium for the masses*. The big window of the bus offers an extraordinary screen for the community of passengers-spectators on which passes a city and with it a History that nonetheless can never be deciphered given that one is usually accustomed to doing something else or going elsewhere. This window can also be understood as a mirror where, as Elisabetta Tesser notes, "it is possible to look for one's identity. While a passenger looks outside, the mirror provides a reflection of himself, thus starting a process of self-analysis."[18]

Here, therefore, digital technology, as an agile and versatile shooting tool, is capable of acting without the need for particular technical details. As for interior shots, digital technology does not need as many artificial lighting devices as are typically used with traditional film stock. This made it easier for Scola to shoot in the confined space of a vehicle in motion like the bus. In this way, the director offers a glimpse of the world that through these window screens naturally activates a real cinematic device and therefore an illusionistic one. As Gore Vidal states at the beginning of Federico Fellini's *Roma* (1972), "Rome is the city of illusions: it is no coincidence that here one finds the Church, the government and cinema, all things that produce illusion."

In *Gente di Roma*, Scola thus traces a path that passes through physical places without sacrificing fantasy, capable of accounting for how the history of a city is again the result of a stratification of (hi)stories, paths, imaginaries, and individual and collective experiences. The very dimension of identity, here associated with a mobile concept of self-definition, reveals its whole fluency, as Tesser has pointed out, ultimately involving more generally the question of Italian identity *tout court*.[19]

In particular, the versatility of both high and low definition cameras makes possible the dynamism of an urban experience told with a "ball pen," or rather *caméra-stylo*, to reclaim the well-known idea of Alexandre Astruc, novelist, critic, and auteur of films often of literary inspiration, considered a forerunner of the *nouvelle vague*. Although hypothesized in a predigital era, Astruc's conception of the camera as a tool of "flexible and subtle writing equal to written language" adapts itself very well to the lightness, maneuverability, and agility of modern and compact camera equipment and therefore seems to find a renewed nourishment and relevance in the ongoing technological horizon.[20] Drawing from this choice, Scola blends documentary and fictional elements into *Gente di Roma* using an approach that he had already experimented with in *Trevico-Torino: Viaggio nel Fiat-Nam* (*Trevico-Turin: Voyage in Fiatnam*, 1973) and *Vorrei che volo* (1982), creating an "impressionist fresco that renounces the support of a dramaturgic structure" and stands halfway between "a sort of amused documentary style and ancient flavors of episode comedies."[21]

The lightness of digital technology here is precisely the "weightless gravity" illustrated by Italo Calvino in his *Lezioni americane*, where at one point he mentions the informatics revolution, speaking in the following terms:

> It is true that software cannot exercise its powers of lightness except through the weight of hardware. But it is software that gives the orders, acting on the outside world and on machines that only exist as functions of software and evolve so that they can work out ever more complex programs. The second industrial revolution, unlike the first, does not

present us with such crushing images such as rolling mills and molten steel, but with 'bits' in a flow of information travelling along circuits in the form of electronic impulses.²²

The digital cameras used by Scola, even being "iron machines," to quote Calvino again, obey "weightless bits," allowing for that free and fluid cinematographic writing, thanks to their manageability and portability. The ability to shoot with a reduced crew and without the heavy apparatus of the traditional set allows for an approach to filming reality—whether shot live or reconstituted—that is less invasive. With this type of cinematographic writing Scola chooses once again to concentrate on small stories of ordinary people, the people of Rome to be precise, reaffirming the principle of microhistory according to which the most significant forces are revealed in that which is small and apparently banal.

An example of a "small" place or situation is the claustrophobic and modest kitchen that opens *Gente di Roma* as the story of a *giornata* (day), no longer "particular," but ordinary, lived by ordinary protagonists in the Eternal City. Meanwhile, the emphasis that Scola places on the "banal" can be found in the gestures made by the woman at dawn, echoing the celebrated awakening of the maid of Vittorio De Sica's *Umberto D.* (1952) who puts a pot of water on the stove and grinds coffee before starting a new day of humble work. The characters of this work in fact almost all belong to the category of those who do not make History but are subjected to its changes. These are the protagonists of microhistory or, as Carlo Lizzani defined it, "sub-history," meaning "the universe of ordinary people."²³

It is in this context that Zavattini's famous teachings of *pedinamento* are explicitly called into question in the sketch in which the freelance journalist, interpreted by Salvatore Marino, recalls the lesson of the great writer and screenwriter and reveals to a Roman passenger (Valerio Mastrandea) on the bus his project to collect a series of interviews with *extracomunitari* (non-EU citizens) living in the capital. Beyond the stressed irony (the character interpreted by Mastandrea will distort the formula of *pedinamento* "as the truth of Trapattoni"), this discussion finds a new momentum in Scola's film thanks to the use of digital *caméra-stylo*. The latter seems to realize Zavattini's dream of direct contact with the pro-filmic but also of that immediacy that was prophesized in 1975 with the idea of a "completely new handheld piece of cinematographic equipment," called "subitol."[24] Scola's digital subitol is thus an ideal interpreter of the mentioned flânerie in the streets of the capital. It takes on the traits of a sort of *deriva situazionista* (situationist drift), a technique of crossing various environments, indissolubly linked to the recognition of psycho-geographic effects, whose substance is precisely that of relinquishing oneself to the stimuli of places and of the encounters that correspond to them.[25] If, however, this concept appears to be linked to a total uncertainty and to the affirmation of a playful behavior, in Scola's cinema meetings with the "people of Rome" always have a social, anthropological, and political purpose. Scola's objective is to tell the story of the encounter-clash of the Eternal City with its new multicultural and interracial dimension.

Special Effects and Multivision of Memory, between Real and Virtual

In a sort of ideal continuity with *Gente di Roma*, exactly ten years later in Scola's last film, *Che strano chiamarsi Federico*, the director returns to activating a prominent movie device aimed at producing visions, which this time are the result of a digital technology understood no longer just as a means of shooting but above all as a visual effect and, therefore, as an infinite possibility of inventing places and configuring situations between fantasy and reality. In a behind-the-scenes video, the filmmaker asserts: "Before we used to go and work from reality, now we choose which sea we want, which sky we want, one that is in one sense better, but with which you are never satisfied."[26] In short the "real" visions of *Gente di Roma* become the artificial images that embody—through the green screen, but also through more traditional special and theatrical effects, such as retroprojection or projection of images on reels—the location par excellence that is a symbol of artifice: Cinecittà's Teatro 5, Fellini's famous set, the heart of the "city of cinema" within the Eternal City. In this film, achieved on the occasion of the twenty-year anniversary of Fellini's death, the special effect becomes the most ideal instrument to convey and represent the "special affection" which Scola held toward his great friend and master.

Che strano chiamarsi Federico aims to offer a "cubist portrait" that mixes archival material, segments of old films, documentaries, and interviews with the two filmmakers. This is, in fact, a work that could be called a "film by convenience" but that in the director's intentions aims to be something entirely different: "a strange non-film, a non-documentary"[27] and "an album that collects photographs, clippings, dry flowers, and maybe even a fly stuck between the pages."[28] It is therefore an extremely multifaceted work that assembles many different materials (photos, cartoons, film clips, cut scenes) and is not just another essay on Fellini's imagination. It is instead an unusual *amarcord* in which Scola recounts his friendship with Fellini and their common initiatory experience—albeit at different times—working on the editorial staff of the humorous newspaper *Marc'Aurelio* as authors and designers.

Unlike what is indicated in the subtitle of the film (*Scola narrates Fellini*), the director recounts not only Fellini but also himself for the first time (and for this, he entrusted his self-portrait to three actors of three different ages, and he dubbed over the adult version of his character with his own voice). The director, however, does not renounce a narration in the third person, delegated in this case to a character outside the story (Vittorio Viviani) whose purpose is to help the viewer "become comfortable in this benevolent film anomaly."[29] He is a narrator out of time and space who traverses the set with an invisible presence, continually breaking the fourth wall with the audience whom he directly addresses, and even interacting with the other characters, including the owner of the bar who, after having served coffee, proclaims: "The narrator does not pay." Through this figure, the director renders explicit the writing and fictitious set in a metacinematographic process that recalls the one utilized through the character of Restif de la Bretonne (Jean-Louis Barrault) in *Il mondo nuovo*. If in *Gente di Roma*, as we have seen, the *caméra-stylo* played a central role, Scola claims (once again recalling Astruc) to view his *Che strano chiamarsi Federico* not so much as a film but instead as a form of *scrittura* (writing) that consists of "thought and memories condensed in cinematic form."[30] The lightness, on the other hand, aims to be the same, touching on something that, as Umberto Mosca writes, resembles a real "comic book."[31]

After the plein air of *Gente di Roma*, Scola opted for virtuality and pure artifice, which are not only digital but which also include the scenery of the movie set, mounted by the faithful Luciano Ricceri in the studio. This practice confirmed, as Stefano Masi notes, "a sort of parallel and uninterrupted writing that constitutes the subtext of the Scola's dramaturgy."[32] In this memory of an epoch and "of a certain cultural style,"[33] more than of a character, such "scenographic writing" becomes once again functional to mark the transition in a closed and protected horizon, in which microhistory is definitely the one configured by the director's personal memories that inevitably end up weaving the plot of a Great History, that of cinema, and more generally of Italian culture of recent decades.

It is no accident, from this point of view, that Scola chose to narrate Fellini just like a Pinocchio (Collodi's *Pinocchio*, moreover, is Scola's favorite book). He is a Pinocchio, however, who never turns into a good boy but as an artist remains a puppet free from all constraints, even death. In the film's finale, which reconstructs the days of the showing of Fellini's coffin in Cinecittà's Teatro 5, "the most memorable and Fellinian image," as the narrator asserts in the film, "remains that of Federico watched over by two tall carabinieri in uniform. The greatest Pinocchio of Italian cinema concluded his last escape without ever becoming a good boy."

The "Pinocchio effect," which Suzanne Stewart-Steinberg discusses in her book, recalls the problematic Italian identity: the strange mix of "anxiety about the potential emptiness of the Italian subject, his fictional and rhetorical quality, his immaturity and even inhuman, puppet nature, and yet also the profundity of Italian interrogations of the social bond in a modern, post-liberal society."[34] Ultimately, this effect has also pervaded the cinema of Scola, an author who, like the beloved Fellini, enters in the groove of a tradition of intellectuals and artists who were able to question the relationship between Italian identity and modernity[35] in its most profound social, cultural, and political implications.[36] Such a discourse, as seen in this chapter, finds in the last part of Scola's filmography an organic correspondence in the way that the new technologies are exemplarily put to the service of dialectics, deeply Scolian, between microhistory and macrohistory, realism and theatricality, the reinvention of places, and continuous experimentation of film language.

Notes

1. Vito Zagarrio, "Se permettete, parliamo di Scola: Introduzione," in *Trevico-Cinecittà: L'avventuroso viaggio di Ettore Scola*, ed. Vito Zagarrio (Venice: Marsilio, 2002), 17–18. Translations throughout the chapter are my own unless otherwise noted.
2. Gianni Canova, "La disgregazione del fuoricampo: gli anni novanta," in Zagarrio, *Trevico-Cinecittà*, 85.
3. According to Freud, the condensation is the dream's tendency to combine several themes into one dream symbol. Freud states: "The dream, when

written down, fills half a page; the analysis, which contains the dream-thoughts, requires six, eight, twelve times as much space." Sigmund Freud, *The Interpretation of Dreams*, trans. A. A. Brill (New York: Dover, 2015), 235.

4. Ettore Scola, quoted in Marco Dionisi and Nevio De Pascalis, "La Roma di Scola," in *Piacere, Ettore Scola*, ed. Marco Dionisi and Nevio De Pascalis (Rome: Edizioni Sabina, 2016), 274. The director refers here to the longstanding accusation against the inactivity and silence by the pope, over the genocide of Jews carried out by the Nazis.
5. Adriano Aprà, "Rossellini oltre il neorealismo," in *Il neorealismo cinematografico italiano*, ed. Lino Miccichè (Venice: Marsilio, 1975), 51.
6. Roberto Silvestri, "Concorrenza sleale," *Il Manifesto*, March 10, 2001, 8.
7. Ettore Scola, quoted in Lino Miccichè, "Il cinema non cambia il mondo ma può farci riflettere: Una conversazione con Ettore Scola," in Zagarrio, *Trevico–Cinecittà*, 28.
8. Millicent Marcus, *Italian Film in the Shadow of Auschwitz* (Toronto: University of Toronto Press, 2007), 113.
9. Ennio Bíspuri, *Ettore Scola: Un umanista nel cinema italiano* (Rome: Bulzoni, 2006), 313.
10. Bíspuri, 313.
11. Stefania Carpiceci, "I labirinti dell'anima nello spazio–tempo familiare," in Zagarrio, *Trevico–Cinecittà*, 179.
12. Marcus, *Italian Film in the Shadow of Auschwitz*, 118. "Hortus conclusus is a circular green space that takes shape in medieval times as a protected place and separated from the outside through a high wall. It is a sort of 'garden of the spirit' that in the convents and monasteries was thought of as a miniature and symbolic representation of the 'garden of the garden,' that is, the Earthly Paradise."
13. Daniela Pecchioni, "Fuori la Storia," in *Drammaturgia*, January 1, 2001, http://drammaturgia.fupress.net/recensioni/recensione1.php?id=2558.
14. Marcus, *Italian Film in the Shadow of Auschwitz*, 115.
15. Marcus, 115.
16. Francesca Giuliani, "Al Ghetto per ricordare," *La Repubblica*, August 11, 1997, http://ricerca.repubblica.it/repubblica/archivio/repubblica/1997/08/11/al-ghetto-per-ricordare.html.
17. Ettore Scola, in Antonio Bertini, ed., *Ettore Scola. Il cinema e io* (Rome: Officina Edizioni, 1996), 186.
18. Elisabetta Tesser, "Gente di Roma: An Exercise of Dérive by Ettore Scola," *Current Issues in Tourism* 15, no. 6 (2012): 581.
19. Tesser, 577. The dimension of Italian identity is both problematic and elusive due to the impossibility of it being defined in solid and unitary terms, as the following scholars have pointed out: Giulio Bollati, *L'italiano: Il carattere*

nazionale come storia e come invenzione (Turin: Einaudi, 2011); Silvana Patriarca, *Italian Vices: Nation and Character from the Risorgimento to the Republic* (Cambridge: Cambridge University Press, 2010); Suzanne Stewart-Steinberg, *The Pinocchio Effect: On Making Italians, 1860–1920* (Chicago: University of Chicago Press, 2007).

20. Alexandre Astruc, "Nascita di una nuova avanguardia: La *caméra-stylo*," in *Leggere il cinema*, ed. Alberto Barbera and Roberto Turigliatto (Milan: Mondadori, 1978), 313.
21. Stefano Masi, *Ettore Scola: Uno sguardo acuto e ironico sull'Italia e gli italiani degli ultimi quarant'anni* (Rome: Gremese, 2007), 117.
22. Italo Calvino, *Six Memos for the New Millennium: The Charles Eliot Norton Lectures, 1985–86*, trans. Patrick Creagh (Cambridge, MA: Harvard University Press, 1988), 8.
23. Carlo Lizzani spoke of "sub-history" in a talk at the Pesaro Conference of 1974. Carlo Lizzani, "Il neorealismo: quando è finito, quello che resta," in *Il neorealismo cinematografico italiano*, ed. Lino Miccichè (Venice: Marsilio, 1999), 100.
24. Stefania Parigi, *Fisiologia dell'immagine: Il pensiero di Cesare Zavattini* (Turin: Lindau, 2006), 72.
25. Tesser, "Gente di Roma," 581–82.
26. DVD bonus, *Che strano chiamarsi Federico—Scola racconta Fellini* (Rai Cinema—01 Distribution, 2014).
27. *Incontro con Ettore Scola a Europacinema 30—The best of*, Europacinema, November 24, 2013, https://youtu.be/vvdDDKzOcLo.
28. Chiara Ugolini, "*Che strano chiamarsi Federico!* Un ritratto," *La Repubblica*, September 6, 2013, 23.
29. Iolanda La Carrubba, "Fellini il mago, secondo Ettore Scola," *Le reti di Dedalus*, November 2013, http://www.retidedalus.it/Archivi/2013/novembre/SPAZIO_LIBERO/5_cineprime/cineprime.pdf.
30. Pierpaolo Festa, *Ettore Scola: "Non dite che sono tornato,"* Film.it, September 7, 2013, http://www.film.it/cinema/venezia-70/dettaglio/art/ettore-scola-non-dite-che-sono-tornato0-38835/.
31. Umberto Mosca, "Che strano chiamarsi Federico," *Panoramiche-panoramiques: Rivista cinematografica quadrimestrale* 56 (2014): 24.
32. Stefano Masi, "I viandanti del teatro di posa: Il viaggio di capitan Luciano e Madame Odette," in Zagarrio, ed., *Trevico-Cinecittà*, 267.
33. Mosca, "Che strano chiamarsi Federico," 24.
34. Stewart-Steinberg, *The Pinocchio Effect*, 6.
35. Andrea Minuz, *Viaggio al termine dell'Italia: Fellini politico* (Soveria Mannelli: Rubbettino, 2011).
36. I would like to express my gratitude to Marco Signoretti for his research contributions.

THE THREE FIGURES OF NOSTALGIA IN SCOLA'S FILMS

Pierre Sorlin

THE 1950S AND 1960S, marked by rapid economic growth and full employment, were the heyday of Italian cinema. Neorealist works and socially engaged comedies, belonging to the so-called vein of Comedy Italian Style, were distributed all over the world. In the early 1970s, the Italian economy and employment entered a period of profound crisis: terroristic acts were on the rise, and television continued to divert spectators from picture houses. Not surprisingly, a bittersweet view of past and present suffuses the cinematic productions of the period. A few phrases uttered by the main characters of Ettore Scola's *C'eravamo tanto amati* (*We All Loved Each Other So Much*, 1974)[1] are often quoted to show that many Italians retained a nostalgia for the golden years of the economic miracle. In the generally recognized meaning of the word, nostalgia is a desire to go back to a previous period of one's past and to restore to life a supposed perfect happiness, as opposed to an unpleasant present. Such sentimental retrospection is oriented toward foregone times, but it is not always mournful. Recent research[2] places nostalgia in opposition to sorrow or melancholy and emphasizes its positive aspects: engaging in nostalgic reflection on the past allows one to think in terms of time and to perceive retrospectively one's life as full of meaning and purpose. While Scola is by no means a theoretician, nor has he written about nostalgia, many of his fictional characters reflect on the passage of time. The present study examines how nostalgia in Scola's work, far from appearing as a mere dysfunction, is a multifarious mood that alternates between being distressing[3] and boosting self-esteem.

FIGURE 18. Ambush scene in *C'eravamo tanto amati*

Scola's films, undoubtedly suffused with nostalgia, illustrate the varied forms that he ascribed to the ill-defined, fluctuating notion of nostalgia.[4]

In *C'eravamo tanto amati*, high-angle shots are limited,[5] and there are even fewer distant shots. Three images taken at a great distance, in high-angle shots, contrast with the dominantly intimate style of the film and, for that reason, hold our attention. All of them, shot in black and white, appear in the first part of the story, the years of the German occupation and the postwar reconstruction. During this time, three young men, Gianni (Vittorio Gassman), Antonio (Nino Manfredi), and Nicola (Stefano Satta Flores), who had met while fighting against the occupying German army, and one young woman, Luciana (Stefania Sandrelli), manage just to get by in a war-torn country.

The first occurrence of a high-angle shot (fig. 18) is of an ambush that Italian Resistance fighters have prepared for a German convoy. The hidden men wait and the armored column advances slowly, but we do not see the combat. The sequence ends with a wide picture: the immensity of a snow-covered landscape, its immaculate whiteness sprinkled with the black silhouettes of the partisans. We abruptly jump forward fourteen months and are confronted with a frenzied crowd: the war is over.

The second high-angle instance (fig. 19) occurs shortly after the young lawyer, Gianni, in the late 1940s, meets with the corrupt real estate developer Catenacci, who offers him a job. Heading into this encounter, Gianni, who had just begun a relationship with Luciana, appears to be upright and principled,

FIGURE 19. Gianni walks through the construction site after agreeing to work for Catenacci in *C'eravamo tanto amati*.

claiming a desire to defend the poor, yet he falls victim to the crook's persuasion. Catenacci advises him, "You are fighting against your conscience. That's good but don't let it win." Thinking that moral principles do not last eternally, Gianni abandons his fiancée and friends, and he accepts the deal. Filmed from high above, Gianni returns home by foot and fades in the background, pleased with his new life. The high-angle shot is doubly symbolic. On the one hand, Gianni walks over a dirty, derelict area, symbolizing the equivocal world he is entering. On the other, the place is a slum soon to be cleared, destroyed, and substituted with middle-class dwellings, symbolizing Gianni's ruthlessness.

The third high-angle shot (fig. 20) occurs after Gianni's rejection of Luciana and her attempted suicide. When Gianni arrives to rescue her, she has already left with Antonio and Nicola, no longer caring about him. The exceptionally long high-angle shot that follows this scene shows a minuscule silhouette of Gianni casting a long shadow across an empty square before disappearing into the foreground.[6] This shot is emblematic as Gianni's slow, solemn walk through this space alludes to the artificial, formal, empty environment the young man has chosen. At the same time, Gianni, who does not even cast a look at the street artist/beggar, is now totally alone. Black-and-white cinematography changes to color, opening the contemporary part of the movie, the 1970s.

These three high-angle shots, alone in the film, illustrate the three configurations of nostalgia that alternate in Scola's works. The first instance is cheerful and optimistic. Gianni's voice-over (which evokes episodes that occurred thirty years before), as well as the dream-like contrast between the white scenery and the black clothes of the partisans, makes it clear that the sequence is a recollection. However, there is no mark of regret in the sequences following this introduction. The freedom fight had been a stimulating adventure, and in peacetime the former partisans draw inspiration from their memories of trying to reconstruct Italy. Leaving apart the dangers of the clandestine struggle, memory only motivates a successful operation against the foe and helps to preserve an undying friendship. Far from making the characters sad, their reminiscences on the past only serve to embellish their present situation. "Do you understand what I'm telling you?" says Nicola. "Instead of looking for an unlikely happiness, better to concoct some pleasurable memory for the future."

While involved in the Resistance movement, Gianni had promised to champion noble causes and defend the poor and weak. He could marry Luciana and enjoy his relationship with his friends, but, in fact, all he wants is to be rich and to play a part in society. Gianni drops his noble ideas when he agrees to work for the crook Catenacci, and in subsequent moments, when he remembers his past, he does not grieve for what he has lost.

Later Gianni arrives at Luciana's home convinced that she has poisoned herself out of love for him. Yet by this point Antonio and Nicola have aided her with great attentiveness, helping her forget her former suitor. Gianni, who

FIGURE 20. Gianni crosses a near empty piazza after Luciana's failed suicide attempt in *C'eravamo tanto amati*.

until now has thoroughly deluded himself, suddenly understands that his link with the others has been broken and that they will not see each other for twenty years. The character's long crossing of the screen in this scene, shot from above, emphasizes the depth of his wistfulness.

C'eravamo tanto amati thus presents three figures of nostalgia—a positive mood, indifference, and mourning—which are also present in other works by Scola. This particular modus operandi will recur on a regular basis in his future productions, exemplifying this full variety of reflective attitudes: a distressing nostalgia in *La terrazza* (*The Terrace*, 1980), a pleasurable one in *Che ora è?* (*What Time Is It?*, 1989), and an indifferent one in *Una giornata particolare* (*A Special Day*, 1977).

A few sequences in *C'eravamo tanto amati* indicate a dark memory of good old days. Following a fortuitous incident, Antonio and Nicola, who had lost touch with Gianni, run into their friend. The three friends go to the local restaurant where they used to eat when they were young and broke. Antonio laments, "We have underrated a great many circumstances that have put us in a quandary: American money, the fear of Stalin, the priests, the nuns, the weeping Madonna, the fear of hell." This line, often quoted as evidence of the film's pessimistic message, must be read in its narrative context. It anticipates Gianni's final and definitive estrangement from his friends. In the film's very short opening sequence, shot in color, Luciana, Antonio, and Nicola pay a surprise visit to Gianni. Abruptly, the movie turns to black and white, presenting a flashback to the ambush sequence mentioned above. The opening sequence closes only at the end of the film; approaching Gianni's luxurious abode, the friends realize that he is no longer among their class. The whole story is therefore a flashback, a vast parenthesis. In the meetings, the three indulge in nostalgia, but the crisis is over. Forgetting the past, they will be able to focus on the present and remain true to their commitment to the causes they care about: justice for Antonio and creative cinema for Nicola.

Only Gianni feels thoroughly discouraged. Unlike his fellows, who think that they will change the world, he is desperate. "Our generation has made a fool of itself, it would have been better to die in the mountains," he says. The film offers a nearly literal illustration of the process Freud called the "return of the repressed." Gianni, despite having disowned his past ideals, remains attached to his comrades and is still in love with Luciana. After her attempted suicide, he tries to win her back, but she rejects him. As he becomes estranged from the trio, he "buries," to use a Freudian term, all relics of the past. Glimpses of his new life show that he has adapted quickly to Catenacci's environment, as he married his boss's daughter and feels happy with his children. The accidental encounter with his friends brings him back to his former existence when the three friends, believing him to be penniless, treat him as they used to do twenty years earlier. Gianni tells Luciana, "During all past years, I have never ceased thinking of you"—a lie but probably a "sincere" one—to which she replies, "Me, no, all that is old stuff!" She does not bemoan her foregone love, whereas he renews his and suffers. He is mistaken not in remembering their romance but in believing that they could resume it given that Luciana has not repressed her past fondness but rather overcome it.

Nostalgia, in the film, takes on two opposite forms. On the one hand, the solidarity built in hardship strengthens a sense of closeness and will carry on among the three comrades. Once Gianni has vanished, the others take pleasure in evoking the past. On the other hand, Gianni's mourning of irrevocably bygone days encroaches on his present, making it unbearable. Contrary to claims by some scholars,[7] Scola's work is not fundamentally pessimistic. If his film calls attention to moral or psychological weaknesses, it is to make their origins comprehensible. In this case, as well as in other examples of dark, sorrowful nostalgia, the movies put forward, behind their fictional construction, a straightforward clinical diagnosis, analyzed differently in *La terrazza*.

La terrazza sketches the worries of five aging Italian intellectuals who realize that they are losing their former influence and, in the eyes of the young, are obsolete. Four of them are prey to an existential uneasiness that they are unable to solve, while the fifth, Luigi (Marcello Mastroianni), loses himself in nostalgia. Fifteen years before, reputed to be a bright columnist, Luigi married the young Carla (Carla Gravina). Today his old-fashioned, pompous style has turned laughable, and his wife, having become an executive in public television, has left the marital domicile. Luigi imagines that if Carla could yield to nostalgia and long for their happy times, she would return home. In the hope of winning her back, he strives to revive the atmosphere of their honeymoon, courting her as he used to do before.

Luigi invites her to the restaurant where they had dinner at the beginning of their relationship, and a striking sequence shows how hopeless his nostalgic strategy is. At first sight, the spectator is taken aback: the image shakes, but it is not the film. It is the old waiter, a vestige of a past irremediably lost, who trembles. Spectators cannot ignore the visual device, which fixes their attention and obliges them to notice that everything in the dining room looks decrepit: furniture, diners, flower salesman. Is it because nothing has changed? Or more likely because the stale memories that Luigi is trying to revive smell musty? Blind to his mistake, fancying an impossible return to olden days, Luigi rejoices and shows Carla that he has ordered the same table, flowers, wine, and dishes she once liked, while Carla, staying out of his dream, does not pay attention to his delusions. Self-delusion allows Luigi to ignore his failure. Later on, he assumes that Carla will enter the house with him, and he is upset when, on the doorstep, she says good-bye.

Gianni (*C'eravamo tanto amati*) and Luigi (*La terrazza*) suffer from two distinct forms of grieving nostalgia. Gianni, unwilling to give up comfort and wealth, mourns a life that he would be unable to carry on. Overwhelmed by the resurgence of the past, he proves acrid, violent, and hopelessly forlorn. Retreating into melancholia, Luigi refuses to acknowledge that bygone days have irrevocably elapsed. The present does not interest him. He accepts overt humiliations as he publicly places himself at Carla's feet, and he does not rebel when two office workers decide he will no longer write the editorial. He also passively consents to being fired from his newspaper. In doing so, Luigi looks for the return of a chimerical happiness. Vaguely understanding this will never happen, he sinks into nothingness. Even though they are different, both Gianni and Luigi lock themselves into a solitary illusion; their nostalgia prevents them from acknowledging that the women they would like to lure into their fantasies have changed. For instance, when Gianni tries to take up with Luciana again, he disregards the fact that since he abandoned her she has been happily married to Antonio. Similarly, Luigi does not understand that his wife, now a bright businesswoman, would like to talk about her professional achievement rather than listen to recollections of a distant past. Scola paid much attention to the psychological damage caused by nostalgia. In *C'eravamo tanto amati* and *La terrazza*, such injuries are partly overshadowed by other themes: the political evolution of Italy, the crisis of the left wing, and the past splendor of Italian cinema, which, having forgotten the inheritance of neorealism, indulges to excess in melodramas and comedies of manners.

Nostalgia as a Welcome Memory of Sunny Times

While Gianni withdraws into discontent, his comrades in *C'eravamo tanto amati* remember with pleasure their Resistance years, a grounding period that made them aware of their inferior social condition and encouraged them to campaign for a better world. Every now and then a short scene in black and white makes a break into the color half of the film, as when the friends take delight in evoking an episode of their clandestine life. Black and white recalls a time when Italians, only just out of a dictatorship and a harsh German occupation, joined forces to rebuild their country, while in the color sequence, affluent people of the 1970s act merely in their own interests. However, for Antonio, Luciana, Nicola, and their comrades who share the same modest condition, such nostalgia is not sorrowful. It instead conjures up a foregone moment that will never happen again, one that was so intense and rewarding that bringing it up makes people feel good about themselves. Nicola maintains that "enjoyable memories" replace the "fleeting happiness" and hardships of ordinary days in peacetime. The dangers of the war created an exceptional camaraderie among partisans, as Antonio contends: "Those who risked death together as we did are united forever." Life was insecure but simple, and doing one's duty was not open to question. Remembering that epoch helps Antonio and Nicola put up with everyday hardships.

Heartwarming nostalgia does not necessarily presuppose unusual events. The curious title of the film *Che ora è?* refers to a minute object, a clock, which brings back a sensation of cheerfulness and merriment experienced in a far-away period. Marcello (Marcello Mastroianni) has lived apart from his son, Michele (Massimo Troisi), for a long time but tries to lure him back to Rome and make him a business partner. Despite listening coldly to his father's proposal, Michele is moved when his father offers him his silver pocket watch. The tick-tock of the watch reminds him of long, tender moments spent with his grandfather as well as the warmth and kindness of the old man. Wistfulness changes his mood. Recalling his granddad's tolerance, he loses all desire to rebuff his clumsy, patronizing father and acknowledges his dad's goodwill and affection. Up to that moment, Scola willingly resorts to trite cinematic formats, medium shots and reverse shots, stressing the coldness of the encounter. The tick-tick wondrously changes the atmosphere. In the background, we now see a bright sun and a pleasant-looking landscape. Long shots, soft focus, and fluid editing evidence Michele's sudden delight. There is no repressed memory in Michele's case. Looking back at a happy youth, he does not mourn but remembers it as a joyous period, establishing thus a state of balance between past and present, admiration for his grandfather and comradeship with his father.

A rewarding nostalgia can be helpful in seeing life from a different angle, as happens to Robert (Jack Lemmon) in *Maccheroni* (*Macaroni*, 1985). This American executive, overcome by familial and professional worries, spends three days in Naples. He has wiped out all memory of a previous stay in the town, as well as a love affair he had with Maria, before he got married and became a successful businessman. Now he will sadly return to the States, get divorced, and work even harder. Maria's brother (Marcello Mastroianni), informed of Robert's visit, drags the American into the family house. Robert is captivated by the warm welcome of a jubilant household, and his confidence in is his own worth is restored by their kindness. He will fly back, but the enchanting memory of his Mediterranean idyll will protect him from domestic or occupational worries. Robert's attitude contrasts with Gianni's (*C'eravamo tanto amati*) and Luigi's (*La terrazza*); the latter two are both hopefully nostalgic but, overlooking the feelings and desires of the women they love, fancy that they will be able to draw them back into a relationship. Robert, much wiser, understands that he alone is moved by a mournful nostalgia, an indirect consequence of his ongoing worries, whereas Maria effortlessly associates her memory of good old days with her merry present life.

After Robert's first return to the United States, Maria did not feel distressed. An interesting feature of *Maccheroni* is the confluence of two different kinds of nostalgia. Far from forgetting its American guest, the Italian family has kept alive the memory of his sojourn for forty years. The depth of such joyful remembrance is cleverly demonstrated by a series of panning shots, recording the surrounding objects in a circular sweep. Robert is surprised by the way the home is decorated: everything relates to America, from the model Statue of Liberty and countless posters to the Star-Spangled Banner. However, these people are not idle dreamers. Realizing quickly that her American boyfriend would never come back, Maria got married and had children and grandchildren. Hers had been a quiet, happy life, and despite Robert's reappearance, she intends to go on along the same path. When Robert arrives, very agitated, she greets him joyfully. She does not need to say anything. Their dialogue is brief, and her attitude conveys what she wants Robert to understand. She accepts his kiss while offering only a cheek and standing aloof, then breaks off his hug and tells him that he is nothing but a wonderful memory.

Nostalgia can be kind and generous, or it can be egocentric and self-indulgent. Scola felt an interest in the second hypothesis that proved difficult to depict. In *La più bella serata della mia vita* (*The Most Wonderful Evening of My Life*, 1972), Alfredo Rossi (Alberto Sordi), a businessman whose car breaks down, spends the night in the home of retired magistrates who amuse themselves by putting their guests through mock trials. Rossi accepts to undergo their role-playing game, and his hosts "convict" him of many crimes. Prey to a histrionic, jubilantly solipsistic nostalgia, without any regret he details truthfully all the misdeeds and crimes that have made him a distinguished businessman. The next day, still pursuing this seductive, chimerical fantasy, he willingly drives his car on an unfinished bridge under construction that collapses, drowning him in an interminable (two-and-a-half-minute) spiral dive, made harsh by his mad laugh. Rossi is a petty criminal, a mean swindler, but his confession hints at corrupted politicians, knaves or conmen in Italy and elsewhere. Could a happy nostalgia be dishonest? By itself, nostalgia is neither moral nor immoral; instead, it is an individual state of mind that does not prevent people from continuing on their way, which is sometimes even an unrighteous one. For instance, overcome by grief, Gianni, in *C'eravamo tanto amati*, does not think even for a single moment that he could give up his crooked activities, recommence a relationship with Luciana, and resume a humble and honest life.

A type of nostalgia that is neither sad nor lighthearted has its best illustration in *Una giornata particolare*. While most Romans participate in a parade in honor of Hitler,[8] Antonietta (Sophia Loren), a modest housewife of an arrogant husband and mother of six spoiled children, remains at home in a multistory building to do household chores. She happens upon another tenant, Gabriele (Marcello Mastroianni), who will be deported to Sardinia the same day because of his homosexuality and his antifascist political stance. They pay a visit to each other and gradually begin an inconsequential flirtation. While Antonietta is at Gabriele's apartment, the camera catches, in the same frame on the left, the expression of the female character alone complaining about her brutal husband and, on the right, the reflection in a mirror of her and Gabriele. These are the two paths opened before her: Will she remain isolated and exploited in the family home or escape with Gabriele? Unfortunately, an image in a looking glass is incorporeal, illusory. There is no choice for Antonietta; even if she wanted, she could not leave her husband and sons, particularly for an outcast.

The nostalgia Antonietta begins to experience on the evening of her ephemeral affair is a conscious chimera, the genesis of which forms the subject of the movie. When they meet by chance, the protagonists feel drawn together by their loneliness. Initially the film lingers on the trivialities of any relationship between neighbors: a few rumba steps, a cup of coffee, a glance at a photo album. The turning point is an elaborate, multifarious sequence in which Antonietta and Gabriele go to the terrace to collect her laundry from the clotheslines. As usual in Scola's films, shots taken above or below the eyeline are rare. Before this scene, there are only two low-angle shots showing the altitude of the building. On the terrace, while Antonietta is gathering undergarments, Gabriele suddenly wraps her in a sheet and, in a high-angle shot, carries her this way and that. She laughs joyfully. The unusual shot is a signal. Only just liberated, she kisses Gabriele passionately. The moment that their lips touch was filmed against the sunlight, and this backlighting could be considered a technical mistake, but clearly it was done intentionally. The submissive housewife has taken the plunge, but Gabriele reacts coldly and confesses his homosexuality. At first indignant, Antonietta, recovering control of her emotions, showers Gabriele with caresses and persuades him to make love to her. He gives in to her wish while remaining unconcerned. If she has been able to perform a personal, independent deed and no longer conceives of herself as a rejected family mother, Antonietta does not seem to regret this ephemeral amorous encounter, even if one-sided, and perhaps not so enjoyable. Hers is a reasonable nostalgia, and she knows that such an opportunity will never arise again.

In the cinema of Ettore Scola, many characters abandon all thought of a better, more pleasant life because they understand that there is no future in such optimism. Two examples illustrate this sad but reasonable renouncement. First, in *La terrazza*, Mario (Vittorio Gassman), an elderly communist congressman, and the young Giovanna (Stefania Sandrelli) fall in love, and their affair is intense, passionate, but both are married. Mario considers adultery treason of communist morality. He could divorce his wife and marry the young woman,[9] but overwhelmed by his wife's sorrow and despised by his comrades, he would be unable to take part in the renewal of the party. After a while, the lovers break up. From now on theirs will be a friendly, distant relationship so that they have no reason for grieving an impassioned but futureless, socially inadmissible relation.

Serene, detached nostalgia serves as a red thread for *La famiglia* (*The Family*, 1987), a dispassionate chronicle covering the long life of Carlo (Vittorio Gassman), from the early 1900s to the last decade of the twentieth century, all shot in the family home in the upper-class Prati district of Rome. Scola privileges the "looping" stories that finish at their point of origin and unfold in a confined space. The film opens when his grandfather welcomes the newborn Carlo and ends when the lineage celebrates Carlo's eightieth birthday. At around age twenty Carlo's first love and fiancée, Adriana (Jo Champa in the first years, then Fanny Ardant), an outstanding piano player, enters an international career, and if Carlo still wants to marry her, he will accept an itinerant existence, unexpected traveling, and long absences. The man does not hesitate; deeply tied to his ancestors' abode, he renounces neither his home nor his comfort and lives happily with his wife and children. In his seventies, he has an open, friendly chat with Adriana. Neither of them has forgotten their juvenile experience and hoped-for bliss. Another destiny was at hand provided she would have sacrificed her vocation or he would have given up his need for security. Filming the encounter was not easy: it was necessary to display at the same time closeness (they were once betrothed) and estrangement (but did not get married). The solution is a shot countershot, in which a wide empty space is managed in front of both characters who face each other but at a distance. In the course of their long nocturnal talk, Adriana and Carlo, now good friends, look back in quiet, pacified terms and come to the same conclusion: their common life might have been a wonderful or an unbearable existence and therefore mourning what did not happen would be profitless. It is better to content oneself with an agreeable memory.

In the films just mentioned, the characters catch a glimpse of the highest degree of liberty and happiness, but either obstacles are insuperable or the cost is too high. There is, between the three cases just mentioned, a gradation that plays astutely on social contingencies and conventions. In *Una giornata particolare*, the housewife Antonietta has no choice, weeping in regret at a lost opportunity that would have been meaningless; something occurred, she will remember, but not lament. Divorcing, Mario would take the risk of upsetting the party and be deprived of his constituency at the next election, but his motivation is mostly ethical, as he cannot disown ideals that have guided his political commitment. In contrast, Carlo and Adriana, both well-off and independent people, act quite freely. Measuring coldly the pros and the cons, they decide what suits them best. Nostalgia, Scola tells us, is a multifarious state of mind.

C'eravamo tanto amati establishes a striking visual contrast between its first and second distant, high-angle shots: the background, luminous, white, and uncontaminated in the former, is black, damp, and muddy in the latter. Such marked opposition is consonant with a widespread interpretation that reads Scola's cinema as a chronicle of "the growing pains, class divisions, and frustrated idealism of 20th-century Italy."[10] The initial vision is a promise of fairness, purity, and cleanness while the other one brings us back to the sordid reality of business. Undoubtedly, a bitter, disenchanted picture of his country is displayed in many of Scola's works. However, in Scola's cinema, symbols are never one-sided; the opposition between snow and mud has another meaning: Gianni has betrayed his moral values, but he has taken a job and wrestles with the dirty materiality of the world, whereas his former friends, Antonio and Nicola, are content with dreaming about a better, faraway society.

The fast, irrevocable passing of time, recurrent in Scola's cinema, creates a feeling of melancholy. Take, for instance, *Ballando ballando* (*Le bal*, 1983), a film without dialogue, which introduces anonymous, storyless people who enter, dance, and change partners; initiate an intrigue; and vanish in the course of years, leaving no trace of their fleeting appearance. Consider also *La terrazza*, in which a mysterious adolescent (Marie Trintignant), who has no part in the story, paces up and down, looking with quiet indifference at the guests: she represents youth itself, part of a generation that does not even take a glance at its predecessors. The has-beens of *La terrazza*, retired from their activities and deprived of prospects, indulge in wistfulness. However, as Scola's films contend, nostalgia is not necessarily a disconsolate brooding over better times lost. Those who sink in regret, like Gianni (*C'eravamo tanto amati*) and Luigi (*La terrazza*), are fragile people who mourn happy bygone periods but do not acknowledge that the price of their illusory bliss was a total submission to a dominating father-in-law or to a much younger wife. Conversely, optimistic nostalgia is to be found among people who admit that what is passed is dead and gone so that yearning about it is no use.

The Italian elite, as represented in many films of the 1970s or 1980s, allowed itself to get caught up in the unfairness and inequality of a materialistic society. "Those who should bring about a revolution don't do it," a character says in *La terrazza*. The satire is cutting. Mario's commitment to an out-of-date ideology prevents him from taking into account the current problems of Italy (money) and allows a Catenacci (*C'eravamo tanto amati*) to corrupt and cheat everyone. Yet, as it is apparent from a glance at his vision of nostalgia, Scola also offers another approach by showing individuals who, making do with their memories and daily concerns, find comfort in the reminiscence of happy times. Michele (*Che ora è?*), enjoys his present life, but a delightful, vivid recollection of a bygone moment helps him become reconciled with his father. Yet, all things considered, is indifference, tinged with a pale smile, not the best solution? Most people, like Antonietta (*Una giornata particolare*), are much too busy to bemoan days gone by.

With a few exceptions,[11] the films mentioned in the chapter, shot between 1972 and 1985, refer to concerns particular to that period. After the two years of social unrest that followed the 1968 student movement, Italy, despite a prosperous economic development, entered a decade of political instability during which many took a nostalgic look at the postwar years. Then, for a short period, right-wing forces, compromised with fascism, were silent, while the "Resistance parties"—communists, socialists, and Christian democrats—collaborated to rebuild the country badly damaged by the war. Italy, with its powerful Communist Party, was soon involved in the Cold War, but the memory of an enthusiastic cooperation between classes lasted and even became a legend.

Scola's films faithfully represent not the late 1940s, a time of hunger and lack of the most elementary means of existence, but the memory of that period that prevailed in the 1970s. This rather fanciful memory attached great value to neorealist cinema, a short-lived experience that had nevertheless given a harrowing vision of a ruined Italy. It is not by chance that Scola, by choosing black-and-white film, adopted a realistic point of view for the retrospective sequences of *C'eravamo tanto amati*. Yet, in the last decades of the twentieth century, people no longer shared the hopes and illusions of the liberation. Scola's lucid nostalgia therefore made allowance for the gloominess of a Gianni who had betrayed his past ideals as well as for the happy memories of the Neapolitan family in *Maccheroni*, which acknowledges that the reasons for living change with the passing of time.

Notes

1. For instance, Nicola states, "We thought we'd change the world; instead the world has changed us," and Gianni adds, "The future passed us by without us even realizing it."
2. See Clay Routledge et al., "The Past Makes the Present Meaningful: Nostalgia as an Existential Resource," *Journal of Personality and Social Psychology* 101 (2011): 638–52.
3. Film critics have often stressed the "feeling of failure and disillusion" experienced by the protagonists of *C'eravamo tanto amati*, who lament lost opportunities and broken promises. Giovanni Ciofalo, "C'eravamo tanto amati: Storia, memoria e industria" in *Memoria, narrazione, audiovisivo*, ed. Silvia Leonzi (Rome: Armandino, 2013), 56. Translations throughout the chapter are my own unless otherwise noted.
4. There is no clinical definition of *nostalgia*, a term that can be understood in many different ways. In Emiliano Morreale, *L'invenzione della nostalgia: Il vintage nel cinema italiano e dintorno* (Rome: Donzelli, 2009), the author maintains that since the 1980s films mourn a fanciful past, a patchwork of images randomly borrowed from television and the Internet, which deviate from what actually happened. Scola's films, firmly linked to Italian history, do not fall into this new conception of the word.
5. Only fourteen, usually spatially limited and very brief, establishing shots introduce a place (restaurant, hospital, building site).
6. The final zoom-in manages the transition from black and white to color and lasts no less than three minutes.
7. See Vito Zagarrio, "La sceneggiatura circolare: Strutture narrative in tre film di Ettore Scola," *Italianist* 29 (2009): 265–80.
8. Hitler actually visited Rome in May 1938. The film opens with seven minutes of newsreels shot on that occasion. It includes German and Italian military hymns sung during the parade.
9. Since 1974, divorce was legal in Italy, but the ethics of the Catholic Church and the Communist Party made it extremely difficult for politicians or opinion leaders to dissolve their marriages.
10. "Films on Display," *Washington Post*, January 20, 2016. The critical, pessimistic stance of Scola's cinema is well analyzed by Stefano Masi, *Ettore Scola* (Rome: Gremese, 2006), who conceives the director's work "a poisoned laugh," 5. Scola's pessimism is also emphasized by Ilario Molè: "The characters embody the emptiness of a society which sees the progressive extinction of all its myths, they are unable to do anything but make us slightly laugh, slightly sadly meditate, slightly pity them." Molè, "Film," *Città Nuova*, March 1980, 64.
11. The exceptions are *Che ora è?*, *La famiglia*, and *La cena*.

LA TERRAZZA ON THE CIRCEO
Ettore Scola, Pasolini, and the Critique of the Roman Intelligentsia in Late 1970s Italy

Francesca Borrione

When in Ettore Scola's *La terrazza* (*The Terrace*, 1980) the journalist Luigi (Marcello Mastroianni) watches Carla (Carla Gravina), his wife, also a journalist, on a televised debate inspired by the Circeo massacre (September 29–30, 1975), he is crassly indifferent to the atrocities of this crime that witnessed the rape and torture of two young lower-class women at the hands of three upper-class neofascist youths. Instead, Luigi cannot see past his own sexual desire for his wife, and he fails to engage these pressing issues of women's rights. The episode with Luigi as protagonist highlights two crucial aspects in *La terrazza*: the mounting anxieties of the Italian patriarchy of the era and the crisis of ideologies within the progressive intellectuals. In doing so, Scola recalls a controversial article by Pier Paolo Pasolini published in *Corriere della Sera* on October 8, 1975, which blames the progressive Left for apathetically observing "cultural genocide" from their ivory tower. In this article, Pasolini asserts that "between 1961 and 1975 something vital changed: a genocide happened, an entire population was destroyed."[1]

Pasolini uses the term *cultural genocide* to signify the death of subproletarian classes whose cultural heritage and identity was becoming compromised by the rise of mass consumerism. The term *subproletariat* in Marxist theory does not refer just to people at the lower scale of the working-class hierarchy but also to outcasts and other unemployed, underemployed, or rejected beings living at the margins of society. Pasolini compares the subproletariat to the larger population by identifying them with the inhabitants of suburban areas known as *borgate*, "working-class neighborhood[s] in a non-working-class city,"[2] where wage-sustaining jobs have yet to be created. Their genocide, Pasolini argues, was determined by the rise of consumerism that colonized the lower classes' minds especially, convincing them they should envy the bourgeoisie and desire to reach the same wealthy lifestyle or an illusion of material prosperity. According to Pasolini, proletarian and subproletarian realities were the object of an anthropological transformation whereby they all became petit bourgeois—in theory, at least— while leaders of the progressive Left were contemplating their own decline. In this articulated context, *La terrazza* marks Scola's completion of a Pasolinian critique of Italian society in the 1970s based on their close intellectual and creative exchange. In fact, the profound connection between Scola and Pasolini is most evident in *Brutti, sporchi e cattivi* (*Down and Dirty*, 1976), an ideal sequel to Pasolini's *Accattone* (1961), for which Pasolini was supposed to have filmed a preface[3] had it not been for his tragic death. Scola's subproletarians[4] still embody Pasolini's prophetic words as a subgroup that is unable to defend their own subculture or that is fascinated by an emerging mass culture. These poor, marginalized people lacked a class consciousness and ingrained sense of institutionalized resistance that could have led them to the revolutionary awakening evoked in the 1920s by such figures as Antonio Gramsci. They allowed consumerism to dictate their new habits, behaviors, and desires; they were "responsible for their own evolution, as they wanted to be colonized and destroyed."[5]

While *Brutti, sporchi e cattivi* depicts the consequences of cultural genocide from the perspective of the Roman subproletariat, *La terrazza* takes a step forward by elaborating a poststructuralist critique of the downfall of the bourgeois intelligentsia, which views reality from a comfortable reserve and does not embody any genuine empathy for proletarian existence. As members of the privileged intelligentsia, they look at life from the remove of a terrace, like mortal gods observing the decay of Rome from their bourgeois Olympus, yet they are unable to offer any actionable solution. Clearly, a correlation between Pasolini and Scola is more explicit in *Brutti, sporchi e cattivi*, but in *La terrazza* Scola recalls and reframes the Pasolinian influences through *commedia all'italiana*, and he emulates Pasolini's example when he intersperses fiction with actual events that were still affecting Italian society and the politics of the time.

In *La terrazza*, a group of five characters—played by famous actors, such as Ugo Tognazzi, Vittorio Gassman, and Marcello Mastroianni, among others, all of whom contributed to the commercial success of the *commedia all'italiana* between the 1950s and 1960s—realize that the time for comedy is over[6] and that the class of (male) intellectuals is also on the verge of breaking down. Screenwriter Enrico (Jean-Louis Trintignant) has a nervous breakdown when he realizes that he cannot write comedic lines or scripts any longer. Enrico's producer Amedeo (Ugo Tognazzi) struggles to make old-style Italian comedies as well and ends up producing a failing feminist film solely to please his wife, who is also a producer. Luigi (Marcello Mastroianni) is a journalist, a Pygmalion figure who is unable to accept his wife's professional success, while Sergio (Serge Reggiani), a RAI (Radiotelevisione italiana, or Italian National Broadcasting Company) manager, reacts to the crisis of his wife's abandonment by literally reducing himself to an anorexic body until he dies, hopeless and lonely, in a TV studio. As a fascinating counterpoint, the film also explores the vicissitudes of Mario (Vittorio Gassman), a congressman of the Italian Communist Party who is torn between his love for a younger woman and his duties as a husband and a representative of the party. These five characters work in the cultural industry, but they never articulate any innovative element that could help move the cultural and political discourse in a new direction. Scola focuses on the ideological crisis these leftist intellectuals face, which has swept away any sense of security and values even as they are cultivating the illusion of power in an Italy still bound to patriarchal tradition.

The decision to focus mainly on the episode with Luigi is based on two instructive elements. First, this character is representative of the cultural and political tensions within Italian society: in fact, Luigi symbolizes middle-aged Italian men's anxieties at the dawn of women's rights movements. Second, in comparing Scola and Pasolini, we can discern one important commonality: Pasolini defined newspapers as "accomplices of politicians,"[7] claiming they were co-responsible for causing the crisis. According to Pasolini, the actors of these political and cultural industries, sitting at a table of compromise, forgot their sense of civic and social responsibility. Committed to their own needs and to the maintenance of the status quo, politicians failed to recognize the anthropological mutation within Italian social classes, while newspapers turned into a propagandistic medium that became the voice of the dominant classes. As ambiguous hypocrites or naive idealists, they became complacent in privilege and lost any contact with the real world. In *La terrazza*, Scola reframes Pasolinian influences and critique through the representation of

Luigi, a journalist deferential to power. The character of Luigi signifies the crisis of the Italian cultural industry in late 1970s and embodies the denied responsibilities of intellectuals after the Circeo massacre of 1975.

Looking Back at 1975: *Pariolini, Borgatare*, and the Indifference of Intellectuals

The five principal protagonists in *La terrazza* regularly meet for dinner on a terrace, overlooking a rooftop in Rome, with views of other rooftops—this privileged view of the world becomes significant because it highlights their social position and reinforces key facets of their personalities. Dinner on the terrace is the occasion for characters to gather, chitchat, and complain about life and politics in Italian society of late 1970s. Their conversations on the terrace are punctuated, emblematically, by a woman in a fancy dress who announces that the next scene is ready to unfold, which marks the beginning of the same protracted lavish dinner and the beginning of each episode.

Thus, *La terrazza* works as an episodic film, in which the five main characters have their own independent story line, but they all meet at regular moments in the narration and finally converge in a collective, choral ending. Scola chooses to develop the story through effective time expansion techniques and subtle repetitions: the dinner on the terrace circularly[8] repeats itself (with small variations) at the end of each single episode. Repetition is also used as a narrative schema that seems to reinforce the immobility and passivity of the characters: prominent intellectuals adrift in a culture with compromised ideals and circumspect values. *La terrazza* does more than explore "anthropological and ideological clichés"[9] inherent to Italian society of the time. As Francesca Cadel argues, Scola emphasizes the "anthropological mutation and complicit silence of leftist intellectuals."[10] That is the same anthropological change Pasolini had identified in an article that first appeared in *Corriere della Sera* on June 10, 1974: "It is the transition of a culture based on illiteracy (the people) and ragged humanism (the middle-class) from an archaic cultural organization into a modern 'mass-culture' organization. Actually, this shift is dramatic, I insist. It is a phenomenon of anthropological 'mutation.'"[11]

From the opening sequence, Scola presents the terrace as a stage: the movie starts the moment in which lights are turned on and the actors enter the scene. On the terrace, in this elegant penthouse with a view on the rooftops of

Rome by night, the five main protagonists live their own personal bourgeois tragedy. Spectators hear the characters' voices first: "He is under investigation, we are waiting for him to be arrested"; "We promised we would not release names nor addresses"; "A new war would be needed!" Those lines are pronounced off-screen by unidentified characters as the camera captures their entrance. Fragmented off-screen voices chat about war, justice, and religion, signifying the pointlessness of conversations that end without specific conclusions. The circular narrative—a characteristic of *La terrazza*—is repeated through the voices as well as in the actors' behaviors as they seem to chase one another around the table.

Through this complex opening scene, Ettore Scola establishes the tone of the film and captures the cynicism of the "affluent society," mentioned by RAI manager Sergio and Luigi in an obvious reference to the theories of American economist John Kenneth Galbraith.[12] In the affluent society—characterized by the massification of goods once labeled as "luxury"—as well as in a consumerist society criticized by Pier Paolo Pasolini, commodities replaced values and ideals, while citizens turned into customers.

La terrazza offers a clear portrait of the Italian upper-class society in transition to the "age of uncertainty."[13] The society depicted is isolated within a petit bourgeois reality, the five male intellectuals from *La terrazza* defend their privilege while longing for the myth of a revolution that never really happened. The anthropological transformation of Italians occurred under the apathetic gaze of the progressive Left, whose revolutionary ideas and ideals had been corrupted by the new radical-chic bourgeois way of life. This complicit silence was fiercely criticized by Pier Paolo Pasolini in a series of articles published in October 1975, in the aftermath of the Circeo massacre, which had occurred a month earlier. Two girls from the *borgata* (working-class suburb) Montagnola, Donatella Colasanti and Rosaria Lopez, were kidnapped, assaulted, and tortured for two days by three young neofascist men, Gianni Guido, Angelo Izzo, and Andrea Ghira. Although left for dead in the trunk of a FIAT 127 in Via Poli in the Parioli neighborhood, close to the home of one of the attackers, Donatella Colasanti survived, denounced her attackers, and clearly identified them, which led to their arrest.

For its cultural and political implications, and for its cruelty, this crime received extensive media attention and caused an immediate sensation among intellectuals, including Pasolini. His article "Il mio Accattone in TV dopo il genocidio" (My *Accattone* [scoundrel] on TV after the genocide), published in the *Corriere della Sera* on October 8, 1975, highlights the responsibilities of the bourgeois intelligentsia for indifferently witnessing the brutal attacks and murder. Pasolini argues that the three neofascist men who attacked Donatella Colasanti and Rosaria Lopez "lost,"[14] but the *pariolini* (Roman bourgeois youth) won as their wealthy lifestyle became a model to subproletarian classes, whose identity had slowly converged into mass cultural conformity.

When Scola introduces Luigi in *La terrazza* as he watches a TV debate about women's rights in Italy during the broadcasting of Loredana Dordi's documentary *Processo per stupro* (1979), the references are clear and the connection with Pasolini is made evident. *Processo per stupro* is RAI's video recording of a rape trial that occurred in 1978 in Latina—only three years after the Circeo massacre—and it marks another important step for the Italian feminist movement and its fight for women's rights. Scola includes footage from the televised trial, which in effect also recalls the Circeo massacre through similar details and symbolic representation. Scola thus offers a twofold critique of Italian culture of the day, from a metaphorically doubled point of view: he not only questions the idea of masculinity in late 1970s Italy, but most important, he reframes Pasolini's bold sociopolitical critique. The four middle-class men who assaulted yet another woman in Latina by luring her with the promise of a job interview are surrogates and directly related to the three upper-class young men who raped and killed Rosaria Lopez and brutally assaulted Donatella Colasanti. These severely disturbed upper-class men acted on their sense of privilege with a relative sense of impunity; they committed these heinous crimes because they could. They embodied their dominant role in the social hierarchy by taking advantage of two *borgatare* (inhabitants of the Roman working-class suburbs) who dreamed about escaping their social class. In her deposition, Donatella Colasanti recalls that when the men were beating her and Rosaria Lopez, the *pariolini* repeatedly called them *accattone*,[15] confirming the political and classist motivations of the crime. In fact, when on November 9, 1975, in a column for the magazine *L'Espresso*, Alberto Moravia compared his 1929 novella *Delitto sul campo da tennis* to the Circeo massacre, he highlighted its sociopolitical implications by defining it as a crime of class ("delitto di classe").[16]

One can easily concur with Italo Calvino who believed the Circeo massacre brought the existence of a "society of monsters"[17] to public attention.

Calvino's article[18] about the Circeo massacre, published in the *Corriere della Sera* on the same day Pasolini published "Il mio Accattone in TV dopo il genocidio," sparked a heated debate among Italian intellectuals and writers. Those *pariolini* are not monsters, Pasolini would argue; they are the product of a criminal environment, and at the same time they represent a dysfunctional role model inherent to a consumerist society. In his article, Pasolini states: "Accattone and his friends silently headed to deportation and the final solution, possibly laughing at their torturers. But what about us, the bourgeois witnesses?"[19] Scola appears to answer the Pasolinian question through the story of Luigi, a journalist who is an accomplice with politicians and power. After briefly introducing Luigi as a cynical middle-aged intellectual who blames society for his own inaction, Scola switches from the exterior scene on the terrace to interiors. A kid dressed up in a white shirt with a black ribbon, who represents a miniature bourgeois, is watching a spaghetti western movie on TV, when Luigi breaks into the room, grabs the remote control from the kid, and turns the channel to a televised panel discussion about sexual violence in Italian society. Luigi's wife, Carla, is a journalist and an advocate for women's rights, and he does not want to miss her as she reports on the incident.

The change is abrupt and dramatic: we move from the violence of a spaghetti western characterized by a loud soundtrack à la Morricone, with cowboys shooting and screaming, to the the footage from the televised trial, *Processo per stupro*. Fiorella, a fictional name for the victim, was sexually assaulted by four men, and she denounces her attackers. A medium close-up shot frames Luigi as he sits in front of the TV and watches the debate: a clip from the documentary *Processo per stupro* is on air. The defendant's lawyer reads Fiorella's statement, in which the rape is recalled in detail. A fancy crystal lamp, situated at the center of the frame right between Luigi in his khaki suit and the black-and-white TV, marks a physical distance between the two, only attracting and therefore illuminating the gaze of the spectator.

Disturbing violence runs throughout the film as Fiorella's lawyer, Tina Lagostena Bassi, and the defendants' lawyer fight over the definition of sexual assault. The fragment is only one minute long, but it is almost unbearable to listen to and watch, though not for Luigi. Initially embarrassed by the presence of the kid, Luigi slightly turns toward him. A medium shot positions Luigi and the kid together in the frame. Again, the crystal lamp—the only source of artificial light—ideally separates the characters while the light appears to frame the kid, somehow directing the spectators' attention to his emotionless facial expression. In fact, the kid has no reaction at all. He does not speak or pose questions but instead passively listens to the lawyer who explains that Fiorella was probably not raped at all, because "sexual assault by fellatio can be interrupted with one small bite."

When the camera moves back to Luigi and the debate, a close-up of lawyer Lagostena Bassi on TV is now central to the frame. Lagostena Bassi, who was also Donatella Colasanti's actual lawyer in the trial that took place in 1976, is a political subject as an activist and a lawyer. This real-life lawyer's portrait is made constantly visible in the background of this telling sequence. With her name, identity, and presence, she directly recalls *Processo per stupro*, but she also functions as a stand-in for the unexplored sociofeminist questions that surround the Circeo massacre. A woman's body is, Foucault reminds us, "directly involved in a political field; power relations have an immediate hold upon it; they invest it, mark it, train it, torture it, force it to carry out tasks, to perform ceremonies, to emit signs."[20]

The woman's body plays a central role in Italian political discourse around women's rights: in the Italian legislative system, sexual violence was merely considered an offense against morality until 1996, when the Parliament deliberated that it should be upgraded to an "offense against the person."[21] Gender hierarchy is still dominant in Italian society, yet Fiorella, Rosaria Lopez, and Donatella Colasanti (and Carla the reporter, here as a capable fictional representation) challenge this concept, insisting that their bodies are political subjects that need to be interrogated and understood within the sociopolitical context of the era.

Scola's interest here is in the debate and in Luigi's reaction, or rather absence of reaction. Lagostena Bassi's outrage toward the reductive rhetoric that first tends to blame the woman for being assaulted and then turns her from victim into attacker (as the defendants' lawyer will later suggest in a fragment not included in the scene) contrasts with and marks Luigi's indifference. He does not show any sign of moral indignation. On the contrary, his eyes reveal that he only waits for Carla to appear on the screen. Within the complex filmic representation of *La terrazza*, as the lawyer mentions fellatio, Luigi crassly lights a cigarette, encoding this symbol of desire into an aggressive phallic metaphor. The unconscious gesture of lighting a cigarette while on TV a man denies that any woman can be sexually assaulted could signify a reprehensible identification between Luigi and the men involved in the trial. By Luigi lighting a cigarette and playing with it as he nervously waits for Carla to show up, he has already objectified and encoded Carla as the circumscribed wife before she makes her screen entrance. Carla is a feminist committed to sensitizing the audience about the oppressive claws of the patriarchal society. Yet Scola strategically depicts Carla through the excited eyes of Luigi, her body gestures as a reflection of Luigi's expectations. Luigi is expecting Carla to pass her cigarette from one hand to another, to breathe, to take a break, to look at the camera. Instead, Carla's voice speaks out loud about men's brutalities and women's rights. Luigi is not listening: to him, Carla's body is a projection of his own possessive love, in a mode reminiscent of other depictions of male–female relations throughout the film. Carla's sexualized projection—contained in the timed and spaced frame of a television—exists only in Luigi's mind, in his desire as he gets closer to actually kissing a close-up of Carla on the TV set. Similarly, in Vittorio De Sica's iconic and sexist comedy *Ieri, oggi e domani* (*Yesterday, Today and Tomorrow*, 1963), Augusto (Marcello Mastroianni) never leaves the bed from which he observes Mara's (Sophia Loren) striptease. Mastroianni may have grown old in that film, but he nonetheless embodies the same reductive archetype. Fortunately, in late 1970s Italy, the satisfaction of sexual desire is denied by Carla, a woman who gained an education, autonomy, and independence. Luigi's disinterest of Carla's ambitions, and his own indifference to a changing society reflect the apathy of a generation of men in crisis in an age characterized by the rise of feminism in Italy and the downfall of ideologies and revolutionary ideals.

The scene in which Luigi and Carla talk about their troubled marriage—Carla considers divorce while Luigi tries to reaffirm his dominant role in their relationship—is emblematic of a complex but changing era. During this pivotal conversation, the camera moves away from Luigi to focus on the characters in the background, Amedeo (Ugo Tognazzi) and Mario (Vittorio Gassman). We hear only Luigi's words as Scola juxtaposes his voice to his friends' faces. In the midst of a cultural shift, Luigi, Amedeo, and Mario are unable to accept that women "all cheek and tenderness"—Luigi's definition—stood up for their rights in a sexist and restrictive Italian society, trying to change from within a personal sphere.

At this turning point in film, Scola abruptly transitions from night to day, from effects lighting to natural lighting, from the terrace that ideally hosted the fight between the old patriarchal structure and the new feminist wave, to a terrace with a view on the urban traffic. Spectators find Luigi with a young woman (Ritza Brown) at his own apartment. This time, the filmic perspective and camera angles are reversed: Scola follows the characters from inside the apartment while his gaze focuses on the outside, on the Roman landscape. The camera stays on Luigi in his comfortable flannel robe as he crosses the living room and reaches the terrace to speak with the woman. The actors turn their backs to the camera and look at the beauty of Rome as they have a casual conversation. The young woman explains that she is from Via di San Valentino, Rome, an upscale neighborhood also in the privileged Parioli district—which becomes an almost invisible but crucial detail that confirms the strong relationship between the episode of Luigi and the Circeo massacre. In Via di San Valentino, Luigi remembers, "my grandfather was attacked by wolves." In Luigi's misguided reverie, Parioli was like any other neighborhood in the mythical and foundational history of Rome. Different kinds of wolves now inhabit Parioli, man-like creatures, assailants named Gianni Guido, Angelo Izzo, and Andrea Ghira, who tortured and brutally assaulted Donatella Colasanti and Rosaria Lopez just five years earlier. And yet Luigi appears to ignore the ongoing political tensions in the area. Luigi's stage is his own house, and his audience is a naive young woman in a man's rumpled dress shirt, her facial traits so similar to young Carla, whose role is just to reinforce Luigi's narcissism and his illusion of hegemonic masculinity.

La terrazza is a metaphor for the mounting anxieties of the Italian patriarchy of the era. Those anxieties, though, are caused neither by women nor by any external factor: they are the consequence of men's inability to relocate themselves in a social and cultural context that had started to change with crucial laws on divorce and abortion, approved in 1970 and 1978, respectively. Women were ready for this change to happen, but men were not. So, when Carla's friend and feminist activist Nicoletta (Angiolina Quinterno)—who is the same age as Luigi and also a widow—reveals she is pregnant, her son-in-law accuses her of being shameless, concerned about what other people will say. To him, every woman who does not align with the moral norms is a *traviata* (literally courtesan, or fallen woman in this context), as the aria "Amami, Alfredo" echoes from the previous scene. In Italian society, separation between church and state never occurred, and pleasure is still considered, to reiterate Foucault, "against the moral norms of sexuality, marriage, and decency."[22] This contradiction inherent to the society is clear in the characters' behaviors and internal struggles. Men, not women, live their lives based on moral norms. Women begin to claim their place in society and their right to exist.

The juxtaposition of feminist ideals and masculine anxieties is particularly obvious in the scene that ends this episode and marks the end of Luigi and Carla's marriage. Luigi and Carla have dinner at an old-fashioned restaurant that exemplifies Luigi's obstinate bond to the past. The mise-en-scène is enriched by small details such as the dark green velvet upholstery on the walls; the presence of an elderly waiter suffering from Parkinson's disease, who is barely able to serve the tables; and the crunching noise of plates and cutlery. The scene is carefully arranged to portray Luigi as a middle-aged bourgeois immersed in his own nostalgic memories, and at the same time it underlines the estranged figure of Carla, now alienated from Luigi's world. The irremediable distance between Carla and Luigi is also effectively emphasized by the use of a shot-reverse shot, right at the moment of the conversation in which Carla starts discussing her future as a TV journalist. Luigi, meanwhile, keeps talking about a time in which his wife was passive and submissive. While Luigi is immersed in the idealization of the past, Carla argues about women's rights, explains her project for a new TV show, and lectures Luigi about what it means to be a female professional in the patriarchal society. Carla clearly tries to engage in a conversation, but Luigi cannot be the interlocutor in a discussion about gender equality: instead he embodies everything Carla is fighting. Luigi represents the patriarchy and its entrenchment with privilege, and he rejects the public discourse to fully embrace the private sphere. His inability to face present and future time—he cannot even stand Carla's gaze—mirrors the Pasolinian critique over the cynical complacency of Italian intellectuals in observing their own decline. Scola appears to criticize the bourgeoisification—to use a term by Marx—not just of proletarians but also of those who once claimed to be revolutionary. After she leaves him at the door of his apartment, Carla walks away from her former life, away from Luigi. Scola uses close-ups and extreme close-ups to capture Luigi's melancholia and his white hair and deep wrinkles, while he turns the camera away from extreme close-ups on Carla's face. Scola is more interested in capturing her dynamic figure as she immerses herself in the traffic and noisy, crowded streets of Rome to fight her battle for women's rights.

Women become capable of acts of true rebellion against the system, while men stay on Parnassus—distant and indifferent in their own heights. And Parnassus is precisely what screenwriter Enrico and RAI manager Sergio discuss in a conversation during the transition from the episode about Luigi to the one about Sergio. "Any wife who emancipates herself also becomes a journalist, director, or architect. No one who wants to be a postal worker—or a kitchen worker from Parnassus," Enrico complains. Sergio replies: "Why not? Several men on Parnassus would look better as sharecroppers or as workers for the railways or in a pasta factory." But even Sergio declares his own incapability of accepting the sociocultural change he originally supported by tragically killing himself. The other male protagonists also stay fixed in their static lives and fail to embrace this changing era. So, too, does Luigi when he melancholically tells Carla that "epochs end this way, suddenly" before he goes back home alone, his masculinity confined behind the fences of a building with a privileged view on the decadent bourgeois class.

A Pasolinian Critique of Cultural Industry

Luigi recognizes their corrupt moral imperatives and troubled responsibilities when it is too late. It is impossible not to consider Scola's analysis of Italian society as a strictly Catholic country in which "the majority's privileges have right of citizenship,"[23] while subproletarians are condemned to their own extinction. *La terrazza* is more than just the story of five characters working in a cultural industry; it is a detailed rhythmic and agonizing portrait of a generation and a well-balanced critique of a group of privileged bourgeois who still control society. When Morando Morandini argues that *La terrazza* "is the result of the narrow point of view of many Roman intellectual filmmakers who believe they are the center of the world, and who ignore the reality of Italian society,"[24] he does not realize that this analysis fails to honor Scola's cinematic style, along with the sophisticated character studies that the director explores. An amplified critique of intellectuals' guilty ignorance is precisely the object of Scola's observations. Amedeo's question, "Revolution is not done by those who are supposed to do it, why should cinema do it?," resonates as an admonition to the Italian film industry. Cinema as a cultural agent has the responsibility to intervene on the "consciousness of the masses,"[25] Scola argues, and Italian style comedies do not simply represent qualities and flaws of Italian society, but they also break down taboos about Catholic morality, corrupted institutions, and the bourgeois intelligentsia. In the wake of a crucial decade for Italian society, *La terrazza*'s pained intellectual stays stubbornly perched on the terrace, unable to communicate his frustration and understand the role he could have played to create a more equal society. Scola shows the interaction between the bourgeois and proletarians on two occasions: when Enrico blames a greengrocer, who is guilty only of speaking too loudly, for distracting him from writing and when Mario asks the train conductor about the ongoing strike at the station. In both scenes, intellectuals speak a perfect Italian language with no inflection, while the *borgatari* speak the local Roman dialect. If subproletarians look to the bourgeois as a reference point, the bourgeois, on the contrary, have no idea about the life of the common people, nor do they care. Gods on Parnassus never look below, nor do they look beyond. Even when they realize that the subproletarians exist, they see them as abstract figures.[26] *La terrazza* is "a trial for a culture, a city, [and] a nation's intelligentsia in crisis,"[27] in which the Pasolinian critique is adapted and translated into images. Scola mirrors what Italy was and has become, a culture that is still inherently sexist; a country intrinsically polarized, whose multiple sociocultural identities were disappearing. Scola offers a compelling and sustained portrait of an intelligentsia detached from reality and leaves judgment to the audience.

Notes

1. Pier Paolo Pasolini, "Il mio Accattone in TV dopo il genocidio," in *Lettere luterane* (Turin: Einaudi, 1976), 154. First published in *Corriere della Sera*, October 8, 1975. Translations throughout the chapter are my own unless otherwise noted.
2. Giovanni Berlinguer and Piero Della Seta, *Borgate di Roma* (Rome: Editori Riuniti, 1976), 156.
3. Ettore Scola, interview by Aldo Tassone, *Parla il cinema italiano*, vol. 2 (Milan: Il Formichiere, 1980), 317.
4. The story of Giacinto Mazzatella (Nino Manfredi) living with his large family in a shack in Monte Ciocci, in Rome, is developed as an ideal sequel to Pasolini's first feature film and includes a deep look at the *borgata* fifteen years later to understand "what stage has been reached in the cultural genocide," to use the words of Ettore Scola, which Pasolini had anticipated in his writings. If in *Accattone* Pasolini portrayed Roman subproletarians

with a deep sense of humanity and compassion for their life (and death) as marginalized people from the suburbs who obey their own system of values, with *Brutti, sporchi e cattivi* Scola proved that the cultural genocide was irreversibly happening. Giacinto's obsession for a small amount of money he got as a reimbursement from the state (which he hides from his greedy relatives) shows the annihilation of subproletarian culture and its consequent mutation into petit bourgeois mediocrity. See Ettore Scola, "I giovani non devono dimenticare Pasolini," interview by Chiara Ugolini, Repubblica TV, October 30, 2017, http://video.repubblica.it/spettacoli-e-cultura/ettore-scola-i-giovani-non-devono-dimenticare-pasolini/216662/215846.

5. Pier Marco De Santi and Rossano Vittori, *I film di Ettore Scola* (Rome: Gremese, 1987), 125.
6. Edoardo Cocciardo, *L'applauso interrotto: Poesia e periferia nell'opera di Massimo Troisi* (Naples: Non solo parole edizioni, 2005), 82.
7. Pasolini, "Il mio Accattone in TV dopo il genocidio," 156.
8. See Vito Zagarrio, "La sceneggiatura circolare: Strutture narrative in tre film di Ettore Scola," *Italianist* 29 (2009): 265–80.
9. Maurizio Grande, *Abiti nuziali e biglietti di banca: La società della commedia nel cinema italiano* (Rome: Bulzoni, 1986), 195.
10. Francesca Cadel, *La lingua dei desideri: Il dialetto secondo Pier Paolo Pasolini* (Lecce: Manni, 2002),167.
11. Pier Paolo Pasolini, "10 giugno 1974: Studio della rivoluzione antropologica in Italia," in *Scritti corsari* (Milan: Garzanti, 1975), 53. First published in *Corriere della Sera* as "Gli italiani non sono più quelli," June 10, 1974.
12. John Kenneth Galbraith, *The Affluent Society* (Boston: Houghton Mifflin Harcourt, 1958).
13. John Kenneth Galbraith, *The Age of Uncertainty* (Boston: Houghton Mifflin Harcourt, 1977).
14. Pasolini, "Il mio Accattone in TV dopo il genocidio," 156.
15. Federica Sciarelli and Giuseppe Rinaldi, *3 bravi ragazzi. Gli assassini del Circeo. I retroscena di un'inchiesta lunga trent'anni* (Milan: Rizzoli, 2006).
16. Alberto Moravia, "Ma che cosa aveva in mente?," *L'Espresso*, November 9, 1975.
17. Italo Calvino, "Delitto in Europa," *Corriere della Sera*, October 8, 1975.
18. *È finita l'età della pietà* by Fabio Pierangeli recollects the history of the Circeo massacre through the articles and essays of Pier Paolo Pasolini, Italo Calvino, Stanislao Nievo, Dacia Maraini, and other prominent Italian writers who engaged in the debate about the crime and its cultural, sociopolitical implications. Fabio Pierangeli, *È finita l'età della pietà: Pasolini, Calvino, S. Nievo e "mostri" del Circeo* (Rome: Edizioni Sinestesie, 2015).
19. Pasolini, "Il mio Accattone in TV dopo il genocidio," 156.

20. Michael Foucault, *Discipline and Punish: The Birth of the Prison*, trans. Alan Sheridan (New York: Vintage Books, 1995), 25.
21. Maura Misiti et al., "La rivoluzione silenziosa delle donne: Cronologia dei diritti," in *Italia 150 anni: Popolazione, welfare, scienza e società*, ed. Sveva Avveduto (Rome: Gangemi, 2005), 113.
22. Michel Foucault, *Power/Knowledge. Selected Interviews and Other Writings 1972–1977*, ed. Colin Gordon, trans. Colin Gordon, Leo Marshall, John Mepham, and Kate Soper (New York: Pantheon Books, 1980), 56.
23. Ettore Scola, "Attenti al buffone: Testimonianze sparse sulla commedia all'italiana," in *Effetto commedia: Teoria, generi, paesaggi della commedia cinematografica*, ed. Claver Salizzato and Vito Zagarrio (Rome: Di Giacomo Editore, 1985), 213.
24. Morando Morandini, "Dal 1968 ai giorni nostri: Agonia, morte e resurrezione," in *Commedia all'italiana: Angolazioni controcampi*, ed. Riccardo Napolitano (Rome: Gangemi, 1986), 92.
25. Ettore Scola, interview by Tassone, *Parla il cinema italiano*, 308.
26. Pier Paolo Pasolini, "Le mie proposte su scuola e TV," in *Lettere luterane*, 175. First published in *Corriere della Sera*, October 18, 1975.
27. Tassone, *Parla il cinema italiano*, 299.

PART 3

SPACE AND PLACE

ITALY MUST BE DEFENDED

Surveillance and Biopolitics in
Una giornata particolare

Brian Tholl

Until recently, films that deal with the fascist *confino*, or internal exile implemented by the Italian fascist regime, as a theme have received little scholarly attention.[1] While many have written about Ettore Scola's *Una giornata particolare* (*A Special Day*, 1977), specifically with regard to gender and sexuality,[2] its relevance to *confino* has been relegated to footnotes and anecdotes. This chapter seeks to fill that gap, situating *confino* at the center of its analysis. I argue for a biopolitical reading of *Una giornata particolare* in order to tease out the ways in which the surveillance apparatus of the fascist regime functioned to induce submissive behavior from Italian citizens during the *ventennio*, or the roughly twenty-year period of fascism in Italy. In the cases in which the regime deemed that citizens were noncompliant, and thus enemies of the state, they were often imprisoned or sent to internal exile in remote areas of Italy, mainly in the south. Drawing on the notion of panopticism, theorized by Michel Foucault through his analysis of Jeremy Bentham's panopticon, I seek to demonstrate how a mode of disciplinary power is inscribed in fascist architecture and further extended beyond physical structures to pervade everyday social life and relations, evolving into what Mark Andrejevic calls "lateral surveillance,"[3] which would allow the regime to spy on Italians through citizen-to-citizen surveillance. The analysis of this chapter centers on the Palazzo Federici—the setting of the entire film and an exemplary case of fascist architecture and the way in which Benito Mussolini sought to control the environment where his subjects lived—as well as the building's caretaker

(Françoise Berd), ultimately demonstrating how the regime managed to erase the distinction between public and private spaces, thus providing a mechanism through which it could practice surveillance and *chirurgia fascista* (fascist surgery), a term Mussolini uses in his Ascension Day speech to justify the removal and exile of those who opposed him. I argue that Gabriele represents the figure of the *homo sacer*, a term borrowed from Giorgio Agamben, who is stripped of his juridical status and exiled from the political community. His political "death" through *confino* and subsequent transformation into a nonperson will pave the way for the fascist New Man—the virile, masculine symbol of Mussolini's Italy—while ironically laying the groundwork for effective antifascist resistance.

Una giornata particolare is set in Rome on the day that Adolf Hitler visits Benito Mussolini (May 6, 1938) and revolves around the chance meeting between Antonietta (Sophia Loren) and Gabriele (Marcello Mastroianni), who both live in Palazzo Federici. Although a historical event is the frame for the story, the film takes place entirely within the walls of the large public housing complex designed by Mario De Renzi and constructed along Viale XXI Aprile in Rome's Nomentano neighborhood. The complex itself may be considered the third protagonist of the film. Indeed, following the newsreel footage that prefaces the film, a survey of the structure of the complex initiates the narrative. Scola's camera pans from right to left in a low-angle shot, establishing the threatening essence of the building, as well as conveying a sense of claustrophobia. As Luciano De Giusti writes, "The scarceness of the spots in which the characters move is accentuated by the stylistic choices that reduce every possibility for openness."[4] Indeed, the camera eye operates in completely enclosed spaces, often denying the audience a view of the sky, as De Giusti also notes. Thus, the Palazzo Federici is reduced to a prison-like structure,[5] in which its inhabitants are suffocated by fascist ideology and iconography. The metaphor of housing complex as prison is a critical part of this chapter, as I draw parallels between the building and Bentham's panopticon.

Following the initial shot, the camera eye dwells on the caretaker of the building, who will be a central figure in carrying out surveillance throughout the film and who furthermore represents the omnipresence of the fascist government. The camera continues to examine the building's residents, who are individually framed in their own apartments. For this reason, we can also read their apartments as prison cells. The camera finally focuses on the housewife

Antonietta who, taking care of six children and a husband who is a Fascist Party official, is living in her own sort of prison. The family prepares for the rally, dressing up in official fascist uniforms. They represent the prototypical fascist family, loyal to the party and its doctrine. Antonietta's husband, Emanuele, upholds fascist doctrine through his appearance and also through his actions. He is the fascist virile man,[6] the dominant head of the family who subjugates his wife and demonstrates his physical strength and athleticism through the exercises he performs shortly after waking up. Sergio Rigoletto notes that Emanuele's virility is a "distinctive public performance,"[7] but we must also note that one of his sons follows in his footsteps, subjugating women through the voyeuristic pleasure he takes in viewing an erotic magazine and drawing on a mustache in order to perform his own masculinity. Emanuele furthermore adheres to fascist language policy, which sought to outlaw foreign words,[8] correcting another son when he uses a foreign word, *pom-pom*, asking him to Italianize the word instead. It is also worth noting that some of the children of the family have names such as Romana and Littorio, which exalt the ideals of imperial Rome. Thus, fascism has invaded every aspect of life in Italy, from daily routines to language use and naming traditions.

As the apartment complex empties and its residents head to the rally, we understand that the complex represents a microcosm of the Italian nation under fascism. Indeed, the spaces that make up the Palazzo Federici are clearly marked as fascist spaces. Aside from the flags of the Fascist and the Nazi Parties that drape from the railings of the raised walkways, above every entrance is the *fascio littorio*, the symbol of the National Fascist Party, designating the pervasiveness of the regime's ideology, even in private spaces. In inhabiting these spaces, the residents participate in and submit themselves to a culture of fascism, through which their identity as Italians in fascist Italy is formed. According to Elena Gorfinkel and John David Rhodes, "Identity is constructed in and through place, whether by our embrace of a place, our inhabitation of a particular point in space, or by our rejection of and departure from a given place and our movement toward, adoption and inhabitation of, another."[9] Gabriele is the only antifascist in the film, and because of his views he is forbidden from occupying certain spaces. He is fired from his job as a radio broadcaster, thus eliminating his vocal presence along the airwaves and replacing it with that of Guido Notari, an actor and radio personality, whose voice fills the diegetic space of the apartments of the Palazzo Federici for most of the film. Indeed, Gabriele's presence in the Palazzo Federici—an inherently fascist space—is only ephemeral, as he awaits his deportation to a *confino* colony in Sardinia.

Confino may be considered as a form of both social engineering and spatial engineering, as those exiled by the regime were interned in remote locations and islands, mainly in the south of Italy, thus allowing the regime to control the demographics, as well as identity, in the areas it deemed appropriate. We can relate this to immunitary protection. Speaking of immunitary protection, Roberto Esposito writes, "Evil must be thwarted, but not by keeping it at a distance from one's borders; rather, it is included inside them. The dialectical figure that thus emerges is that of exclusionary inclusion or exclusion by inclusion. The body defeats a poison not by expelling it outside the organism, but by making it somehow part of the body."[10] Exclusion by inclusion, the fact of existing both internal to and external to Italy is what comes to define the *confinati*. This is necessary, however, in order to construct the fascist state desired by Mussolini. By removing the infecting agent, through the "death" of the antifascist, the regime is able to construct a pure space in which life—understood as the new fascist subject—might thrive. Despite this effort, *confino* colonies would effectively become "schools of antifascism," as Alberto Jacometti writes, and the intellectuals and antifascists who made up their population would lay the groundwork for a postwar Italy and Europe that had been ravaged by the ideology of fascism.[11]

The regime relied heavily on surveillance in order to eliminate from its spaces antifascists and those whom fascist ideology deemed "subversive." If we are to understand the Palazzo Federici as a microcosm of the nation, then the control over space and the determination of who may or may not occupy certain spaces (the control over bodies) functions to shape the new Italian. Architecture plays a crucial role in this practice, as it is an instrument that, according to Sven-Olov Wallenstein, "is an essential part of the biopolitical machine."[12] In Wallenstein's words, "architecture is no longer *like* a body . . . but *acts upon* the body," and thus we may affirm that the architectural structure finds meaning only through the body that moves through or is eliminated from its space.[13] The relationship between architecture and the policing of the Italian body features prominently throughout the film; Scola provides various shots of the Palazzo Federici throughout the film, and his camera reveals that the building is constructed in a manner that obliterates privacy. The structure's transparent windows and stairwells allow for effortless surveillance of the movements and actions of its inhabitants.[14] In considering this, we must reflect on Foucault's notion of panopticism, an internal surveillance mechanism that through its disciplinary power may also assist in fulfilling the biopolitical aims of a nation. This notion is derived from Jeremy Bentham's idea of the panopticon, a type of prison that would maximize the efficiency of surveillance specifically by allowing a prison inspector to observe a detainee without being observed himself. Bentham imagined that through the structure of the prison (through the power of architecture itself) he would possess a new psychological tool, referring to the practice of panopticism as "a new mode of obtaining power of mind over mind, in a quantity hitherto without example."[15] We may compare the idea of the panopticon to the omnipresence of God himself. Indeed, the name given to this structure (deriving from Greek), roughly translates to "all seeing." Outlining the structure of the panopticon, Bentham writes:

> The building is circular. The apartments of the prisoners occupy the circumference. You may call them, if you please, the *cells*. These *cells* are divided from one another, and the prisoners by that means secluded from all communication with each other, by *partitions* in the form of *radii* issuing from the circumference toward the centre, and extending as many feet as shall be thought necessary to form the largest dimension of the cell. The apartment of the inspector occupies the centre; you may call it if you please the *inspector's lodge*.[16]

Although it would be impossible for the inspector to observe all prisoners and all cells at the same time, the structure was designed in a way that would render it impossible to determine whether or not one was under surveillance, thus soliciting complacency at all times. Indeed, Bentham writes, "Perhaps it is the most important point . . . that the persons to be inspected should always feel themselves as if under inspection, at least as standing a great chance of being so."[17] In this way, then, each detainee must consider the weight of the "*apparent omnipresence* of the inspector" combined with the "extreme facility of his *real presence*."[18] Those living under the fascist regime, then, had to assume that they were constantly under surveillance; although this was physically impossible, it was very much a conceptual plausibility, for they had no way of knowing whether or not they were being observed, or would have been at a future time.

While the Palazzo Federici is certainly not the panopticon that Bentham imagines, the purpose of the building is similar to that which he theorized. Scola's camera adopts the perspective of the prison inspector, lingering on the various residents of the building in the opening shots of the film. Throughout the film, there are various shots that demonstrate the view that the building's residents have from inside their own apartments, such as Gabriele's view from his desk at the beginning of the film and Antonietta's view from her apartment's kitchen. These shots show that the Palazzo Federici is a completely enclosed structure, as the views from each window reveal a snapshot into the apartments of the other inhabitants, demonstrating the limited privacy that is easily undermined by wandering eyes, such as those of the building's caretaker. Thus, De Renzi's architecture allows for ordered and facilitated surveillance, erasing the distinction between public and private spaces. The residents of the Palazzo Federici, then, must always be aware of the possibility of being surveilled. Indeed, as the complex clears out, we observe the movement of its residents, who are visible through transparent glass panes as they utilize the stairwells. Then, when the complex is empty, Antonietta's bird, Rosmunda, repeats her name, thus reminding her that someone is always watching. It is this same bird that sets the plot of the film into motion, escaping from Antonietta's apartment and flying to Gabriele's. Before arriving at Gabriele's apartment, the bird flies around the complex as the camera cuts back and forth between shots of Antonietta at her window and shots of the bird's wide flight path, demonstrating the ease with which one may carry out surveillance throughout the complex. Later in the film, Gabriele will observe, at length, his own apartment from Antonietta's, remarking how strange it is to see it from someone else's viewpoint, allowing us to reflect on the possibility of past surveillance performed on Gabriele specifically.

We must furthermore consider the concept of "lateral surveillance," put forth by Mark Andrejevic. Lateral surveillance is described as "peer-to-peer monitoring, understood as the use of surveillance tools by individuals, rather than by agents of institutions public or private."[19] Bentham's panopticon, then, ceases to be a prison and morphs into a free-roaming apparatus, which may exist in both public and private spaces. Indeed, as Foucault writes, "[T]he Panopticon must not be understood as a dream building: it is the diagram of a mechanism of power reduced to its ideal form; its functioning, abstracted from any obstacle, resistance or friction, must be represented as a pure architectural and optical system: it is in fact a figure of political technology that may and must be detached from any specific use."[20] Foucault recognizes the malleability of the panopticon and its ability to additionally function in spaces outside of the penal dimension: "The panoptic schema, without disappearing as such or losing any of its properties, was destined to spread throughout the social body; its vocation was to become a generalized function."[21] The most threatening embodiment of this type of surveillance power in the film is exemplified by the building's caretaker, who, in addition to Gabriele and Antonietta, stays home from the rally. Luciano De Giusti notes that the caretaker is akin to a prison guard,[22] although we may argue that any resident in the Palazzo Federici may fulfill this role. Her presence is always felt throughout the film—she oversees the behavior of the residents of the complex, saluting them as they leave for the rally and greeting them as they come back, ensuring that they have fulfilled their duty as members of fascist Italy. Even when she is not physically present, we are reminded that she is near; the sound of the rally blaring from her radio is audible throughout most of the film. Although the caretaker is completely ignored by the other residents of the complex, and her interaction with Antonietta and Gabriele is limited—she represents the fear of Italians of the pervasive surveillance of the regime. This fear is evident throughout the film—when Gabriele first comes to Antonietta's apartment, he remarks that she does not seem happy to see him, to which she responds, "I just get a bit scared when the doorbell rings; if you ask who is there, they say 'friends.'" Aware of the intelligence-gathering power of the Organization for Vigilance and Repression of Anti-Fascism (OVRA)—the fascist secret police—Italians had to fear the omnipresence of the regime. Michael Ebner writes that "the myth of an omniscient and omnipotent OVRA . . . was perhaps not entirely overblown, if one considers the interconnectedness of OVRA with the offices of the *polizia politica* and the network of informants surrounding the *questure*."[23] Ebner, moreover, notes that the network of informants was recruited from a wide pool of Italians, including former socialists and communists, family members, and private businesses, with some individuals being offered employment;[24] thus, ordinary citizens always had to worry about the threat of surveillance, as seemingly anyone could be an informant.

Scola does not hesitate to demonstrate this threat: the next time the bell rings, it is the building's caretaker—the symbol of the citizen surveillance apparatus of the fascist regime—who is standing outside. Antonietta is visibly frightened each time the caretaker comes to her door and each time the conversation centers around the idea that Gabriele is an antifascist. The caretaker also implies that someone is always watching when she says, "Hanging around certain people can get you in trouble. . . . The sixth-floor tenant is a no-good naysayer, a defeatist, an antifascist." Thus, to be seen with someone whom the fascist regime deemed subversive was cause for concern and precaution. Consequently, both Antonietta and Gabriele seek to avoid surveillance as they move throughout the complex, using the rooftop, the complex's boiler room, and other locations to remain hidden from the building's caretaker and, by extension, the eyes of the regime.[25]

Gabriele is aware that he cannot escape the eyes of the regime, and throughout the day we are reminded that he is preparing to be sent to *confino*. As Antonietta retrieves her escaped bird from Gabriele's apartment, Gabriele's phone rings. Through the phone conversation, we understand that Gabriele is preparing to leave somewhere, and this is the first allusion to *confino* in the film. Later, we learn that Gabriele's friend, who he states is "a subversive like me," is interned in Carbonia in Sardinia, and thus we are to expect that Gabriele faces the same fate because of his homosexuality.[26] Exiled to these remote locations, the *confinato* represents the *homo sacer*, stripped of his political existence, or *bios*, and reduced solely to his biological existence, or *zoē*.[27] The *confino* colony, then, is a camp, which Agamben recognizes as the paradigm of the state of exception of the twentieth century. The camp is opened when the state of exception—"a temporary suspension of the rule of law on the basis of a factual state of danger"[28]—becomes a permanent fixture. Because of this suspension of the rule of law, the *confinato* is allowed to be "killed," as he is forcibly removed from the political community in Italy.

Gabriele's phone conversation specifically reveals the measures taken by the fascist police with regard to those who were considered subversive in the eyes of the regime and demonstrates how the state of exception is slowly becoming permanent in fascist Italy. Gabriele says, "They always do it when there are these ceremonies. . . . You'll see that in a couple of days they'll let him go," thus demonstrating how the regime implemented the state of exception by temporarily suspending the law and detaining Italians without trial, and revealing the extent to which fascism policed bodies and restricted movement and productivity, understood in political, intellectual, or sexual terms. We may understand this through the concept of biopolitics put forth by Michel Foucault in *Society Must Be Defended*. Foucault conceptualizes the role of power in the nineteenth century, citing "power's hold over life," which he further explains as "the acquisition of power over man insofar as man is a living being, that the biological came under State control, that there was at least a certain tendency that leads to what might be termed State control of the biological."[29] In further explaining this concept, Foucault asserts that a fundamental change occurred in the nineteenth century, that the sovereign's right to "take life and let live" was supplemented by the right to "make live and let die."[30] This new power did not address the individual man, man as body, as Foucault says, but rather man as an overall mass, man as species. In contrast to the sovereign power, then, which allowed the sovereign to take life, the concept of biopolitics was related to "a set of processes such as the ratio of births to deaths, the rate of reproduction, the fertility of a population, and so on,"[31] a concept of power that would make life.

Mussolini was quite concerned with the fertility of the Italian population and its birthrates, initiating the "battle for births" in 1927, which ultimately proved unsuccessful.[32] Although Foucault argues the right to take life is retreating in favor of the right to make life, with the advent of fascism, we see both the right to take life and the right to make life and, in some cases, the right to take life *in order to* make life. Foucault addresses this in his same lecture when describing the functions of racism.[33] The defense of the Italian race, specifically through the creation and maintenance of a new, inherently fascist race, was at the center of Mussolini's national security policy. To create and maintain this race, then, the antifascist race had to die. We are not necessarily speaking of death and killing in biological terms but rather in the terms that Foucault subsequently lays out: "the fact of exposing someone to death, increasing the risk of death for some people, or, quite simply, political death, expulsion, rejection, and so on."[34] Therefore, the fascist regime is able to make life through the kind of social and spatial engineering discussed earlier in this chapter, *confino*, the embodiment of the regime's power to take life in fascist Italy.

As a homosexual in fascist Italy, Gabriele faces rejection and political death—he is fired by the EIAR (Ente Italiano per le Audizioni Radiofoniche,

Italian National Radio) because he is not a member of the Fascist Party, and he is not deemed a member of the Fascist Party because it is "a party of men." In addition, Gabriele notes that his voice "did not meet EIAR requirements: solemn, martial, and conveying Roman pride." As we learn that he is waiting to be sent to *confino*, we must understand that he faces complete expulsion from the Italian community. In Mussolini's speeches, however, this expulsion is framed not only in political terms but also in medical terms. He adopts a rhetoric of hygiene, portraying Italy as a sick body of which Rome is the literal and figural heart that needs to be cured of its illness. Thus, the medical and the pathogenic will become the central subjects around which fascist national security policy revolves. In his "Discorso di Udine" (Udine speech) delivered in preparation for the fascist March on Rome, Mussolini states, "We hope to make Rome the city of our spirit, a city purified and disinfected of all the elements that corrupt and dirty it. We hope to make Rome the beating heart, the zealous spirit of the imperial Italy that we dream of."[35] Italy, then, is a sick body, and the only way to cure itself of its illness is through the exclusion of the infecting agent—the antifascist. Mussolini asserts his violence over the antifascists through *confino*, through the physical control over rejected bodies. In this same speech, he asserts that "when our violence is the resolution for a cancerous situation, it is extremely moral, sacrosanct, and necessary."[36] Thus, for Mussolini, this violence is a question of public health, of a pure community, to borrow from Foucault.

As we see above, Mussolini's rhetoric is used to paint himself as a medical professional who may track a contagious disease. In fact, in a later speech in which Mussolini expands on his national security policy, especially in relation to *confino*, he asserts: "I am the clinician who does not neglect the symptoms, and these are symptoms that should make us seriously reflect."[37] Thus, Mussolini follows the symptoms that threaten the regime and the public hygiene of the country, ultimately resorting to *chirurgia fascista*[38] to cleanse the nation. Concerning the practice of forced exile, he maintains the medical metaphor: "Terror, gentlemen, this? No, it is not terror, it is barely rigor. Terrorism? Not even, it is social hygiene, national prophylaxis, these individuals are removed from circulation as a doctor removes a contagious subject from circulation."[39] *Confino*, then, may best be described as a form of quarantine, implemented to guarantee the health and safety of the general population.[40] To better understand this, it is useful to consider Foucault's discussion of quarantine in *Discipline and Punish*, in which he writes about seventeenth-century plans and "measures to be taken when the plague appeared in town," the purpose of which "is to sort out every possible confusion: that of the disease, which is transmitted when bodies are mixed together; that of evil, which is increased when fear and death overcome prohibitions."[41] The spread of "disease" is central to the idea of *confino*, and the rhetoric of infection surrounding this topic is the concept through which exile, quarantine, and surveillance are justified. In this same chapter, Foucault notes the distinction between the goals of the "exile of the leper" and the "arrest of the plague." He writes: "The first is that of a pure community, the second that of a disciplined society."[42] I believe, however, that we cannot make a distinction between the leper and the plague; in the eyes of the fascist regime, they are the same, and thus the political goals of a pure society and of a disciplined society are intertwined. To reach these goals, then, surveillance becomes a defense mechanism not only in maintaining a disciplined society but also in assisting in the purification of society. Thus, when we speak of fascist surgery, we are speaking of social cleansing through the removal and thus the "death" of the other.

The fascist concepts of biopolitics and public hygiene as they relate to Gabriele are present throughout the film. In juxtaposing Gabriele's homosexuality with Antonietta's fertility (she is the mother of six children), Scola emphasizes the regime's characterization of Gabriele as a sterile figure, one who will neither reproduce the ideology of fascism nor participate in the biological reproduction of the new Italian, modeled on Mussolini himself. Indeed, Gabriele himself does not fit into the definition of the fascist New Man.[43] As Gabriele flips through Antonietta's picture album, we learn what a man and a woman are in the eyes of the regime. The first caption on which the camera focuses reads, "Fascist women, you must be the keepers of the hearth." Antonietta performs the role ascribed to her by the regime well, whereas Gabriele does not: on a page in which we see photos of Mussolini with his family, as well as photos of Mussolini dressed in military garb, we read, "The man who is not a husband, father, and soldier is not a man." Gabriele is not any of these things: in fact, we learn in a conversation between Antonietta and him that because he is single, he must pay a bachelor tax. In considering the significance of his existence for the public hygiene of the country, we are furthermore reminded of fascism's other public health projects. In a scene inside Antonietta's apartment, Gabriele moves about the room, observing the various objects hanging on the wall. The camera, before falling back on Gabriele, lingers over a framed certificate that reads "Italian National Fascist Federation for the Struggle against Tuberculosis." This juxtaposition forces us to consider Gabriele in medical terms, as a disease that may be controlled and eliminated by fascism.

Fascism's control over Gabriele's body is demonstrated as he dances the rumba in his apartment. As he starts dancing, the caretaker of the building turns on the radio broadcast of the rally, which drowns out Gabriele's music. The song playing on the radio is "Giovinezza," which was the official hymn of the Italian National Fascist Party. The song not only suggests the omnipresence of fascism in the lives of all Italians (the radio broadcast is heard in every part of the complex), but it also demonstrates the control that the regime has over the bodies of Italians. Gabriele turns off his own music, and as the fascist hymn plays, he notes that "you can't really dance to that one." The radio broadcast will continue to play nonstop throughout the film, up until the point in which Gabriele and Antonietta engage in sex. The film demonstrates not only the regime's control over the bodies of potential subversives but also over the bodies of the loyal practitioners of its ideology. After Gabriele finishes looking through the album, Antonietta describes the time she crossed paths with Mussolini. She depicts him in terms of the virile fascist man, recounting a story in which Mussolini gallops by her on horseback, which causes her to become dizzy and subsequently faint. She learns that day that she is pregnant with her son, Littorio. It is as if Antonietta becomes pregnant through the will of Mussolini and his regime. As Duggan notes, Mussolini himself was an example of the fecund Italian, with five children[44] and, as noted previously, the New Man on which Italians were to model themselves. Through the mythology surrounding Mussolini, then, Scola demonstrates the power that the regime held over fertility and the rate of reproduction of the Italian population.

However, the regime's control over the bodies of the Italian population is challenged in the climax of the film when Antonietta and Gabriele engage in sex. Up until this point, the patriotic music and the broadcast from the rally—the incessant presence of fascist rhetoric and ideology—is audible as it plays from the apartment of the caretaker. Only after Antonietta and Gabriele have sex does the radio go silent, perhaps indicating that Antonietta—by virtue of her chance meeting and bonding with Gabriele—is capable of seeing past and challenging the rhetoric of the regime. Antonietta's position on top of Gabriele—who remains relatively passive throughout the encounter—demonstrates her power and control and asserts her dominance in the sexual encounter, thus reversing traditional gender dynamics in fascist Italy. Sergio Rigoletto suggests that this encounter indicates "the recovery of a part of that sexual agency that she had to give up to fulfil her role of fascist mother and wife . . . the rediscovery of her body and of the terms of her oppression."[45] Scola, however, is quick to remind us that this type of reversal is not permitted by the regime. As the film concludes, both Gabriele and Antonietta are forced to accept the positions ascribed to them in fascist Italy. Antonietta watches from her apartment as Gabriele is taken from his own in order to be sent to *confino*. Gabriele, a future *confinato*, is the *homo sacer* of the fascist regime, reduced to bare life and stripped of his political existence. His detainment in the camp, "the materialization of the state of exception" of the twentieth century,[46] his inclusion through exclusion, allows the virile fascist to thrive. Despite her sexual reawakening with Gabriele, Antonietta returns to her role as the submissive housewife and child bearer. Her husband, Emanuele, alludes to sex and remarks that they will call their seventh child Adolf. At first, the film's concluding shot—overlapped by the anthem of the Nazi Party, the "Horst Wessel Lied"—seemingly offers little hope. The camera eye rests on Antonietta, who walks into the bedroom and undresses, reinscribing her role assigned to her by the regime and reasserting its control over her body. But the seed has been planted—moments earlier, we see Antonietta tucking away the book gifted to her by Gabriele, suggesting that she will continue her resistance and learn to oppose the tyranny of fascist ideology.

Although *Una giornata particolare* demonstrates the power of fascist surveillance and biopolitics, it most importantly shows that it is possible to resist the influence and control of totalitarian politics. The film reveals that even though power may flow one way, this does not eliminate the possibility of engaging in acts of resistance that may someday bear fruit. Indeed, many of those sent to *confino* would eventually become the main actors in the literary and political community following World War II, laying the groundwork for the reconstruction of Italy and the (re)birth of the European community. The timing of the film and its message arrive during a significant moment in history; it was released in the heat of the international struggle for gay rights, a time in which many were fighting for freedom and control over their own bodies.[47] Perhaps Scola's intention is to highlight that even in the face of oppression, resistance *is* possible. After all, one encounter, one event, or one special day is enough to spark the change needed to achieve liberation.

Notes

1. For a recent essay that addresses this concern, see Dana Renga, "Screening *Confino*: Male Melodrama and Exile Cinema," *Journal of Italian Cinema and Media Studies* 5, no. 1 (2017): 23–46. A version of this essay and other commentary on the representation of *confino* appear in Piero Garofalo, Elizabeth Leake, and Dana Renga, *Internal Exile in Fascist Italy: History and Representations of* Confino (Manchester: Manchester University Press, 2019).
2. See Millicent Marcus, "Un'ora e mezzo particolare: Teaching Fascism with Ettore Scola," *Italica* 83, no. 1 (2006): 53–61; Sandra Ponzanesi, "Queering European Sexualities through Italy's Fascist Past: Colonialism, Homosexuality, and Masculinities," in *What's Queer about Europe? Productive Encounters and Re-enchanting Paradigms*, ed. Mireille Rosello and Sudeep Dasgupta (New York: Fordham University Press, 2014), 81–90; Sergio Rigoletto, *Masculinity and Italian Cinema: Sexual Politics, Social Conflict, and Male Crisis in the 1970s* (Edinburgh: Edinburgh University Press, 2014), 93–100; and Szymon Pietrzykowski, "Gay as a Stranger: Homosexuality during Fascism in Ettore Scola's *Una Giornata Particolare*" ["A Special Day"]," in *Maska* 24 (2014): 75–88.
3. I am grateful to Daniel Grinberg who pointed me to lateral surveillance.
4. Luciano De Giusti, "La lunga durata di *Una giornata particolare*," in Vito Zagarrio, ed., *Trevico—Cinecittà: L'avventuroso viaggio di Ettore Scola* (Venice: Marsilio, 2002), 278. Translations throughout the chapter are my own unless otherwise noted.
5. See also Christian Uva, "Un borgo nella metropoli: Ettore Scola a Palazzo Federici," *The Italianist* 35, no. 2 (2015): 284–90.
6. For a discussion of virility in fascist Italy, see Barbara Spackman, *Fascist Virilities: Rhetoric, Ideology, and Social Fantasy in Italy* (Minneapolis: University of Minnesota Press, 1996).
7. Rigoletto, *Masculinity and Italian Cinema*, 95.
8. See Gabriella Klein, *La politica linguistica del Fascismo* (Bologna: Il Mulino, 1986).
9. Elena Gorfinkel and John David Rhodes, "Introduction," in *Taking Place: Location and the Moving Image*, ed. Elena Gorfinkel and John David Rhodes (Minneapolis: University of Minnesota Press, 2011), ix.
10. Roberto Esposito, *Immunitas: The Protection and Negation of Life*, trans. Zakiya Hanafi (Cambridge: Polity Press, 2011), 8.
11. Alberto Jacometti, *Ventotene* (Genoa: Fratelli Frilli Editori, 2004), 31. See also

Illaria Poerio, *A scuola di dissenso: Storie di resistenza al confino di polizia (1925–1943)* (Rome: Carocci editore, 2016).
12. Sven-Olov Wallenstein, *Biopolitics and the Emergence of Modern Architecture* (New York: Princeton Architectural, 2009), 20.
13. Wallenstein, 25; see also 46n33.
14. See also Paul Baxa, "Ettore Scola's *A Special Day*," AMU on Film, Ave Maria University Film Society September 8, 2011, https://amufilm.wordpress.com/2011/09/08/ettore-scolas-a-special-day.
15. Jeremy Bentham, *The Panopticon Writings* (London: Verso, 1995), 31.
16. Bentham, 35.
17. Bentham, 43.
18. Bentham, 45.
19. Mark Andrejevic, "The Work of Watching One Another: Lateral Surveillance, Risk, and Governance," *Surveillance and Society* 2, no. 4 (2004): 488.
20. Michel Foucault, *Discipline and Punish: The Birth of the Prison*, trans. Alan Sheridan (New York: Vintage Books, 1995), 205.
21. Foucault, 207.
22. De Giusti, "La lunga durata di *Una giornata particolare*," 278.
23. Michael Ebner, *Ordinary Violence in Mussolini's Italy* (New York: Cambridge University Press, 2011), 56.
24. Ebner, 56–57.
25. See Baxa, "Ettore Scola's *A Special Day*," for more commentary on the role of space in the building.
26. At least three hundred Italians were interned for their homosexuality, although this number is mostly likely higher. See Gianfranco Goretti and Tommaso Giartosio, *La città e l'isola: Omosessuali al confino nell'Italia fascista* (Rome: Donzelli Editore, 2006), viii.
27. See Giorgio Agamben, Homo Sacer: *Sovereign Power and Bare Life*, trans. Daniel Heller-Roazen (Stanford, CA: Stanford University Press, 1998), 1.
28. Agamben, 169.
29. Michel Foucault, *Society Must Be Defended: Lectures at the Collège de France, 1975–1976*, trans. David Macey (New York: Picador, 2003), 239–40.
30. Foucault, 241.
31. Foucault, 243.
32. For an in-depth discussion of fertility and birthrates in fascist Italy, see Christopher Duggan, *The Force of Destiny: A History of Italy Since 1796* (London: Penguin Books, 2007), 469–74.
33. See Foucault, *Society Must Be Defended*, 254–55.
34. Foucault, 256.
35. Benito Mussolini, *Opera Omnia*, vol. 18 (Florence: La Fenice, 1951–63), 412.
36. Mussolini, 18:413.

37. Benito Mussolini, *Opera Omnia*, vol. 22, 367.
38. Mussolini, 22:373.
39. Mussolini, 22:378.
40. For more commentary on social hygiene, see David G. Horn, *Social Bodies: Science, Reproduction, and Italian Modernity* (Princeton, NJ: Princeton University Press, 1994), 46; and Spackman, *Fascist Virilities*, 143–55.
41. Foucault, *Discipline and Punish*, 195, 197.
42. Foucault, 198.
43. See Lorenzo Benadusi, *The Enemy of the New Man: Homosexuality in Fascist Italy*, trans. Suzanne Dingee and Jennifer Pudney (Madison: University of Wisconsin Press, 2012).
44. Duggan, *The Force of Destiny*, 471.
45. Rigoletto, *Masculinity and Italian Cinema*, 99.
46. Agamben, *Homo Sacer*, 174.
47. The film was released less than ten years after the Stonewall riots of 1969, which kicked off the international gay rights movement. Subsequently, the 1970s proved to be an important period for the gay rights movement in Italy as well. FUORI! (Fronte Unitario Omosessuale Rivoluzionario Italiano), the first Italian gay rights association, was born in 1971 in Turin. For more on this and the gay rights movement in Italy, see Gianni Rossi Barilli, *Il movimento gay in Italia* (Milan: Feltrinelli, 1999).

TREVICO-TORINO: VIAGGIO NEL FIAT-NAM

Metamorphoses of Urban Space and the Multiplication of the Factory in the Age of the Anthropocene

Emiliano Guaraldo and Federica Colleoni

Trevico-Torino: Viaggio nel Fiat-Nam (*Trevico-Turin: Voyage in Fiatnam*) by Ettore Scola, shot in 1970–71 and released in 1973, was largely produced by the director and completed with funds from Unitelefilm,[1] the film production company of the Partito Comunista Italiano (PCI, or Italian Communist Party). It chronicles the story of Fortunato Santospirito, a young man who leaves his hometown of Trevico (Scola's hometown), forty miles from the city of Naples, for the northern Italian industrial city of Turin. There, the huge FIAT car factory (also called *la città-fabbrica*, the factory-city) recruited workers from every part of the country, particularly the southern regions. In a time of massive internal migration, Fortunato's story is representative of a wide phenomenon of displacement of entire villages, families, and individuals from south to north. His story also comments on the destiny of a generation who found work and hope but also felt lost in industrial urban areas that bore no resemblance to their rural background. Scola chose to narrate the political awakening of a young poor southerner in an estranged cultural context, where the meeting between students and workers was inevitable but also ultimately problematic. Its release was immediately followed in 1974 by Scola's much more successful political comedy *C'eravamo tanto amati* (*We All Loved Each Other So Much*). *Trevico-Torino* constitutes an important experiment in the art of political documentary and a rather faithful representation of the Italian political and social climate of the time, with references to student movements and workers' uprisings.

This chapter is divided into two complementary portions. In the first part, we analyze the film's historical and sociological references, and in the second we attempt to problematize the role of Turin in the film, its configuration as a factory-city and how this is expressed formally by Scola. From our contemporary perspective, both the aesthetic and the ideological domains of the film, in addition to its development and historical contextualization, offer a unique chance to gaze into a specific moment of mutation of Turin's urban spaces. More specifically, the historical moment immortalized by Scola represents the intersection of three macroevents that involve numerous passive actors and agents: the multiplication of the city space (which includes the political and the material spheres), the displacement and management of groups of people (a shift that required both migrants from the north and Turinese natives to adapt), and the proliferation of the automobile (both as a commodity and as the main product of Italian factories). The consequences of these macroevents are still visible in contemporary Italian life, even if the early 1970s cannot be considered the generative moment for all these phenomena. Given its dual fictional and documentary form, we can approach *Trevico-Torino* as an ideal document for understanding the interaction between such assemblages in the age of the Anthropocene.[2]

Trevico-Torino: Journeys by Ettore Scola and Fortunato

The title itself, *Trevico-Torino*, refers to a path or a journey. The hyphen between the two places seems to symbolize the railway that immigrants traveled in search of a better future, from Trevico, in the Campania region, toward Turin, in the northern region of Piemonte, in the 1960s and 1970s. The subtitle that follows, *Voyage through Fiat-nam*, seeks to explain that journey, contextualizing it in terms of the protests and slogans of a fraught historical period, in which opposition to militarism (in reference to the Vietnam War) meets opposition to Fordism (here noted by the *Fiat* wordplay). It is, therefore, more than a title: it is a symbol of a place, an itinerary from the Italian south to north, and a displacement, of which the film depicts both trauma and hope.

In those years, the city of Turin, home to the largest factory in Italy—and one of the largest in all of Europe—was a key destination for many young people who were driven by the dream of factory jobs that would free them from a new, modern nightmare: unemployment. Italy's other large industrial city, Milan, had previously been examined in Luchino Visconti's 1960 masterpiece, *Rocco e i suoi fratelli* (*Rocco and His Brothers*). Visconti's film tells the epic tale of a family of Campanian migrants who live in Milan and confront the difficulties of internal migration for the first time in Italian cinema.[3] Scola was born in Trevico in 1931, but his family soon moved to Rome, where he completed his collegiate studies. He was no stranger to the rural southerner's sense of displacement, so when he decided to shoot a film that discussed internal migration in Italy, he centered it around a fictional character, Fortunato, from his own hometown. In the film, Carbona, another migrant from the South, says to Fortunato, "But you know that coming from the South, the first thing that we lose—unfortunately it's painful—we lose our home, [then] friendship, loved ones, the road, the street. . . . We become disoriented. I have been here for twelve years." These words communicate the sense of disorientation and loss of identity experienced by migrants from the south who reached the cities of the north. The feeling of disoriented bewilderment is present throughout the movie in different scenes, as we often see Fortunato wandering through Turin alone, experiencing the northern cold for the first time. In some scenes, drivers and pedestrians ignore him, making the urban landscape appear alien and distant. Scola is able to visualize this sense of estrangement by using perspective camera shots in which we see Fortunato from behind while he is walking away toward farther vanishing points. Throughout the film, these types of shot compositions have a perspective convergence point placed at the center of the image. Fortunato's profound displacement demonstrates that the unification of Italy, which took place about a century before, had not extended to the disparate cultures in the young nation's north and south. Fortunato experiences this incomplete unification firsthand. His arrival in the great factory-city represents a traumatic moment, an identity crisis that is meticulously described in the documentary film. The camera follows him from the moment he arrives by train and chronicles his efforts to find a job, a place to live, and friends. Fortunato is continuously disappointed by the working conditions and precarious nature of life for migrants.

As he worked to complete the postproduction of *Trevico-Torino*, Scola explored another story of displacement and migrant struggles in his 1971 film *Permette? Rocco Papaleo* (*My Name Is Rocco Papaleo*). This film, starring Marcello Mastroianni, narrates the story of a Sicilian immigrant in the United States, whose tragedy entails a failure to realize a dream, even in America where he finds himself poor and alone. The film presents an opportunity for the director to illustrate various problems with American society at the time, primarily the marginalization of the underclass but also racial conflict and class divisions. The city of Turin (as both a concrete and cultural notion), with its urban crisis, is a true costar of the film. Fortunato's individual and allegorical journey allows the director to highlight the urban landscape of the capital of Piemonte, a region that at the time was considered, together with Lombardy and its capital Milan, the most industrialized area of Italy. Turin represents the modernity that simultaneously fascinates and disturbs the young protagonist as soon as he arrives.

The film's opening scene takes place at the train station. As Fortunato descends from the train and leaves the station, he notices noise, traffic, and fog, and his first request for information is, naively, "Is it the Fiat?"[4] and then, "Is this where they hire the FIAT workers?" When he asks a stranger, "Where are you from?" using the second person plural *voi*, the man looks at him, surprised at his use of the *voi* term, and asks him, "Voi chi?" (You who?) and Fortunato responds, "Voi . . . voi tu!" (You . . . you you!)[5] The use of the formal pronoun (*voi* vs. *Lei*) is a typical Italian marker of regional difference between the north and the south. This scene represents an important moment because it shows that Fortunato must learn a new (modern, northern, industrial European) way of inhabiting urban space, together with a new grammar (the language of the northerners) that is merely a piece of the vast, intricate, and pervasive lexicon of industrial capitalist modernity.

Fortunato meets Vicky, a girl from the Lotta Continua group (Continuous Struggle),[6] while she distributes leaflets to the workers at the factory gates, and he strikes up a friendship with her that initially spurs him to understand his own situation. In the end, though, their bond cannot survive their cultural differences. Assigned to a harder job after a dispute with his manager, the young man launches himself into a desperate cry. This final scene depicts Fortunato's failure in both work and relationships, demonstrating how the "political" and the "personal" are strictly intertwined. According to critic Tullio Masoni, Fortunato and Vicky's relationship is about "an attempt to forge a connection on a political but also human and personal level, between a somehow 'classic' proletariat-laborer experience and the radicalizations of the new left in the student and bourgeois matrix,"[7] an attempt that seems destined to fail.

The urban dimension of Turin is already in itself a cause for disorientation among those who come from the small villages of the south. Scholar Nicola Pizzolato, who found similarities between the two motor cities of Turin and Detroit, asserts: "Fordism, like any regime of accumulation, exhibited its own economic geography. Through its agglomeration of manufacture in specific urban concentrations, it created large peripheral or semi-peripheral areas, both within and beyond the core states of the world economy, that had unemployment, low wages, and 'backward' social organization. The American South and the Italian Mezzogiorno both fit this description."[8]

The presence of Southern migrants in Turin in the 1960s and 1970s in Scola's film seems to suggest a "city within the city." The student riots of 1968[9] were followed by the unions' and workers' struggles in 1969 across the peninsula, since that year coincided with the expiration of the metalworkers' labor contract. The autumn of 1969, remembered as the "hot autumn," marked the meeting of the workers' demands (with the emergence of a new figure, the *operaio-massa*, or mass worker—young, southern, and unskilled) and the demands of the students. In the film, these conflicting demands are exemplified by the relationship between Vicky and Fortunato; while they develop a friendship, he continues to harbor unrequited feelings for her.

On the one hand, the film documents the social climate of the time when it was filmed, thanks to footage of the workers' meeting places[10] and to various interviews. On the other hand, it inserts a fictitious plot containing literary and cinematic references. One can see how Fortunato's initial trip toward the city, in particular at the railway station at night, has Dantesque echoes as these scenes suggest that it is necessary to cross a dark and painful space in order to achieve a greater awareness and resume one's life. The camerawork, which constantly follows the protagonist throughout the city, also reflects the ideas of *pedinamento*[11] by Cesare Zavattini—the Italian screenwriter and frequent collaborator with Vittorio De Sica—about filmic narration.

After searching unsuccessfully for nightly shelter at the train station, Fortunato, afraid of the nocturnal and strange characters who live there (a demented worker, prostitutes, and transvestites who deride him), escapes to the streets, almost inebriated by the light of bright signs, until he is left hypnotized by the enormous luminous FIAT sign. The insistent, extra-diegetic flute music underlines the urban environment's hypnotic power over the protagonist. The camera lingers artistically on this almost hallucinatory, dream-like vision, then returns to the "realism" of the documentary. This night scene stands out as a temporary break from the realist tones of the rest of the movie because it is also the scene in which the interaction among the background characters seems more traditionally cinematic and even slightly grotesque. In this scene, some homeless people start a fight while a lady who is talking to Fortunato tries to intervene and placate them. Scola's editing betrays a certain degree of scene construction as this highly theatrical fight scene is composed of alternating shots of the altercation with close-ups of Fortunato's eyes and of the woman's face. The latter, somewhat unconvincingly, yells at the homeless people, "Basta!" (Stop!) and "Arrivano neh!" (They are coming!), before resuming her discussion with Fortunato. The "staged realism" of the composition and the amateurish theatricality of the nonactors involved in it, contribute to the general feel of alienated dreaminess in the film's night sequence.

Fortunato quickly finds refuge at an institution, the EISS (Ente Italiano Servizio Sociale, or Italian Social Service)—Centro Immigrati Meridionali (Southern Migrant Center)—whose sign is easily readable in the frame, signaling the didactic and informative intent of the director Scola. The EISS is also a symbolic place of salvation, an oasis of comprehension in the middle of an urban desert that elicits fear.

At this point in the film, there is a transition into documentary-style talking-head interviews, with a focus on Don Allais, a real priest linked to the center, who offers us his crude account of the situation: "The issue of lodging [for the workers] is grave, but it is not the only one." The priest informs Fortunato that in the past the EISS had sent a letter to all the bishops of southern Italy so that they could warn those who intended to come to Turin about the great problems that they would encounter. "The risk of coming to Turin," says the priest, "is too great. These are absurd things that happen in a society that knows very well how to progress from the technical point of view, but cannot solve human problems." The priest is tasked with giving a voice to the critical consciousness of the film, to its revolutionary message: "[You] will realize that you are actually a pawn called from a thousand or one thousand five hundred kilometers away because production needs you, and you will be the last to have the advantages of this society that called you. This is the sad situation."[12] From this point of view, the film manages to ably combine the denunciation typical of political cinema in the 1960s and 1970s in Italy (with authors like Francesco Rosi, Gillo Pontecorvo and Elio Petri, to give a few examples) and the social denunciation style that was valued in investigative journalism during those years. But Don Allais' scene seems to serve an additional educational purpose. Directly addressing Fortunato—and implicitly the viewers,[13] who are mostly workers like Fortunato—Don Allais is warning the southern masses waiting for their chance to move north.

Peter Bondanella asserts that *Trevico-Torino* "represents a nod to Italy's neorealist heritage in cinema" and "creates compelling reconstruction of the alienated existence of southern immigrants in Turin who work on the assembly lines in Italy's most important industrial complex."[14] This nod to the ways and the ideological domain of Italian neorealist heritage comes together with Scola's intimate southern identity and consciousness. As a southerner himself, he seems to be even more invested in trying to use the cinematic medium as a way to improve migrants' lives in the north and, more important, to convince the underdeveloped masses of the south to work toward a better and more just society back home.

Trevico-Torino, with its commitment to denouncing the inhuman conditions of migrant workers, ended up being perceived as excessively political and didactic. Ennio Bíspuri notes that *Trevico-Torino* was neither appreciated on the left nor on the right: "Paolo Valmarana caught an excess of gloom and pessimism in the film, while Goffredo Fofi judged it 'a film for children' due to an 'excess of spectacular craftiness.' It is as if, perhaps as a result of the epoch when the film was conceived and shot ... the story, very linearly and elementarily told, exhibits a clear prejudice that, in presenting us a predictable product, detracts from the final result."[15] Diego Novelli,[16] who had worked on the film, highlights this "demonstrative" function, affirming that the young Fortunato, by Scola's intention, was the pretext for helping the viewer to understand "the reality of Turin in those years: a city plagued with deep issues, where individualism and egotism had abated their own popular conscience."[17]

Scola's 1982 documentary *Vorrei che volo* was conceived as a return to the setting of *Trevico-Torino*. Turin once more became a protagonist, seen through the eyes of a young child of southern migrants, who crosses the city a bit like Bruno in *Ladri di biciclette* (*Bicycle Thieves*, Vittorio De Sica, 1948).

This time, however, the child commits petty thefts instead of searching for his father's stolen bicycle. The camera in *Vorrei che volo* follows the child, and in the meantime adults and children tell their stories, sometimes about their successes and sometimes about their failures at integration and social advancement. Interviewees make references to petty crime, prostitution, and the death of a young person at the hands of the police, but they also tell stories of urban housing cooperatives, experiments in socialization of artistic and cultural activities, restructuring buildings to create cultural places, reception centers for young mothers, and so on.

Turin, Factory City of the Anthropocene

Trevico-Torino is a film that narrates (a journey into) the alienation of the average factory worker, but more specifically, it presents a process that we may call the "multiplication of the factory" and the emergence of the *fabbrica sociale* (literally, social factory), which are made visible to the audience. This critique of industrial capitalism is aimed at individuating and underlining the effects of factory life *outside* the manufactory plants. The existence of this dynamic was something that had been posited in Italy in the late 1960s by workerist theorists such as Mario Tronti and Toni Negri and by the Autonomia Operaia radical movement, which even today has an impact on some analyses of the relationship between work and everyday life spaces.[18] As Tronti states: "When the factory seizes the whole of society—all of social production is turned into industrial production—the specific traits of the factory are lost within the generic traits of society. When the whole of society is reduced to the factory, the factory—as such—appears to *disappear*. It is on this material basis that is repeated and concludes, at a real higher level, the maximum ideological development of bourgeois metamorphoses."[19] For Tronti and the workerists, the factory transcends its material walls and conquers the spaces of everyday life. When there is no longer a discernible internal-external divide between private life and the processes of production, alienation of the worker can happen outside of the factory spaces as well. However, the autonomists were not the only ones who understood the problematic relationship between factory and social life. Henri Lefebvre, in *The Production of Space*, studies how the flows and the operations of capital construct space on both local and global levels:

In the traditional industrial production process, the relationship to space had long been comprised of discrete points: the place of extraction or origin of raw materials, the place of production (factory), and the place of sale. Only the distribution networks of this system had a wider spatial dimension. Now that the "elements" themselves are produced and reproduced, however, the relationship of productive activity to space is modified; it involved space now in another way, and this is as true for the initial stages of the process (for example, the management of water and water resources) as it is for the final stages (within urban space) and for all the steps in between.[20]

Following Lefebvre's reasoning and adopting his perspective to rethink Turin and its evolutions through the twentieth century, we can start to map the various effects that a colossal factory such as FIAT has had on its urban texture. More important, FIAT's productive output itself (cars) from one side required a mobilization of immense resources, both living (the workers and their families and the proliferation of the so-called *indotto*[21] industry) and nonliving (metal, hydrocarbon fuels, plastic materials, etc.), and from the other side created one of the necessary conditions for the multiplication of the urban space itself (fast, individualized transportation) along with the aesthetic connotations connected with modern urban living (traffic, engine noises, the smell of burnt petrol). The separation of the spaces of production, consumption, and living is made problematic by the dynamics of labor division in post-Fordist societies, as Lefebvre points out:

> The urban fabric, with its multiple networks of communication and exchange, is likewise part of the means of production. The town and its multifarious establishments (its post offices and railway stations—as also its storehouses, transportation systems and varied services) are fixed capital. The division of labor affects the whole of space—not just the "space of work," not just the factory floor. And the whole of space is an object of productive consumption, just like factory buildings and plants, machinery, raw materials, and labor power itself.[22]

The concept of a social factory, in which the social sphere of everyday life is captured by the productive forces of capital and eventually transforms the subconscious of workers, is portrayed in Scola's film through cinematic devices such as juxtapositions and montage and by a skillful use of the mise-en-scène, as Scola's camera explores several public and intimate spaces in Turin. What we see in the film is not just the story of Fortunato's struggle to integrate in a new city but also the simultaneous metamorphoses of the urban landscape of Turin turning itself into a giant, infinite factory. This dual transformation is made even more evident by the fact that Scola was unable to film inside the actual FIAT assembly lines in Mirafiori, forcing him to express Fortunato's journey using exclusively the nonindustrial spaces of Turin, such as private houses, train stations, marketplaces, churches, and of course the gates of the factory. *Trevico-Torino* emerges as a film about industrial labor told from the perspective of someone who is excluded from it. Watching Scola's film, Harun Farocki's study on the fascination of early cinema with the factory's external space comes to mind:

> The first camera in the history of cinema was pointed at a factory, but a century later it can be said that film is hardly drawn to the factory and is even repelled by it. Films about work or workers have not become one of the main genres, and the space in front of the factory has remained on the sidelines. Most narrative films take place in that part of life where work has been left behind. Everything which makes the industrial form of production superior to others—the division of labor into minute stages, the constant repetition, a degree of organization which demands few decisions of the individual and which leaves him little room for maneuver—all this makes it hard to demonstrate changes in circumstances.[23]

In a way, *Trevico-Torino* proves that such a fascination did not cease because of the evolution of cinematic tastes and themes but rather because the factory disappeared into the fabric of society itself. The gates of the FIAT are not the gates of Mirafiori anymore, but as we sense from watching *Trevico-Torino*, the new gates of FIAT come to be represented by the train station of Porta Nuova (literally, New Gate) itself. In the numerous dialogue and interview scenes, Scola's camera and his cinematic vision try to blend in with the environment, as what we see in *Trevico-Torino* is a piece of industrial fiction represented through the use of cinema verité aesthetics. In this sense, the film becomes even more compelling considering what is left outside of the shot and what constitutes the background of the film's scenes: passersby, cars, pollution, workers leaving the factory, urban noise, and the semiotic complexity of the city. Considering the richness of life in the urban landscape, can we still consider this landscape a mere backdrop and not, instead, the embodiment of the coemergence of all the subjects and agencies involved in the industrial capitalist project? This is a participated, intertextual example of storytelling set inside a bigger, all-encompassing factory in which the productive relations are staged: Turin the factory-city. The film, together with Fortunato's journey, tells the story of its constant mutation and transformation.

Curiously enough, a similar metamorphosis had been previously shown in a completely different film: the 1969 British comedy *The Italian Job*, directed by Peter Collinson. In some of its most memorable scenes, three Mini Coopers appropriate Turin's spaces of everyday life (the market place, the Subalpina, and the San Federico gallery, the Valentino Park, and the *portici* of Piazza Vittorio) in an act of subversion of urban spaces. Once nonliving products of the industrial city itself, now the cars dominate and impose their spatial logic on the urban texture. *The Italian Job* has a well-known sequence of a police chase, in which a fast-paced montage (so ideologically and radically opposed to Jean-Luc Godard's famous *Weekend* (1967) horizontal traffic shot) shows the Mini Coopers making use of sidewalks, parks, and all sorts of surfaces normally limited for human use while at the same time depicting the suburbs of Turin as sprawls of cheerful, playful, gray concrete.

But if *The Italian Job* aims to show a joyful, nonalienated version of Turin as the industrial motor city par excellence, *Trevico-Torino*, by contrast, critiques the invisible and silent propagation of the factory as the main spatial logic of industrial capitalism. The expansive dynamic of the factory is, of course, not just allegorical or ideological, but it is also material, as it presents itself, among other things, through the effects of atmospheric pollution, the creation of waste materials, and the development of new neighborhoods. It is to be noted that forty-four years after the film was shot, Turin—once the quintessential industrial city but now the emblem of Western postindustrial urban renewal efforts—still suffers from its troubled relationship with the automotive industry. This relationship becomes evident, for example, if one analyzes the recent pollution crisis of 2017[24] or the unstoppable demographic decline of Turin.[25]

The mise-en-scène and the double nature (documentary and fiction) of *Trevico-Torino*, helped Scola translate into images a difficult bundle of ideas. In a certain sense, the film can be seen as a strategic tool for critiquing the factory space rather than exclusively the equally important issue of southerners' diaspora. Scola understood well the ideological potential of film for social inquiry, and he moved toward a cinematic medium that is more of a hybrid educational piece of technology than a means of purely creative expression. *Trevico-Torino* mixes interviews with fiction, diegetic and nondiegetic sound, actors, and real workers (and real homeless people) as a way to convey ideological meaning. The film openly becomes an educational tool for the masses to be shown to target audiences in specific places (labor unions, PCI houses, *dopolavoro* [the union's recreational programs], etc.)

The voyage into and through "Fiat-nam" has deep consequences. The transformations coming from this journey emerge in the film both as mise-en-scène and as allegorical devices, which illustrate the hybridizing and the melding of the human (represented by Fortunato and his companions) with the industrial, inorganic, polluted reality of Turin. The city's pollution is never explicitly addressed in the movie, but it is, of course, always present. In the panoramic shots of Porta Palazzo and the Mirafiori factory complex we can see and feel the grayish presence of burnt carbon fossils. In other scenes, we see the smog generated by thousands of cars, specifically, in parts of the city that today are closed to traffic (due to the antipollution city policies of the 1990s). Visual culture theorist Nicholas Mirzoeff proposes that the Anthropocene can be visualized by changing the way we look back at visual art. For example, addressing pollution (of water and air) in New York and London, he writes in his study of Bellow's 1907 painting *Forty-Two Kids*: "While the 'great unwashed' working classes might have been expected to be willing to live with dirt and smells, so too were New York's elites. It appears that the desire to live in the modern city was so great that it literally anaesthetized the senses, or at least allowed people to disregard what they saw and smelled in the water. . . . London was afflicted with dense smogs produced by burning coal. . . . This persistent smog became a feature of London life."[26] Mirzoeff concludes that by subtly invading the representations of the modern metropolis and anesthetizing its inhabitants to the inevitability of its existence, air pollution becomes a marker for acquired modernity, as the "imperial smoke is a positive sign of the energy and vitality of the modern metropole."[27] In *Trevico-Torino*, the pollution has a similar function. It is a mute agent, constantly present, signifying the postwar conquest of Italian modernity. Fortunato wanders in a pre-postapocalyptic[28] Turin, suffocated by carbon dioxide emissions, is still a city that is vital, growing, and thriving.

The process of manufacturing always intrinsically corresponds to a process of transformation of raw materials into commodities. Moreover, the automobile, a quintessential symbol of urban life, is itself the object that thousands of young workers from the rural south came to assemble, in a sort of quest for the conquest of modernity. The assembly line, though, does not exclusively turn metal into cars; it also has serious psychological and physical effects on workers.[29] This double relation of capital and labor, in which the manipulation of matter and the dematerialization of the human happen simultaneously in the factory-city, is represented in *Trevico-Torino* through Fortunato's unfortunate struggles to fit in.

Through Fortunato's misfortunes, we see the effects of this process on Turin's landscape (coincidentally soundscape, as the car engines' noises are constantly present in the film) and on the bodies that inhabit it. Workers' survival in such a hellish milieu is completely dedicated to the functioning of the factory, represented by Scola as the beholding eye of FIAT surveilling the land and the workers like an assembly-line panoptical device. The immigrant workers in the film are gradually characterized as tools of production, similarly to how animals could have been depicted in a preindustrialized world. Their life and well-being are devoted to and depend on the volume of industrial production and the successful propagation of the city-factory itself. Through their labor and their bodies, FIAT configures itself as an agent of geological proportions, an active assemblage of the Anthropocene that transforms inorganic matter and *bios* (the living matter, both human and nonhuman) alike into machines and commodities that are ultimately microscopically and biochemically responsible for the geological transformations of the planet itself. FIAT transforms the bodies of the workers into tools for production while at the same time allocating spaces for their material existence, multiplying the space of the city itself. Through the management and manipulation of workers and of inorganic and living matter—exponentially multiplied by the basic algorithmic operations of capital—the city-factory grows, transforms itself, and ultimately establishes itself as the hegemonic chronotope of industrial capitalism. As represented by Scola, humans and machines coexist as their voices intertwine in the diegetic and nondiegetic soundscapes of the movie.

Like postapocalyptic antiheroes who roam the scorched earth looking for shelter and food, Fortunato wanders from location to location looking for accommodation and human interaction but eventually fails. In this journey, he meets other wretched denizens of the interstitial spaces of Turin: prostitutes, thieves, and lunatics. They inhabit the same train stations, squares, and streets that today have been repurposed by postindustrial capital into shopping centers, fancy nightlife spots, luxury department stores, and so forth. The city is the paradigmatic place where we visualize the story of the individual clashing and melding into the history of the material phenomena produced by the ruling and the exploited classes through the centuries. Fortunato wanders through medieval, baroque, and neoclassical milieus that in different ages hosted narratives of exploitation and liberation, played by the conflicting historical agents that gave shape to the following metanetworks: feudalism, capitalism, aristocracy, religious power, bourgeoisie, fascism, the rise of the industrial complex, and the hegemonic cultural apparatus.

Fortunato is offered a room to rent by a Piedmontese-speaking Torinese, but it turns out to be a mere tool shack, an unhospitable coal chamber. This scene establishes a strong connection between Fortunato's body and its configuration as a source of energy for the functioning of FIAT. The Anthropocene, here represented by the city-factory sprawl, is a geological expression of a structure of power, in this case industrial capitalism. Following Serenella Iovino's analysis of Calvino's *Marcovaldo*,[30] we can say that Fortunato, like Marcovaldo in the book,[31] is part of the processes of the Anthropocene, but he cannot be the *anthropos* of the Anthropocene because he has barely any conscious or active part in it—he can only struggle to survive in a new planet reconfigured by industrial capital.

The final scene of the film, more than any other, helps us understand this narrative. In it, Fortunato expresses all his frustration and sense of failure derived from his experience as an immigrant and factory worker in Turin. His closing monologue is a final assessment on what he has lost and what he has gained by moving to the north and becoming a dehumanized tool of the FIAT assembly line. The form of a spoken, open letter to other potential immigrants from the south adds a dramatic tone to the scene before transitioning into a bitter, more general reflection of the situation of the working class in Italy.

The most interesting technical aspects are the interaction of montage, sound, and pace, as well as the use of geometry in the construction of the scene. The straight lines traced by the factory buildings and the steel infrastructure serve as the spatial demarcation and boundaries of Fortunato's run. The camera alternates frontal and side shots of Fortunato, presenting the perspective vanishing point at the center of the image in a fashion similar to Giorgio De Chirico's metaphysical paintings. All these elements are used to express the final loss of his human dignity and his definitive, humiliating transformation into a production commodity owned by the factory.

Fortunato is running alone on a street, without a purpose or goal. He is carrying a briefcase and seems to have a direction, although that direction is very much circumscribed by the physical environment around him: a line of cars, a wall, and the junkyard. His run alludes to a sort of escape effort, and a factory crane carrying unidentified metallic junk follows the movements of Fortunato in a parallel way. The camera moves along with Fortunato, eventually closing up on his gradually grieving face. Montage cuts alternate close-ups of Fortunato's face and images of quickly passing buildings, parked cars, and the moving crane itself. Simultaneously, and interacting with the montage, increasing industrial sounds produce a distressing feeling in the viewer, who can feel Fortunato's existential anguish. The industrial percussion noise works like a metronome directing the timing of the editing cuts and general pace of the scene. Climax is suddenly reached at the moment when the crane stops and releases all the iron and metallic junk it was carrying. At the same time, Fortunato collapses to the ground as if he had been shot in the chest, but the camera delays its own stop, hinting at an expression of nonhuman surprise. This is an example of Scola's humanized camera gaze; it is as if the camera were Fortunato's companion following his run. When Fortunato falls to the ground, the camera slows down and directs its gaze back at him, then slowly zooms in on him. Even if different possible interpretations can be made of the first part of the final scene, they all point in the same direction. Montage and close-ups create an effect of socioallegorical representation between Fortunato and the crane, suggesting that he is now just as much a tool of production, a mechanized drone of FIAT. An additional, more convincing interpretation is plausible. Fortunato is indeed a tool, but the director encourages the viewer to compare Fortunato's condition with the metallic junk carried by the crane: life in the city-factory will turn Fortunato's human body into an old, obsolete and unusable piece of junk. It is worth noting that on Fortunato's left we are shown the raw material (the metallic junk of the *ferriere*) and on his right we see a long, interminable line of new Fiat 500s. This placement represents the transition of the worker from being a free individual to being a disposable resource for industrial production. At the same time, a new layer of meaning is added to the title *Viaggio nel Fiat-nam*. The director evokes the Vietnam War in order to impel the viewer to consider the similarities of the conditions of the factory workers and soldiers, who are both disposable and bound to obedience to a higher bourgeois hegemonic ideology. Fortunato's definitive "absorption in the every-day silent, ruthless and with no-way-out war that is the Vietnam of the working class becomes the symbol and the conclusion of a story that allusively synthetizes the dramatic existence in a world dominated by the profit logic."[32] The fall of Fortunato can be indeed compared to the fall of a soldier in a war movie, and it is uncannily similar to the famous sequence of Pina's death from Rossellini's *Roma città aperta* (*Rome Open City*, 1945) in that Fortunato's fall is captured by the camera from a similar point of view. But if the cold-blooded murder of Pina, a woman and a mother, in *Roma città aperta* was Rossellini's way to expose the brutality of Nazi-fascist occupation (and the impotence of an entire city)[33] in *Trevico-Torino*'s ending, Fortunato runs, then falls, but eventually gets back on his feet. This final, dignified deed of endurance serves as Scola's tribute to the southern immigrants' resilience. Montage, parallel images and movement, the fast pace, and the ascending climax are all effective strategies in Scola's project of denouncing the alienating dynamics of factory life.

In the second part of the scene, Fortunato stands up from the ground and while crying reaches for his food, but this extreme human act is interrupted once again by the intervention of the crane and its release of metal waste. Emotional collapse is irreversible now. Fortunato screams and cries, "Basta! Basta!" but his voice is covered by industrial noise, and he ultimately understands that he only has two paths ahead: one path leads back to the poor life in the south; the other is giving up and resuming his new life in the factory-city system. The crane relentlessly "watches" his desperate struggle, and similar to the logo earlier in the film, it stands as a representation of FIAT itself or of its metaphorical surveillance function, an animus. Initially, Fortunato starts walking back, but a montage cut shows the crane moving in the opposite direction, as if it were imposing an order. Fortunato then changes his path and, obeying the higher authority of the crane/FIAT, he slowly walks away and back into a life of alienation while the word *Fine* (The end) appears on the screen. The second segment is formally opposite to the first one. If the first one comprises of fast movement and dynamic montage, the second basically consists of a single, very slow, long shot. The camera does not move; it stops when Fortunato falls to the ground and does not follow him anymore. He walks away from the viewer and from the camera. We are not able to see him while he walks back into the factory. We now have a static point of view as opposed to the fast dynamism of the previous part of the scene, contributing to a strong feeling of abandonment. In addition, in the second part of the scene the incoherent relationship between image and sound is even more evident. We see Fortunato screaming and we understand perfectly the words that he is trying to express, but there is no sound (or at least, there is no human sound). The sound editing overlaps the metallic noises with Fortunato's screams, creating the astonishing effect of giving a new inorganic, metallic voice to the flesh-and-blood immigrant worker. In this way, Scola expresses industrial alienation on an intimate level and Fortunato's slow automatized, dehumanized, defeated walk toward the end is just the obvious outcome of this process.

Often disregarded as an excessively ideological and didactic movie, *Trevico-Torino* has received little critical attention and scarce scholarship thus far. The strengths of Scola's cinematography, beyond the way it represents its main story and characters, are also to be found in what it represents in its background. *Trevico-Torino* is indeed a unique piece of genuine storytelling that, thanks to its dual form of fiction and documentary filmmaking, is able to capture a crucial moment of the development of urban life in Italy and, more specifically, the huge transformations of Turin. In the postindustrial, multicultural present of the city, it is easy to forget its dramatic past in which thousands of Fortunatos journeyed toward Fiat-nam. Today the city's leaders try to cope with the constantly diminishing presence of the factory in the life of the city. What is the future of a factory-city that loses its factory? Looking back at *Trevico-Torino* and the warnings that Scola tried to voice, we are left with the bitter realization that the Turinese who were born after the 1970s have known only a version of the city that owes its momentary economic stability and its exponential growth to the sacrifice of the many Fortunatos who served in the FIAT assembly lines. Today FIAT has abandoned Turin, but the radical transformations that it imposed on it (in order to function properly) will remain, just like structures of past hegemonic forces such as baroque churches, the nineteenth-century squares, and the tombs of the Savoy dynasty.

Notes

1. Founded in 1963, Unitelefilm was tasked by the PCI with collecting and conserving the party's film production. It also produced its own autonomous content. See Archivio Aamod, Archivio Audiovisivo del Movimento Operaio e Democratico, www.aamod.it.
2. The Anthropocene is the epoch in which humans become a transformative geological force, following Paul J. Crutzen's original formulation in his "Geology of Mankind: The Anthropocene," *Nature* 415 (2002): 23.
3. Gianni's Amelio's *Così ridevano* (*The Way We Laughed*, 1998) tells the story of Sicilian brothers in Turin during the years of the economic boom.
4. All film quotes are taken from the original script: Ettore Scola, *Trevico Torino. Testo*, Archivio Luce, 1972, http://image.archivioluce.com/dm_o/IL/luceAamod/allegati/860/000/2014/860.000.2014.0002.pdf.
5. See also Paola Micheli, *Ettore Scola: I film e le parole* (Rome: Bulzoni, 1994), 32. Micheli notes that Scola makes it clear to the viewer that his protagonist is out of place, not only through images of the young immigrant's arrival to the city but also through this linguistic contrast. Translations throughout the chapter are our own unless otherwise noted.
6. Lotta Continua, a far-Left extraparliamentary organization, was constituted in 1969 by members of the student-worker movement of Turin.
7. Tullio Masoni, "La commedia: Primi segnali di decadenza," in *Storia del cinema italiano*, ed. Vito Zagarrio, vol. 13, *1977–1985* (Venice: Marsilio, 2005), 111. Regarding the "incommunicability of class" between Vicky and Fortunato, see Italo Moscati, "*Trevico-Torino* di Ettore Scola," *Letture 1973* 27, no. 12. (1972): 889–91, 890.
8. Nicola Pizzolato, "Workers and Revolutionaries at the Twilights of Fordism: The Breakdown of Industrial Relations in the Automobile Plants of Detroit and Turin, 1967–1973," *Labor History* 45, no. 4 (2004): 419–43, 421. Pizzolato continues in reference to the close relationship between immigrants and the city: "The intense pace of new arrivals heightened competition for the insufficient housing, providing migrants with expensive and shabby accommodations. Because newcomers arrived often through a migratory chain, overcrowding of single-family units further dilapidated the city's housing stock. Likewise, in the job market, migrants entered in competition, primarily among themselves, for hazardous and intermittent occupations" (423).

9. Antiauthoritarian protests and social conflicts erupted in 1968 in many capitalist countries. In Italy in particular, a clash between students and police (known as the battle of Valle Giulia) took place in Rome on March 1, 1968. Italian students closed the University of Rome for many days during an antiwar protest. Following the students' protests, in 1969 factory workers went on strike in many areas of Italy. The historical upheaval of those years is referred to as "Il '68," "The '68."
10. FIAT prohibited shooting film inside the factory, so the director used only external shots. To give a sense of the interior, he turned to a photograph that served as the background of the titles of the film's various chapters.
11. "Pedinamento" (shadowing, or stalking) was a concept used by Cesare Zavattini to describe a new model of filmmaking after World War II. He believed that the time was ripe to throw away scripts and follow (*pedinare*) men in the streets with a camera, meaning that life was going to appear on the screen by itself, without filters. See Cesare Zavattini, *Neorealismo ecc.*, ed. Mino Argentieri (Milan: Bompiani, 1979).
12. Don Allais continues: "The immigrant is not accustomed to the work setting, not prepared to confront the conditions and rhythms of the work, to work indoors; therefore . . . he will suffer grave discomfort at the beginning . . . you prepare for this and you talk about it with your friends, they inform you. You make sure to join them . . . at all of those protests, just in case at one protest, today you will win and the factory will provide better working conditions."
13. The film was intended to be shown in Labor Union and PCI clubs and films festivals.
14. Scola shot the film with Diego Novelli, who at the time was the editor in chief of the communist newspaper *L'Unità* and later was elected mayor of Turin. For more on the relationship between Italian filmmakers and the PCI, the labor union Confederazione Generale Italiana del Lavoro (Italian General Confederation of Labour), Unitelefilm, and Cesare Zavattini's animated newsreels, see Goffredo Fofi et al., eds., *Storia del cinema: Dalle nouvelle vagues ai nostri giorni*, vol. 3 (Milan: Garzanti, 1988), 374.
15. Ennio Bíspuri, *Ettore Scola: Un umanista nel cinema italiano* (Rome: Bulzoni, 2006), 206–7. As Bíspuri himself recalls, Scola knew well which ideas he wanted to convey in *Trevico-Torino*: "The civility of the automobile has given Italy another record: the European city with the most highways and the fewest hospitals, least schools . . . least efficient public services. . . . The degradation of the nation has its eye on Turin." Aldo Tassone, *Parla il cinema* italiano, vol. 2 (Milan: Il Formichiere, 1980), 311.
16. Novelli was the mayor of Turin from 1975 to 1985. As a member of the PCI, he founded the magazine *Nuova Società* and published several books about Turin and FIAT.

17. Novelli continues: "The original characteristics of the Turin laborer were lost thanks to tumultuous, disorganized growth (wrongly labeled 'development') that only obeyed the demands of industrial production, breaking, shattering unity in the community." Diego Novelli, "Il caso Trevico-Torino," in *Trevico-Cinecittà: L'avventuroso viaggio di Ettore Scola*, ed. Vito Zagarrio (Venice: Marsilio, 2002), 116–19, 117.
18. For example, see the outstanding Melissa Gregg, *Work's Intimacy* (New York: John Wiley, 2011).
19. Tronti, Mario. "Factory and Society," *Operaismo in English*, June 13, 2013, https://operaismoinenglish.wordpress.com/2013/06/13/factory-and-society/.
20. Henri Lefebvre, *The Production of Space* (Malden, MA: Blackwell, 1991), 330.
21. Secondary autonomous factories that manufacture items needed by the primary factory (in this case FIAT).
22. Lefebvre, *Production of Space*, 347.
23. Harun Farocki, "Workers Leaving the Factory," *Senses of Cinema* 21 (July 2002), http://sensesofcinema.com/2002/harun-farocki/farocki_workers/. Harun Farocki in his 2002 essay and in his 1995 documentary *Workers Leaving the Factory* references many instances in which film directors turned their attention toward the external spaces of the factories, both in European and in American cinema. The first film ever by the Lumiere brothers, *La sortie de l'usine Lumière à Lyon*, 1895 (*Exiting the Factory*), was a forty-six-second recording of the Lumiere factory workers ending their workday and leaving for their homes.
24. "Smog-Hit Turin Blocks Euro 5 Cars," Ansa.it, October 20, 2017, http://www.ansa.it/english/news/2017/10/20/smog-hit-turin-blocks-euro-5-cars-3_cddeaec2-4558-44f8-bfb8-0658fe9b45bf.html.
25. Total population changed from 1,167,968 to 872,367 in the 1981–2011 period. See "Censimento popolazione Torino 1861–2011," Tuttitalia.it, accessed January 24, 2019, http://www.tuttitalia.it/piemonte/72-torino/statistiche/censimenti-popolazione/.
26. Nicholas Mirzoeff, "Visualizing the Anthropocene," *Public Culture* 26, no. 2 (2014): 213–32, 224.
27. Mirzoeff, 226.
28. The city of *Trevico-Torino* is pre-postapocalyptic in the sense that it eerily shows the signs of a disaster about to come (pollution, alienation, etc.), while at the same time presenting it in a moment in which these signs do not signify an imminent danger yet.
29. This dual relationship between the assembly line and the worker has been the topic of several classic films such as Charlie Chaplin's *Modern Times* (1936) and Elio Petri's *La classe operaia va in paradiso* (1971). The latter is fittingly known as *Lulu the Tool* in English-speaking countries.

30. Serenella Iovino, "Sedimenting Stories: Italo Calvino and the Extraordinary Strata of the Anthropocene," *Neohelicon* 44, no. 2 (2017): 315–30.
31. Italo Calvino, *Marcovaldo, ovvero le stagioni in città* (Milan: Mondadori, 2002).
32. Bíspuri, *Ettore Scola*, 211.
33. In *Trevico-Torino*'s ending, the parked cars on the side of the road are nonhuman witnesses to Fortunato's fall. In Pina's death, the city of Rome, represented by the faceless, formless people in the crowd who are being held back by German soldiers, must impotently watch her death. The connection here can be found in their equal lack of agency.

GENTE DI ROMA UNDER THE EFFECT OF FEDERICO FELLINI'S ROME

Marina Vargau

THE FILMS OF FEDERICO Fellini and Ettore Scola play a critical role in making Rome a cinematic city par excellence.[1] In many of their films, the city provides the setting and serves as a protagonist, taking up a central and powerful position in their cinematic poetics. Even though the respective poetics of these two auteurs have been analyzed separately in the past,[2] bringing them together invites new reflections. Scola intended through several of his films, especially in *Gente di Roma* (*People of Rome*, 2003), to establish and develop a dialogue on Rome with Fellini. This filmic dialogue is the result of the complex encounter between their personalities, their careers, and their cinemas.[3] After briefly discussing the analogies between their careers and their cinematic poetics with regard to Rome and its people, this chapter examines the effect of Fellini's Rome on *Gente di Roma* and illustrates how Scola responded in particular to Fellini's portrayal of Rome in *Block-notes di un regista* (*Fellini: A Director's Notebook*, 1969) and *Roma* (1972). Scola's Rome is constructed with the same primordial elements as Fellini's Rome: flânerie, spectacle, and memory.[4] Moreover, the Felliniesque effect is present in both the form and in the structure of *Gente di Roma*—which are fragmentary and discontinuous— in which we recognize familiar Felliniesque figures and sequences, realized or only ideated.

From the start, it is important to specify that the present study uses the concepts of encounter, dialogue, and effect in their respective Deleuzian meanings. As Gilles Deleuze illustrates in his dialogues with Claire Parnet, the absolute solitude necessary for philosophical work is populated by encounters with people, movements, ideas, events, and entities, all things that have proper names that designate an effect, "something which passes or happens between two as though under a potential difference."[5] In his vocabulary, encounters are the same as "becomings" or "nuptials," when "to become is never to imitate, nor to 'do like,' nor to conform to the model."[6] Founded on dialogue, the effect supposes "finding, encountering, stealing instead of regulating, recognizing, and judging."[7]

Inspired by these Deleuzian concepts, I interpret cinematic work as being similar to philosophical work. In this sense, I propose to read the relations between Scola's cinematic Rome and Fellini's Rome as an encounter and a dialogue. I interpret the effect of Fellini's Rome on Scola's vision of the city in terms of finding, encountering, and appropriating. Contrary to the concept of influence, highly criticized in the recent past by Michel Foucault, Harold Bloom and Umberto Eco,[8] the effect is a dynamic process, a "becoming," in Deleuzian terms, which supposes the production of a new type of creation, from something already existing. Furthermore, effect also implies analytical work on the continuing potentialities in a work of art, which can resurface at different degrees of intensity. Consequently, these processes imply a series of repetitions. Inspired always by Deleuze, for whom repetition, in its complexity, is rich, differentiated, and never the same,[9] I analyze how Scola succeeds in making an original work by repeating some elements, sequences, and figures of Fellini's Rome. In order to exemplify this meaning through my analyses, I argue that while at first Fellini's Roman poetics is appropriated by Scola, the latter finally delivers in *Gente di Roma* a new cinematic vision of Rome.

The choice of the term *flânerie* is inspired by Walter Benjamin in his seminal texts on the figure of the flâneur.[10] Thanks to his theoretical work, the nineteenth-century Parisian idler has become the emblematic and paradigmatic figure of urban modernity. In Benjamin, this urban figure allows us to correlate the flânerie, or stroll, as a practice of urban space with the spectacle of the street and arcades and also with the memory evoked by the spaces traversed. Through this conceptual work, Fellini's films appear all the more relevant, since his flâneur shows similarities to Benjamin's, notably in how it links flânerie, spectacle, and memory and how it is composed of a series of characters: aesthete, physiognomist, sociologist, journalist, detective, suspect, archaeologist, and collector. However, the differences between Benjamin's and

Fellini's flâneurs are worth noting: for example, in Fellini's Roman films, we find the presence of a new character, the flâneur-filmmaker. In addition, the flâneur of Fellini comes from a long series of Roman flâneurs that dates back to ancient Rome.[11] Scola's *Gente di Roma* reworks some ideas appropriated from Fellini in order to create his own cinematographic flâneur.

Fellini, Scola, and Rome

The paths of Scola and Fellini show surprising parallels: first as draftsmen and caricaturists for the satirical magazine *Marc'Aurelio*, subsequently as authors of radio texts and cowriters for many films, and eventually as internationally recognized filmmakers.[12] Ennio Bíspuri identifies some common aesthetic and ethical characteristics in their films, such as the assimilation of and transcending of the neorealist lesson, the concern for spectacle and variety theater, the comic and satirical dimension typical of their cinematic signatures, and an interest in the psychology of the characters. Bíspuri also emphasizes that the idea of a cinema founded on creation and fantastic invention is common to both directors.[13]

Beyond these analogies, both filmmakers made Rome the privileged space of their filmographies. As Bíspuri notes, this city is the core of the Felliniesque poetics and the "ideal geography" for Scola,[14] who anchors here the thematics that constantly interest him, such as friendship, love, time, history, and social problems. Fellini and Scola show an unconditional lifetime attachment to their adoptive city, which they constantly explored throughout their filmographies. As two provincials who arrived in Rome—Fellini from Rimini in 1938, Scola from Trevico in 1936—both filmmakers made their provincial gaze an asset in their filmographies when addressing the city, which appears for them to be more marvelous than in reality. In films by both auteurs—Fellini's *La dolce vita* (1960), *Roma*, and *Intervista* (1987) and Scola's *C'eravamo tanto amati* (*We Loved Each Other So Much*, 1974) *Brutti, sporchi e cattivi* (*Down and Dirty*, 1976), *Gente di Roma*—the city of Rome, with its architecture, squares, monuments, theaters, *borgate* (working-class suburbs), and so on, is presented as much a protagonist as the human characters. For instance, Via Veneto—with its lively nightlife at luxurious hotels, restaurants, and cafes, frequented by foreigners, stars, and paparazzi—functions as a key protagonist in *La dolce vita*.[15] Correspondingly, the imposing structure of the Palazzo Federici in

Scola's *Una giornata particolare* (*A Special Day*, 1977), which allows residents to watch one another's movements, acquires an important status in the film, almost on the level of a human protagonist as it frames and enhances the solitude of Antonietta (Sophia Loren) and Gabriele (Marcello Mastroianni).

Apart from these similarities, a comparison of their respective filmographies allows us to identify clear differences between their poetics of Rome. Fellini, although interested in several temporalities of Rome, from antiquity until the twentieth century, built a highly poetic and unitary vision of the city. In Fellini's vision, historical realities are glimpsed through the dense veils of fiction, invention, and dream, the result being a personal work with universal appeal.[16] By contrast, in Scola's films, this unity of vision is absent because, over time, he proposes several distinct images of Rome. Their diversity is not explained by the fact that Scola deals with discrete periods of the past (in his Roman films, he focuses primarily on the twentieth century), but by the fact that he explores different aesthetic registers, such as the *commedia all'italiana*, the grotesque and the monstrous (*Brutti, sporchi e cattivi*), and documentary style in fictional works (*Gente di Roma*). This diversity also manifests itself in the time of narration in Scola's films, which varies from an action concentrated in one day (*Una giornata particolare, Gente di Roma*) to historical frescoes covering several decades (*C'eravamo tanto amati, La famiglia/The Family*, 1987).

Another difference between their poetics concerns the choice of shooting in the studio or in natural settings. While Fellini, from *La dolce vita* onward, always re-creates Rome at Cinecittà, Scola alternates between filming in the studios (*La terrazza/The Terrace*, 1980; *La famiglia*; *La cena/The Dinner*, 1998) and on location (*Dramma della gelosia—tutti i particolari in cronaca/The Pizza Triangle*, 1970; *C'eravamo tanto amati*; *Gente di Roma*).[17] With these characteristics and qualities, although Scola's Rome appears less coherent than Fellini's, it also seems more verisimilar. For example, in *Gente di Roma*, Scola at times adopts a documentary style of filmmaking as he films numerous street scenes full of extras (bus passengers, pedestrians, etc.) with a handheld digital camera. Discussing this difference, Scola specifies that his inspiration is "more neo-realistic, more in direct contact with life and reality, thus with the city"; Fellini instead "has to relinquish Rome as it is: he re-creates it, and the one that he creates in the studio is sometimes more true than the real city."[18] Emphasizing that he is a realistic filmmaker, Scola adds: "In my movies, Rome is always present because I make a type of cinema not invented by me; it is one that represents not merely my inner poetic world, and it does not give way to fantasies born from my imagination."[19] This difference compared to Fellini's cinematographic poetics was widely exploited by Scola in his latest film dedicated to the city of Rome.

By adopting Deleuzian vocabulary, we can take a retroactive look at the proximities between the professional paths of the two filmmakers and identify Fellini's effect on Scola from the beginning, which Scola shows in *Che strano chiamarsi Federico* (*How Strange to be Named Federico*, 2013), a film that presents Fellini as a guide and as a source of inspiration. This early encounter is therefore decisive for Scola's entire career and is coherent with the presence of the Fellini effect on his cinematic poetics, including his cinematic portrayal of Rome.

Scola's *Che strano chiamarsi Federico* featured eminently among the cinematic tributes paid to Fellini twenty years after his death.[20] Following his announcement in 2003 that he would no longer make films, Scola went back on his decision and directed a film dedicated to Fellini. In it, Scola explicitly proposes reading together their careers and their cinemas. *Che strano chiamarsi Federico* is a hybrid of documentary and fiction and also of biopic and autobiographical film. In reconstructing Fellini's early Roman years, it shows the young Ettore Scola, whose career closely follows that of the young Federico.[21] To create a "cubist" portrait of Fellini in *Che strano chiamarsi Federico*, Scola uses numerous photos, extracts from documentaries and filmed interviews, and also some clips from the directors' respective films, including Fellini's *La dolce vita* (1960) and Scola's *C'eravamo tanto amati*. This material is interlaced among sequences shot at Cinecittà that reconstitute, in a fragmentary way, important moments of their careers and their encounters. The mnemonic dimension that crosses the movie, due to Scola's incursion into his own memories, reactivates the founding elements of Fellini's cinematic poetics of Rome, including the evocation of the nocturnal flâneries of Federico in search of film locations, his congenial relations with the studios of Cinecittà and the Teatro 5, and his interest in the world of spectacle.

C'eravamo tanto amati[22] marks Scola's first direct encounter with Fellini's Rome and with *La dolce vita* in particular. The female protagonist of Scola's film, Luciana (Stefania Sandrelli), dreams of becoming a famous actress like Anita Ekberg, who interprets the diva Sylvia in *La dolce vita*. Recalling a sequence from the film *Una vita difficile* (1961) by Dino Risi[23] (which gathers together on the same set of Cinecittà Vittorio Gassman, Silvana Mangano, and Alessandro Blasetti), Scola reconstitutes the shooting of the famous Trevi Fountain sequence in *La dolce vita*, by showing Fellini and Mastroianni who interpret, with an ironic distance, their own roles. Stealing this famous sequence from *La dolce vita*,[24] thereby enabling the encounter with Fellini and his cinematic Rome, is both an invitation to dialogue and an act of appropriation by Scola.

The Effect of Fellini's Rome on *Gente di Roma*

With *Gente di Roma*, Scola pays a vibrant tribute to Italy's capital and to Fellini's cinematic Rome. By making the city the film's true protagonist, Scola proposes a "portrait" of the city by showing it "not only as a place, but as a soul, as a mentality, as a psychology, as a substratum for the Romans."[25] Scola viewed the film as being "very close to reality, shot in natural settings . . . a project focused on a kind of documentation" of Rome and also as "a more personal notebook."[26] *Gente di Roma* can be interpreted as a response to Fellini's documentary *Block-notes di un regista*, as another personal film, in which the director narrates himself and his own Rome along with his way to make a movie.

While Scola himself considers *Gente di Roma* in line with his own previous production, both in style and meaning, the film is different with respect to his other Roman films in terms of narrative structure, as it replicates that of Fellini's *Block-notes di un regista*, *Fellini Satyricon* (1969), and *Roma*. Like these films, *Gente di Roma* has a fragmentary nature and its autonomous episodes succeed each other like "a series of paintings,"[27] in which each episode provokes a different emotion while becoming integrated into the general framework. The aesthetic of the fragment also characterizes the visual description of the characters, sketched as if Scola had applied the technique of *bozzettismo*[28] to cinema. Like the aforementioned films by Fellini, *Gente di Roma* is open to possibilities without a clear beginning and conclusion.

The technique of fragmentation is announced by the credits, which run over the background of the typical and characteristic Roman pavement made from beveled stones of black basalt called *sampietrini*. Their shape and arrangement announce the organization of the stories, which, taken separately, like the pieces of pavement, resemble each other without ever being the same, while together forming a mosaic. This image is symbolic for what is seen in the film: a mosaic of stories, spaces, objects, figures, cultures, civilizations, languages, colors, sounds, songs, and architectures. The *sampietrini*, by their arrangement and utility, also announce the primordial meaning of the film, which is that of strolling around the city. The practice of the flânerie in Scola's film, as in the Roman filmography of Fellini, recalls the theoretical observations of Walter Benjamin concerning the fragmentary perception of the city.[29] The image of the *sampietrini* also recalls the symbolic passage of the Rubicon in the film *Roma*, which, in turn, repeated in a caricatural way the historical crossing of the river by Caesar and his army. This way, from the beginning of *Gente di Roma*, Scola connects his Rome to both ancient Rome and Fellini's invented Rome.

In this film, Scola's Rome is a whirlwind of disparate figures (the Roman, the immigrant, the tourist, the actress, the homeless, the unemployed, etc.), interpreted largely by nonprofessional actors and several professional actors (Stefania Sandrelli, Valerio Mastandrea, Arnoldo Foà). The references are cinematic (Fellini, Zavattini), literary (Shakespeare, Belli, Dostoevsky), political (the protest march in Piazza San Giovanni), and historical (World War II). *Gente di Roma* sometimes takes on the formula of a gag,[30] which allows for a great variety of expressive registers, such as the comic burlesque (the declamation in the Palace of the Senators), the tragic (the old woman who has returned from the concentration camps), or comic drama (the woman who wants to leave her spouse). The topics addressed are also very diverse: work, unemployment, family, marriage, love, adultery, homosexuality, poverty, war, immigration, tourism, old age, sickness, and death. All these elements contribute to create a heterogeneous image of Scola's cinematic Rome, strongly recalling the city that Fellini had shaped in *Roma*.

Under the effect of Fellini's Rome, in *Gente di Roma* Scola retrieves some ideas realized by Fellini. Among the Felliniesque characters that circulate in the film, there is an excessively made-up woman who, treated rudely in the restaurant, is a reference to the Felliniesque female character of the prostitute, without, however, the same evocative strength. Another Felliniesque figure in Scola's film is the man who walks in the cemetery; although the dialogue between the busts and the photographs reproduces the short story "Bobok" of Dostoevsky,[31] the character recalls Ivo Salvini (Roberto Benigni), the protagonist of *La voce della luna* (*The Voice of the Moon*, 1990), while the staging recalls *Block-notes di un regista*. Bernardino Zapponi,[32] in recounting the scene from *Block-notes* in which Fellini invites Genius to help him discover the mysteries buried under Via Appia Antica, points out that the clairvoyant, in contact with dead persons, told him to see and to hear the centurions. In these cases, too, considering the idea of remake or imitation in the Deleuzian sense, one notes Scola's efforts with respect to Fellini's characters, images, and ideas, reappropriated in an original way. This sequence brings the two filmmakers closer in the representation of death on the screen. Fellini explained his wish to shoot a scene in the Verano cemetery by claiming that in Rome death always has a familiar appearance, like a relative.[33] Similarly, Scola noted in an interview that Romans regularly see dead people and that on November 2, the Day of the Dead, "families invade the pathways in the cemeteries, with the little children running and cheering each other joyfully between the graves."[34] For Romans, death is not the dramatic end of life but another spectacle in which dead people speak, quarrel, and love each other as in life. The dream-like episode filmed by Scola is therefore a tribute to Fellini's cinema and to Dostoevsky's short story. In addition, both filmmakers insist on the familiar character of the cemetery as a "big apartment you can stroll through in pajamas and slippers"[35] and a "city in the city."[36] During his stroll in the Verano cemetery and among the funerary monuments and statues, Scola's solitary man (Rolando Ravello) listens to parts of conversations between the dead, which are strikingly banal. While Fellini does not include an episode dedicated to the cemetery in *Roma*, he does present a dream-like sequence in *8½* that features a normal conversation between Guido Anselmi (Marcello Mastroianni) and his deceased father. This appropriation of public space also recalls the experiences of flâneurs for whom the city would transform under their footsteps "into one great interior—a house whose rooms are the neighborhoods."[37]

At the beginning of Fellini's *Roma*, the village idiot, standing next to a mutilated statue of Julius Caesar, improvises a poem in which the historical figures of Mussolini and the emperor are confused. This sequence was revisited by Scola: in the Palace of Senators, after having dusted Julius Caesar's statue, the cleaning person—a nonprofessional actor and real-life janitor—recites a fragment of Mark Antony's speech from Shakespeare's *Julius Caesar*. Scola specifies that this idea was inspired from real life because "many Romans, even of modest condition, have this fixed idea to play comedy, to make a spectacle of themselves."[38] For a moment, the platform from which the Italian senators are speaking becomes a theater stage for the employees of the town hall, who turn into actors and spectators, just as before, in the cinema of Fellini, the urban space had functioned as an ad hoc performance space.

Likewise, *Gente di Roma*'s final scene evokes the ending of Fellini's *Roma*. At first, the camera moves in a circle, capturing the agitation of the city by night, with its sounds produced by automobiles, buses, and motorcycles. Then, in Piazza di Spagna, the camera focuses for a few seconds on Via del Corso, exactly where Fellini's cinematic Rome had begun, in *Luci del varietà* (*Variety Lights*, 1950). In Piazza Navona, late at night, Scola films a meeting between two elderly men, one homeless, the other an aristocrat. The architecture of the square and Gian Lorenzo Bernini's fountain are filmed in an extreme long shot, while the two men are filmed in a full shot. This alternation shows that people are as important as urban objects for Scola, an intention already announced in the film's title, whereas Fellini, in his final sequence of *Roma*, emphasizes the city's monumentality. In Fellini's sequence, one recalls the Baroque and hallucinatory vertigo of the monuments, statues, and fountains of Rome filmed in a fragmentary style, in brief shots, as motorcycles speed through the historic center. The monuments and statues appear as silent and impassible guardians of the place: whereas young motorcyclists are passing through the city, urban architectural objects are there to stay.

The finale of the long-take sequence reveals Scola's humanistic approach: after the two men greet like old friends, they silently share a bench next to the fountain. Indifferent to their disparate social conditions, they let themselves be carried away by the charm of the Roman night and the architecture of the piazza, accepting serenely their human condition, which is ephemeral compared to the Eternal City. With this finale, Scola agrees with Fellini, who in the sequence dedicated to Festa de'Noiantri in the finale of *Roma* has the American writer Gore Vidal say that there is not a better place than Rome to reach for the end of the world.

In *Gente di Roma*, Scola revives subjects that Fellini left out of the final version of *Roma*, such as the journey on the night tram, the "eternal" confrontation between Lazio and Roma, the Roman women, the clouds of Rome, and the Verano cemetery.[39] In response to a sequence that Fellini drastically cut from *Roma*—a prostitute reciting Giuseppe Gioachino Belli's 1832 poem "La madre de le sante" (she appears for only a few seconds before the sequence dedicated to Grande Raccordo Anulare)—Scola has an old Roman (Fiorenzo Fiorentini) on a bus recite Belli's famous vulgar poem "Er padre de li santi" (1832). In these instances, both filmmakers reappropriate an emblem of Roman popular identity: the poet Belli, who authored more than two thousand sonnets in Roman dialect.[40] In this way, Scola updates Fellini's cinematographic intentions by projecting them into the daily life of twenty-first century Rome.

Scola recalls, always in different ways, certain Roman emblems already seen in *Roma*. The city's anthem "La società dei magnaccioni," exalting the beautiful life and the *dolce far niente* ("ma che ce frega, ma che ce importa" [but what do we care? does it matter?]) is heard in the sequence of Fellini's *Roma* dedicated to the Festa de' Noiantri,[41] while in *Gente di Roma*, it is sung by Valerio Mastandrea in one of the sequences filmed on the bus. The ways in which the anthem is introduced and sung in both films stand in contrast: whereas in Fellini the singing voice-over accompanies images that extol the beauty and diversity of the neighborhood, Scola's character visibly disturbs other passengers on the bus. Thus, if in the context of Trastevere's popular culture the anthem still invokes a Roman community, in the other case it no longer has the power to bring together Romans and new immigrants.

The dialogue between Scola and Fellini is also apparent in their shared determination to find an actress who would offer a cinematic face of Rome. The appearance of Anna Magnani in Fellini's *Roma* becomes an event: her face and body become an anachronistic palimpsest of signs. Like a she-wolf and a vestal, she connects twentieth-century Rome with ancient Rome. In addition, thanks to her exemplary career, Anna Magnani also connects Fellini's cinematic Rome to those of Roberto Rossellini, Luchino Visconti, and Pier Paolo Pasolini and also with the tradition of the *teatro di rivista* (variety show). Meanwhile, Scola chose Stefania Sandrelli[42] as his "face" for Rome to establish links between different moments of his filmography[43] and, implicitly, the history of Italian cinema. Although the two actresses are filmed in the natural setting of Rome, Sandrelli in *Gente di Roma*, in a park in full sun having fun with her granddaughter, contrasts with Magnani in *Roma*, solitary in the night in front of her home. Without the evocative power of Magnani, Scola's actress nonetheless remains linked to the representation of the city.[44] The presence of these two actresses, although short lived as cameo appearances, is one of the strategies that help to enhance the metacinematographic dialogue between by the two filmmakers. Anna Magnani invites Federico Fellini to go to sleep, so as to keep dreaming of cinema, while Stefania Sandrelli speaks of a cinema made of lies. The discourse of these two prominent figures of cinematographic memory thus conveys the same idea: that of a cinema made of illusions.

Flânerie, Spectacle, Memory: From Fellini to Scola

The effect of Fellini's Rome is also reflected in the repetition of the three founding elements of Felliniesque Roman poetics: flânerie, spectacle, and memory. The flânerie as a practice of space, as the art of surveying the city, and as a state of mind is intrinsic in the approach of Scola, who, as an invisible wanderer, traverses the eternal city to record the ordinary moments of its existence. Unlike Fellini, who films himself in *Block-notes di un regista*, *Roma*, and *Intervista*, Scola never shows himself directly. For this reason, his flânerie as a filmmaker in search of locations is further enhanced by the use of a digital camera. His strolling, facilitated by the lightness of the apparatus, is repeated in the heavier movement of the bus, which, by contamination, becomes a "*metaphorai*"[45] of the city. Scola exploits the meanings of the bus as "vehicle," according to its etymology (Latin *vehiculum*, means of transport, from *vehere*, to transport), as well as its figurative sense, as something that serves to transmit, to move from one place to another, to drive. And when the physical urban flânerie is redoubled by the narrative one, thanks to the fragmentary stories that form the film and that transform the traveled places into spaces,[46] the strolling bus also plays the role of conductor between the "spatial stories." As a flâneur, the bus traverses the city, from Pietralata to the historic center, crossing streets and squares and allowing the director to show also the Capitoline Square and Coliseum, Termini Station, and the Verano cemetery. When it stops, it is the camera's turn to enter everywhere, in public and private spaces: apartments, *palazzi*, small restaurants, bingo halls, health clinics, schools, and so on. By filming in this manner, Scola puts into practice Zavattini's method of *pedinamento*, a shadowing by the camera, or watching without being noticed (similar to the way that detectives follow suspected criminals), which is used to offer a semblance of ordinary people in real life.[47] This shooting technique also recalls the behavior of the flâneur, described by Benjamin, who can be perceived at the same time as detective and suspect.

Moving camera shots of Rome are scattered throughout the film, especially in moments of transition: the camera shows the streets, the ruins, the buildings, and the people of Rome, all accompanied by the musical *ritornello* (refrain) composed by Armando Trovajoli. The camera similarly strolls in such transitional sequences. Sometimes the images of Rome are in black and white, in a documentary style. One example is the sequence on the bus in which the spectator, by a mise en abyme structure, can see on the screen of the computer what the journalist had filmed. This nested sequence contaminates the next one (still in black in white), in which the spectator watches Piazza Vittorio and its passersby in real time through the window of the bus.

Zavattini speaks of cinema as the medium that captures the flow of reality, a conception that anticipates Siegfried Kracauer, whose flâneur experiences the flow of life in the city, looking at "taxi cabs, buildings, passers-by, inanimate objects, faces," along with the fragmentary happenings incidental to them.[48] Scola practices both theories in his film, thanks to the use of the urban flânerie, which allows the invisible camera to record the flow of life in a succession of objects, figures, faces, and events.

These cinematic techniques enable the metamorphosis of the bus into a motorized flâneur that runs through the city. One understands that it is a flânerie, with random or invented trajectories, by looking at the numbers displayed on the front of the bus at the onset of each sequence. In fact, it is the same bus, with the same female driver. This silent and indifferent woman, who drives confidently, lends itself to several interpretations. She could be a survival, vestige of antiquity,[49] or a vestal virgin disguised in a uniform, or a *genius loci*, an ideal guide, like the engineer of *Roma*. Also, this black-haired woman who knows all the streets of the city could be considered a response to the series of black-haired women[50] who play the role of the *lupa* (she-wolf) in Fellini's *Roma*. Or indeed, the female driver could be an image of the city, as depicted in the sequence in which the bus leaves the Coliseum and a camera shot from above shows the woman in profile: for a moment, the image of her face and the monumental edifice overlap, in a confusion of flesh and stone. With these multiple interpretations, Scola's female figure also becomes a palimpsest of powerful signs, like the face of Anna Magnani in Fellini's film.

Similar to Fellini in his Roman films, Scola makes theatricality an intrinsic dimension of the city and its people. The streets and the squares become the scene of artistic manifestations, where Romans perform in the spectacle of everyday life. This heterogeneous spectacle often consists of dance, music, literature, rhetoric, politics, and soccer. Scola's film shows how in the evening the city turns into a dance scene. Projected on giant screens, an elegant contest is transmitted live from the Baths of Caracalla, once the dance space of Sylvia in *La dolce vita*. After filming the graceful waltz, the camera records the joy of older people dancing in a Roman square, while the young people perform at the Gay Village, where muscular professional male dancers and female dancers with fabulous hairstyles and costumes move to the rhythm of electronic music. This last example shows the difference between the current situation in which homosexuality is portrayed nonjudgmentally and the time of *La dolce vita*, the early 1960s, when the church was scandalized by the striptease performed by Nadia Gray. In another sequence, the spectator observes a left-wing demonstration in San Giovanni square, where Nanni Moretti and Dario Fò address Romans from an improvised stand. This political spectacle is mixed with a musical one as Scola films Francesco de Gregori, a well-known contemporary songwriter, generally associated with the musical scene of Rome. The presence in the film of these emblematic personalities for the artistic life of the capital reinforces Scola's idea of documenting his city and, at the same time, constitutes the director's tribute to them.

To reinforce the images of Rome as a city of spectacle and of Romans as actors, Scola films people around the Colosseum dressed as centurions and legionaries, who appear more ridiculous and pathetic than the Felliniesque survivals from ancient Rome in *Block-notes di un regista* and in *Roma*. An anachronistic Rome is fabricated by Fellini. In it, figures, situations, and encounters, enveloped in an aura that enhances their original meanings, are repeated on other layers of the past, and transformed into mythological and legendary appearances and events. We note a contrary tendency in the case of Scola, who shows, without artifice, how these figures, situations, and encounters evolve in the normality of everyday life. In Scola's Rome, the past does not have the strength it had in Fellini's. The monuments, the ruins, and the *lupa* are objects and figures that no longer reawaken the gaze as in Fellini's films; rather, Scola's concern is to "dust them off," as in the symbolic cleaning of the statues of Julius Caesar and the *lupa* in *Gente di Roma*.

In the construction of the cinematic Rome of Fellini and Scola, the metacinematic dimension is also of central importance. In *Roma* and *Intervista*, Fellini shoots on the Roman streets, in the subway, and on the Great Ring Road (*Grande Raccordo Anulare*), all re-created at Cinecittà, deliberately showing the camera, the equipment, and the crew. In *Gente di Roma*, at the beginning of the twenty-first century, the Roman streets are always used as natural cinematic settings, as in the sequence with the realistic reconstruction of a moment of Jewish deportation. This cinematic dimension of Rome operates as a sort of carnival in that it features a reversal of roles: if the Romans become actors instantaneously, actors and filmmakers descend into the streets and squares, either to have fun, like Sandrelli, or to get involved politically, like Moretti.

Unlike Fellini, who approaches the question of memory like a palimpsest, formed by layers of personal, urban, and cinematic memories, Scola's *Gente di Roma* problematizes the relationship between memory and oblivion in two contrasting scenes. For example, in one scene, an old Jewish woman who has not forgotten the traumas of the Nazi occupation faints before a cinematic reconstitution of the deportation of Jews, while in another scene we encounter Alzheimer's patients at a medical center who have forgotten everything. In this way, human memory is presented by Scola in all its fragility, especially in its relation to the memory of the city, inscribed as *ab urbe condita* (from the founding of the city) in its form and its stones.

Pursuing Fellini's interest in marginalized and excluded people,[51] Scola focuses on such problems as unemployment, poverty, the difficulty of communication, the dissolution of the family, lack of housing, and immigration. Scola's social and engagement is evidenced in scenes such as the one with the husband who pretends to leave the house for work but instead goes to the park because he cannot bear to tell his wife that he lost his job. The most distressing sequence in *Gente di Roma* features a dozen homeless persons. It re-creates a scene from Fellini's *Le notti di Cabiria* (*Nights of Cabiria*, 1957), in which vagrants, sitting in front of the ancient ruins as on a theater stage, drink, smoke, read newspapers, quarrel, and reconcile as friends. The desolation of the place is all the greater because the stone ruins correspond to these human ruins. Surrounded by the remains of vegetation, cartons, abandoned cars and furniture, these characters live on the margins of society. Like the poor shown in Fellini's films of the 1950s, who lived in the dens of the earth, the homeless filmed by Scola feed on leftovers and wear worn clothing. The male nurse who acted as a guardian angel in *Le notti di Cabiria* is no longer there, thereby leaving an empty place and little hope. Treated as human waste by the consumer society, these people are excluded, but, as a result of their marginal status, they have become the guardians of the place, the protectors of the ruins.

The flânerie split between the camera and the bus is once more replayed in the sequence centered on multiethnic and multicultural cohabitation in today's Rome. The protagonists are a migrant (Salvatore Marino), who works as a freelance journalist, and a Roman (Valerio Mastandrea). With the character of the journalist in *Gente di Roma*, Scola re-creates a key figure of Fellini's cinema, present from *La dolce vita* to *Intervista*; yet, while Marcello in *La dolce vita* is interested in mundanities, Scola's journalist of the twenty-first century investigates social issues, such as recent immigration. Much has changed in Rome between the late 1930s, as depicted in Fellini's *Roma* and *Intervista*, showing the curious gaze of the young Fellini, and the new millennium, when Scola's journalist conducts the inquiry on foreigners and the Eternal City according to Zavattini's method: the cityscape; its leaders; its inhabitants, technology, and manners. Nonetheless, Scola's journalist reactivates certain characters of the flâneur: the sociologist, the detective, and the collector. The aesthetic perspective on the city and on its architecture and the investigation of the past do not interest him anymore. Concentrated exclusively on the present, this modern-day Virgil films daily life in the streets of Rome with his minicamera, and his gestures reproduce those of Scola himself, as a filmmaker in search of locations. These recordings documenting everyday life in the city contain a collection of faces and gestures of its passersby and of inscriptions written on the walls, which constitute "the voice of the city." In this manner, Scola's journalist represents a tribute not only to Fellini's flâneurs but also to nineteenth-century authors of panoramic literature, to Franz Hessel and to Benjamin, who as flâneurs read and interpreted the messages of urban modernity in signs and posters.

All these repetitions and the effect of the cinematic poetics of Fellini's Rome identified before in the film *Gente di Roma* do not take away from its originality. From this perspective, the relation of Scola's cinematic work to Fellini's appears even more important. As Deleuze showed us, such repetition is productive, creative, and always takes place in the difference.[52] Therefore, repeating certain characters, sequences, qualities, and ways of making a film presupposes a double work that is more arduous. In dialogue with Fellini's Rome, appropriated and assimilated through the creative process, Scola delivers a new cinematic vision of Rome. The effect of his Rome on future cinematic images of the eternal city remains to be seen.

Notes

1. Many studies have been published on Rome as a cinematic city. Recent works include: Flaminio Di Biagi, *Il cinema a Roma: Guida alla storia e ai luoghi del cinema nella capitale* (Rome: Palombi Editori, 2007; first published 2003); Richard Wrigley, ed., *Cinematic Rome* (Leicester: Troubador, 2008); and Gabriel Solomons, ed., *World Film Locations: Rome* (Bristol: Intellect Books, 2014).
2. Peter Bondanella, *The Cinema of Federico Fellini* (Princeton, NJ: Princeton University Press, 1992); Paola Bernardini et al., eds., *Federico Fellini: Riprese, riletture, (re)visioni. Atti della North American Conference on the Italian Master of Cinema* (Florence: Franco Cesati Editore, 2016); and Vito Zagarrio, ed., *Trevico-Cinecittà: L'avventuroso viaggio di Ettore Scola* (Venice: Marsilio, 2002).
3. This encounter is also explored in the latest work of Scola, *Che strano chiamarsi Federico* (*How Strange to be Named Federico*, 2013), though the main focus of this chapter is on *Gente di Roma*.
4. The relationship among three elements is the basis of Fellini's poetic cinematography on the city. In the constellation of Roman films by Fellini, strolling as a reflexive practice to browse, watch, and interpret the city allows one to see the city's architectural wonders and also to access the different spaces of professional performances (e.g., cabaret, cinemas, streets, piazzas), which are inexhaustible sources for a plural and palimpsestic memory.
5. Gilles Deleuze and Claire Parnet, *Dialogues*, trans. Hugh Tomlinson and Barbara Habberrjam (New York: Columbia University Press, 1987; first published 1977), 6.
6. Deleuze and Parnet, 2.
7. Deleuze and Parnet, 8.
8. Perceived for some time now as problematic (Michel Foucault, *L'archéologie du savoir* [Paris: Gallimard, 1969]), distressing (Harold Bloom, *The Anxiety of Influence: A Theory of Poetry* [New York: Oxford University Press, 1973]), and dangerous (Umberto Eco, "Borges e la mia angoscia dell'influenza," in *Sulla letteratura* [Milan: Bompiani, 2002, 128–46]), influence implies the superiority of the original work over the others who follow it chronologically and, consequently, supposes a tree-like relationship. In contrast, the effect assumes a rhyzomatic relationship, based on encounters and dialogue. In this meaning, Deleuze and Parnet write: "We constantly oppose the rhizome to the tree, like two conceptions and even two different ways of thinking. A line does not go to from one point to another, but passes between the points, ceaselessly bifurcating and diverging, like one of Pollock's line" (*Dialogues*, viii).
9. See Gilles Deleuze, *Difference and Repetition*, trans. Paul Patton (New York: Columbia University Press, 1994; first published 1968), 6. According to

Deleuze, one of the propositions to oppose repetition to all forms of generality is "make something new of repetition itself" (6).

10. Walter Benjamin, *The Arcades Project*, trans. Howard Eiland and Kevin McLaughlin (Cambridge, MA: Belknap, 1999; first published 1982); and Walter Benjamin, *The Writer of Modern Life: Essays on Charles Baudelaire*, ed. Michael W. Jennings, trans. Howard Eiland, Edmund Jephcott, Rodney Livingstone, and Harry Zohn (Cambridge, MA: Belknap, 2006).
11. For more information about the Roman flâneur during antiquity, see Marina Vargau, *Romarcord: Flânerie dans la cine-città*, Université de Montréal, 2016, 41–61. https://papyrus.bib.umontreal.ca/xmlui/bitstream/handle/1866/18457/Vargau_Marina_2016_these.pdf?sequence=2.
12. To this date, Bíspuri and Manuela Gieri are the only scholars to have utilized a comparative approach to analyze the careers of the two filmmakers. See Ennio Bíspuri, *Ettore Scola: Un umanista nel cinema italiano* (Rome: Bulzoni, 2006); and Manuela Gieri, *Contemporary Italian Filmmaking: Pirandello, Fellini, Scola, and the Directors of the New Generation* (Toronto: University of Toronto Press, 1995).
13. Bíspuri, 345–52.
14. Bíspuri, 352–53. Translations throughout the chapter are my own unless otherwise noted.
15. Moreover, Via Veneto is the space that ensures the unity of Fellini's first Roman films, *Luci del varietà*, *Notti di Cabiria*, and *La dolce vita*.
16. For example, *La dolce vita* triggered an "earthquake" among audiences and reception in general; see Tullio Kezich, *Federico Fellini: La vita e i film* (Milan: Feltrinelli, 2007), 203–11. According to Emanuel Levy, *Cinema of Outsiders: The Rise of American Independent Film* (New York: New York University Press, 1999), 32–33, in 1960, the film earned $10 million, and in 1999 the box office receipts equaled about $70 million.
17. See Franco Montini, "La Roma di Scola," in Zagarrio, *Trevico-Cinecittà*, 218–22.
18. Ettore Scola, "Rome, ville de passage et de saccage," in *Cités-cinés* (La Villette: Ramsay et Grande Halle, 1987), 52.
19. Scola, 52.
20. Another filmic tribute is Paolo Sorrentino's *La grande bellezza* (*The Great Beauty*, 2013).
21. The protagonists are interpreted by the grandsons of Scola, Tommaso (playing the young Federico) and Giacomo Lazotti (playing the young Ettore).
22. In the case of *C'eravamo tanto amati*, beyond featuring Fellini and his film *La dolce vita*, Scola also provokes an encounter with De Sica and the films *Battleship Potemkin*, *Ladri di biciclette*, *Una vita difficile*, and *L'eclisse*.
23. Scola wrote various and important films for Dino Risi, but this one is by Rodolfo Sonego.

24. Scola is not the only filmmaker to react to the phenomenon of *La dolce vita*. For example, in 1961, Sergio Corbucci proposed a parodic version of Fellini's film in *Totò, Peppino e ... la dolce vita* (*Totò, Peppino and ... the Sweet Life*) while Pietro Germi, in *Divorzio all'italiana* (*Divorce Italian Style*, 1961) showed the effect of Sylvia's dance on the spectators in a Sicilian movie theater.
25. Ettore Scola in Jean A. Gili, "Propos d'Ettore Scola," Bonus feature, DVD, *Gente di Roma*, 2004.
26. Scola in Gili.
27. Scola in Gili. As Gili notes, these scenes "are detached from one another, but in a relationship of osmosis, each scene transmits to the other an additional meaning."
28. Scola defines this technique, already used in his caricatures, as "the first draft of something that must then be developed, but which already has a certain value in itself"; Scola is quoted in Aldo Tassone, *Le cinéma italien parle* (Paris: Edilig, 1982), 234. "The outline of something that must be developed, but which already has a certain value in itself."
29. Benjamin, *The Arcades Project*.
30. One recognizes this minor cinematic genre in two silent sequences, filmed in the streets of Rome and featuring protagonists who communicate through written cartoons or gestures in the tradition of cinematic gags of 1920s.
31. Fyodor Dostoyevsky, "Bobok" (1873), in *White Nights and Other Stories*, trans. Constance Garnett (New York: Dover Thrift Editions, 2017; first published 1873), 134–48.
32. Bernardino Zapponi, *"Roma" di Federico Fellini* (Bologna: Cappelli, 1972), 31.
33. Federico Fellini, *Making a Film*, 232.
34. Gili, "Propos d'Ettore Scola," 2004.
35. Federico Fellini, *Making a Film*, trans. Christopher Burton White (New York: Contra Mundum Press, 2015), 233.
36. Scola in Gili, "Propos d'Ettore Scola," 2004.
37. Benjamin, *The Arcades Project*, 422.
38. Gili, "Propos d'Ettore Scola," 2004.
39. Fellini notes: "As far as my movie is concerned, a lot of things from the screenplay were left out." Fellini, *Making a Film*, 232.
40. Giuseppe Gioachino Belli, *I sonetti romaneschi*, vol. 1 (Città di Castello: S. Lappi tipografo editore, 1889), 289.
41. I refer to the full sequence, presented only in the first version of the film (130 minutes).
42. See Elio Girlanda, *Stefania Sandrelli* (Rome: Gremese, 2002); and Daniela Brogi, *La donna visibile: Il cinema di Stefania Sandrelli* (Pisa: Edizioni ETS, 2016).
43. Sandrelli played for Scola in *C'eravamo tanto amati*, *La terrazza*, *La famiglia*, and *La cena*.

44. It is a sad coincidence that the appearance of Alberto Sordi, Magnani's masculine counterpart as the cinematic face of Rome, is missing in both *Roma* and *Gente di Roma*. Fellini had made a brief sequence—cut in the definitive version of the film—with the actor, who delighted in the street spectacle on a terrace, surrounded by women and admirers. On his part, Scola wanted Sordi to arrive by horse-drawn carriage in Piazza Navona, to meet the tramp in the final sequence (see Gili, "Propos d'Ettore Scola"). The actor's death during the shooting makes his appearance impossible, so Scola dedicates the film to him.
45. Certeau begins the chapter about spatial stories with a provocative association: "In modern Athens, the vehicles of mass transportation are called *metaphorai*. To go to work or come home, one takes a 'metaphor'—a bus or a train. Stories could also take this noble name: every day, they traverse and organize places; they select and link together, they make sentences and itineraries out of them." See Michel de Certeau, *The Practice of Everyday Life*, trans. Steven F. Rendall (Berkeley: University of California Press, 1984), 115.
46. According to Certeau, the space is a "practiced place" (*The Practice of Everyday Life*, 117).
47. See Cesare Zavattini, "Basta con i soggetti," in *Neorealismo ecc.*, ed. Mino Argentieri (Milan: Bompiani, 1979).
48. Siegfried Kracauer, *Theory of Film: The Redemption of Physical Reality* (Princeton, NJ: Princeton University Press, 1997; first published 1960), 170.
49. Concerning the meaning of this term, I follow Georges Didi-Huberman, *The Surviving Image: Phantoms of Time and Time of Phantoms. Aby Warburg's History of Art*, trans. Harvey Mendelsohn (University Park: Pennsylvania State University Press, 2016). According to him, the survival is an old image that can irrupt into the present in a fragmentary and chaotical manner. This term corresponds to Aby Warburg's concept of *Nachleben*, which supposes the return of the images.
50. In the film *Roma*, the women who meet this criterion are the woman waiting on the platform of the train station, the prostitute who lives in the large apartment, and the woman who goes down in the piazza to sit next to her fiancé.
51. During the nineteenth century already, Charles Baudelaire, poet of modernity and loafer, was interested in urban figures of marginality, such as ragpickers prowlers, prostitutes, lesbians, who constituted the "rejects of the society." See Benjamin, *The Writer of Modern Life*, 109.
52. See Deleuze, *Difference and Repetition*.

PART 4

SCOLA AND POLITICS

SENTENCED TO DEATH

The Proto-Berlusconi of *La più bella serata della mia vita*

Nicoletta Marini-Maio

ETTORE SCOLA'S FILMIC AND narrative "architecture" explores the microhistories of phenomenal human types, stories, and settings in the attempt to represent, in the director's own words, the "history of human beings, their confrontations and battles with the reality of those big events looming around them."[1] This emblematic "dance of history" moves along historical continuums, from fascism to the contemporary age, and sways across the social spectrum, from the lumpenproletariat to the bourgeoisie.[2] It is a long-range investigation that depicts the faces of power through bittersweet, if not gloomy, stories. Although in his last years, at odds with Italian media tycoon and former prime minister Silvio Berlusconi's all-pervasive system of power, Scola's creative arc declined, his cinema nonetheless did not fail to discern the emergence of *berlusconismo*. As historiographical research indicates, the socioeconomic, cultural, and historical factors that eventually converged to produce *berlusconismo* in the 1990s were at work long before the premier's economic and political climax. This chapter captures Scola's ethical and artistic sensitivity to symptoms of *berlusconismo* percolating in Italian society since the early 1970s, and it does so by way of a polyvalent approach. Grounded in

---

This chapter develops a preliminary analysis of Ettore Scola's *La più bella serata della mia vita*, published in Nicoletta Marini-Maio's *A Very Seductive Body Politic: Silvio Berlusconi in Cinema* (Milan-Udine: Mimesis, 2015), 29–39. © Mimesis International www.mimesisinternational. com. I would like to thank Mimesis for granting me permission to use parts of that work in this chapter.

a cultural studies methodology, it centers on the film *La più bella serata della mia vita* (*The Most Wonderful Evening of My Life*, 1972) as a meditation on the relationships among representation, sociocultural discourses, and the Italian historical context.

After some introductory considerations of Scola's intellectual and professional position within the context of Berlusconi's 1990s Italy, this chapter argues that *La più bella serata* presents a proto-Berlusconi character years before the actual historical figure cast a populist spell on the country. This does not suggest an actual physiognomic resemblance between the protagonist, Alfredo Rossi (Alberto Sordi), and Silvio Berlusconi. Similarly, the aim is not to demonstrate that Scola intentionally thought of Berlusconi while developing the script or casting Sordi. In fact, *La più bella serata* is neither a biopic nor a fictional story proffering a Berlusconi avatar.[3] Rather, it is a tragicomic condemnation of the average Italian (the *italiano medio*, or Everyman), a semiotic and cultural construct that portrays contempt for legal and moral rules, a dishonest work ethic, inflated individualism, the illusory performance of masculinity, and the obsessive pursuit of sexual conquest.[4] Exploring the film's mise-en-scène and cinematography, the chapter focuses specifically on the symbolism of the film's narrative, the characterization of Alfredo, and the cultural discourses surrounding the *italiano medio*, embodied on a macrotextual level by Silvio Berlusconi. Alberto Sordi's performative body, in concert with the film's dark plot, allows Scola to pursue (proto)*berlusconismo* in *La più bella serata*, something he would emphasize years later, commenting on the film. Seen from this perspective, the trial and the apocalyptic ending of *La più bella serata* foreshadow Scola's moral and intellectual position vis-à-vis the wave of *berlusconismo* that changed the culture of the nation from the early 1990s.

Ettore Scola and *Berlusconismo*

Silvio Berlusconi, a Milanese entrepreneur and media tycoon, first entered the political arena during Italy's Second Republic in January 1994 to be precise, when he founded the new Right-tending party Forza Italia and addressed the nation in a notorious speech now known as his *discesa in campo* (entering the field), which aired on the TV networks constituting part of his media empire. In the national elections of March 1994, the coalition led by Forza Italia won the majority in Parliament, and Berlusconi was named prime minister for the first time. He served as prime minister again from 2001 to 2006 and 2008 to 2011.

Recent historiographical studies assert that Berlusconi's emergence in Italian politics cannot be isolated solely within the context of the late 1980s and early 1990s.[5] His political leadership reflected a shift in cultural paradigms—commonly defined as *berlusconismo*—that became visible in the political and socioeconomic coordinates emerging toward the end of the 1980s and that shaped Berlusconi's power system.[6] It was the redefinition of the international political scene following the collapse of communism in 1989 that legitimated *berlusconismo*. However, changes in public opinion, aspirations, and desires that *berlusconismo* brought to the fore can be traced back to the period following the economic boom and student movements of the 1960s.[7] Giovanni Orsina projects the figure of Berlusconi onto a logic of *longue durée*, arguing that *berlusconismo* is the consequence of a historical trajectory beginning with the failure of the nineteenth-century moderate Right that led to fascism, the subsequent lack of a modern conservative party, the forty-year-long political dominance of the Christian Democrats, as well as left-wing cultural hegemony in postwar Italy.[8] The judicial investigation known as *Mani pulite* (Clean Hands), which indicted the leadership of the Christian Democratic and Socialist parties in the 1990s on corruption charges, wiped away the two major moderate parties. The political void on the Right was ripe for the filling by Berlusconi, who stated that he could "save" the country from the rise of left-wing political forces (i.e., the Democratic Party of the Left and the Communist Refoundation Party), which he vilified as "illiberal."[9] Berlusconi styled himself as a pragmatic businessman determined to dismantle the political rules and rigid bureaucracy that had dominated the First Republic. In addition, through the exhibition of Berlusconi's exaggerated sexual appetite and performative masculinity, *berlusconismo* established itself as a *regime del godimento* (regime of pleasure), calling attention to symbolic processes of pleasure enthusiastically accepted by a substantial part of the electorate.[10]

Scola experienced Berlusconi's ascent to power with great concern. Since the media magnate's second electoral victory in 2001, Scola decided not to make any more fictional films, and the sense of purpose he assigned to fictional cinema seemed to fade away. He worked on several collective documentaries and directed two features, including *Gente di Roma* (*People of Rome*, 2003) and *Che strano chiamarsi Federico* (*How Strange to Be Named Federico*, 2013), neither of which film is strictly narrative in form. *Un drago a forma di nuvola* (*A Dragon-Shaped Cloud*), a fictional film that Scola was considering to stage and shoot in France, remained in project form when the director learned that Berlusconi's media company Medusa was set to produce it.[11] Scola's withdrawal from narrative cinema at such a critical moment of Italian history was an unexpected but firm decision, and in the ensuing years the filmmaker continued to voice his Balzacian "accusation," or, as Paoli called it, his "anathema," pointing to production issues and lack of freedom.[12] Grounded in his long-term communist faith, Scola's aversion to Berlusconi transformed into open hostility concerning the media tycoon's monopoly of the Italian film industry. However, the filmmaker's decision to stop making films was also motivated by other factors related to *berlusconismo*.

Berlusconismo had a profound impact on the ways in which authors, directors, actors, and producers had been working in Italy since the end of the war and, overall, on the intellectual context in which Scola's cinema had thrived. In a 2009 interview, Scola admitted:

> Cinema is not like the work of a writer or painter, who can say what he likes without worrying about external financial support. All they need is a canvas or a blank page. Cinema is also an industrial endeavor. Among other things, Berlusconi controls the press, and TV, even cinema, to a large extent, depends on him. . . . I think that, in order to be able to work, in whatever job . . . even a carpenter must have a rapport with his client. He needs to feel part of a creative family. So working with someone you're against . . . I didn't think it would go very well, in the end.[13]

In addition to his reluctance to abide by Berlusconi's systemic control of the film and media industry, Scola's emphasis on collaborative partnerships (i.e., "have a rapport," "feel part of a creative family," "working with someone you're against") brings to consideration ethical and psychological factors. Italian critic and writer Andrea Pomella argues that changes in the cultural industry had traumatic repercussions for Scola's work as well as his personal life:

> It was like what happens in the psyche of a man who has his first heart attack in life, that is, he has a feeling of displacement, the idea that nature

has suddenly become hostile, that he is not safe anymore, that he is exposed to removal, collapse, and extinction. The ugly things of berlusconismo, the trauma of the realization of not being able to communicate any longer with the ethical and social subjects, the young, and the masses blurred by cultural homologation: this was the black hole in which his generation had precipitated.[14]

Scola's "feeling of displacement," adds Pomella, relates to the collapse of his politically engaged world: "Perhaps Berlusconi did not have much to do with it. It was more because of the disintegration of the left and the agony and endless destruction of the world that had been communist, an agony of which Berlusconi was not the cause, but the consequence."[15] The decline of the Left's cultural leadership invalidated the Gramscian paradigm of the organic intellectual—that is, of the "constructor, organizer, convincer," whose purpose was to serve the proletariat's struggle by educating from the inside.[16] Scola's cinema of the 1970s and 1980s, claims Pomella, is the "live narration of that crisis."[17] Making a bitter comedy of "*berlusconismo* could have represented for Scola the opportunity to come full circle, an opportunity that he missed nonetheless."[18]

From the perspective of *longue durée* of Italian historiography, the horizon of Scola's cinema clearly incorporates—although in a very original way—the sociocultural constructs that caused *berlusconismo*, from *C'eravamo tanto amati* (*We All Loved Each Other So Much*, 1974) and *Signore e signori, buonanotte* (*Ladies and Gentlemen, Goodnight*, 1976), to *I nuovi mostri* (*Viva Italia!*, 1977) and *La terrazza* (*The Terrace*, 1980).[19] All these films reinterpret past and present Italian society in a way that interrogates "the established structures of power (and of the shared image that we have of it)," yet there is one, specifically *La più bella serata della mia vita*, that has not only intercepted the cultural figurations that Italian society has constructed of itself, the system(s) of power it has created, and its underlying symbols, but that has also powerfully foreshadowed Silvio Berlusconi before the real political figure entered the public stage.[20] *La più bella serata* is not usually regarded as part of Scola's mainstream production. Indeed, the film has been almost forgotten because of its lack of commercial success. Nevertheless, it deserves attention for its artistic mise-en-scène and creative cinematography, for the contextual relevance of the drama it stages, and, most important, for its uncanny prefiguration of the amoral proto-Berlusconi entrepreneurial character performatively created by Alberto Sordi. As I mentioned earlier, Berlusconi's figure cannot be historically identified in the film according to any naturalistic register of representation owing to the absence of the resemblance between Sordi and Berlusconi or any references to Milan or to Berlusconi's career in construction or media. Still, as Scola noted retrospectively and I will discuss later, the film stigmatizes the issues of rampant Italian capitalism in the 1970s, pointing to their iconic imminent incarnation, Silvio Berlusconi.

La più bella serata della mia vita, or the Tragic Comedy of (Proto)Berlusconismo

La più bella serata represents a turning point in Scola's cinema. Ennio Bíspuri notes that this film is "one of his most anomalous works, most distant from the classical grammar of comedy Italian style and from realism" because of its emphasis on the grotesque and its surreal narrative aspects.[21] Gianni Canova maintains that more than any of Scola's films, *La più bella serata* is a "work of self-critical reflection and transition" insofar as it stages a trial against the mediocre self-made man of rampant Italian capitalism, whose death sentence reverberates on the *commedia all'italiana* as a whole.[22] An analysis of this film may illuminate Scola's representation of the cultural and ethical dimensions signifying Berlusconi's emergence and also this transformative moment of Scola's cinema.

A dark comedy drawn from the 1956 short story by Swiss writer Friedrich Dürrenmatt, *Die Panne* (*Traps*, 1960), *La più bella serata* is Scola's second literary adaptation.[23] The film transforms Dürrenmatt's austere parable of guilt into a tragicomic narrative. From the opening sequence, in which the Italian businessman Alfredo Rossi (Alberto Sordi) drives to Switzerland to illegally transfer funds, up until the man's catastrophic death in the Alps, the plot deserves attention. After the money-laundering operation, Alfredo's Maserati breaks down on a mountain road in the Alpine countryside while chasing an attractive and enigmatic female motorist. Seeking help, he arrives at a sinister, isolated castle (Tures Castle in Brunico, Italy), where he meets four noblemen retired from legal professions (Michel Simon, Charles Vanel, Claude Dauphin, and Pierre Brasseur), who, to entertain themselves, hold mock trials for historical characters and, occasionally, for real guests. They invite him to stay and partake in his own trial. Alfredo accepts the strange invitation only because he is lured by the attractive waitress Simonetta (Janet Agren), who works in the castle. During the mock trial, the four hosts question Alfredo about his life and work and then debate their findings.

The grotesque trial dissects the myth of the self-made man that Alfredo would like to incarnate and in so doing unveils a disturbing reality. In a "climate of incumbent tragedy," Alfredo's eloquent speeches progressively construct a striking portrait of a con man who has privileged cheating, expedience, and fraud in his personal and professional life.[24] He candidly admits that his financial fortunes are the outcome of a carefully designed plot to lay hands on his former boss's company. Alfredo won his boss's favor by trafficking call girls for him, seducing his wife, exploiting his health issues to orchestrate his death, and, finally, inheriting his patrimony. In the closing arguments of the mock trial, the "prosecutor" portrays Alfredo as a shameless, corrupt, and depraved criminal and advocates for the death penalty. In contrast, Alfredo's defense "attorney" paints the picture of an inept man whose riches are not the product of any talent of his own. As Jacqueline Reich has shown in her discussion of the *inetto* (the inept man), this contradictory characterization is a typical trait of the male protagonist of the *commedia all'italiana*.[25] Alfredo is both a cynical egotist who pursues only his own interests and an inept bumbler, ill equipped to achieve his goals. Ineptitude in Alfredo goes hand in hand with the attributes of the *nuovo ricco* (nouveau riche) of modern Italy's consumerist society.

The mock trial, which extends for almost the entire length of the film, dramatizes Alfredo's inconsistencies. It takes place in the dining room of the castle, in what Gian Piero Brunetta has defined as "the most refined dinner in Scola's films, in which he familiarizes us with his wine and food culture."[26] The prevalence of interiors and frontal shots shape a theatrical space detached from the outside world, which viewers glimpse in the opening sequence, and from the Alpine landscape, the background of Alfredo's escapades. A variety of elements come together to create a claustrophobic and surreal atmosphere, in which reality recedes and becomes symbolic, something achieved by the meticulously decorated interiors (by set designer Luciano Ricceri), the hosts' costumes and mannerisms, the color palette dominated by shades of red, and the low-key lighting. Playing with the conventions of the horror genre, these elements evoke mysterious rituals from an ancient past and foreshadow dark and bloody events. Christian Uva sees a dialectical tension between off-screen and on-screen space in Scola's cinema. What remains "unseen" from the former, Uva argues, symbolically gravitates on and gives meaning to the microhistories artificially re-created by the latter.[27] This formulation holds for *La più bella serata*, where Alfredo's personal history unfolds as emblematic of a sociocultural type—well contextualized in the 1970s—prone to tax evasion, flight of capital, ostentation of status, corruption, and uncontrollable social aspirations. *La più bella serata* also abides by an Aristotelian sense of tragic unity of place and time, a recurring pattern in Scola's films that allows him to create powerful chronotopes. Brunetta points out that the narrative unity of place and time in Scola allows for a closer investigation not only of the characters' personalities but also of the traces that history has left "on their gestures, words, and masks, and below their masks."[28] In *La più bella serata*, Alfredo Rossi is such a mask and the one-evening trial inside the castle is the powerful dramaturgical device deployed to investigate it.

From a philosophical and ethical perspective, the trial allegory revolves around the Kafkaesque idea of controlling authority and incumbent punishment of *Die Panne*. It is symptomatic of a larger issue, as Antonio Rosario Daniele suggests, that the trial is also a central narrative device of other contemporary films, such as Marco Bellocchio's *Nel nome del padre* (*In the Name of the Father*, 1972), Marco Ferreri's *La cagna* (*The Bitch*, 1972), and Damiano Damiani's *Confessione di un commissario di polizia al procuratore della Repubblica* (*Confession of a Police Captain*, 1971).[29] The moral trials presented in these films interrogate society's expectations for institutional justice (the Catholic Church and the police), challenge the hierarchical power relations in a dysfunctional society, and condemn the inhumanity of authority as a whole. Overall, the trope of the trial in the Italian cinema of the 1970s points to the ethical role staged by the law in mediating among the social, civic, and political codes that shape the idea of social justice. The mock trial of *La più bella serata* goes beyond the ethics of justice. Focusing on the clash between Alfredo's amoral disposition, tacky vanity, and mediocrity, it exposes the sociological features that his mask encapsulates and calls attention to the cultural socioeconomic markers that characterize Italian society in the 1970s, revealing the incipient symptoms of *berlusconismo*.[30]

La più bella serata ends gloomily. After the mock death sentence, the sinister events foreshadowed during the trial start to unfold. Alfredo goes to sleep and has a nightmare in which the waitress Simonetta takes him on a motorcycle ride around the castle and eventually brings him to his own grotesque,

FIGURE 21. The long slow-motion shot of the Maserati precipitating from the ravine in *La più bella serata della mia vita*

medieval-style execution ceremony. The following morning, Alfredo leaves the castle in his Maserati with a roll of parchment containing the entries of the mock proceedings. Along the way, he sees the anonymous female motorist who led him there, and he chases her once more at full speed. As he tries to brake for a road closed for construction, the parchment falls and gets jammed between the gas and the brake, forcing him to step instead on the gas. The Maserati accelerates and Alfredo falls into the ravine, thus executing himself according to the sentence handed down by the "mock" trial. During the fall, he sees the female motorist remove her helmet, revealing herself as the waitress Simonetta. The sexual power emanating from Simonetta, who plays the seductive angel of death, and Alfredo's farcical failure as a womanizer guarantee the death narrative. The final scene turns the comedy into a dark tragedy that epitomizes the condemnation of Alfredo and the unbridled and individualistic bourgeoisie he represents.

The long shot of the Maserati falling through the air, repeated three times from different angles, is filmed using a special camera for car crash tests that produces an extreme slow-motion effect and shows the Maserati dramatically suspended in the air (fig. 21).[31]

The editing juxtaposes extreme low-angle close-ups of Simonetta contemplating Alfredo's death from a position of domination (fig. 22) with extreme high-angle close-ups of Alfredo's face looking at her from inside the

FIGURE 22. Extreme close-up, high-angle shot of Simonetta staring at Alfredo in the death scene in *La più bella serata della mia vita*

FIGURE 23. Extreme close-up, low-angle shot of Alfredo's laughter while he is precipitating and looking at the woman in *La più bella serata della mia vita*

car (fig. 23). This complex cinematography, in ironic contrast to Armando Trovajoli's graceful score that accompanies the flight of the car, emphasizes and expands the last moments of Alfredo's life, in which he becomes aware of his destiny and bursts into interminable, sardonic laughter.

This dramatic finale evokes Federico Fellini's *Toby Dammit*.[32] The two films share their central narrative and several aesthetic features: the high-speed car ride from the driver's perspective, the blonde female character leading the death narrative, the protagonist's laughter before his death, and the mise-en-scène of part of the death sequence. However, Dammit's and Alfredo's motivations and ethical choices diverge substantially. Dammit's laughter stems from the awareness that he is unable to free himself from the artificial image that the media has set for him. To escape this artificial and—pretty Felliniesque—subhuman landscape, he purposefully chooses a self-inflicted death.[33] Alfredo, on the contrary, lacks a moral universe. Even if his death, too, is essentially a self-execution, it is not the result of Alfredo's decision, but the outcome of an external force—destiny or a superior justice. Alfredo remains impervious to moral judgment and to any notion of self-improvement or redemption, and he dies in an almost ridiculous way while chasing an unknown woman.

Alfredo's laughter during the spectacular car accident stems from his awareness that the death penalty has been performed, synecdochally, through the parchment containing the transcript of the mock trial. Regardless of his ironic destiny, he shows a sense of fulfillment and pleasure. Scola comments that "he laughs because he knows that he's indestructible, the little Italian bourgeois knows . . . that he will never die. . . . After all, he was very confident in his destiny, in his role in human history. . . . Therefore, he was so amused and satisfied that he dies laughing."[34] In other words, the philosophical focus of *La più bella serata* is not Alfredo's moral degeneration but the enjoyment he feels at the moment of his symbolic death.

The adaptation from Dürrenmatt's *Die Panne* confirms this perspective. The script that Scola wrote with Sergio Amidei is more pessimistic than the Swiss original because it describes Alfredo as a cynical moneymaker who values his Maserati above all else, including friendship, love, and loyalty.[35] Alfredo Traps, the Swiss petty travel salesman of *Die Panne*, sees the mock trial as a compelling moral judgment that forces him to reassess his life. Eventually, he has the revelation of a superior sense of justice and hangs himself in the attempt to overcome his guilt and pay for his crimes. The symbolic departure of Scola's finale from Dürrenmatt's alters the story's original dramaturgic center and focuses on the negative potential of the cultural construct incarnated by Alfredo Rossi, the *nuovo ricco* whose ruthless profile has characterized Italian society since the economic boom and found its socioeconomic and political epitome in Silvio Berlusconi.[36] This finale is an "umbilical scene," as defined by Millicent Marcus, insofar as it deviates from its literary parent text, exposing the derivative process and making the filmmaker's "interpretive strategy" explicit.[37]

Scola, in an interview, recalled discussing with Dürrenmatt the Italian script's drastic deviation from the original finale, arguing that Alfredo Rossi's committing suicide would have been unsustainable: "We are Catholic and not Lutheran. . . . For the sinner there will always be a punishment, but he'll die laughing because he knows that his bourgeois mentality, which is infinitely stronger than any religious credo, will never die."[38] In the same passage, Scola commented on how Alfredo Rossi's character foreshadowed Silvio Berlusconi: "He [Dürrenmatt] didn't like my explanation very much, but the final result, although very distant from his work, persuaded him. Besides that, Sordi resembled Berlusconi and foreshadowed his motifs in an impressive manner. Some lines sound like [they were] written by him [Berlusconi]."[39] The parallel that Scola draws between Berlusconi and Sordi raises questions not only about the sociocultural construct of Alfredo's character, which Scola relates to Catholicism and the bourgeois mind-set, but also about the impersonation of this construct through Sordi's body. "In that film [Sordi] is a 'little Berlusconi,'" Scola insists in another interview speaking of Sordi's performance, "so proud of his dirty tricks that he takes pride in exposing them to the judges."[40] Scola casts Sordi in *La più bella giornata* because he is a "maschera tragica" and his performance as Alfredo Rossi captures the dramaturgic and ethical force of a tragic Shakespearean hero:[41] "It is a tragic character worthy of Shakespeare: a man of power, a wealthy man who is desperate. . . . He is a man that made himself inconsolable, by his very personal contemplation of the abyss. He certainly does not think of the salvation of the soul or of the mind."[42]

It is significant that the correlation that Scola draws between Sordi/Rossi and Berlusconi entails performative, symbolic, dramaturgic, and sociocultural factors. In fact, from a sociocultural and historical perspective, Alfredo Rossi foreshadows Berlusconi in a number of ways. There are striking social and biographical analogies between the character and Berlusconi's historical persona: in Italian society, Berlusconi is the nouveau riche par excellence, and his patrimony is of notoriously unclear origin; he is outspoken about being a womanizer; and he is apparently obsessed with sex. Comprehensive exegeses of *berlusconismo* and Berlusconi's media empire, patrimony, and alleged relationship with the Mafia have been published. Some claim this relationship gave Berlusconi the financial means to jump-start his career in the early 1980s.⁴³ Ginsborg and Asquer provided the first overarching vision of *berlusconismo* as a power system shaped by historical, sociological, and economic factors as well as cultural and discursive practices.⁴⁴ Antonio Gibelli emphasizes how *berlusconismo* reflects the individual and collective changes that occurred after the economic miracle, the student and sexual liberation, and the collapse of communism in 1989.⁴⁵ A problematic relationship with justice is also central within Berlusconi's life. Berlusconi's trials for corruption, fraud, and sex offenses led to a vote of no confidence against his government and, consequently, to his resignation in 2011. Two years later, a court's verdict sentenced him to four years in jail and banned him from holding public office until 2019. The verdict was commuted to one year and, ultimately, to performing social work once a week for ten months in a community for the elderly in Cesano Boscone (Milan), since at the time of his sentence Berlusconi was too old to go to jail under Italian law.

The final execution of Alfredo orchestrated by a silent but dominating Simonetta also foreshadows Berlusconi's ignominious downfall, prompted by a series of sexual scandals, his wife's public denunciation, and his being sentenced to seven years of detention for charges stemming from an alleged sex-for-hire affair with Karima El Mahroug, a young Moroccan woman known as "Ruby Rubacuori" (Ruby the Heart Stealer) while she was a minor. "Several female voices shouted that 'the king is naked,'" writes Ida Dominijanni, and brought about his progressive elimination from Parliament.⁴⁶ Most important, Alfredo embodies a symbolic mix of the stereotypical *italiano medio* traits that make him a powerful proto-Berlusconi figure. Alfredo is the Italian Everyman, but he also embodies a constant oscillation between ineptitude and Machiavellian behavior and displays an uncontrollable craving for sexual enjoyment.

As Silvana Patriarca has observed, Berlusconi's persona has been linked to the stereotypical elements of what is perceived as the Italian "national character" or the *italiano medio*.⁴⁷ In fact, he has used his own persona to occupy the Italian public stage with a grotesque "hedonistic body" that is deeply rooted "in the nation's autobiography and collective imaginary."⁴⁸ Both his appeal as the epitome of the "national character" and the strategic message emanating from it have been perceived as a conglomerate of ideas, experiences, contexts, and lifestyles that public opinion has largely both recognized and embraced as its own. In other words, Berlusconi has deliberately created a public performance of his own self that overlaps with the construct of the *italiano medio*, and this has consequently affected the electorate's reactions to his political agenda. It is this junction between his performance and the paradigm of the Italian "national character" that establishes parallels between Berlusconi's body and that of Alberto Sordi, the corrupt and immature Italian Everyman character in *commedia all'italiana*, and, especially, with the impersonator of Alfredo Rossi in *La più bella serata*.

As Albertazzi and Rothenberg maintain, *berlusconismo* is not the culmination of the Italians' democratic immaturity and natural propensity to corruption.[49] On the contrary, it is the biopolitical project devised through Berlusconi's body and *berlusconismo* that incorporated symbols of popular culture that had been circulating for some time prior to his arrival on the national stage. In his analysis of the *italiano medio* within the sociocultural context of the economic miracle, Sergio Rigoletto compellingly interprets this figure as embodying a discursive process that delimits normality and ordinariness and that creates the "cinematic construct as an image of potential collective identification for the nation."[50] This logic, I argue, is at play in Berlusconi's public performance. Here, the resemblance to Alfredo Rossi is truly striking. Scola and Amidei identified these symbols and created a character that would crystallize into a cultural icon. On the other hand, Berlusconi was able to intercept these symbols and propose his own body—political and private—as the incarnation of a construct that already existed and was socially accepted.

Silvio Berlusconi's Embodiment of the *Italiano medio*

Berlusconi's official biography from 1995 listed the chief features of the Cavaliere's personality and leadership. Some of these included "stubbornness, volubility, unpredictability, unscrupulousness, ambiguity, a self-reliant walk across the labyrinth of secrets . . . , sense of clan, taste for command, propensity to control, attention for the attractive gesture, desire to please."[51] During the 2001 electoral campaign, Forza Italia sent each Italian household *An Italian Story* (2001), a glossy 128-page biography of the leader, accompanied by a letter signed by Berlusconi himself. *An Italian Story* praises Berlusconi for his "irrepressible and outgoing vitality," "cult for family," blind devotion to his mother, enthusiastic passion for soccer, and ability to make money even if in slightly dishonest—but socially acceptable—ways, such as doing homework for his classmates while in high school.[52] The volume also emphasizes the envy Berlusconi's young friends felt because of his charm, fashion sense and self-presentation, intense social life, talent for performing and singing, and purported success with girls. These last two attributes subtly hint of Berlusconi's performance to follow of Don Juan figure engaging in a vigorous sexual life, which would later fully emerge as the sex scandals, the bunga bunga parties, and allegations about underage prostitution.[53]

In other words, since the beginning of his political career, an image has been discursively created of Berlusconi as a resourceful self-made man bearing the psychological traits, social behavior, and drives associated with the stereotypical idea of Italianness. These qualities also include the negative attributes approved and accepted as positive by Italian society. In his discussion of Berlusconi's ascent to power in the national and international context, Perry Anderson elaborates on Berlusconi's principal quality, his *spregiudicatezza*, a word with no English equivalent but that roughly connotes a mix of conflicting qualities signifying "indivisibly, both admirable open-mindedness and deplorable ruthlessness."[54] "In theory," Anderson remarks, "the context indicates which [one] applies. In practice, common usage erodes the distinction between them."[55]

Spregiudicatezza in all matters is the defining characteristic of both Alfredo Rossi and Silvio Berlusconi. Its conflicting meanings underscore the tension between two dialectic forces— namely, the drama of the individual who struggles to adapt to social conventions while simultaneously recognizing society's revulsion of him.[56] This conflict emphasizes, albeit in a hyperbolic fashion, the "aberrant, abnormal everyday life, [which is] dominated by the most unbridled individualism and by a surplus of subjectivity that results in failure and defeat."[57] In other words, it is in the discursive construction of Italianness and in the *spregiudicatezza* of comedy Italian style that the proto-Berlusconi mask offers its finest performance as well as its ability to model moral degradation.

To conclude, I would like to recall Vincenzo Susca's suggestion that the figure of Berlusconi is an "extraordinary pre-text to give meaning to our past and future history."[58] The proto-Berlusconi type of *La più bella serata della mia vita* is one such pretext in Scola's cinema. It is in fact an opportunity to discuss, retrospectively, the impact of *berlusconismo* on Italian society, while at the same time it offers a textual illustration of *berlusconismo* before the advent of Berlusconi. Scola's condemnation of Alfredo's amoral *spregiudicatezza* not only adopts a strong moral stance in the context of contemporary Italian society and politics but also constitutes the director's attempt to eliminate the proto-Berlusconi mask from his artistic horizon. As Scola allowed in 2012, "In 1972, we didn't think that what we were reinventing . . . while we were writing to make jokes and have fun . . . would ever occur in the reality."[59]

Notes

1. Zagarrio emphasizes the complexity of the filmic and narrative "architecture" of Scola's cinema in "La sceneggiatura circolare: Strutture narrative in the film di Ettore Scola," *Italianist* 29 (2009): 265–80; 272, 276–77. The quote from Scola comes from "Conversation with Ettore Scola," Rome, March 1, 1986, in Pier Marco De Santi and Rossano Vittori, *I film di Ettore Scola* (Rome: Gremese, 1987), 42. Translations throughout the chapter are my own unless otherwise noted.
2. The definition of Scola's cinema as the "dance of history" is by Vito Zagarrio. I am quoting from my notes taken during Zagarrio's presentation "Scola e la storia del dopoguerra in Italia" at the Ettore Scola symposium in Venice, October 2016.
3. It is the case, for example, of Harrison Ford's resemblance to Ronald Reagan in *Raiders of the Lost Ark*, shot in 1981, the first year of the Reagan presidency. I thank the anonymous reader who suggested the cinematic reference and raised the avatar question, giving me the opportunity to clarify my argument.
4. For a theoretical discussion of the construct of *Italiano medio* in comedy Italian style, see Vittorio Spinazzola, *Cinema e pubblico: Lo spettacolo filmico in Italia, 1945–1965* (Rome: Bulzoni, 1985); Sergio Rigoletto, "The Italian Comedy of the Economic Miracle: *L'italiano medio* and Strategies of Gender Exclusion," in *Italy on Screen: National Identity and Italian Imaginary*, ed. Lucy Bolton and Christina Siggers Manson (London: IGRS, 2007); and Silvana Patriarca, *Italianità: La costruzione del carattere nazionale* (Rome-Bari: Laterza, 2010).
5. See Giovanni Orsina, *Il Berlusconismo nella storia d'Italia*, Kindle ed. (Venice: Marsilio, 2013).
6. See Paul Ginsborg and Enrica Asquer, eds., *Berlusconismo: Analisi di un sistema di potere* (Bari: Laterza, 2011).
7. See Antonio Gibelli, *Berlusconi passato alla storia: L'Italia nell'era della democrazia autoritaria* (Rome: Donzelli, 2010).
8. For the linkage with fascism, see also Gianpasquale Santomassimo, ed., *La notte della democrazia italiana: Dal regime fascista al governo Berlusconi* (Milan: Il Saggiatore, 2003); and the two special issues of the political magazine *Migro Mega*, "Berlusconismo e fascismo" (January 2011) and "Berlusconismo e fascismo" (February 2011).

9. See Silvio Berlusconi's speech of the *discesa in campo*, in "'L'Italia è il paese che amo': La discesa in campo sul video," January 22, 1004, Repubblica.it, http://www.repubblica.it/2004/a/sezioni/politica/festaforza/discesa/discesa.html.
10. On *berlusconismo* as a biopolitical "regime of enjoyment," see Ida Dominijanni, *Il trucco: Sessualità e biopolitica nella fine di Berlusconi* (Rome: Ediesse, 2014), 25–55. Dominijanni's analysis is inspired by Žižek's theoretical perspective on enjoyment as a political factor. See Slavoj Žižek, *For They Know Not What They Do: Enjoyment as a Political Factor* (London: Verso, 2002).
11. Scola coauthored the script for *Un drago in forma di nuvola* with Furio Scarpelli and Silvia Scola. He then published *Un drago* as a graphic novel in 2013 with the artistic collaboration of Ivo Milazzo.
12. Enrico Paoli uses the word *anathema* to define Scola's stance on Berlusconi in "Il maestro rosso," *Libero*, January 20, 2016, http://www.pressreader.com/italy/libero/20160120/282033326204057/TextView.
13. See Giovanni Magi's "Interview—Ettore Scola," Euronews, May 9, 2009, https://www.youtube.com/watch?v=nSTBchUcs00&feature=fvw. A transcription of the interview is available at http://it.euronews.com/2009/05/08/ettore-scola-finche-c-e-berlusconi-al-potere-io-film-non-ne-faccio, and the English translation may be accessed at http://www.euronews.com/2009/05/08/scola-i-won-t-make-films-while-berlusconi-rules.
14. Magi.
15. Magi.
16. Magi.
17. Magi.
18. Magi.
19. *Signore e signori, buonanotte* is a collective film produced and directed by Cooperative May 15: Agenore Incrocci (Age), Leonardo Benvenuti, Luigi Comencini, Piero De Bernardi, Nanni Loy, Ruggero Maccari, Luigi Magni, Mario Monicelli, Ugo Pirro, Furio Scarpelli, and Scola. *I nuovi mostri* is an episodic film directed by Dino Risi, Monicelli, and Scola and refers back to *I mostri* (*The Monsters*, 1963), directed by Risi on a script by Petri, Age, Scarpelli, and Scola.
20. For the concept of cinema as a form of interrogation of power, see Pier Paolo Antonello, "I due corpi del divo: Le maschere del potere: Andreotti, Thatcher, Elisabetta II," *Bianco e Nero* 576, nos. 2–3 (2013): 163.
21. Ennio Bíspuri, *Ettore Scola: Un umanista nel cinema italiano* (Rome: Bulzoni, 2006), 212.
22. Gianni Canova, "Ettore Scola," *Belfagor* 41, 3 (1986): 284.
23. Scola's first adaptation is *Il commissario Pepe* (*Police Chief Pepe*, 1969), inspired by the eponymous novel by Ugo Facco De Lagarda (1965).

24. Stefano Masi, *Ettore Scola: Uno sguardo acuto e ironico sull'Italia e gli italiani degli ultimi quarant'anni* (Rome: Gremese, 2006), 50.
25. See Jacqueline Reich, *Beyond the Latin Lover: Marcello Mastroianni, Masculinity, and Italian Cinema* (Bloomington: Indiana University Press, 2004).
26. See Gian Piero Brunetta's chapter, "Dancing and Drinking with the Muses—the Cinema of Ettore Scola," this volume.
27. See Christian Uva, "Un borgo nella metropoli: Ettore Scola a Palazzo Federici." *Italianist* 35, no. 2 (2015): 287. Uva's analysis focuses in particular on the settings of *Una giornata particolare* (*A Special Day*, 1977) and *Romanzo di un giovane povero* (*The Story of a Poor Young Boy*, 1995).
28. Giampiero Brunetta, *Il cinema italiano contemporaneo: Da "La dolce vita" a "Centochiodi,"* ePub e-book (Bari/Milan: Laterza, 2007).
29. Antonio Rosario Daniele, "Meccanismi iperparodici dalla narrazione al cinema: *La panne* di Dürrenmatt fra Ettore Scola e Alberto Sordi," *Between*, 6, no. 12 (2016), http://ojs.unica.it/index.php/between/article/view/2204.
30. On Alfredo's mediocrity and its parody in the film, see again Rosario.
31. See Masi's description of the sequence in *Ettore Scola*, 46.
32. *Toby Dammit* is a chapter of *Tre passi nel delirio* (*Spirits of the Dead*, 1969), featuring three shorts inspired by Edgar Allan Poe's tales and directed, respectively, by Roger Vadim, Louis Malle, and Fellini. Ennio Bíspuri refers to *La più bella giornata* and to *Toby Dammit* in *Ettore Scola*, 215. Millicent Marcus also suggested this comparison to me.
33. In Fellini's visionary adaption from Poe's "Never Bet the Devil Your Head," Toby Dammit (Terence Stamp) is a British actor casted for an Italian spaghetti western. Dammit uses alcohol and drugs in the attempt to survive the mediatization of reality and his personal life. In a mise-en-scène dominated by hallucinatory and dark undertones, Dammit escapes in his Ferrari from a television studio to chase an ominous young blonde girl. Literally driven to madness, he arrives to a closed road with a bridge under construction and bursts into laughter. He decides to jump across the bridge and is decapitated. The girl picks up his head and looks into the camera, revealing a devilish gaze and raising questions about Dammit's moral choice.
34. "Serate di Cinevino: Ettore Scola presenta *La più bella serata della mia vita*," YouTube, January 20, 2012, 9:58, posted by CinetecaBologna, https://www.youtube.com/watch?v=L3rTw6oCyg4.
35. See Masi, *Ettore Scola*, 45–46.
36. Another important variation from the original, as Daniele rightly emphasizes, is the transformation of Simone, the middle-aged skillful housekeeper in Dürrenmatt's story, into Simonetta, a young and sensual maid played by Janet Agren, the future starlet of Italian sexy comedy. See again Daniele, "Meccanismi iperparodici," 6.

37. See Millicent Marcus, "Umbilical Scenes: Where Filmmakers Foreground Their Relationships to Literary Sources," *Romance Languages Annual* 10, no. 1 (1998): xix–xxiv.
38. Malcom Pagani and Fabrizio Corallo, "'Fosse stato per me non sarei mai diventato regista': Intervista a Ettore Scola." Traffico di parole, May 16, 2014, http://www.trafficodiparole.com/wordpress/fosse-stato-per-me-non-sarei-mai-diventato-regista-intervista-a-ettore-scola-di-malcom-pagani-e-fabrizio-corallo/. First published in *Il fatto quotidiano*.
39. Malcom Pagani and Fabrizio Corallo, "'Fosse stato per me.'"
40. Marco Spagnoli, *Alberto Sordi: Storia di un italiano* (Rome: Adnkronos, 2003), 99.
41. Spagnoli, 98.
42. Spagnoli, 99.
43. Among others, see Alexander Stille, *Citizen Berlusconi* (Milan: Garzanti, 2006).
44. See Ginsborg and Asquer, *Berlusconismo*.
45. See Gibelli, *Berlusconi passato alla storia*.
46. Dominijanni, *Il trucco*, 26.
47. Patriarca, 266.
48. Dominijanni, *Il trucco*, 19.
49. Daniele Albertazzi et al., eds., *Resisting the Tide: Cultures of Opposition under Berlusconi (2001–2006)* (New York: Continuum, 2011), 10.
50. Rigoletto, "Italian Comedy," 34.
51. Giuseppe Fiori, *Il venditore: Storia di Silvio Berlusconi e della Fininvest* (Milan: Garzanti, 1995), 41.
52. Forza Italia, *Una storia italiana* (Milan: Mondadori, 2001), 9–19.
53. Berlusconi allegedly learned from Muammar al-Gaddafi how to organize bunga bunga parties—that is, orgies with nude young women dancing and performing sexual games for him and his male guests.
54. See Perry Anderson, "Land without Prejudice," *London Review of Books*, March 21, 2002, http://www.lrb.co.uk/v24/n06/perry-anderson/land-without-prejudice.
55. Anderson.
56. Maurizio Grande, *La commedia all'italiana*, ed. Orio Caldiron (Rome: Bulzoni 2003), 45.
57. Grande, 55.
58. Alberto Abruzzese and Vincenzo Susca, eds., *Tutto è Berlusconi: Radici, metafore e destinazione del tempo nuovo* (Milan: Lupetti, 2004), 55.
59. "Serate di Cinevino."

FACING THE FAILURE
Characters as Political Allegories in *La terrazza*

Dario Marcucci and Luca Zamparini

LA TERRAZZA (*THE TERRACE*, 1980), although less celebrated and studied than other works by Scola,[1] stands out as a crucial step in the director's career for it illustrates clearly how the filmmaker's artistic and human trajectory is intertwined with the history of Italian society, politics, and culture. This chapter considers *La terrazza* as the movie that, by portraying the failure of the left-wing intelligentsia associated with the Partito Comunista Italiano (PCI, or Italian Communist Party), and prefiguring the so-called *riflusso nel privato* (retreat into the private sphere) of the early 1980s, emblematically concludes the 1970s.

Following his directorial debut, *Se permettete parliamo di donne* (*Let's Talk about Women*, 1964), Scola gradually set aside the stereotypical situations of Italian comedy to address more urgent social and political issues.[2] The intensification of political struggles in Italy in the late 1960s and early 1970s, along with the Left's inability to fulfill its historical role, pushed Scola to more intensively reflect on Italy's recent history. Beginning with *C'eravamo tanto amati* (*We All Loved Each Other So Much*, 1974) and continuing up to *La terrazza*, he attempted to essentialize the mechanics of both the cultural industry and the politics of his time. Within this context, we investigate the main rhetorical device through which Scola dealt with the complexity of these subjects: the use of allegorical characters. We argue that the characters of Scola's political season are not significant as individuals but rather as the embodiments of social actors of contemporary Italian history. This is most evident in *La terrazza*, a movie that marks a turning point in Scola's career and, by tackling the deep identity crisis of the 1970s, concludes the era of *commedia all'italiana*.

The so-called *anni di piombo* (years of lead) opened emblematically with the Piazza Fontana bombing in Milan in December of 1969 and with the birth of the Red Brigades in August of the following year, thereby bringing a climate of violence and social tension that affected every facet of Italian society. Amid this political turmoil, the global economic crisis peaked in October 1973 with the oil crisis and subsequent embargo. This crisis especially struck Italy, still reeling from the recession following the 1960s economic boom. Combined with the emergence of a new competitor in television alongside an old competitor like Hollywood, the economic crisis also struck the film industry, which up until that time was one of the most productive and successful branches of the Italian economy. All these factors affected the structure, characteristics, and mood of Italian comedy, which during the 1970s remained the most profitable genre at the box office.[3] The main reason for its unchallenged success was the intrinsic nature of the genre, which, far from having a rigid, well-defined structure, was characterized by openness and elasticity.

Italian comedy of the 1970s has been defined by Scola as a "supergenre"[4] for its potential to cross different genres and to frame different content without losing its essence. Film historian Gian Piero Brunetta defines it as a "container for carrying all types of materials and assembling complex codes and systems."[5] Such a quality allows Italian-style comedy—a genre originally related to a specific historical period (namely, the economic boom)—to reinvent itself and to adapt to a society deeply changed in its dynamics and balances of power. Throughout the seventies, the political struggle in Italy intensified as did social turmoil over long-held conservative values embedded in traditional institutions such as the family and church, particularly with respect to marriage and the patriarchal structure. This struggle, which began mainly as a social conflict, extended to generational and gender-based conflict and resulted in a radicalization of political involvement.[6] In this context, auteurs such as Mario Monicelli, Dino Risi, Luigi Comencini, and Scola continued to explore the potentialities of comedy, developing the tendencies begun in the previous decade, in order to address a more complex social and political milieu.

During the 1960s, comedic cinematic discourse became an instrument with which to investigate reality, with a focus on recent national history. As Brunetta writes, at the time "film-makers address[ed] the recent history of the nation and recover[ed] the collective memory. . . . Rather than adopting grand style and drama, they opt[ed] for comedy, but they deeply change[d] its morphology."[7] In other words, comedy of the 1960s unveiled social dynamics and desacralized institutions by addressing important episodes of recent Italian history through the lens of what might be called "humor Italian style."[8] This idea of critical humor played a key role in the 1970s as well, yet at that time pessimism and disenchantment prevailed.

Among the intellectuals who described this crisis, one of the most powerful voices was Pier Paolo Pasolini's. In 1975, he directed *Salò o le 120 giornate di Sodoma* (*Salò or the 120 Days of Sodom*), a dramatic testament and desperate *j'accuse* to modern society. That same year, he published *La nuova gioventù*, a collection of his poems, including selections from *La meglio gioventù*, written during the 1950s in Friulan dialect. In light of the deep pessimism that characterized the decade, the author rewrote some of his old poems. In *Versi sottili come righe di pioggia* (*Lines as Thin as Streaks of Rain*), Pasolini retraces the origin of the historical pessimism that prevails during the 1970s and states the impossibility to escape it:

> Equally severe sentence must be pronounced on anyone who
> Loves the sub-proletariat and who therefore
> Has no class-consciousness.
> . . . .
> The words of condemnation began to be heard
> Midway in Fifties and are still resounding.
> Meanwhile: innocence, which in fact existed,
> Has begun to lose itself in corruption, denials, neuroses.[9]

These lines exemplify the pervasive loss of faith in leftist ideology common to several intellectuals. Despite the ideological differences between Pasolini and Scola, the mood and the themes of the poem seem to echo those of Scola's political comedies. Indeed, Scola suggested that comedy was the most suitable genre to portray the pessimism of the decade: "[Comedy] grew up and addressed reality; it abandoned its consolatory role and became disquieting and provocative."[10] In describing the evolution of *commedia all'italiana*, the director retraced his own parabola, from early, innocuous comedies, to progressively more political films.

By 1969, in *Il commissario Pepe* (*Police Chief Pepe*), Scola was already attempting to problematize the basic narrative of comedy. Here, Scola deploys the trope of the hypocritical Italian bourgeoisie defined by immoral clandestine behaviors in order to expose a corrupt political judiciary system that does not hesitate to punish the weak to preserve itself. The attention dedicated to the structural injustices of postwar Italian society, linked to the usual caustic portrait of Italian bourgeoisie, denotes a new aspect of Scola's comedy, and it affects the whole mood of the film, pervaded by melancholy and sad resignation.

However, it was with the 1973 film, *Trevico-Torino: Viaggio nel Fiat-Nam* (*Trevico-Turin: Voyage in Fiat-nam*), that Scola turned his cinema more directly to politics. With this film—produced by the PCI-managed Unitelefilm—Scola follows the stylistic lesson of Free Cinema and Direct Cinema and decides to shoot a low-budget film in 16 mm. In portraying the struggle of Fortunato, a migrant from Trevico in southern Italy, the director attempts to fill the gap between camera and the object filmed. Taking advantage of the mobility of the 16 mm camera, Scola places the spectator within the crowd of the working class. The strong stylistic rupture from the standard mise-en scène and cinematography of Scola's former films is, however, framed within a well-defined narrative structure. The film was ostracized by the Agnelli family (the founders of FIAT) and was prevented from being distributed successfully. These vicissitudes likely led Scola to return to comedy. Yet the need to deal with urgent social, political, and historical issues continued to affect the substratum of his next production, resulting in what Scola would call "commedia provocatoria" (provocative comedy).

C'eravamo tanto amati epitomizes this new phase of Scola's production, in which the director analyzes the first thirty years of the Italian Republic through the story of three friends who fought together in the Resistance but then followed very different paths. The stylistic sophistication of the characters and situations of the *commedia all'italiana* allowed Scola to offer an articulate criticism of the contradictions of a republic that was supposed to be founded on the ideals of the Resistance. The strength of Scola's approach is in his overarching effort, which encompasses and scrutinizes different segments of society and cultural institutions. His caustic look lies on boorish parvenus (Aldo Fabrizi as Romolo Catenacci), social climbers (Vittorio Gassman as Gianni Perego), and egocentric intellectuals (Stefano Satta Flores as Nicola Palumbo). Through the representation of the characters and their interplay with cultural and social processes of this time period, the filmmaker develops the cynical mode that will become one of his main stylistic features. Gianni Perego's parabola from antifascist idealism to cynical opportunism, although accompanied by a few moments of melancholic self-awareness, embodies Scola's new attitude toward the traditional traits of the genre. Moreover, in *C'eravamo tanto amati*, Scola starts focusing on the Left's inability to tackle the actual needs of the people, seen as a consequence of both the isolation of intellectuals and the bourgeoisification of the political class.[11] This theme becomes central in the filmmaker's following work.

In *Brutti, sporchi e cattivi* (*Down and Dirty*, 1976), Scola created an extreme portrait of those who would be later defined as "proletarians without revolution."[12] The misadventures of a family living in a *baraccopoli* (shantytown) outside Rome are employed to expose the conditions of subproletarians in the years of the economic boom. Nino Manfredi plays Giacinto, the crude patriarch of a large family who migrated from Puglia. Abuses, deceptions, and degeneration revolve around a sum of money Giacinto hides from his relatives and their attempts to steal it. The comedic element is developed through the filter of an unprecedented grotesque style, which allows Scola to deepen his political discourse and define his cultural stance within a tragicomic context. In doing so, the director criticizes the misrepresentations of the lower classes as they have been produced by a certain leftist populism, which found it more convenient to romanticize these marginal people than to critically address their actual situation. For Scola, to succeed politically, the Left could not avoid a constant process of self-analysis and self-criticism, especially with regard to its cultural politics. Although the response of critics was not unanimously good,[13] the movie exemplifies the ideological crisis of the Left and the sociological changes at play in Italy. It is worth noting that in the same years Pasolini, whose influence in the making of *Brutti, sporchi e cattivi* is evident,[14] was addressing the same themes. In a well-known essay titled "Abiura dalla trilogia della vita" ("Abjuration of the Trilogy of Life," April 1975), Pasolini reconsidered his once romanticized view of the subproletariat and laid the foundation for the concept, developed some months later,[15] of cultural genocide, the loss of the cultural and historical identity of subproletarians classes.

Even when dealing with the fascist period, as he does in his next film, *Una giornata particolare* (*A Special Day*, 1977), Scola addresses urgent contemporary issues, such as the marginalization of particular groups. The two main characters in *Una giornata particolare* represent two identity groups, women and homosexuals, who were particularly oppressed during the *ventennio* (fascist period) yet were still struggling in 1977 to find their own political space within the strongly class-oriented political narrative of the extraparliamentary leftist groups. Again, Scola's work underlines the distance between a left anchored to theoretical dogmas and the actual individual needs of the people.

In *La terrazza*, Scola—who would retreat to literary cinema with an adaptation of Iginio Ugo Tarchetti's *Fosca* (1869) the very next year with *Passione d'amore* (*Passion of Love*, 1981)—finally acknowledges the impossibility of any real social and cultural change through film. Such an artistic disposition will define his production during the 1980s. The terrace of the title is a symbolic space that resembles the Buñuelian dining room of *El Ángel Exterminator* (*The Exterminating Angel*, 1962), where weary social rituals and class privileges emblematically trap the high-society characters in a surreal cage without walls. Similarly, in Scola's terrace the tired and empty interactions between characters coming from both the cultural and political realm embody the dead end of enthusiasm that first followed the Resistance and later the political movements of 1968.

La terrazza is a pessimistic portrait of the failure of leftist intellectual typologies, thereby marking a bitter close to Scola's political comedies of the seventies. Events from the very same night are repeated and shown from different perspectives, interrupted by the backstories of five characters linked to each other. The camerawork conveys two different narrative temporalities: on the one hand, there are the backstories with narrative-oriented standard representation; on the other hand, there are the long takes during the party on the terrace, when time appears to be slowed down and the camera indulges in exposing the repetition of rituals and ceremonials of a society that is ineluctably detached from history. All the elements of Scola's mise-en-scène convey the crystallization of a specific intellectual milieu—the aging Roman intelligentsia—in a sterile cultural aristocracy. Nevertheless, in the representation of the younger generations of intellectuals and directors, there is a little grudge, translated into characters who are often voluble and ridiculous in their efforts to repudiate the works of the previous generation.

Like his previous political comedies, *La terrazza* presents characters that unfold the director's vision of Italian society in allegory. Scola focuses more on their representative function than on their psychological coherence. Far from creating empty containers for political or social actors, Scola often adds layers to his representation and problematizes it by using extratextual elements. His political films frequently employ signifiers that are both historically and culturally charged and that transcend fictional borders, providing further meanings to the filmic text. For instance, in *C'eravamo tanto amati*, cinema and neorealism are not simply referenced as important cultural aspects of Italian postwar history, but also symbolize a moral counterpoint to the corruption that began to spread in Italian society and politics just after the war.

The characters of *La terrazza* are complicated and stratified by the paratextual structure surrounding the actors' personas. Sometimes the process is transparent—as when Galeazzo Benti, playing himself, exposes the decline of his career; other times, it is more complex, with actors whose real and fictional personas interact seamlessly. Tognazzi's role in *La terrazza* is also a commentary on his own career, while Mastroianni's character is, instead, a tired and sloppy evolution of Marcello from Fellini's *La dolce vita* (1961).[16] Revisiting the traditional *maschere* (types) of *commedia all'italiana*, Scola constructs systems of references and relations between characters with specific functions and actors popularly recognized as representative of certain kinds of roles. All the main male actors are from the generation that contributed to the success of Italian comedy (and cinema). Besides their single roles and allegorical functions, they are supposed to embody the pessimism and resignation of those people who had aimed for a real social and artistic change but instead found themselves trapped in institutionalized narratives. Tognazzi, Gassman, Mastroianni, and Trintignant are usually defined as *istituzioni del cinema* (mainstays of cinema), and Scola uses their established images to make a statement on a specific type of Italian cinema. Their inability to keep up with the changes promoted by the new generations is also a melancholic acknowledgment of the obsoleteness of the classic *commedia all'italiana*, of which Scola was—both as a screenwriter and director—one of the main representatives.

Whereas the stock characters of postwar old-style comedies were heirs of a dramatic tradition grounded in the works of Plautus, playing their roles within prearranged narrative contexts, Scola's allegorical characters are deeply steeped in society. To those critics who accused him of superficial representation, Scola answered: "If in a movie a filmmaker roughly outlines the human and psychological features of a character, then I don't think that such a flat character would be less valid than a round character. Critics do not use the term 'bozzettismo' as synonymous of notation but of superficiality. But we can find 'bozzettismo' even in *The Betrothed*."[17] With the term "bozzettismo," Scola means an apparently superficial representation, which emphasizes the stereotyped peculiarities of a character. The reference to Alessandro Manzoni's novel, *I promessi sposi* (*The Betrothed*, 1827), is significant, as the novelist often adopted the same device to depict reality and its mechanisms. For example, in chapter 5 of *I promessi sposi*, Manzoni stages a banquet at Don Rodrigo's palace. Here, the dinner guests represent the society portrayed in the novel: Don Rodrigo and Count Attilio embody aristocratic oppression; the *podestà* (chief magistrate) of Lecco represents political power; and Azzecagarbugli personifies bureaucracy, seen as an instrument of power. To complete the scene, two anonymous commensals simply eat and nod to whatever the others say; they embody the populace, which, far from having any right to speak, accepts domination in return for something to eat. Manzoni's representation is static and theatrical, following that same principle of correspondence between the employment of allegorical characters and the theatrical style that we find in *La terrazza*.

The first segment from the party on the terrace, shows the screenwriter, Enrico, hiding from Amedeo, a producer who has been waiting for months in vain for Enrico's latest script. The movie Enrico is working on is supposed to be an anthology film, one of the most iconic narrative structures of Italian comedy. The writer's block affecting Enrico is symptomatic of the more general creative sterility affecting the Italian film industry, mainly the *commedia all'italiana*, which exhausted its satiric function and confined itself in repetitive and tired formulas and situations.[18] Enrico is victim to an anachronistic industry that does not want to change and looks at past successes nostalgically, losing along the way the ability to represent contemporary society. Scola uses allegory to depict such creative impasse through the famous and powerful sequence of Enrico's self-mutilation: in the grip of writer's block and as a form of intellectual castration, the screenwriter puts his finger in an electric pencil sharpener. Enrico's act epitomizes the dead end in which Italian comedy found itself, and it leads us to consider his idiosyncratic relationship with Amedeo; this allegoric rupture between a screenwriter and a producer mirrors the crisis of a cultural institution that lost the pivotal role it played in the past.

The subject of the film Enrico is supposed to write is typical of a series of works made in the aftermath of the economic boom, which aimed at illustrating the clash between the new ways of life and the old social structure. When

Enrico, talking on the phone with Amedeo, is forced to improvise an episode of the (nonexistent) screenplay, he cannot create anything different from the usual depiction of the "pizzichettaro" parvenu,[19] together with all the clichéd stereotypes seen on the screen of the previous decade. Of course, according to Enrico, Alberto Sordi was supposed to be the main character, reinforcing the predictability of the episode and evoking Nanni Moretti's famous statement in *Ecce Bombo* (1978), "You deserve Alberto Sordi!," thus epitomizing the attitude of the new directors toward the former generation of colleagues.[20] During the phone conversation crosscutting, both the mise-en-scène and the actors' performances participate in describing the traditional *commedia all'italiana* as a collection of empty signifiers. Enrico, improvising the story, enters a frantic stream of consciousness of stereotypical comedic situations, which drains him physically and mentally. He finally loses control and empties a glass of orange juice on his head. Amedeo, while listening, is floating in his dirty pool, sprawled on an inflatable lounge chair. His laugh is hysterical and exaggerated, as improbable as the story and the characters narrated by the screenwriter, and it symbolizes a desperate reaction to one of the main tendencies of Italian comedy of the seventies—namely, the fading of the comical function, and its substitution with cynicism, bitterness, or grotesqueness. Paradoxically, in the comedies of the 1970s, laughter seems no longer necessary or at least loses its pivotal role. As Manuela Gieri puts it, in those years laughter "became a grimace,"[21] which, rather than performing an amusing function, aimed to uncover the dynamics at play in Italian society.

Amedeo's concern with Enrico's writing was primarily about the profitability of the screenplay, which, in his mind, was related to its ability to make people laugh. Amedeo's constant asking "Does it make one laugh?" becomes Enrico's obsession and will cause him to lose his mind. Amedeo represents the producer who is willing to sacrifice any artistic aspiration to make a greater profit. On an allegorical level, though, the character is more complicated and historically connoted. Amedeo is also a lost and melancholic figure, incapable of making sense of the social and cultural changes under way and unwilling to realize that the gap between his generation and the younger ones has made him obsolete.

The representation of this generational distance becomes more problematic when it deals with the relationship between men and women and the emancipation of the latter. Amedeo, like other characters of the film, cannot really accept the fact that his younger wife, Enza (Ombretta Colli), has a full-time career and cannot spend time at home with him. She works in film production as well, but she looks at her husband with contempt, as she is more involved with artistic and (pseudo)intellectual projects. This dynamic is a narrative leitmotiv of the movie: the sudden decrease of power gap within the workplace, together with the social emancipation of women, is perceived by the male characters as an attack on their virility and as a threat to their privileges.

Nevertheless, Scola perceives the possibility of some negative consequences in the renegotiation of gender relations. In the following quote, he explains why in the film he could not give a positive representation of the only two women who have a career in fields dominated by males: "If a woman follows the same path of men and perpetrates the same servilities, and she is not able to create harmony between her private life and her work, she will be nothing but another man-like figure in career; like Gravina [Carla], who is more driven by journalistic careerism than by serious professionalism, or Colli [Enza] who is a film producer for mundane reasons and intellectualism."[22] Even more significant is the fact that Enza works together with a younger, pseudointellectual director, Giorgio Campi (Fabio Garriba). They both take advantage of Amedeo's solitude to produce a movie that is presented as pretentious and uselessly provocative. Scola's sympathy for Amedeo is absent for Enza and Giorgio, who are depicted as opportunistic and lacking all the moral qualities that, in spite of their contradictions and weaknesses, are present in each of the characters from Amedeo's generation.

The problematic relationship between an older man and a younger career woman is also at the core of the episode of Luigi, an aged journalist in professional and personal crisis. As stated above, it is significant that the character is played by Mastroianni, who, almost twenty years prior, played the most famous journalist of Italian cinema: Marcello in *La dolce vita*. Ruthlessly defined by younger colleagues as "accommodating, possibilist, and repetitive," Luigi is relegated to a minor role in the newspaper. Still clinging to the past and unable to interpret the dynamics of modern society, he embodies an older type of intellectual: in an age of protests, engagement, and strong political standpoints, his lack of values and his superficiality make him a living anachronism. The decadence of the character also arises from his awareness of this condition. "Here is the past, look at me!" Luigi says in an awkward attempt to seduce a young girl he has just met on the terrace. Such a lucid and plain sentence is the actualization of the allegorical function of the character; Scola provides the key to interpret the episode in Luigi's own words.

Luigi's struggle with his wife, Carla (Carla Gravina), again exemplifies the uncertainties and worries of a masculine society facing the feminist movements growing in Italy throughout those years. Deeply involved with her job, Carla takes a break in the relationship and moves back with her family. Luigi's attempt to save the marriage is unproductive, and the episode closes with the definitive break and Luigi's bitter and telling sentence: "I believe that epochs end like that: suddenly!" Despite Luigi's claims, Carla maintains that her husband stood in the way of her emancipation. Scola dealt with a similar dynamic in *C'eravamo tanto amati*, with Elide (Giovanna Ralli): Gianni's (Vittorio Gassman) wife and Catenacci's (Aldo Fabrizi) daughter. Compared to Carla, Elide still represents an incomplete, or embryonic, feminist, for her effort at emancipation merely aims to please her husband.[23] Furthermore, the difference in reactions between Gianni and Luigi in dealing with their wives—the former, cynical and neglectful; the latter, imploring and frightened—epitomizes a deep change in gender roles that occurred in Italian society throughout the 1970s.

The decade was indeed characterized by the birth of several associations, groups, and feminist *collettivi* (political organizations), which together fostered the fight for the liberalization of contraceptives and abortion. An echo of the law on abortion (1978)—the highest achievement of these movements—is in the brilliant sequence about the pregnancy of Carla's aged mother. As she tells her son, Tizzo (Stefano Satta Flores), a left-wing film critic and feminist intellectual, about her condition, he gets uncontrollably angry and, despite his supposed progressive views, proposes as a solution to the forthcoming, unexpected birth, to leave the baby "on the stairs of a church." In this sequence, perhaps the most openly comical of the movie, Scola ironically targets the contradictions of a masculine society, still unready and unable to process the urgent matter of women's rights.

The following episode is possibly the most tragic in *La terrazza*. The protagonist is Sergio Stiller (Serge Reggiani), the depressed and anorexic manager at RAI (Radiotelevisione italiana, or Italian National Broadcasting Company) who, like all the other intellectuals hanging out at the terrace—but surely with a greater intensity—feels irredeemably outdated. Sergio constantly weighs himself and rejects food; such an obsessive and self-destructive behavior leads him to a spectacular—and, most important, allegorical—death on the snowy set of a modernized remake of *Captain Fracasse* by Théophile Gautier. An old-school intellectual, still committed to a traditional idea of culture and aesthetics, Sergio listens with disdain to the proposal of a young director who asks a RAI executive to produce his tortuous, intellectualized version of *Captain Fracasse*.

Surrounded by a world whose values and cultural references have changed drastically, Sergio finally sees the meaninglessness of his life and lets starvation overcome him. His gradual and inexorable loss of weight, as the cynical sequence of the reduction of his office, is an allegory for the loss of importance and the failure of an entire generation of intellectuals. Given that Scola often develops a metacinematic discourse in his films, Sergio's death on a set is particularly significant; he sinks in the fake snow like Matamoro, a character in *Captain Fracasse*, thereby ultimately exemplifying another trend of 1970s Italian comedy: the presence of death.[24]

Death enters the realm of comedy as a consequence of the climate created by the *anni di piombo*, which made it a daily presence in Italian society. It is significant that even in a movie such as Monicelli's *Amici miei* (*My Friends*, 1975), which restores laughter to its former centrality, a bittersweet mood prevails, and death, although mocked by the playful protagonists, still plays a key role. Scola had already addressed this morbid issue in the last episode of *I nuovi mostri* (*Viva l'Italia!*, 1977), titled "Elogio funebre." The sequence presents the funeral of a comic actor, which turns into an entertaining celebration of the "good old times" of comedy when a friend and colleague of the deceased starts remembering old gags and stories. Through his typical allegorical style, Scola stages the funeral of the old comedy genre, and it is telling that the man who gives the eulogy is played by Alberto Sordi, the face of traditional comedy par excellence. Sergio's tragedy is the loss of a specific role within the new social and cultural dynamics—in other words, a loss of personal and social identity. Sergio does not join the young RAI workers in their protests, nor does he commit to the ideas of his chief; he is stuck in a limbo of apathy and uncertainty, an institutional intellectual who does not understand his institution anymore.

These four male characters (Enrico, Amedeo, Luigi, and Sergio) suffer from the same alienation from a public sphere that does not consider them relevant anymore. It is quite clear that the disquiet portrait created by Scola is inspired by the impossibility of fulfilling the ideals that animated the political activism of his generation. At the same time, the feeling of being constantly threatened by the younger generations emerges from Scola's skepticism toward the political iconoclasm of the 1977 movement. This movement, although still composed primarily of young people, was different from that of 1968, as its raison d'être was the deep and irreparable fracture with the PCI. Such a fracture became visible in all its urgency on February 17, 1977, when Luciano Lama, the secretary of the Confederazione Italiana del Lavoro (CGIL, or Italian General Confederation of Labour)—a trade union influenced by the PCI—was forced by students to interrupt an assembly he was supposed to hold at the University of Rome.[25]

The last episode of *La terrazza*, in which Vittorio Gassman plays Mario, an old member of the PCI, carries the traumatic consequences of that event. Mario is progressively marginalized in the party that has been his home for the last thirty years of his life, excluded from important meetings and uninformed about important decisions. It is interesting that Scola does not portray the young protesters at all, representing, instead, the marginalization of Mario as something exclusively caused by generational conflicts within the party. Such an approach, unable to deal with the complexity of the period, was defined by Lino Miccichè as a peculiar trait of Italian cinema of the second half of the 1970s:

> [In the second part of the decade] movies [that were] somehow related to contemporary events disappeared: that was a decade made of extremely harsh protests and bloody events in the universities, in the factories and in the streets; those events are not traceable at all in coeval cinema. Because of the difficulty to understand the present and to choose valid alternatives . . . movies started to be mostly about historical reenactment, paroxysmal withdrawals into the private sphere and themes of no importance; depoliticization became the very basis of any aesthetic research.[26]

The characters' inability to deal with the younger generations is also Scola's inability to represent them. According to Alberto Tovaglieri, what characterized the "movimento del '77" was not only the violent rejection of old political institutions and practices but also the constant search for "new ways of language and communication as a crucial battleground against power."[27] Scola and his generation could not make sense of this new language, as they were anchored to older political practices. In such an impasse, it was impossible to have some form of resolution, and the only possible ending was what was going to be defined as *riflusso nel privato*: the retreat to a private dimension outside the permanent politicization of daily life. The movie's last episode portrays such a phenomenon, which deeply affected the interplay between politics and society throughout the late 1970s.

In that final installment, Mario falls in love with Giovanna (Stefania Sandrelli), a much younger woman he meets at the terrace. The character of Giovanna shows the limits of Scola's representation when dealing with the new political subjects: she embodies the new leftist generation, ferociously critical of the old members of the PCI and still unable to offer a constructive solution to recent failures. Again, Scola represents the conflict between two generations of comrades, but in this episode he paradoxically does it by staging a tender and impossible love story. The only resolution Scola can find is to turn Giovanna into the familiar figure of the young lover Stefania Sandrelli played successfully in other masterpieces of Italian cinema, such as Pietro Germi's *Divorzio all'italiana* (*Divorce Italian Style*, 1961) and *Sedotta e abbandonata* (*Seduced and Abandoned*, 1964), and Antonio Pietrangeli's *Io la conoscevo bene* (*I Knew Her Well*, 1965) to name a few. The quarrel between Mario and Giovanna when they first meet offers one of the most brilliant dialogues of the entire movie. Angrily, Giovanna says, "You believe yourself to be the last and only revolutionary . . . but I'm much more a leftist than you are." Mario's answer is a great sample of Scola's cynical humor: "Of course, you guys are the real revolutionaries. We know you! What time is the revolution, miss? Will you serve a refreshment?"[28] However, despite their deep differences (and their respective marriages), they start an affair, which appears from the beginning to be without future.

In a dream sequence Mario publicly discusses his relationship in a speech delivered to the PCI assembly. Mario's speech, which is shot during an actual PCI congress, is a crucial segment of the movie, for here Scola reveals his allegorical style and, through his character's words, directly faces the very issue of the episode: the contrast between private and public life. Mario asks: "Is it permissible for an old comrade like me, to fall in love? . . . Is it permissible to be happy, if this causes unhappiness [for others]?" The transition from public to private is visually translated: when Mario asks the assembly for the permission to address his private concerns, the camera slowly zooms in from a medium shot to a close-up, thus excluding the audience and further isolating Mario from his comrades. Mario's last question is reminiscent of Gianni's in *C'eravamo tanto amati*: "Will we choose to be honest or to be happy?" Six years later, Scola's characters deal with the same problem, and they still seem hesitant and dazed, while the split between the private and public spheres has become much more profound. Now there is only one possible choice: Mario's personal crisis mirrors the public crisis of a political and intellectual class in the midst of the *anni di piombo*. The aftermath of the June 1976 elections[29] together with the failure of the 1977 movement, triggered an ideological pessimism to which the retreat to a private dimension seemed the only "safe exit."[30]

In *La terrazza*, Scola represents the *riflusso nel privato* as a condition imposed by the very political situation of Italy in the late 1970s. Whereas in *C'eravamo tanto amati* the ending leaves the spectator with some hope in the possibility of community solidarity, in *La terrazza* the camera wanders around looking in vain for a character that could give a glimpse of positivity, a little optimism about the future. The last sequence shows all the characters gathering around a piano and singing old popular songs, in a weak attempt to forget their emptiness at least for a minute. The general tone of irony and pessimism relies on the ineptitude of the characters who, despite being in a position of cultural hegemony, are unable to foster real social change. Bourgeoisification and bureaucratic assimilation prevent them from fulfilling the hopes of the Italian people in the aftermath of the Resistance. Yet the new generation does not provide a plausible alternative: though eager to replace the old protagonists, they merely offer a counterproductive iconoclasm and a vague, detached rhetoric.

In his depiction of an ideological fracture, Scola does not shy away from sociopolitical concerns: he acknowledges, rather, the failure of a certain kind of political cinema. Later, by shifting toward a disengaged literary cinema with *Passione d'amore*, the director ostensibly sets aside social and political critique in his final fiction films. As a stylistic consequence, this shift resulted in a different approach to characters: the allegorical function employed to depict the macrodynamics shaping Italian society is now replaced by characters significant as individuals.[31] Scola's gaze turns from a structural inquiry into a more intimist and psychological narration. Nonetheless, at the same time, the director's involvement in 1989 Achille Occhetto's shadow government[32] and his participation in some collective political documentaries[33] attest to his belief that other forms of political engagement were possible outside popular fiction cinema. The will to revive the active role of the intellectual was not shared by most of the generation embodied by the characters of *La terrazza*, who were unable to escape the symbolic space of the terrace, which, for them, was a claustrophobic gilded cage.

Notes

1. Among the film's most eminent critics was Morando Morandini, who wrote: "*La terrazza* is still a movie in which one wallows in self-pity, weeping about midlife crisis, the irreversible passing of time, the heroic years of the Resistance, capitulations, disappointments and betrayals." Morando Morandini, "Dal 1968 ai giorni nostri: Agonia, morte e resurrezione," in *Commedia all'italiana. Angolazioni controcampi 1986*, ed. Riccardo Napolitano (Rome: Gangemi, 1986), 91. Translations throughout the chapter are our own unless otherwise noted.
2. Scola's first movie that problematizes and develops the potentiality of the genre before the turn of the seventies was *Riusciranno i nostri eroi a ritrovare l'amico misteriosamente scomparso in Africa?* (*Will Our Heroes Be Able to Find Their Friend Who Has Mysteriously Disappeared in Africa?*, 1968). Through a plot largely inspired by Conrad's *Heart of Darkness*, Scola portrays a satire against the "civilized" Western world. He targets the shallow and tired social dynamics that lead a wealthy middle-aged man (Manfredi) to leave his safe but monotonous life in Rome and research his identity and freedom in the African jungle.
3. From 1968 to 1976—the only exception being Francis Ford Coppola's *The Godfather* (1972) in 1972–73—Italian comedies topped the box office: 1968–69, *Serafino* (Pietro Germi, 1968); 1969–70, *Nell'anno del signore* (*The Conspirators*, Luigi Magni, 1969); 1970–71, *Per grazia ricevuta* (*Between Miracles*, Nino Manfredi, 1971); 1971–72, *Continuavano a chiamarlo Trinità* (*Trinity Is Still My Name!*, E. B. Clucher, 1971); 1973–74, *Altrimenti ci arrabbiamo* (*Watch Out, We're Mad*, Marcello Fondato, 1974); 1974–75, *Fantozzi* (Luciano Salce, 1975); 1975–76, *Amici miei* (*My Friends*, Mario Monicelli, 1975). In addition to the new voices of comedy, such as those of Lina Wertmüller (*Travolti da un insolito destino nell'azzurro mare di agosto* / *Swept Away* 1974) and Sergio Corbucci (*Di che segno sei*, 1975), and the *filone* (thread) starring Terence Hill and Bud Spencer, the old masters of *commedia all'italiana*, such as Dino Risi (*Straziami ma di baci saziami* / *Torture Me But Kill Me with Kisses*, 1968; *Vedo*

nudo, 1969; *La moglie del prete / The Priest's Wife*, 1971; *Sessomatto*, 1973) and Luigi Zampa (*Il medico della mutua / Be Sick . . . It's Free*, 1968), kept placing films in the yearly box office top ten.
4. Roberto Ellero, *Ettore Scola* (Milan: Il Castoro, 1996), 9.
5. Gian Piero Brunetta, *Cent'anni di cinema italiano*, vol. 2 (Rome: Laterza, 2004), 426.
6. The electoral turnout of June 1976 has been defined as an "earthquake." Celso Ghini, *Il terremoto del 15 giugno* (Milan: Feltrinelli, 1976); and Marco Caciagli, "Terremoti elettorali e transazioni fra i partiti," in *L'Italia repubblicana nella crisi degli anni settanta: Partiti e organizzazioni di massa*, ed. Francesco Malgeri and Leonardi Paggio (Soveria Mannelli: Rubbettino, 2003), 143–68.
7. Brunetta, *Storia del cinema italiano*, vol. 4 (Rome: Editori Riuniti, 1998), 181.
8. For instance, at the beginning of the decade Risi's *Una vita difficile* (*A Difficult Life*, 1961) portrays the climate of political opportunism and disenchantment of postwar Italy. In *La marcia su Roma* (*March on Rome*, 1962), Risi addresses, through the lens of comedy, one of the darkest periods of Italian recent history: the fascist march on Rome. A few years before, Monicelli did the same with the massacre of World War I, in *La grande guerra* (*The Great War*, 1959). Germi's *Divorzio all'italiana* and *L'immorale* (1967) desacralized the institution of marriage, addressing crucial topics such as divorce and crimes of honor.
9. Translation in François Bondy, *European Notebooks: New Societies and Old Politics, 1954–1985* (London: Transactions Publishers, 2005), 175. See Pier Paolo Pasolini, *La nuova gioventù* (Turin: Einaudi, 1996), 252. The original text of Pasolini's poem is:

   > Bisogna condannare
   > altrettanto severamente chi
   > ami il sottoproletariato
   > privo di coscienza di classe
   > . . . .
   > Queste parole di condanna
   > hanno cominciato a risuonare
   > nel cuore degli Anni Cinquanta
   > e hanno continuato fino a oggi.
   > Frattanto l'innocenza,
   > che effettivamente c'era,
   > ha cominciato a perdersi
   > in corruzioni, abiure e nevrosi.

10. Ellero, *Ettore Scola*, 6.
11. The most obvious example is the didascalic tripartition of the heritage of the "Resistenza" in *C'eravamo tanto amati*. Gianni Perego (Vittorio Gassman) is

the idealistic lawyer who betrays his prior engagement and joins the shrewd and small-minded Romolo Catenacci (Aldo Fabrizi), while Nicola Palumbo (Stefano Satta Flores) is the intellectual in the ivory tower. Both are opposed by the naiveté and goodness of Antonio (Nino Manfredi).

12. Roberto Ellero defines Scola's main characters as "proletari senza rivoluzione" ("proletarians without a revolution") from *Permette? Rocco Papaleo* (*My Name Is Rocco Papaleo*, 1971) up to *Brutti, sporchi e cattivi*. Ellero, *Ettore Scola*, 34.
13. For instance, Morando Morandini called the movie "populist" (*Il Giorno*, January 22, 1976), and Ermanno Comuzio described it as a "commedia degli straccioni" in "Monty Python—*Brutti, sporchi e cattivi*," *Cineforum* 159 (November 1976).
14. Scola stated that *Brutti, sporchi e cattivi* was originally thought about and written as *Accattone*'s (1961) sequel. The movie should have opened with a prologue in which Pasolini himself appeared and explained how subproletarians and suburbs have changed in the years separating *Accattone* and *Brutti, sporchi e cattivi*. On this matter, see Francesca Borrione, "La terrazza on the Circeo: Ettore Scola, Pasolini, and the Critique of the Roman Intelligentsia in Late 1970s Italy," this volume.
15. *Corriere della Sera*, October 8, 1975.
16. Similarly, in *Una giornata particolare*, Scola builds the two main characters by establishing an extratextual reference to the stardom status of the two actors, Marcello Mastroianni and Sophia Loren. The deconstruction of their solidified images as Italian sex symbols amplifies the significance of their performance.
17. Ellero, *Ettore Scola*, 8.
18. See, for instance, the exploitation of the outdated anthology film genre: Marco Aleandri's *Tanto va la gatta al lardo . . .* (1978) and *Ridendo e scherzando* (1978), as well as Domenico Paolella's *Belli e brutti ridono tutti* (1979).
19. In Roman dialect, the term *pizzichettaro* generally describes a lower-class, uneducated grocer.
20. A famous debate that took place in 1978 during a RAI show between Mario Monicelli (the old master of *commedia all'italiana*) and Nanni Moretti (the young emerging director) exemplified the clash between traditional and new comedic style.
21. Manuela Gieri, *Contemporary Italian Filmmaking: Strategies of Subversion* (Toronto: University of Toronto Press, 1995), 173.
22. Antonio Bertini, ed. *Ettore Scola: Il cinema e io. Conversazione con Antonio Bertini* (Rome: Officina Edizioni, 1996), 154–55.
23. After the marriage, Elide tries to grow intellectually in order to please her husband. She asks Gianni after her death, in a dream-like sequence: "Am I important to you now?"

24. See Rémi Fournier Lanzoni, *Comedy Italian Style: The Golden Age of Italian Film Comedies* (New York: Continuum, 2008), 160–61; and Masolino d'Amico, *La commedia all'italiana* (Milan: Il Saggiatore, 2008), 221–34.
25. The symbolic impact of the episode was clear from the beginning. It led Alberto Asor Rosa, one of the most influent intellectuals revolving around the PCI, to write his famous essay, *Le due società: Ipotesi sulla crisi italiana* (Torino: Einaudi, 1977), a reflection on the split between the traditional, organized Left and the new spontaneous movements of young people. The relationship between Mario and Giovanna in *La terrazza* addresses such an issue.
26. Lino Miccichè, *Il cinema del riflusso: Film e cineasti italiani degli anni '70* (Venice: Marsilio, 1997), 10–11.
27. Alberto Tovaglieri, *La dirompente illusione: Il cinema italiano e il Sessantotto* (Soveria Mannelli: Rubbettino, 2014), 366.
28. His line in Italian is: "Lei crede di essere stato l'ultimo giovanotto con la patente di rivoluzionario . . . io sono molto più a sinistra di lei" "figuriamoci, vi sappiamo, siete voi i rivoluzionari! A che ora è la rivoluzione? Come bisogna venire? Già mangiati?"
29. The attempt first and the failure later of the *compromesso storico* (historical compromise) further alienated the leftest components of the PCI, and resulted in an increase of political violence.
30. Tovaglieri, *La dirompente illusione*, 366.
31. For instance, the characters of *Passione d'amore* and *Il viaggio di Capitan Fracassa* (*Captain Fracassa's Journey*, 1990) are structured on two specific literary traditions: decadent/*scapigliatura* in the former and picaresque in the latter. In *La famiglia* (*The Family*, 1987), although history is a constant presence, the emphasis is on the intimate and psychological dimensions of the characters. The same approach can be found in the portrayal of the relationship between father and son in *Che ora è?* (*What Time Is It?*, 1989); the generational conflict between Michele (Massimo Troisi) and Marcello (Mastroianni) is not developed on an emblematic and allegorical level but is defined through the lens of the private sphere. Only exception to this tendency is *Mario, Maria e Mario* (1993), where Scola deals with the dissolution of the PCI.
32. In 1989, Occhetto, the secretary-general of the PCI, inspired by the British shadow cabinet, created a shadow government that was supposed to present the PCI as a valid alternative to the Christian Democratic official government. For a brief period, Scola served as shadow minister of culture and entertainment.
33. *L'addio a Berlinguer* (1984), *Roma 12 novembre 1994* (1995), *Un altro mondo è possibile* (*Another World is Possible*, 2001), *La primavera del 2002—l'Italia protesta, l'Italia si ferma* (2002), *Lettere dalla Palestina* (*Letters from Palestine*, 2003).

SCOLA'S LEGACY

A Statesman for Italian Cinema

Edward Bowen

THIS CHAPTER FOCUSES ON an often-ignored part of Scola's biography and legacy: his political activism as a spokesman and defender of Italian cinema. When addressing Ettore Scola's legacy, the typical points of departure for journalists and critics have been his masterpieces and the role he played in the evolution of Comedy Italian Style as both screenwriter and director. His legacy as a filmmaker is immense, as he directed twenty-seven feature films, numerous documentaries, shorts, and episodes in joint projects and wrote or collaborated on the screenplays of over eighty films (including those he directed). However, Scola aimed to leave behind much more than a large body of films. He was politically active for most of his life, especially from 1968, when he joined the Partito Comunista Italiano (PCI, or Italian Communist Party), until his death in 2016. Most of his activism focused on culture. Scola also served as an active member of the National Association of Cinema Authors (ANAC) for nearly fifty years.[1] Understanding the precarious state of the Italian education system and the threats to free thought in the media, he worked to improve the state of Italian cinema and ensure its role in the cultural formation of future generations. His agenda, especially later in life, focused on preserving the memory of Italian cinema and safeguarding Italian film production and exhibition. Scola believed that filmmaking, film viewing, and the study of film history play a key role in the growth of a critical conscience in young people and thus contribute to the public good.

There were many moments in Scola's life when he put politics first. For example, on April 17, 1996, he wrote a letter to German filmmaker Wim Wenders in which he explained that he would miss a meeting of the European

Film Academy because he needed to campaign for the left-wing candidate Romano Prodi against Silvio Berlusconi: "I am sorry that I cannot come to Berlin—as I had planned—but I believe that I am more useful here, in the hope of having a government more sensitive to culture [the arts] and to democracy."[2] A more significant example occurred in 2003 when Scola decided to abandon a film project (*Un drago a forma di nuvola / A Dragon-Shaped Cloud*) with Berlusconi's production and distribution company, Medusa, after the prime minister bragged in parliament that he was open-minded for producing a film by the "communist Scola." Scola explained in an interview: "I wrote to Medusa that I had never had sponsors, that I did not want them, and that I would not make the film."[3] Frustrated with a media landscape dominated by Berlusconi, Scola abandoned feature filmmaking for a ten-year period, until he made his last film, *Che strano chiamarsi Federico* (*How Strange to be Named Federico*), in 2013.

Yet journalists, scholars, and documentary filmmakers have downplayed, and at times ignored, Scola's social and political activism. Many articles and obituaries dedicate no more than a sentence or two to his political commitment, though a few exceptions can be found.[4] Even the documentary *Ridendo e scherzando* (*Laughing and Joking*, 2016), directed by Scola's daughters Silvia and Paola, barely discusses politics. Scola's daughters had filmed him responding to questions on politics but chose to leave these scenes out of the film. In this unused footage, shared with me by Scola's grandson, Marco Scola di Mambro, Ettore states that politics are of supreme importance as they touch on all aspects of our lives, and they constitute "the highest form of cohabitation, of organizing human cohabitation."[5] He further explains that politics have become a difficult and uncomfortable topic for people today: "And instead today 'politics' has become a bad word, a thing to not even name. . . . It is certain that people are guarded against politics given that politics quickly becomes [a question of] political parties, this face, that other face, that person who corrupts, that other person who corrupts, that injustice, that mafia, and therefore, politics has lost its [role] as a distinctive characteristic of man."[6] Politics is indeed an uncomfortable topic, which partially explains why his political activism has been marginalized in examinations of his legacy. It is also presumable that scholars and journalists have paid less attention to Scola's political views because in his feature films they were most often expressed through comedy and satire, typically viewed as less serious forms of ideological commitment than can be found, for example, in the militant, documentary-style works of Gillo Pontecorvo and the films of investigation into political corruption by Francesco Rosi.

Though scholarship on Scola's political engagement is scant, recent works, including several articles in this volume, address the political commentary in his films, especially in the period ranging from *Trevico-Torino: Viaggio nel Fiat-Nam* (*Trevico-Turin: Voyage in Fiat-Nam*, 1973) through *La terrazza* (*The Terrace*, 1980). Further, the recent publication *Piacere, Ettore Scola* (*Pleasure to Meet You, Ettore Scola*, 2016), edited by Marco Dionisi and Nevio De Pascalis, linked to a traveling exhibition of documents on Scola, partially fills the gap, as it touches on his ties to the Communist Party and his activism as a shadow minister for the PCI (1989–92).

This chapter underscores the principles of Scola's political activism and explains how he emerged as a statesman for and defender of Italian cinema in the latter part of his life. Definitions vary slightly as to what constitutes a statesman, but typically it entails being a skilled political or public figure, with considerable experience, who is well respected nationally and at times internationally. According to the scholar Rufus Fears, politicians and statesmen differ in that the latter are free leaders who promote the public good.[7] Scola never viewed himself as a politician, even though he engaged in many battles of political significance, especially in the realm of culture. Scola had the four qualities that Fears identifies as fundamental for all statesmen: "a bedrock of principles, a moral compass, a vision, and the ability to build a consensus to achieve a vision."[8] This chapter, beyond briefly introducing Scola's shift to political filmmaking in the early 1970s and his later service as shadow minister of culture, will primarily focus on his political and social activism during the last five years of his life (2011–16): most notably his efforts to protect film production jobs at Cinecittà and the zoning permits of closed cinemas in Rome, and his advocacy for a tuition-free film school in Rome (the Scuola Volonté) and the Museum of Neorealism in Fondi. Thus, the major emphasis of this study is not on Scola's films but rather on his advocacy to protect and improve the state of Italian cinema. Sources include a variety of primary documents and original interviews. Scola's family generously shared letters and the texts of speeches not part of the traveling exhibition *Piacere, Ettore Scola*. Scola had kept these documents, along with many newspaper clippings, in the cabinet behind his desk. Given that not all the documents were dated, nor from all periods of his life, I chose to fill in the gaps by interviewing his collaborators, close friends, and family members.

Scola's commitment to the PCI and his interest in addressing political issues grew in the late 1960s and early 1970s. According to scholar Stefano Masi, Scola was rather "disengaged"[9] politically in his early adulthood. Gigliola Scola, Ettore's wife since 1956, affirmed in an interview that he became interested in politics in the early 1960s, "much before the movements in 1968."[10] His early screenplays do not, however, reveal this interest, and he did not become politically committed as an artist until the fall of 1969, known as the *autunno caldo* (hot autumn), when workers throughout Italy fought for better contracts.[11] The movement inspired Scola to begin preparing *Trevico-Torino: Viaggio nel Fiat-Nam*, a film shot in documentary style that recounts the story of a young man (Fortunato) from southern Italy (Trevico—Scola's hometown) who faces difficult living and working conditions at the FIAT factory in Turin. Scola shot the film in 1970 and 1971, largely using his own money after his producer, Pio Angeletti, abandoned the project. Angeletti likely wanted to avoid criticizing the powerful Agnelli family, which owned the FIAT factory and had ties to banks throughout Italy.[12] In an interview, filmmaker Ugo Gregoretti, head of the PCI's production company, Unitelefilm, in the early 1970s, described Scola as rather hesitant to become a fervent party member when he first asked the PCI for funds to complete the postproduction of *Trevico-Torino*.[13] Even though Unitelefilm had limited funds, according to Gregoretti, "the party did what it could to fund the film which addressed important subjects for the debates of the time."[14] Gregoretti encouraged Scola's increased participation in the party because he knew Scola "would be a big acquisition that would bring more prestige to the party."[15] According to Gregoretti, the distribution of *Trevico-Torino* in 1973 at cine-clubs and at communist meeting houses brought Scola into greater contact with the working class and solidified his commitment to the party.

Scola's political cinematic production peaked during the 1970s,[16] but it did not end with *La terrazza* (1980) as he continued to make documentaries on a variety of political issues until the early 2000s. Scola returned to Turin in 1980, nearly a decade after shooting *Trevico-Torino*, to film another hybrid documentary–fiction film *Vorrei che volo* (*I Would Like to Fly*, 1982) focusing on the challenges that the city faces, including racial tensions, crime, drug addiction, and discrimination. *Vorrei che volo* presents a viewpoint of hope from communist mayor Diego Novelli, who responds to letters by residents and defends initiatives that have the aim of improving integration, education, and urban revitalization. Made for Novelli's reelection campaign, the underlying message is that greater assistance programs and a more progressive mind-set among city residents would benefit marginalized peoples, including the film's protagonist, Massimino, a poor immigrant child and petty thief, who expresses a desire for a better life. Scola also participated in collective documentaries on major historical moments, such as L'addio a Enrico Berlinguer (*Farewell to Berlinguer*, 1984), which features the last major speech by Enrico Berlinguer, the longtime general secretary of the PCI (1972–84) and the large gatherings that followed his death, including his funeral in Piazza San Giovanni attended by over one million people.¹⁷ Scola's contributions include an interview with Mikhail Gorbachev, then second secretary of the Communist Party of the Soviet Union, who expressed admiration for Berlinguer despite the latter's decision to distance his party from the Communist Party of the Soviet Union. The collective documentary *Un mondo diverso è possibile* (*A Different World is Possible*, 2001), which features footage from over thirty Italian directors, including Scola, covers the protests at the G8 summit in Genoa in July 2001. Scola was seventy years old at the time. His wife recalled that Ettore went to Genoa to participate in the protest and "document" the event. In Genoa, he was teargassed and subsequently his "mouth would swell," at times, thereby affecting his ability to breathe normally.¹⁸ In 2002, Scola traveled to Palestine to make another collective documentary, *Lettere dalla Palestina*. Each of the ten directors filmed a segment on the desperate living conditions that many Palestinians face in Jerusalem. Of Scola's feature films after *La terrazza*, the one that offers the most political commentary is *Mario, Maria e Mario* (*Mario, Maria and Mario*, 1993), which presents the emblematic story of a married couple in crisis during the years of transition for the Communist Party in Italy, between the fall of the Berlin Wall in November 1989 and January 1991, when 65 percent of party delegates voted to dissolve the party and form the Partito Democratico della Sinistra (PDS, or Democratic Party of the Left).¹⁹

During this transitional moment, Scola served as a shadow minister of culture and entertainment from March 1989 until June 1992 in a shadow cabinet led by Achille Occhetto. Occhetto was secretary of the Communist Party until its dissolution in early 1991 and leader of the newly formed PDS.

The cabinet comprised twenty-one members and was formed in opposition to Prime Minister Giulio Andreotti's administration. At the time, the PCI faced many challenges, as it had experienced a decline in votes since the late 1970s,[20] and Occhetto, a centrist in the party, formed the shadow cabinet to offer "alternative ideas and projects" and not simply monitor closely the moves of the administration in power.[21] Scola accepted the role, while finishing up work on *Che ora è?* (*What Time Is It?*, 1989), because he felt the urgency of saving Italy's cultural patrimony:

> There is a need for urgent interventions. . . . The decay of cultural and artistic patrimony, the problems of publishing where one witnesses today phenomena of monopolistic concentrations, the unresolved relationship between [the industries of] cinema and television are only a few examples that place us in this Europe that we are forming as a country [that is] certainly not among the most advanced. And let's bear in mind that in Italy the [chief] raw material is certainly not coal, but instead artistic and creative patrimony, today which is not adequately protected.[22]

Walter Veltroni, a member of the secretariat during those years, stated that Scola took his role as shadow minister seriously during a time of "profound changes in peoples' habits, including their film consumption."[23] These changes included the growing popularity of viewing films on television and on home video. Veltroni added that Scola's political initiative in those years "concentrated on the need for support of cinema and the Italian cultural industry and for the defense of its contents."[24]

Scola advocated regulations "on the flow of films, commercial breaks during films on TV, and irrevocable quotas of European [film] production."[25] He did not see his plans as "protectionistic," but he argued that "protectionistic is the regime of the uncontrolled market that has forced us to undergo cultural dependence on the USA and Japan."[26] On October 11, 1989, Scola spoke at a meeting of the shadow government on the need for a "systematic law for cinema" that would "invest in the defense of the identity and cultural autonomy of products of Italian cinema and television."[27] He endorsed a plan that would ensure a balance in the programming of films on both public and private TV channels, allowing films from Italy and Europe to have at least half of the programming time. He also argued that tax credits would not be sufficient to "guarantee greater creative liberties"[28] to Italian films if more space were not granted to them in movie theaters.

Scola, as shadow minister and a leading figure in the ANAC, became one of the most prominent figures to join Federico Fellini in the fight against TV ad interruptions. Fellini began this campaign in May 1985, after Berlusconi's Canale 5 bought the distribution rights to some of his films, then excessively interrupted them on TV.[29] The battle reached one of its high points on February 14, 1989, when hundreds of directors and film workers protested at the Teatro Eliseo in Rome in support of a new law, proposed by the PCI, to block commercial interruptions.[30] One of Scola's contributions was to secure an endorsement from his socialist friend, Jack Lang, the French minister of culture. Symbolically this endorsement was important, understanding that Lang's viewpoint differed from that of many Italian socialists, including former prime minister Craxi, who had taken several steps in the mid-1980s to support his friend Berlusconi's near monopoly of commercial TV stations.[31] Statesmen have an ability to build support for causes, and Scola certainly possessed this quality, using his knowledge of French and his reputation of shooting films in France to build an alliance with Lang on this issue, even if the end result of the parliamentary debates was not so satisfactory. The "Mammi law" passed in August 1990 established the following regulations: advertisements could exceed neither 15 percent of the entire day of programming nor 18 percent of any given hour.[32] A national referendum in 1995 on whether to prevent advertising breaks during televised film screenings did not pass: more than 55 percent voted to keep the interruptions legal, making this a major victory for Berlusconi and his advertising firm Publitalia, which controlled nearly 85 percent of TV ads.[33]

Before examining Scola's activism in the last five years of his life, it is worth adding that during the years that Walter Veltroni served as minister of culture (1996–98) and as mayor of Rome (2001–8), Scola served as an important interlocutor. Veltroni remarked that Scola "did not have formal roles (nor did he want them), but he was . . . one of the people whom I listened to the most, with whom I weaved together a constant dialogue."[34] The two worked to secure investments from Radiotelevisione italiana (RAI, or Italian National Broadcasting Company) and Mediaset in Italian film production to combat the dominance of imported films. Another significant project of Mayor Veltroni's was the creation of the Rome Film Festival, which Scola endorsed as an attempt to "construct a great occasion for Italian cinema and for Rome."[35] As a statesman for Italian cinema, Scola believed in the importance of film festivals and awards for emerging directors (such as the Dolly d'Oro/Golden Dolly), and he served as president of both the Fondi Film Festival and the Bari International Film Festival.

As an activist in the cultural realm, especially in all the initiatives discussed below, Scola aimed to defend and promote opportunities for young people to have greater access to quality Italian films and to succeed as filmmakers. His commitment to the future of Italian cinema was inextricably tied to his goal of helping young people grow. This belief in the power of cinema to be a key part of one's education can be seen in Scola's short film '43–'97, in which a Jewish boy finds refuge in a cinema during a roundup by Nazi's on October 16, 1943, and subsequently watches a lifetime of films there up until 1997. This point is reinforced at the film's finale when an out-of-breath migrant boy enters the same space in duress and sits next to and exchanges glances with the elderly Jewish man. Scola's wife, Gigliola, confirmed in an interview her husband's commitment to helping young people. She stated that although "he did not like meeting critics and journalists to give interviews, he always made time to meet with young people."[36] Gigliola added: "He had a particular interest towards young people because he maintained that only in this manner could cinema renew itself in the moment that it served to help people grow in some way. He was very sought after. He often met with young people from universities, from high schools, the kids of friends, and those who wanted to work in the film industry, who wanted directions from him, this he always did."[37] Felice Laudadio, current president of the Centro Sperimentale di Cinematografia and founder of the Casa del Cinema of Rome, remembered that Scola used to come regularly to the Casa del Cinema to have coffee with his wife or to help "young students who wanted to write theses on the maestro."[38] Marco Spagnoli, vice director of the Bari Film Festival, affirmed that "Scola loved young people" and that despite his cynicism and excessive irony, "in truth he was motivated by a profound optimism."[39] This optimism emerges in all the initiatives discussed below.

Scuola Volonté

Scola's support for the tuition-free Scuola d'Arte Cinematografica Gian Maria Volonté, inaugurated in 2011, demonstrates his interest in leaving a legacy of opportunities for future generations of filmmakers from all economic backgrounds. The school, in the Magliana neighborhood of Rome, was originally planned by filmmakers Daniele Vicari and Andrea Porporati, actor Valerio Mastandrea, and critic Antonio Medici. After this group wrote a proposal for the project, they contacted Scola for his feedback. The school's artistic director, Daniele Vicari, discussed Scola's contributions to the project in an interview:

> He listened, he made his own comments about the project, and then he decided to commit to it, because the idea alone of a public and free school, according to him, made the project necessary and urgent. From that moment, he accompanied us for the entire journey, from the encounters with administrators of the former province of Roma (at this point abolished by a constitutional reform), to the [school's] inauguration, and to the identification of members of the scientific committee on which he himself participated. Ettore even wanted to make the first choices [of students] for the course on directing. He was close to the school until the end.[40]

Vicari explained that in meetings Scola regularly advocated that the group not waver from its original idea of keeping the school tuition-free.[41] The launch of the school was officially announced in October 2010, during a time when the Berlusconi administration had decided to make cuts of approximately 40 percent to arts funding for the following year. Scola viewed this assault on the arts as an attempt by Berlusconi's administration to reduce opposition, especially by hindering the growth of young critics. In this context, Scola referred to the Scuola Volonté as a revolutionary project because it offered opportunities to less fortunate and less connected young people, including second-generation immigrants. Following a press conference for the Scuola Volonté in October 2010, Scola told reporters: "There are many film schools that cost upwards of 16,000 euros for each student.... Instead here [at this school] even children of immigrants know that they too can contribute to the growth of the country through cinema."[42] To appreciate the significance of this project, it is important to look at the school's growth. The school, which offers three-year degrees, is open to ages 18 to 28. Its first class in 2011 consisted of 66 students, six in each of the school's eleven fields of study. The school has since slightly increased class sizes. At the Romics Convention on October 2, 2016, Vicari announced that approximately 150 students had graduated in the school's first five years and that approximately half of these have succeeded in making a living in the film industry.[43]

The Struggle to Protect Historic Cinemas, Theaters, and Cinecittà

Ettore Scola became involved in a movement to protect cultural spaces in Italy, which took off in late 2010 following the Berlusconi administration's move to drastically cut arts funding. The battle was centered in Rome, where Mayor Gianni Alemanno, like Berlusconi, viewed privatization and building projects as a way out of the economic crisis. In protest, film workers occupied the red carpet at the Rome Film Festival in October 2010, accompanied by workers from Cinecittà, who opposed a plan by the leaders of Cinecittà Studios to build a hotel, new offices, a new studio, parking decks, and a fitness facility on the property. Artists from many fields united, and within six months a number of occupations began to galvanize considerable support from residents in Rome. In April 2011, activists occupied the Cinema Palazzo to prevent it from becoming a gambling facility, and two months later activists occupied the government-owned Teatro Valle to prevent it from being privatized. With free film screenings, theatrical performances, speeches, round-table discussions, and debates, these occupied spaces became important cultural venues in the city for a couple of summers. Meanwhile, in July 2012 technicians at Cinecittà symbolically occupied the entrance to the studios for eighty days in opposition to plans for job transfers, layoffs, and new construction. Ettore Scola lent support to many of these protests by making public appearances, speaking to the press, writing letters to politicians, galvanizing the support of other artists, and even assuming the role of mediator at times.

In the following pages, I will focus mainly on Scola's support for the Cinema America and Cinecittà protests, though he also endorsed the Teatro Valle occupation. On June 16, 2011, two days after the Teatro Valle was occupied and shortly after Roman citizens voted against the privatization of water in a referendum, Scola urged the occupiers to maintain their energy and passion for defending culture. His speech emphasized the same arguments of the occupiers that culture was a public good, like water, "because it [culture] belongs to everyone and because it is necessary. It needs to be free."[44] Scola worried greatly about the loss of cultural spaces, the precarious state of Italian film production, and what these developments would mean for the future of the country.

Cinema America Protest

Scola became particularly involved in the Cinema America protest, led by a group of high school and university students. The group occupied the Cinema America in Trastevere from November 2012 until September 2014 in an effort to prevent it from being demolished and replaced by luxury apartments. The occupiers regularly organized film screenings to draw supporters and to strengthen community ties in a neighborhood under assault by tourism and gentrification. The idea of young people standing up to defend film exhibition and the quality of life in a neighborhood fit perfectly within the principles of his political activism. The utopic vision of the young activists must have greatly impressed the elderly director, who had told Lino Miccichè many years before in an interview that "man without utopia is nothing."[45] The protest reflected a sort of response to the ending of his 1988 film *Splendor*, in which townspeople occupy seats in the Cinema Splendor as workers attempt to remove the seats in preparation for its impending conversion. Scola did not present a film at the occupied cinema, but he maintained contact with the group by phone during the occupation.

He became a more active supporter of the protest after the group was evicted from the building on September 3, 2014, and moved their protest to nearby Piazza San Cosimato. There they organized a film series and protests attended by well-known directors. In total, Scola made three public speeches on behalf of the group in 2014 and 2015. Valerio Carocci, leader of the Cinema America protest, explained that Scola functioned as a sort of adoptive parent to the young group:

> He was never missing, not in one moment: he always responded to phone calls, he followed us, he yelled, advised, and congratulated us. He was

like a second adoptive parent, severe, but honest and loving. He wrote and signed [letters and petitions], and contacted numerous colleagues asking them to support us. When it was necessary, he was the first to "show up in the square." He was the first to confirm his willingness to protest in person against the Comune of Rome in our defense.[46]

Press coverage of the protest put pressure on Mayor Ignazio Marino and the city council. In January 2015, the city council released its plan to stimulate the recovery of abandoned cinemas. Despite this response, on February 17, 2015, Scola and eighteen other filmmakers wrote an open letter to Marino, in which they criticized the city's plan as vague and not incentivizing cinema rebirths.[47]

Two weeks later, on March 6, 2015, Scola delivered one of the longest speeches at a rally in front of the Cinema America (fig. 24). Seated in the middle of a table of well-known directors, in front of the banner "Let's Save Movie Theaters," he appeared as a statesman for Italian cinema. As in other speeches, he emphasized the role that films can play in the growth of a critical consciousness in young people. Scola began his speech by pointing to a boy in the audience. He argued that cinema "is a service that is useful to help that boy [over there] grow, that serves to protect his personality, his rights to choose, to change, to attempt changing things."[48] Scola explained that films had the potential to provoke scorn and criticism, which could be productive for society:

> Through cinema ideas, thoughts, and criticism can be formed. Okay here, criticism above all. We are in the situation we are in today truly because criticism is lacking. We accept almost everything. We give up, and therefore we see a country that is crumbling away truly because disdain is lacking, [and] criticism is lacking. Okay, here, disdain and criticism need to be watered, we need to help [young people] grow, certainly from kindergarten on, from the first years of their contact with reality.[49]

Months later, on June 5, 2015, Scola presented *Splendor* in Piazza San Cosimato, and he asserted in a speech at the event that Mayor Marino and the *assessore alla cultura*, Giovanna Marinelli, needed to reflect more on the importance of cultural activities for children.

FIGURE 24. "Let's Save Movie Theaters" rally in front of the Cinema America, March 6, 2015 (photo courtesy of Piccolo Cinema America Association)

Scola and other filmmakers pressured the minister of culture, Dario Franceschini, to maintain his promise to protect the Cinema America as a site of cultural interest. Their activism also influenced the city's decision to open a competition in August 2015 for the reuse of the city-owned Sala Troisi (former Cinema Induno). Scola did not live to see the positive results of the protest. In April 2016, the city awarded the Sala Troisi to the young activists. When I asked Valerio Carocci what Scola's legacy was for the group, he responded: "Calmness, temperance, and political calculation of every move. He knew the city, its terraces, its dance halls, but also its shantytowns. Ettore Scola . . . taught us to be panthers, but also lions. When we needed to attack, he would say, 'Don't spare anyone—now you must show them the strength of your ideas.'"[50] Near the end of a lifetime of cultural battles in Rome, Scola had much to share with the twenty-year-olds regarding local politics, including strategies on when and how to pressure political leaders. In May 2016, the group paid homage to Scola by screening *Brutti, sporchi e cattivi* (*Down and Dirty*, 1976) on Monte Ciocci, where it had been filmed forty years before. Although the renovation project that the group envisions will take time, they hope to open the Sala Troisi by early 2020. Carocci explained that the space will be a lively cultural center, a "training ground for democracy, a workshop for social relations, a citadel for young people who safeguard the area and values such as antifascism and anti-racism" and much more.[51] The group plans to screen classic and contemporary Italian films, and carry on the project Scola so greatly valued.

Cinecittà

The battle to protect the historic studios of Cinecittà from property speculation and to prevent layoffs of workers lasted from late 2010 until 2017. Scola had a great interest in supporting this protest given that he shot many of his films there, including his last, *Che strano chiamarsi Federico*, and had formed close relationships with many longtime technicians on the site. The studios opened in 1937 under Mussolini. Following World War II, as the second-largest complex of studios in the world and home to national and international productions, Cinecittà earned the nickname "Hollywood on the Tiber." Following a major crisis for the Italian film industry from the mid-1970s through the mid-1990s, the studios were privatized in 1997 under the rationale that the private sector would have more success revitalizing them. Luigi Abete, president of Cinecittà Studios, SpA, and also president of the Banca Nazionale del Lavoro, was the lead proponent of the redevelopment projects.[52] Abete attempted to add a megaplex cinema, a hotel, and stores on the site in 1998, a move Scola, Carlo Lizzani, Mario Monicelli, and many other directors strongly opposed. Warner eventually decided to build the megaplex elsewhere to avoid negative press.[53] Twelve years later, Abete continued to pursue his plan to construct a hotel and other commercial facilities on the property. He also began a project to build a major theme park, Cinecittà World, on the site of Dino De Laurentiis's studios at Pontina (it was eventually constructed in 2012–14). By mid-2011, technicians at Cinecittà became concerned about having their jobs transferred or cut. Many scenographers were transferred to a location at Pontina. The battle intensified on July 4, 2012, when workers occupied the entrance to Cinecittà and went on strike for eighty days, with the support of multiple trade unions.[54]

During the strike, Ettore Scola and representatives of ANAC lent their support and functioned as mediators. Ugo Gregoretti, president of ANAC at the time, explained that ANAC's role was that of "open support,"⁵⁵ including writing letters to president of the Republic Giorgio Napolitano and Prime Minister Mario Monti. Gregoretti added that the members of ANAC "attended the protest in large numbers and the star of the group was Ettore Scola. He was adored by the workers."⁵⁶ According to Gregoretti, ANAC wanted a "decisive battle, but without exaggerating ... and Scola at a certain point put a brake on the furies of several union leaders who were excessive to the point of risking consensus among the workers."⁵⁷ Scola and Citto Maselli succeeded in having the protest covered in the foreign press, and they played a role in convincing *Le Figaro* to publish a supportive statement from French filmmakers.⁵⁸ Union representative and Cinecittà electrician Massimo Corridori stated that "at that point they [leaders of Cinecittà Studios] could no longer ignore our discussion."⁵⁹

Scola used the press during the occupation and after to speak to the larger Italian public on the potential consequences of a dismantled Cinecittà beyond the loss of jobs: "It needs to be made clear to citizens that their interests are at risk: if one allows Cinecittà to be dismantled and the ruins of Pompeii to be destroyed, which are also at risk these days, that which will be lost is their patrimony, something that belongs to their history and it will be denied to their children, to future generations."⁶⁰ The strike had some success, as ninety workers were able to protect their jobs by signing a contract of solidarity. They accepted a 40 percent cut in their salaries but at least could remain active and hope that efforts to relaunch the studios would allow them to later return to full salary. Nonetheless, within a year and a half, many again feared job losses and others worried that they would be placed in *cassa integrazione*, meaning that they would receive government subsidies to make up for reduced or suspended work. In response to this crisis, technicians held a rally outside of the Ministry of Fine Arts headquarters on March 19, 2014.

Scola not only participated in the March 19 rally, but he, Gregoretti, and some union leaders were received by the secretary of MiBAC (Ministry of Cultural Heritage and Activities and Tourism), Antonia Pasqua Recchia, and the cinema director of MiBAC, Nicola Borelli.⁶¹ On this day of protest, the statesman Scola criticized the government's stance against social movements and also its inability to address serious problems. He told the press: "The studios are dying, the workers get fired, salaries [are] drastically reduced, and everything happens without the government, the city, political parties, and unions speaking up. For this reason, as a director and as a representative of ANAC... I feel that it is my duty to intervene and to denounce a situation of decay that risks eliminating Europe's oldest and most prestigious studios."[62] He accused the government of not looking out for subsequent generations: "[The government] does not think about its children, putting the problems of culture at the back of the line, while they need to think precisely about Italian culture, the only great patrimony that we have."[63] Technicians at Cinecittà periodically held protests for the next several years.

Several important victories took place in the battle to save Cinecittà in 2016 and 2017. First, the Italian government passed a new law for the film industry on November 3, 2016, which allows for the greater use of tax credits to stimulate film production at Cinecittà and elsewhere in Italy. Second, Abete decided to leave his role as president of Cinecittà Studios, succumbing to pressure for not paying rent to the Ministry of Fine Arts for Cinecittà and for announcing further layoffs. In July 2017, the Ministry of Fine Arts announced that the Istituto Luce would take over the direction of the studios, meaning the twenty-year stint of privatized studios had ended. The newly passed law was positively received by filmmakers, by the new directors of Cinecittà and by exhibitors. The law dedicated up to 120 million euros over the next three years to the renovation of shuttered movie theaters,[64] a measure of the kind Scola had championed as a shadow minister nearly thirty years prior. These recent developments prove that Scola's political battles in the cultural field were not in vain.

Museum of Neorealism

Up until his last days, Ettore Scola continued to fight for projects dear to his vision for preserving the memory and ensuring the future of Italian cinema. As the longtime director of the Associazione Giuseppe De Santis, from its inception in 1999, Scola was greatly invested in the group's project to open a Museum of Neorealism in Fondi, where De Santis was born. The first in the world dedicated to neorealism, the museum was originally Tullio Kezich's idea, but the project was piloted by Ettore Scola, Carlo Lizzani, and other members of the association from 2007 on, and they chose the ex-convent of San Domenico, owned by the region, as an ideal location. The Lazio region approved the project, and the museum was expected to open in 2009, but the initiative turned out to be much more drawn out than Scola and other supporters could have ever imagined.

Frustrated from waiting over seven years, Scola wrote a letter to the president of the Lazio region, Nicola Zingaretti, and personally met with Lidia Ravera, the region's *assessore alla cultura* in November 2015. He hoped that the museum would open in time for the centennial celebration in 2017 of Giuseppe De Santis's birth. On the night of Scola's death, Ravera wrote a warm remembrance of his visit to her office and promised: "Dear Ettore, we will open it, the Museum of Neorealism. We will open it soon. . . . It will be a place of meeting, of study, of exchange, of memory of cinema's past, for the development of future cinema. It will be beautiful, and it will speak of you."[65] Despite this promise, in July 2016 the budget committee of the Lazio region removed several articles from the upcoming budget, including one in support of the Museum of Neorealism.[66] New directors of the Associazione De Santis, Giuliano Montaldo, Gianni Amelio, and Mario Martone, began to carry forward the torch that Scola bore for years and continued to put pressure on the Lazio region.

In an October 9, 2017, interview, the secretary of the Associazione De Santis, Marco Grossi, explained that the museum would carry out activities ranging from conservation and educational programs to multimedia production, with "particular attention to the engagement of young people."[67] Thus, the museum's core goals reflect Scola's interest in preserving the memory of Italian cinema and his hope that future generations would benefit from viewing, studying, and making films. Marco Grossi added that "the museum would constitute one of the most important bequests by Ettore Scola for the Association that he directed with great self-sacrifice and his great contribution regarding the knowledge of Italian cinema by younger generations."[68]

It took until August 5, 2017, before the Lazio region recommitted itself to funding the museum, and this support came in the wake of pressure from the local administrations of five towns in Lazio—Fondi, Lenola, Sperlonga, Itri, and Monte San Biagio—and subsequently the provincial councils of Frosinone and Latina. The region's approval of the project was celebrated as a long-awaited success, and Scola's unwavering support for the project was noted in interviews by bipartisan supporters, including regional councilmen Giuseppe Simeone of the right-wing Forza Italia Party and Enrico Forte of the left-wing Democratic Party.[69]

In conclusion, Scola was more than a casual supporter of initiatives or protests, and his endorsement carried significant weight. He did much more than simply add his name to a petition or a letter. He remained active in a range of cultural protests until his last days. He regularly attended meetings, participated in protests, wrote letters, offered advice, and arranged meetings with local politicians. Scola's tireless activism is a key part of his legacy, as he set an example for filmmakers and artists of all ages of the importance of defending sites of historic memory and promoting education and initiatives geared toward the young. One of Scola's political principles was that it was important to wage a battle for one's convictions and to make an opposing voice heard, even if the results were not guaranteed. Reflecting on his role as shadow minister of culture, Scola recalled:

> I was "shadow minister" of culture, "shadow" meaning that you didn't count for anything. A minister without a budget or power. More than anything else it was an attempt to say that we could govern in another way, but with the distance of many years I can say with resoluteness, also looking at the experience of Renzi, that it is not possible. However, it was an attempt: life is made of attempts and battles. Battles that I define as "happy," maybe like for my job at *Marc'Aurelio*, in which we were convinced of what we were doing. They were battles that were certainly not without bloodshed, because power knows what it is and fighting it is not easy. Being a mosquito that irritates has all the same its own function.[70]

In his final battles, Scola knew that his presence at protests and his interviews with the press drew attention to the failure of government to protect Italian film production, exhibition spaces, and cinematic landmarks. He encouraged future generations of filmmakers to become more active politically in the cultural sphere, and he proved that waging battles is worthwhile. Scola did not get a chance to see resolution in the cases of the Cinema America protest, the Museum of Neorealism, the battle to protect Cinecittà, or the passage of a new law on cinema, but his friends, collaborators, and followers have seen the legacy of his activism.

Notes

1. Scola joined ANAC in 1967. ANAC was formed in 1952 as an association for screenwriters and directors. The association has defended the freedom of expression for authors and authors' rights to their work.
2. Ettore Scola, Ettore Scola to Wim Wenders, April 17, 1996, letter, from Ettore Scola's private archive, access and rights granted by his family.
3. Ettore Scola, interview by Maria Pia Fusco, "'Ho avuto tanto, basta col cinema non chiudo la carriera in bruttezza,'" *La Repubblica*, July 23, 2011, http://ricerca.repubblica.it/repubblica/archivio/repubblica/2011/07/23/ettore-scola-ho-avuto-tanto-basta-col.html.
4. See "La scomparsa di Ettore Scola è come un pugno in faccia," Archivio Audiovisivo del Movimento Operaio e Democratico, January 26, 2016, http://www.aamod.it/2016/01/26/la-scomparsa-di-ettore-scola-e-come-un-pugno-in-faccia/.
5. Ettore Scola, recorded by Marco Scola di Mambro on the set of *Ridendo e scherzando: Ritratto di un regista all'italiana*. Translations throughout the chapter are my own unless otherwise noted.
6. E. Scola.
7. Jason Harris, "Lincoln and Freedom: A Lecture by Rufus Fears," Oklahoma History Center, accessed July 25, 2017, http://www.okhistory.org/pdf/lincoln.pdf.
8. Harris, 3.
9. Stefano Masi, *Ettore Scola: Uno sguardo acuto e ironico sull'Italia e gli italiani* (Rome: Gremese, 2006), 38.
10. Gigliola Scola, interview by Edward Bowen, June 14, 2017.
11. For a more detailed discussion of the "hot autumn," see Paul Ginsborg, *A History of Contemporary Italy: Society and Politics 1943–1988* (London: Penguin Books, 1990), 311–20.
12. Masi, 38.
13. Ugo Gregoretti, interview by Edward Bowen, May 25, 2017.
14. Gregoretti.
15. Gregoretti.
16. Beyond *Trevico-Torino*, some of Scola's early political documentaries include the short films *"Lotta Continua" a Napoli* (*"Continuous Struggle" in Naples*, 1971) and *Festa dell'Unità a Roma* (*Festival of L'Unità in Rome*, 1972), which focused on political rallies and meetings. In the mid-1970s, he also made a short on the question of divorce, titled *Cortometraggio a favore della campagna per il referendum sul divorzio* (*Short Film in Favor of the Campaign for the Referendum on Divorce*, 1974) and a documentary titled *Confronto, partecipazione, unità* (*Debate, Participation, Unity*, 1975), which advocates

for the greater presence of the PCI in parliament. Scola's best-known feature films—*C'eravamo tanto amati* (*We All Loved Each Other So Much*, 1974), *Brutti, sporchi e cattivi* (*Down and Dirty*, 1976), and *Una giornata particolare* (*A Special Day*, 1977)—comment on political delusions, marginalization, and oppression.

17. For this film, which features material shot by forty directors, Scola was one of eight to make selections for the final cut. The other seven directors who selected the material were Franco Giraldi, Carlo Lizzani, Luigi Magni, Francesco Maselli, Bernardo Bertolucci, Gillo Pontecorvo, and Giuliano Montaldo. Ugo Gregoretti edited this collective film, produced by Unitelefilm.
18. Gigliola Scola, interview.
19. Dissidents formed the Rifondazione Comunista (Communist Reform Party, RC) later that year. Paul Ginsborg, *Italy and Its Discontents: Family, Civil Society, State, 1980–2001* (New York: Palgrave Macmillan, 2003), 161.
20. Donald Sassoon, *Contemporary Italy: Economy, Society and Politics since 1945* (London: Longman, 1997), 252.
21. Pasquale Giordano, "Le idee dell'alternativa," *Paese Sera*, July 20, 1989.
22. Raffaele Rosselli, "Scola: Tuteliamo la creatività," *Paese Sera*, July 20, 1989.
23. Walter Veltroni, interview by Edward Bowen, October 5, 2016.
24. Veltroni.
25. Ettore Scola, quoted in Raffaele Rosselli, "Scola: Tuteliamo la creatività," *Paese Sera*, July 20, 1989.
26. E. Scola.
27. Ettore Scola, speech, Meeting of the Shadow Government, October 11, 1989. From Ettore Scola's private archive, access and rights granted by his family. This document is typed with Scola's edits and additions.
28. E. Scola.
29. For an extensive discussion of Fellini's battle against advertisements, see Andrea Minuz, *Political Fellini: Journey to the End of Italy*, trans. Marcus Perryman (New York: Berghahn, 2015), 175–80.
30. Marco Dionisi and Nevio De Pascalis, eds., *Piacere, Ettore Scola* (Rome: Edizioni Sabinae, 2016), 266.
31. Ginsborg, *Italy and Its Discontents*, 155–56.
32. Dionisi and De Pascalis, 267.
33. Carlo Marletti and Franca Roncarolo, "Media Influence in the Italian Transition from a Consensual to a Majoritarian Democracy," in *Democracy and the Media: A Comparative Perspective*, ed. Richard Gunther and Anthony Mughan (Cambridge: Cambridge University Press, 2000), 230–31.
34. Veltroni.
35. Veltroni.
36. G. Scola, interview.

37. G. Scola.
38. Felice Laudadio, interview by Edward Bowen, September 21, 2016.
39. Marco Spagnoli, interview by Edward Bowen, September 17, 2016.
40. Daniele Vicari, interview by Edward Bowen, September 13, 2016.
41. Vicari.
42. UniromaTv, "Presentata la Scuola provinciale del Cinema," October 28, 2010, https://www.youtube.com/watch?v=LHpa4Fm8PaY.
43. Scuola Volonté, Facebook page, video. October 2, 2016, https://www.facebook.com/comitato.promotore.7/videos/1788868071359676.
44. Ettore Scola, speech at the Teatro Valle, video by Nicola Moruzzi available on "Ettore Scola: 'Serve un referendum permanente per la cultura,'" June 17, 2011, http://www.ilfattoquotidiano.it/2011/06/17/ettore-scola-%E2%80%9Cserve-un-referendum-permanente-per-la-cultura%E2%80%9D/118889/.
45. Vito Zagarrio, ed., *Trevico-Cinecittà: L'avventuroso viaggio di Ettore Scola* (Venice: Marsilio, 2002), 31.
46. Valerio Carocci, interview by Edward Bowen, May 7, 2016.
47. "Cinema America, l'appello dei registi a Marino," *La Repubblica*, Rome, February 17, 2015, http://roma.repubblica.it/cronaca/2015/03/02/news/cinema_america_l_appello_dei_registi_a_marino-108572902/.
48. Piccolo Cinema America, "Chiude il Piccolo America—Virzì Scola Verdone e Bruni," YouTube, posted March 24, 2015, https://www.youtube.com/watch?v=omecU4agv6E.
49. Piccolo Cinema America.
50. Carocci, interview.
51. Isabella Borghese, "Roma, la Sala Troisi ai ragazzi del Cinema America Occupato: Un altro spazio restituito alla città," *Il Fatto Quotidiano*, April 14, 2016, https://www.ilfattoquotidiano.it/2016/04/14/roma-la-sala-troisi-ai-ragazzi-del-cinema-america-occupato-un-altro-spazio-restituito-alla-citta/2636671/.
52. Abete's partners at Cinecittà Studios included Diego Della Valle, Aurelio De Laurentiis, and the Haggiag family.
53. Sandra Cesarale, "I registi contro la Melandri," *Corriere della Sera*, November 27, 1999.
54. The trade unions involved in the protest were Cgil, Cisl, Uil e Ugl. "I lavoratori degli Studios di Cinecittà hanno vinto: Intervista a Massimo Corridori Rsu," Rifondazione Comunista, April 30, 2017, http://www.rifondazione.it/primapagina/?p=28880.
55. Gregoretti, interview.
56. Gregoretti.
57. Gregoretti.
58. Daniele Rocca, "Salviamo Cinecittà" ha vinto: Accordo Studios-Can, *Daily*

Storm, February 7, 2013, http://dailystorm.it/2013/02/07/salviamo-cinecitta-ha-vinto-accordo-studios-cna/.
59. "I lavoratori degli Studios di Cinecittà hanno vinto."
60. Néstor Tirri, "Che cosa ne sarà del cinema senza Cinecittà," Italia dall'Estero, August 31, 2012, http://italiadallestero.info/archives/16393.
61. "Salviamo Cinecittà," sit-in MiBAC con Scola. Franceschini: "Impegno per il rilancio degli studios," *La Repubblica*, March 19, 2014, http://roma.repubblica.it/cronaca/2014/03/19/news/cinecitt-81397038/.
62. Franco Montini, "'Cinecittà, la protesta di Ettore Scola': Gli studios stanno morendo e il governo tace," *La Repubblica*, March 24, 2014, http://roma.repubblica.it/cronaca/2014/03/24/news/cinecitta_ettore_scola-81772036/.
63. "Tra i film e il cemento: Battaglia per Cinecittà," *Il Tempo*, March 20, 2014, http://www.iltempo.it/cultura-a/2014/03/20/gallery/tra-i-film-e-il-cemento-battaglia-per-cinecitta-932486/.
64. "Cosa c'è nella nuova legge sul cinema," *Il Post*, November 4, 2016, http://www.ilpost.it/2016/11/04/nuova-legge-sul-cinema/.
65. Quoted in "Fondi il Museo del Neorealismo si farà: Parola dell'Ass.re Lidia Ravera della Regione Lazio," January 21, 2016, http://www.lenola.it/2016/01/21/fondi-il-museo-del-neorealismo-si-fara-parola-dellass-re-lidia-ravera-della-regione-lazio/.
66. Comunicato Stampa, "Museo del Neorealismo a Fondi: Dietrofronte della regione; non si fa più," August 10, 2016, http://www.h24notizie.com/2016/08/museo-del-neorealismo-a-fondi-dietrofront-della-regione-non-si-fa-piu/.
67. Marco Grossi, interview conducted by Edward Bowen, October 9, 2016.
68. Grossi.
69. "Fondi, ok della Regione al Museo del Neorealismo: Votato l'emendamento a firma Simeone-Forte," *Latina Editoriale Oggi*, August 8, 2017, http://www.latinaoggi.eu/news/attualita/55018/fondi_-ok-della-regione-al-museo-del-neorealismo-votato-lemendamento-a-firma-simeone-forte.
70. Quoted in Dionisi and De Pascalis, 265.

CODA

DANCING AND DRINKING WITH THE MUSES

The Cinema of Ettore Scola

Gian Piero Brunetta
Translated by Marguerite Shore

THIS CHAPTER ATTESTS TO a long friendship and describes some encounters with Ettore Scola that have been illuminating for me. And it is meant as an act of respect, affection, and gratitude. It is also an attempt to follow some thematic and narrative threads that have been present throughout all of Scola's work. Followed separately, and then in various ways tied together, these threads compose the weft and warp of most of his films and form their distinctive and characteristic qualities.

February 1975. In Asiago, at the Lux Cinema, there was an 8:30 p.m. screening of *Amore in Città* (*Love in the City*, 1953), a tribute to Cesare Zavattini as part of a memorable conference to celebrate his seventy-fifth birthday. After the manager apologized that the heat wasn't working—it was 14 degrees Fahrenheit outside—Ettore Scola took the microphone, facing an audience of a few score conference-goers, all chilled to the bone. His carefully articulated words transmitted not only the sense of Zavattini's magical omnipresence in Italian cinema but also such affectionate warmth, such demonstrative esteem and gratitude, that the chill in the room, bit by bit, seemed to melt away. Scola began by thanking Zavattini in the name of Italian cinema, where for over forty years he had been able to play many roles: father (or mother) of the

---

This chapter is a modified version of "Ballando e brindando con le Muse a Casa Scola," in Gian Piero Brunetta, *Attrazione fatale: Letterati italiani e letteratura dalla pagina allo schermo. Una storia culturale* (Milan: Mimesis, 2017), 359–91.

neorealist family and guide and explorer of new narrative paths, both in the direction of realism and moving toward fairytale-like and surreal dimensions. And Scola did not neglect the fact that Zavattini was a discoverer of talents, someone who transported many humorists from the pages of magazines to those of Italian scripts and screenplays in the 1930s. But Scola also credited Zavattini for his ability to attend to every detail—including those of others, often playing the role of midwife or nurse, in charge of every aspect of cinematographic cuisine—and to think of Italian cinema as a whole, participating in the same flows and tensions amid a plurality of voices and components.

Although already an acknowledged master, Scola seemed like a student, thrilled to be speaking on behalf of a vibrant cinematographic community. There was added emotion when he turned his thoughts to Vittorio De Sica, who though had recently died was still present in various ways, including in *C'eravamo tanto amati* (*We All Loved Each Other So Much*, 1974), which had just been released and was dedicated to him.[1] That authentic feeling of gratitude would always accompany Scola, along with a profound sense of connections, values, energy, passions, tensions, and shared ideals, in which he was proud to have partaken. He expressed his gratitude to all the masters of Italian postwar cinema,[2] along with the editorial staff of *Marc'Aurelio*; to Ruggero Maccari, with whom he would form a more than thirty-year friendship; to Steno, Umberto Mosca, and Pasquale Festa Campanile; to Sergio Amidei, to whom he dedicated *Il mondo nuovo* (*That Night in Varennes*, 1982); to Federico Fellini, Antonio Pietrangeli, and Luigi Zampa; and to all those who had guided him during his long apprenticeship phase, allowing him to master the necessary professional tools[3] and gradually to nurture his own abilities as a journalist, a designer, a humorist, and an inventor of jokes, dialogues, comical, and dramatic situations, and stories: "With [Antonio] Pietrangeli, [Dino] Risi, and [Luigi] Zampa," Scola explained, "I encountered other screenwriters (Age, [Furio] Scarpelli, Maccari) from whom I learned to closely examine the story and the psychology of the characters, the sense of history, the definition of atmospheres."[4] Among those on his congratulatory list, he expressed gratitude above all to Pietrangeli and Zampa, who wanted him by their side during filming and from whom he learned, day by day, the fundamentals of directing; to Age and Scarpelli, who taught him how inspiration could come from reading; and to Amidei, from whom he learned the ethics of work that was destined to remain invisible.

Few artists know how to think "in the name of," renouncing, with conviction and a sense of understatement, their own role as an author, but Scola did this even when he began receiving recognition in the early 1970s (although Goffredo Fofi, Calvino-like, calls him a "nonexistent director"[5]). He did so in order to support his fervent attachment to his cinematic family, without whom he would not have been able to accomplish what he did.[6] Competing from the start with artists such as Roberto Rossellini, De Sica, Zavattini, Luchino Visconti, and Fellini, he immediately emerged as a moderate and controlled presence, more inclined to stay in a group than to shine with his own light. Scola very much saw himself as a dwarf on the shoulders of giants. Time spent with other actors, from Alberto Sordi to Vittorio Gassman, from Marcello Mastroianni to Nino Manfredi, was decisive, and they would have significant influence on the creation of his stories, often conceived and made to measure for them.[7]

For Scola, laying claim to authorship always emerged from the activity of a workshop, with the enhancement of many types of knowledge, the result of skills that successfully come together to create a product capable of making the most of dialogue and interaction. Thanks to a sense of sharing and belonging to the same space and to the same creative process, he succeeded in constructing cinema that is consistent, recognizable in its recurring motifs and the presence of actors and other collaborators, rich in questions, doubts, uncertainties, and capable of mixing and blending different levels and genres.

In a forgettable pamphlet from the early eighties, Paolo Bertetto finds fault with Italian comic films, deeming them revelatory not of the directors' feelings but of "different collectives." In Scola's work, this becomes a fundamental and characteristic element.[8] He would lament that this sense of belonging was something that younger generations felt no need for, or had no experience with,[9] precisely because for them the affirmation of authorship was more important than the sense of being part of a cultural community. Moreover, on the set, Scola would also take on the role of orchestra director and audience. For him, it was important to recognize the places and moments where he could condense and recognize a true sharing of values, emotions, feelings, and perceptions—his own and those of others—and where he could transmit knowledge from one generation to another.[10]

Scola, like few other artists of his time, was a hands-on worker, not only a director-"weaver," proud of revealing his roots, developed in different material and immaterial spaces, able to devise and untie narrative knots and to create new arcs and connections but also a balladeer capable of mixing styles and different levels social representation, uniting and hybridizing languages, grasping their dynamics, from dialects to gibberish, to distinctive languages, to regional Italian, to the neo-Italian created by television, to the admission of foreign forms that had come into use via the mass media.[11] While he took pleasure in morphological distortion, accepted nonstandard usage, expressive characterization, and lexical invention, he was careful about linguistic and phonetic mimesis—something not found in the work of other directors of comedy. He possessed an extraordinary ability to take on dramatic writings and adopt them as his own, tainting them and refusing to respect territorial limits.

Well read as a screenwriter and director,[12] he immersed himself in different levels of comedy, which, since noting a gradual "decline of passions and tensions"[13] making their way through Italian society, he would interweave in progression with a melancholic vein and pessimistic tones and nuances. And he was not afraid to push himself to the highest levels of tragedy, such as addressing the racial laws of 1938 in *Concorrenza sleale* and the pact between Hitler and Mussolini in *Una giornata particolare*. An artist endowed with a manifest capacity for assimilation and the promotion of his own sources, he was an inventor of stories who knew how to grasp and receive inspiration from the present, but (as in the visual spectacle of *Il mondo nuovo*,[14] staged on a barge on the banks of the Seine) he used all possible sources to describe and put in perspective both the minor history of events and Great History ("Behold the great Machine. It is the mirror of History").[15] Using lenses with variable spatial-temporal focuses, Scola succeeded in recomposing human comedy in all its variety and complexity, in its chronotopes and its chrono-utopias, observing it through the past to examine the possible horizons that the present allowed him to imagine. He left the role of background noise, the grand setting, both implicit and depicted, to Great History, to epic deeds, or to tragedy.

Scola was an artist who wanted to invent stories in which he disseminated the tale through almost invisible, uninterrupted autobiographical traces,[16] which included signposts that showed perceptible connections of characters with the culture of their time and that revealed the extent of the influence and sometimes invasive presence of all sorts of expressions—literature, poetry, music, theater, photography, cinema, radio, television, cartoons, illustrated magazines, photo-strip stories, and even record players, jukeboxes, Cineboxes (coin-operated film projection devices), and video games in the real and the imaginary lives of the characters. It is no accident that I consider his work to have been created under the influence of the Muses,[17] especially Clio, muse of history; Thalia, muse of comedy; Terpsichore, muse of dance; Melpomene, muse of musical harmony; Erato, muse of choral music, lyric poetry, and tragedy; Urania, muse of astronomy and mathematics.[18] This is something that can be said of very few other directors throughout the entire history of cinema.

Literature, cinema, music, theater, and popular entertainment in all forms, and also food and dining, are themes and signature motifs, conscious acts, that are consistent connective elements in Scola's work. He roamed the world, all of which he considered deserving of his attention, on all levels, and he dedicated stories to crossroads or central junctions, almost seeking, if possible, to respect the poetics of Aristotle and the unity of time, place, and action. His unmistakable style and the emergence of his personality also consist in his narrative, lexical and theatrical use of elements tied to the manners and rituals of eating and drinking, separate or interwoven with various forms of theatrical representation and the transmission of media culture.

Thus, in the narrative fabric that makes up the totality of his films, these are structural elements, objects of reflection, points of intersection and exchange, motifs that follow one upon another and overlap, circumstantial clues, keys for better defining the characters in their social roles and political convictions as well as in their passions. But these also *synesthetically* convey to us the perfumes, scents, and sounds of the time. Or they are guides for grasping an idea before directly knowing the actual places where the stories are set.[19]

I don't intend to discuss music, which is a fundamental inspirational presence in Scola's films and a source of both great inventive and feasible happiness and personal pleasure. Nor will I touch on political themes.[20] Instead I will limit myself to mentioning that his approach to these elements clearly did not meet with broad consensus. And while Fofi (understood as an essential example of the critical-ideological intolerance in the 1970s) accused his films of "vulgar Fascism and anti-popular racism,"[21] I will attempt to bring together some significant traces of other themes from throughout the entire creative arc of his career. For better or worse, books, comic books, popular performances, and films live in and inhabit real spaces, as they do the imagination of his characters, starting with the period of his screenplays for *Un americano a Roma* (*An American in Rome*, 1954) and *Un giorno in pretura* (*A Day in Court*, 1954). They influence and characterize the characters' behavior and serve as a unit of measurement, as elements for examining people's social position; for many, they also define forms of corruption and aspirations to a social-cultural upgrade.

Scola, more than being interested in the translation of the word to the screen (although certain subjects come from literary texts), drew on the imagination of many writers. He incorporated their inventiveness and tried to assimilate their spirit, adopting their structural models. Thus, his tutelary spirits and inspirations can be found in numerous sources: Plautus, the comedic playwright of ancient Rome, from whom Scola took the figure of the *miles gloriosus* (the vainglorious soldier), who would be reincarnated in many characters played by Vittorio Gassman, particularly for films written for Risi; the picaresque Spanish novel (from Miguél de Cervantes to Francisco de Quevedo); and, in random order, Carlo Goldoni, Théophile Gauthier, Edgar Allan Poe, Joseph Conrad, Fyodor Dostoevsky, Luigi Pirandello, Bertolt Brecht, and Edoardo De Filippo, to name a few. Thanks to these and other authors, Scola questioned how to gauge the strength of characters' feelings, how to make their passions and ideology coexist, how to represent their individual problems before X-raying them and condensing their behavior in light of ideological schemes and interpretations. In doing this, it is above all music and books that guided him—Giacomo Puccini, most of all.

In addition to the authors who helped him imagine the structure of his stories, Scola gave books a fundamental role, finding in them "necessary angelic presences." He used them as subjects of action and vehicles for feelings, and he brought them to the forefront, perused them with interest, particularly when they depicted licentious images;[22] he turned them into an indispensable source of nourishment for more than a few characters. In his films, private and public libraries appear, where the protagonists meet or work; household libraries and print shops seem to live outside time. Books are simultaneously a magical helper, a hippogiff that allows a character to flee his claustrophobic habitat and live a more fulfilling life in a prison, a drug to alleviate solitude, and a trusted resource to increase self-knowledge. Literature is symbolic of recognition, almost a social-cultural marker of the characters, and it is also, in film after film, a way to reveal the roots that are most deeply submerged in the territory from which the director drew his sources of inspiration.

Scola's cinema is rooted in Rome and in Cinecittà, but his cultural compass pointed beyond national boundaries, above all to France, which is a permanent reference point, a place of cultural, cinematographic, and ideal love that is always fully exchanged. His films provide autobiographical clues through evocation and appearance within the setting of a book or comic book, or a book immediately replaced by a comic book, as in *La congiuntura* (*Hard Time for Princes*, 1964), in which Prince Giuliano Nicolini Borga (Gassman), lying in bed, begins reading William James's *Principles of Psychology* but soon replaces it with a *Nembo Kid* comic. Some of these books are the ones the director, as a child, read to his grandfather, a notary who had gone blind. The memory of this fundamental moment in his life is transferred into his conception of the story of *Un drago a forma di nuvola* (*A Dragon-Shaped Cloud*): for years the bookseller, father of a girl paralyzed in an accident, reads books to her in the evening, before they fall asleep.

Indeed books, quotations, and names of writers have a pervasive presence throughout his filmography. Scola prefers French novels but also has a penchant for books of poetry, adventure, historical novels, masterpieces of Enlightenment thought, and books he had read as a child, thanks to the family library and to his mother, a professor of French. I will cite only a few examples: the quote from Horace ("Sicut erat in votis" [This was my desire]) in *La cena* (*The Dinner*, 1998); the reference to *Pinocchio*, brought up by one of the three aunts in *La famiglia* (*The Family*, 1987); mention of *The Three Musketeers* by Alexandre Dumas, which appears in both *Una giornata particolare* (*A Special Day*, 1977) and in *C'eravamo tanto amati* (in the latter, Elide is pushed by Gianni to read a "very tough" book, and she devotes herself first to Carl Sagan and then ends up reading *Siddhartha*). The poets and writers whom Scola references include Giosuè Carducci, who the grandfather of the protagonist and narrator of *La famiglia* admires; Guido Gozzano, whom Nicola brings up at the table in *C'eravamo tanto amati*; Giacoma Leopardi, whom Fosca (in *Passione d'amore/Passion of Love*, 1981) quotes in his speech to the PCI convention ("In 1821, Leopardi wrote . . .") in which he speaks of the right to pursue happiness in the American Constitution, mentioned again in the letter of the female student to her professor's wife in *La cena*.

In addition to books and writers, we often chance upon readers—compulsive, almost vampiric readers, like Fosca, the protagonist of the film taken from Igino Ugo Tarchetti's story, and readers who manage to sneak time during the day to turn reading into a moment of self-care (Antonietta in *Una giornata particolare*). Comic books are ever present, with equal dignity to books (and not merely children's books). Even the florist Adelaide, protagonist of *Dramma della gelosia—tutti i particolari in cronaca* (*The Pizza Triangle*, 1970), tells her psychoanalyst that she reads "a bit of everything." The most tragically typical moment that illustrates the importance of comic books in a character's life is found in the story of Baroloni in *Romanzo di un giovane povero* (*The Story of a Poor Young Boy*, 1995) in which he tries to reconstruct a comic book from the 1930s, which his wife has torn to bits, along with the rest of his collection. "She tore them all up? Out of pure evil, because she knew that it was my treasure. Everything I had, from 1935 to the present: *The Katzenjammer Kids*, *Bringing Up Father*, *The Phantom*, *Mandrake the Magician*, *Cino e Franco*, *Nembo Kid*, *Tex Willer*. All numbered, all catalogued. In the evening I would leaf through them, read them." Elide in *C'eravamo tanto amati* discovers reading as a way to feel she has enhanced her social status. When Fosca, the protagonist of *Passione d'amore*, encounters Captain Giorgio for the first time, after thanking him for lending her *La nouvelle Héloïse* ("That novel by Rousseau thrilled me") and explaining why she has underlined very sad passages ("I know how to recognize unhappiness, I have some experience of it"), she asks him: "Is it true that my cousin has accused me of being an intemperate reader?" And this bibliophile goes on to explain: "I read to forget, to know the joys that the world dispenses to those who are happy. Everything that I can do to escape reality, to feign other existences, to dream a lot." In *Un drago a forma di nuvola*, Albertine, the daughter of the bookseller on the Île Saint-Louis, who lives at home, paralyzed, also speaks of the importance of books in her life: "Books are the existence I haven't lived, the loves I haven't had, the happiness I have not dared to hope. Since I was a child, hundreds of books have allowed me to move about through the world."

    The increasingly invasive presence of the mass media and attention paid to the role of modifying and creating surrogate and dependent lives is one of the many themes, depicted in various ways, in Scola's films. But more than this, I would like to address how Scola constantly uses cinema by putting himself in the role of both author and viewer.

    Cinema is a daily source of nourishment and an element whose presence is breathed in everywhere. It is also a source of inspiration: film characters go to the movies, they watch movies on television, they quote films or imagine them, they read about the lives of stars in illustrated magazines. And they want to participate in films as subjects. In *Splendor* (1988), in the microcosm of a movie hall in a village in Basso Lazio, there is an attempt to create a collective autobiography, to tell history through the histories of different groups—spectators, participants in the *Cineforum*, and filmmakers (including moments of Scola's own life)—all blended with a commentary on the history of genre cinema and the myths that cinema has produced.

With modesty and engagement, Scola succeeds in reconstructing his own primal scene. The boy goes into the village square with his stool and tries to find the perfect geometric point where the body and the glance can enter the screen, creating an ideal *homo cinematographicus* (heir to Leonardo's *homo vitruvianus* in the Accademia museum in Venice). This is where his perfect alter ego lies: "I was four or five years old when I saw a real film for the first time: *Frà Diavolo*, in Trevico, a little mountain village, 1,200 meters above sea level. It was cold out, even on a summer evening. They hung a big tarp between two linden trees. Each audience member arrived with his own chair. We children arrived in the afternoon, to claim the best spots. And a frenetic wait began. Once a year!"[23]

It is a memory and a popular custom that, a decade before, in *C'eravamo tanto amati*, the director already saw disappearing and blurring, as evidenced in the scene in which the Sifar colonel says to Fellini while the latter is shooting the Trevi Fountain scene in *La dolce vita* (1960): "I am proud to shake the hand of the great Rossellini." This extraordinary gag also functions as an affectionate jab at the aggrandizement of Fellini's ego. Rossellini is a pontifical figure, present in *C'eravamo tanto amati* and alluded to in the final images in *Brutti, sporchi e cattivi* (*Down and Dirty*, 1976), which cast St. Peter's Basilica in the background. In *C'eravamo tanto amati*, however, it is De Sica and Zavattini who are evoked: Professor Nicola Palumbo, participating in the television game show *Lascia o raddoppia* (*Double or Nothing*), must respond to a trick question about *Ladri di biciclette* (*Bicycle Thieves*, De Sica, 1948). In this same film, Luciana comes to Rome from a village in Friuli ("Trasachis, vicino Peonis" [Trasachis, near Peonis]), hoping to work in cinema. Introduced to Fellini, who asks her if she has ever worked in cinema, she responds, "Qualcosina" (a little bit). Zavattini and De Sica and the ending of *Miracolo a Milano* (*Miracle in Milan*, 1951) are referenced again at the end of *La cena*, when the accountant, Marchetti, flees on a broomstick, along with Adam the magician. Neorealism was indeed his North Star, his obligatory point of reference.[24]

The example of Fellinian life expands the spaces of desire of the suburbanites in *Brutti, sporchi e cattivi*: "We owe something to *La dolce vita*," Giacinto says to Iside, opening up future paradisiacal horizons. "We have to get rid of all our whims. I am taking you to Trastevere to buy watermelon, we'll go to the Via Veneto at night to eat sweet shaved ice and, if we feel like it, we even go by car."

Fellini, in person, becomes the protagonist of Scola's last work, *Che strano chiamarsi Federico* (*How Strange to be Named Federico*, 2013), which describes the paths of two leading figures in Italian cinema, Fellini and Scola, mixing biographical, autobiographical, and collective biographical elements and parting ways with a type of cinema that Scola had greatly loved.

Visconti's *Senso* (1954), in particular, serves as a point of reference for *Passione d'amore*. Scola had such great respect and admiration for Visconti that he would never want to parody his way of working or style. Antonioni, instead, precisely because of the aura surrounding him and his "alienated" characters, is a multifunctional presence, parodied with affection and used as an anti-intellectual target. Antonioni had already made an appearance in a memorable speech by Bruno Cortona in *Il sorpasso* (*The Easy Life*, 1962).[25] In *C'eravamo tanto amati*, Elide uses the microphone of a recorder to feel as though she can identify with the characters in Antonioni's films.[26] Finally, Antonioni is the inspiration for an entire scene in *Splendor*, when the police commissioner calls in Jordan and Luigi, saying he wants to advise the town to hang this sign in front of the movie theater, to commemorate a historic date: "On 25 February 1976 eight hundred citizens, defying rain and wind, exited their houses and rushed into this movie theater to see *Professione: Reporter* (*The Passenger*, 1975), directed by Michelangelo Antonioni."

If De Sica is the maestro to whom *C'eravamo tanto amati* is dedicated, Pasolini is the inevitable reference point the following year, when Scola conceived *Brutti, sporchi e cattivi*. But even earlier, the final long shot in *C'eravamo tanto amati*, in which Nicola, Antonio, and Luciana discuss the significance of the phrase "Boh?," recalls Mao's words at the end of Pasolini's *Uccellacci e uccellini* (*The Hawks and the Sparrows*, 1966): "Where is humanity going? Boh?"[27]

The history of cinema is obviously present in *Splendor*, articulated over the forty-year time span of the story, but small references, necessary for more precisely setting the period of a film's action, appear continually in nearly every one of his films.

Finally, there is a gesture to a great metaphorical reflection on Italian cinema and its destiny, recounted by the Italian comedians' journey to Paris in *Il viaggio di Capitan Fracassa* (*The Voyage of Captain Fracassa*, 1990). Made during a period in which Scola felt less moved by ideological and aspirational passions and tensions, the picaresque journey of the small company of comedians who, despite everything, manage to reach their goal, still seems to give him some ray of hope for the future of cinema.

Which brings us to the last motif: the table, the crux of the action of the private and public inner dynamics of the characters, a bourgeois and proletarian secularization of the ritual meal, a place of sharing and staging for interindividual and social relationships, a thermometer for measuring changes in taste or manners. In Scola's films, an astonishing variety of foods and beverages play a supporting and connective role, no less than the themes considered thus far. In terms of cuisine, his films respect tradition, paying homage to Pellegrino Artusi (best known for having written *La scienza in cucina e l'arte di mangiar bene* / *Science in the Kitchen and the Art of Eating Well*), Auguste Escoffier, and the Michelin guides, but they also give due consideration to evolutions in taste, fears, and the loss of certain fundamental pleasures in feasting rituals.

Table, food, and the material culture tied to them allow the director to describe, in the most articulate and characteristic fashion, the characters, places, times, and transformations taking place in twentieth-century Italy. In all his films, there is a precision of details regarding the setting, which allows wine-and food-culture to shine through and which sometimes overlaps with, sometimes maintains a distance from, the characters; sometimes conveys emotions; and sometimes transmits a widespread sense of loss and neglect on all levels. From one film to another, depictions of home-style, family cooking (described best in *La famiglia* and also in the local trattoria in *La cena*) alternate with those of epic-level cooking (the head chef in *La cena* evokes the five thousand meals served at the annual festivals of *L'Unità*—as fundraisers for the Communist Party newspaper) and those of fine dining and rich buffets represented in *La terrazza*. Scola does not neglect street food, as evidenced by the man who buys his grandchildren cooked pears from a street vendor in *Concorrenza sleale* (*Unfair Competition*, 2001); the enormous, stuffed sandwich, more than a meter long, that Rocco Papaleo buys in Chicago *Permette?*

Rocco Papaleo (*My Name Is Rocco Papaleo*, 1971); and the *baba au rhum* with whipped cream and cherry glaze, eaten on the street in *Maccheroni* (*Macaroni*, 1985), accompanied by detailed theorizing and demonstrations on how it should be eaten.

Without flaunting it, Scola sends signals that inform us about his private passions and the ways that these passions, together with reasonable expertise, are sources of inspiration that, to varying degrees, engage him with memories or mere declarations of personal taste. Sharing food at the dining table provides an occasion for his characters to tell their stories, or to evoke episodes of history that memory cannot erase (e.g., in *Che ora è?/What Time Is It?*, 1989, Marcello, sitting at the table, tells his son, Michele, the story of the disappearance of the Jewish man, after the racial laws were enacted in Rome, who used come to his house to redo the mattresses), or as indicators of status and transformations under way in Italian society. Without bringing up Marcel Proust, who in any case influenced Scola's various ways of representing time (particularly in *Ballando ballando/Le Bal*, 1983, and in *La famiglia*), it must be noted that for Scola, the table references a totality of sensations—tactile, emotional, gustatory, olfactory—which he attempts to convey through the characters, who may appraise, comment on, or even ignore what they are eating, absorbed as they are in their discussions. "Food and drink symbolize the very human condition, a poet friend of mine, a Greek from 2,000 years ago, said. . . . Any table whatsoever, with strangers or friends, contains something that has more to do with the heart than with the stomach. . . . After all, conviviality means living with others," Maestro Pezzullo says in *La cena*, a film that can be considered the summation of ways of observing behavior at the table. Scola's prevailing tastes lead to an appreciation of the simplest things, such as eggs, the most perfect food for him.

No film Scola has written or directed has any character who, sitting at a table, through the simple gestures of drinking and eating, fails to reveal a great deal about himself, his social identity, and his present and past life. In a kitchen scene in *La cena*, the head chef, Duilio, while preparing various dishes, speaks of other things, particularly politics. We have an opportunity to see or hear about, with various levels of appreciation, a number of dishes that the cooks are now compelled to prepare in place of traditional Roman fare since they must satisfy the vagaries of peoples' diets and tastes (memorably conveyed by the members of a Japanese family who ask for ketchup to pour over their carbonara). Thus, macrobiotic meals, spaghetti seasoned with oil, white rice, and some consommé are served with obvious frustration, while boiled meat and a breaded cutlet are scoffed at. Furthermore, *carciofi alla romana*, Roman-style artichokes, emblem of local culinary tradition, are confused with *carciofi alla giudia*, Jewish-style artichokes, after being carelessly dropped on the floor, gathered up, and nonchalantly put back on the plate of an unfortunate customer.

The scene of the most refined dinner in Scola's films, in which he familiarizes us with his wine and food culture, appears in *La più bella serata della mia vita* (*The Most Wonderful Evening of My Life*, 1972). Alfredo Rossi (Alberto Sordi), who has ended up by chance in Count Brunetière's castle, thinks he is being offered dinner by the owner, who has also invited three of his friends, retired magistrates. During dinner, one course follows another, precisely described by the Rossi's fellow diners and by the owner of the castle, in an homage to grand French cuisine: gigantic trout from the Lys River; kidneys Bordelaise; a pheasant that sits enthroned on its eggs on a serving dish; partridges that are cooked in the kitchen on a skewer, basted with antlers. (The partridges, it is revealed, were hunted by the Count himself, who at the beginning of the film describes how they must be struck in order to avoid damaging their flesh.)

There is a progression of food and drink, traditional Italian and international fare, served on a wide range of tables, spread out over time and space: noble tables where representatives of three generations are seated, along with the dog, the grandfather's favorite breed, and where the diners are served by white-gloved waiters (*La congiuntura*); tables where officers in a garrison gather every day to speak about weapons, female conquests, and food (*Passione d'amore*),[28] middle-class and lower middle-class tables, where the characters respect rituals and roles; buffets around which there gather real and imaginary spokespeople for left-wing political conformity, Roman spectacles, and culture; proletarian and lower-class tables; tables in a castle transformed into a deluxe hotel; tables at restaurants and inns; kitchen tables in palaces and apartments in large public housing complexes; large long tables outdoors (the scene of a birthday celebration for Romolo Catenacci, a building speculator whose daughter Gianni has married in *C'eravamo tanto amati*) onto which a gigantic pork roast is hoisted with a crane; tables at which the diners can sample ("aggustare," as Iside will say, in *Brutti, sporchi e cattivi*) dishes of every type, which define their social status and economic conditions. These are tables around which almost a century of family life and the story of a nation revolves. These are tables spread with personal and collective stories, around which tragic or happy memories surface, resentments explode, insults fly, relationships are born or die, and personal convictions or political crises are declared.

Numerous menus feature true home cooking and, taken together, can be seen as a sign of Artusi-inspired cuisine: the tortellini in *brodo* in the first meal depicted in *La famiglia*; the risottos ("If there isn't any bone marrow in the risotto, it isn't risotto," *Passione d'amore*); vegetable and fish soups; pasta with chickpeas (*C'eravamo tanto amati*); spaghettis; typical Italian dishes;[29] razor clams; and tagliatelle with tomato sauce and Parmesan (now taboo for the eighty-year-old Carlo, but which his grandson Carlino offers him a taste of in *La famiglia*). Then there is macaroni: pierced with forks, which Antonio, Nicola, and Gianni cross like three swords in *C'eravamo tanto amati*, quipping like the musketeers, "All for one, one for all," and doused in sauce and pecorino, at the table where they await the miracle of Antonio's third resurrection in *Maccheroni*. Obviously, one cannot fail to mention the macaroni scene in *Un americano a Roma* (surely written by Scola) in which Nando Moriconi assails his plate of food: "Macaroni, you provoked me and now I will destroy you, macaroni! I'm going to eat you!" The most touching dishes of *spaghetti al sugo* are the one prepared by Nicola for Luciana in the garret in *C'eravamo tanto amati* (eaten in between such reflections as "Spaghetti, great comforter of every suffering. More than love)" and above all the one in *Ballando ballando*, prepared by the Italian barista for the Jewish violinist who has sought shelter during a bombing raid in occupied Paris. Equally memorable are depictions of meat: *involtini* with green beans or rabbit *alla cacciatora* with potatoes, cooked in the terra-cotta pan in *La famiglia*; the *picchiapò* (Roman-style braised beef) and the enormous pork roast in *C'eravamo tanto amati*; and the meat hanging down, eaten raw during the family reunion at which they decide to poison the father, in *Brutti, sporchi e cattivi*.

While Scola shows discretion and respect for his characters' sexual activity, he does not hesitate to expose their personalities, vices, and virtues, using the dining table as a therapeutic alternative that is more economical and widespread than the psychoanalyst's couch. The way they stick a fork into a morsel of food before eating it attests to their physical exuberance and appetites.

Moving his gaze along an ideal table that occupies nearly the entire space of the twentieth century, Scola records and describes the dynamics and transformations in individual and group behaviors of Italians in terms of food. Alongside the splendors of a beautifully set table and the celebration of the ritual that accompanies many moments in *La famiglia*, he observes the ways in which the characters go from frugal consumption, hunger (which is often evoked), and destitution to abundance, excess, waste, and, as the century seems to come full circle, to a return to poverty and widespread social malaise. While in the late 1930s, food is rationed but the rules of hospitality nonetheless prevail over the racial laws, in the immediate postwar period it is possible to enjoy unlimited credit in restaurants, as "il re della mezza porzione" (the king of the half portion) did, without ever paying the bill.[30] This is an Italy that is famished but still open to all gastronomic adventures, which Scola stages, starting with his earliest films. His characters have no problem making their habits and tastes public knowledge. In some of his screenplays from the early 1960s, next to a table laden with dishes that are explicit indicators of the new state of affluence given the inflated costs of some foods,[31] we already begin to see a quest for forbidden foods, such as *casu marzu*, a traditional Sardinian cheese infested with maggots, which denotes "success"; and the memory of authentic dishes begins to vanish, as they become victims of the transformation of the food industry.

Food increasingly suffers from the economic, environmental, social, and production changes that are under way. Finding authentic foods can seem like a utopia, and the dining table does not escape the eye of this director who, beginning in the late 1980s, takes a darker view and removes any aura of pleasure from dining and from the faces of characters involved in eating. Physical and moral deviation from the *bon ton* and from the rules of common education, brutishness, environmental degradation, and pollution accompany the contamination and loss of the natural properties of food, still mythicized and idealized in the boom years, when the first negative signs were already appearing. Junk food and chemical adulteration are described, for example, in *Il successo* (1963), when, at the dinner table, Sergio, the character played by Jean-Louis Trintignant, reveals the results of some of his analyses of food.[32]

Beverages are very typical temporal indicators. In *Ballando ballando*, they add elements of contextualization that describe transformations in tastes and habits over the decades. Sharing drink is a natural way to stay together, to tell stories, to get to know one another. Wine has a special place here, even compared to coffee, which also plays a very important role. In *Permette? Rocco Papaleo*, when Jenny invites Rocco to a restaurant for the first time, there are allusions to caviar and champagne. *Ballando ballando* pays homage to two famous champagne brands, Moët Chandon and Perrier-Jouët; the latter, brought home, is substituted for the former. In *La più bella serata della mia vita*, the judges cannot help but recognize the crimes of the accused because of his wine expertise. At a certain point during dinner, when six types of wine have been consumed and Alfredo Rossi complains that he is not accustomed to mixing wines, the waiter opens a bottle of Brunello di Montalcino, a Biondi Santi label. Rossi impertinently declares: "I have heard about it, but I have never had any. Stuff like this costs 5,000 or 6,000 lire a bottle." "It could also cost 200,000," one of the judges corrects him. "It is a 1936 vintage." The wine brought out before the end of dinner will be a 1952 Château Haut-Brion: "A robust and lively wine, with a classic aroma, a sedate perfume, a pedigreed taste," the Count comments. We cannot forget that a bottle of 1942 Delaforce vintage port was opened as an aperitif.

Speaking of vintages, I would like to conclude by offering up one final memory of a particular year in Scola's career: 1988, the year that he made *Splendor*. In September of that year, which was proclaimed the "Year of Cinema and Television" in Europe, Scola, as head of the Italian delegation, had contributed to the editing of the "Delphi Declaration," a document signed by approximately three hundred European figures in the film and TV world in defense of freedom of expression and in opposition to restrictions and advertising influences on film and television. Perhaps sensing the spirit of the place, that occasion was the first time I thought that Scola was one of the few directors to consistently enjoy the presence and support of nearly all the Muses. They have all inhabited his work, acting as godparents to one or more of his films.

In Delphi, where it was possible to feel in touch with the roots of European culture, Ettore started speaking in defense of these subjects and the values connected to them, which I have finally addressed, in particular "the right for each person to enrich his personality through emotions, experiences lived and shared, and through understanding." It was a battle that was lost in the short term, but Scola felt that it was being fought, in any case, for future generations. Even then, it seemed to him that this battle would be key for the cultural configuration that the European Community, whose birth was imminent, would be able to assume. And it was something that he had prophesied back in 1982, through the final words of Restif de la Bretonne in *Il mondo nuovo*: "Europe will have a single government."

Notes

1. In the first screenplay, there was a role for De Sica. See Jean A. Gili, *Ettore Scola: Une pensée graphique* (Enghien Les Bains: Centre des Arts, 2008; first published March 1976 in *Ecran* 52).
2. "I remained staggered by *Ladri di biciclette* (1948) and *Roma città aperta* (1945). But a somewhat neglected movie, which struck me because it represented a turning point, was *Una domenica d'agosto* by Emmer," Ettore Scola told Antonio Gnoli. "Every director always makes the one movie too many. That is why I stopped at the penultimate." "Ettore Scola," *La Repubblica*, January 13, 2013, https://ricerca.repubblica.it/repubblica/archivio/repubblica/2013/01/13/ettore-scola.html. Translations of quotations throughout the chapter are Marguerite Shore's unless otherwise noted.
3. From pens and pencils to the typewriter to the dolly, lift, cart, and zoom of *Una giornata particolare*.
4. Ettore Scola quoted in Silvio Danese, *Anni fuggenti: Il romanzo del cinema italiano* (Milan: Bompiani, 2003), 426.
5. Goffredo Fofi, *Il cinema italiano servi e padroni* (Milan: Feltrinelli, 1971), 140.
6. "Not limiting my work as a director I've always been very much concerned about the private dimension, for example, the feeling of friendship," Scola said in 2011. See Ettore Scola, "Ho voluto raccontare la mia generazione," interview by Piero Spila and Bruno Torri, *Cinecritica* A.16, no. 63 (2011): 20.
7. Ennio Bíspuri, *Ettore Scola: Un umanista nel cinema italiano* (Rome: Bulzoni, 2006).
8. Paolo Bertetto, *Il più brutto del mondo* (Milan: Bompiani, 1982), 129.
9. Scola stated: "When Metz and Marchesi asked me if I wanted to work with them, well, I felt like a happy guy. The first film I collaborated with was *Totò Tarzan*. They handed me the script for which I had to add jokes and gags, anonymously. I would write it on a business card. That would be impossible today. Nobody would go for this kind of delivery. Today no young writer is willing to work without recognition of his/her work." Danese, *Anni fuggenti*, 425.
10. "After all there is a form of autobiography in my movies, one that does not concern my person, but a more general biography.... My presumption, sometimes successful, sometimes no, is to make the biography of others, to tell

a common, generational story." Scola, "Ho voluto raccontare la mia generazione," 21.
11. An accurate analysis of the language in some Scola movies can be found in Paola Micheli's *Ettore Scola, i film e le parole* (Rome: Bulzoni, 1994).
12. A "humanist," as happily defined by Bíspuri, *Ettore Scola*.
13. Ettore Scola, letter to Gian Piero Brunetta, July 24, 1988, cited in Gian Piero Brunetta, "Come splendor ha illuminato il mio buio in sala," in *Trevico-Cinecittà: L'avventuroso viaggio di Ettore Scola*, ed. Vito Zagarrio (Venice: Marsilio, 2002), 105.
14. On this visual spectacle and the time of history, see Orio Caldiron, "Il tempo della storia: Il 'Mondo nuovo'" in Zagarrio, *Trevico-Cinecittà*, 146–56.
15. As stated by the character of the Italian clown (interpreted by Enzo Jannacci) in *Il mondo nuovo*.
16. Two examples: (1) the notebook with his drawings of the small protagonist-narrator of *Concorrenza sleale* (*Unfair Competition*, 2001) and (2) making Trintignant in *Il sorpasso* a law student, as Scola was, and having Gassman and Trintignant's characters travel to a home where Scola spent his childhood.
17. To which may be added the Neo-Muse of the new media, which, like Fellini, warns and tries to combat the influence and the evil and deadly power since *Il commissario Pepe*'s time.
18. In *Riusciranno i nostri eroi a ritrovare l'amico misteriosamente scomparso in Africa* (*Will Our Heroes Be Able to Find Their Friend Who Has Mysteriously Disappeared in Africa?*, 1968), for example, Fausto De Savio (Alberto Sordi) says: "The Equator crossed. We are under the constellation of the south, light emotion." And in the final scene of *La cena*, the Japanese boy stares at the starry sky with the figures of his video game.
19. On the metalanguage in Scola's cinema, see Vito Zagarrio, "Introduction," in Zagarrio, *Trevico-Cinecittà*.
20. For this purpose, I refer to Paolo D'Agostini, "Commedia (e comunismo) all'italiana," *Cinecritica* A.16, no. 63 (2011): 32–37.
21. Fofi, *Il cinema italiano servi e padroni*, 140.
22. As is the case in *Il mio calendario*, the forbidden and polemical book of Restif de la Bretonne, seen at the beginning of *Mondo Nuovo*.
23. Ettore Scola, *C'eravamo tanto amati*, in Silvio Danese, *Anni fuggenti: Il romanzo del cinema italiano* (Milan: Bompiani, 2003), 424.
24. "Neo-realism," according to Scola, "was not just a cinematic phenomenon. It was a style, a model, a cultural tension that invested writers, painters, musicians, filmmakers. The dialogue between the artists was a value, the habit of meeting was fundamental. The young people of the next generations were missing the conversation with their fathers." Danese, *Anni fuggenti*, 422.
25. "I always like Modugno," says Bruno. "That song 'Uomo in frac' makes me go

crazy, because it seems nothing and then it has everything: loneliness, incommunicability, then that other thing, that's in fashion today . . . the alienation, like in Antonioni's films. Have you seen *The Eclipse*? I slept . . . took a nice nap . . . nice filmmaker that Antonioni."

26. Says Elide: "I saw *The Eclipse* of Antonioni and thought it was strange. Others also fall into the depths of the female soul, illuminating the loneliness and incommunicability with the rest of mankind. Sagan, Volpini and even myself, while living in comfort, have great communication difficulties and therefore I speak with myself and confide myself. It may be due to alienation but I feel more warmth in cold objects than in men."
27. In 1976, Scola and other directors dedicated a documentary titled *Le borgate di Pasolini* in tribute to Pasolinian boroughs.
28. One of the officers "boasts gastronomic knowledge that he cannot fully assert for the usual lack of the right ingredients."
29. But whose carbohydrates in excess ruin the diet. From *Romanzo di un giovane povero* (1995): "It's what happens to all foreigners who come to Italy. They discover pasta and go crazy."
30. "I could not afford to enter a modest restaurant without first having made a careful budget estimate," says Gianni in *C'eravamo tanto amati*.
31. See *Il sorpasso*, the invitation to eat the fish soup. Gassman says: "Eat . . . it's good" and "But what did they eat before us? Crème caramel, Mamma mia . . . gross!" and in *La congiuntura*, still Gassman: "A portion of shrimps, 2200 lire!"
32.

    SERGIO: Just now in the lab we examined a sample of fettuccine.
    LAURA: So?
    SERGIO: If you knew what was inside you would not ask for it.
    GIULIO: Don't tell me because I want to eat.
    SERGIO: Corn flour, lemon peel, dirt from Siena.
    LAURA: Is it possible that whenever we sit at the table you have to tell us the analysis you've made?
    SERGIO: It's my job.
    GIULIO: Fortunately, you are not a gravedigger.

BIBLIOGRAPHY

Abruzzese, Alberto, and Vincenzo Susca, eds. *Tutto è Berlusconi: Radici, metafore e destinazione del tempo nuovo*. Milan: Lupetti, 2004.
Agacinski, Sylviane. *Le passeur de temps. Modernité et nostalgie*. Paris: Éditions du Seuil, 2000.
Agamben, Giorgio. Homo Sacer: *Sovereign Power and Bare Life*. Translated by Daniel Heller-Roazen. Stanford, CA: Stanford University Press, 1998.
Albertazzi, Daniele, Clodagh Brook, Charlotte Ross, and Nina Rothenbergh, eds. *Resisting the Tide: Cultures of Opposition under Berlusconi (2001–2006)*. New York: Continuum, 2011.
Anderson, Perry. "Land without Prejudice." *London Review of Books*, March 21, 2002. http://www.lrb.co.uk/v24/n06/perry-anderson/land-without-prejudice.
Andrejevic, Mark. "The Work of Watching One Another: Lateral Surveillance, Risk, and Governance." *Surveillance and Society* 2, no. 4 (2004): 479–97.
Andrew, Dudley. *André Bazin*. New York: Columbia University Press, 1990.
———. *Concepts in Film Theory*. New York: Oxford University Press, 1984.
Antonello, Pierpaolo. "I due corpi del divo: le maschere del potere: Andreotti, Thatcher, Elisabetta II." *Bianco e Nero* 576–77, nos. 2–3 (2013): 160–67.
Antonello, Pierpaolo, and Florian Mussgnug, eds. *Postmodern Impegno: Ethics and Commitment in Contemporary Italian Culture* (Oxford: Peter Lang, 2009).
Aprà, Adriano. "Rossellini oltre il neorealismo." In Miccichè, *Il neorealismo cinematografico italiano*, 313–16.
Asor Rosa, Alberto. *Le due società: Ipotesi sulla crisi italiana*. Torino: Einaudi, 1977.
Astruc, Alexandre. "Nascita di una nuova avanguardia: La *caméra stylo*." In *Leggere il cinema*, edited by Alberto Barbera and Roberto Turigliatto, 313–16. Milan: Mondadori, 1978.
Bakhtin, Mikhail. *L'opera di Rabelais e la cultura popolare*. Turin: Einaudi, 1995.
———. *Rabelais and His World*. Bloomington: Indiana University Press, 1984.
Barattoni, Luca. *Italian Post-neorealist Cinema*. Edinburgh: Edinburgh University Press, 2012.
Baxa, Paul. "Ettore Scola's *A Special Day*." AMU on Film. Ave Maria University Film Society, September 8, 2011. https://amufilm.wordpress.com/2011/09/08/ettore-scolas-a-special-day.

Belli, Giuseppe Gioacchino. *I sonetti romaneschi*. Vol. 1. Città di Castello: S. Lappi tipografo editore, 1889.

Benadusi, Lorenzo. *The Enemy of the New Man: Homosexuality in Fascist Italy*. Translated by Suzanne Dingee and Jennifer Pudney. Madison: University of Wisconsin Press, 2012.

Benjamin, Walter. *The Arcades Project*. Translated by Howard Eiland and Kevin McLaughlin. Cambridge, MA: Belknap, 1999. First published 1982.

———. *The Writer of Modern Life: Essays on Charles Baudelaire*. Edited by Michael W. Jennings. Translated by Howard Eiland, Edmund Jephcott, Rodney Livingstone, and Harry Zohn. Cambridge, MA: Belknap, 2006.

Bentham, Jeremy. *The Panopticon Writings*. London: Verso, 1995.

Berlinguer, Giovanni, and Piero Della Seta. *Borgate di Roma*. Rome: Editori Riuniti, 1976.

"Berlusconismo e fascismo." Special issues, *Migro Mega*. January 2011 and February 2011.

Bernardini, Paola, Joanne Granata, Teresa Lobalsamo, and Alberto Zambenedetti, eds. *Federico Fellini: Riprese, riletture, (re)visioni. Atti della North American Conference on the Italian Master of Cinema*. Florence: Franco Cesati Editore, 2016.

Bertetto, Paolo. *Il più brutto del mondo*. Milan: Bompiani, 1982.

Bertini, Antonio, ed. *Ettore Scola: Il cinema e io. Conversazione con Antonio Bertini*. Rome: Officina Edizioni, 1996.

Bertoni, Clotilde, and Massimo Fusillo. "Tematica romanzesca o topoi letterari di lunga durata?" In Moretti, *Il romanzo*, 4: 31–38. Turin: Einaudi, 2003.

Bíspuri, Ennio. *Ettore Scola: Un umanista nel cinema italiano*. Rome: Bulzoni, 2006.

———. *Interpretare Fellini*. Rimini: Guaraldi, 2003.

Bloom, Harold. *The Anxiety of Influence: A Theory of Poetry*. New York: Oxford University Press, 1973.

Bollati, Giulio. *L'italiano: Il carattere nazionale come storia e come invenzione*. Turin: Einaudi, 2011.

Bondanella, Peter. *The Cinema of Federico Fellini*. Princeton, NJ: Princeton University Press, 1992.

———. *A History of Italian Cinema*. New York: Continuum, 2009.

Bondy, François. *European Notebooks: New Societies and Old Politics, 1954–1985*. London: Transactions, 2005.

Borghese, Ilaria, Mariapia Comand, and Maria Rita Fedrizzi. *Sergio Amidei, sceneggiatore*. Gorizia: Grafiche Goriziane, 2004.

Brogi, Daniela. *La donna visibile: Il cinema di Stefania Sandrelli*. Pisa: Edizioni ETS, 2016.

Bruner, Jerome. *Actual Minds, Possible Worlds*. Cambridge, MA: Harvard University Press, 1986.

Brunet, Catherine. *Le monde d'Ettore Scola: La famille, la politique, l'histoire*. Paris: L'Harmattan, 2012.

Brunetta, Gian Piero. *Cent'anni di cinema italiano*. Vol. 2. Rome: Laterza, 2004.

———. *Il cinema italiano contemporaneo: Da "La dolce vita" a Centochiodi*. Bari: Laterza, 2007.

———. *The History of Italian Cinema: A Guide to Italian Film from its Origins to the Twenty-First Century*. Translated by Jeremy Parzen. Princeton: Princeton University Press, 2009.

———. *Storia del cinema italiano*. Vol. 4. Rome: Editori Riuniti, 1998.

Bruscolini, Elisabeta. *Roma nel cinema tra realtà e finzione*. Rome: Quaderni della Cineteca, 2000.

Buck-Morss, Susanne. *The Dialectics of Seeing: Walter Benjamin and the Arcades Project*. London: MIT Press, 1989.

———. "Le flâneur, l'homme-sandwich et la prostituée." In *Walter Benjamin et Paris*, edited by Heinz Wismann, 361–402. Paris: Cerf, 1986.

Bufalino, Gesualdo. *Il malpensante: Lunario dell'anno che fu*. Milan: Bompiani, 1987.

Butler, Judith. *Gender Trouble: Feminism and the Subversion of Identity*. New York: Routledge, 2007.

Caciagli, Marco. "Terremoti elettorali e transazioni fra i partiti." In *L'Italia repubblicana nella crisi degli anni settanta. Partiti e organizzazioni di massa*, edited by Francesco Malgeri and Leonardi Paggio, 149–54. Soveria Mannelli: Rubbettino, 2003.

Cadel, Francesca. *La lingua dei desideri: Il dialetto secondo Pier Paolo Pasolini*. Lecce: Manni, 2002.

Caldiron, Orio. "Il tempo della storia: Il ondo nuovo." In Zagarrio, *Trevico-Cinecittà*, 146–56.

Calvino, Italo. "Delitto in Europa." *Corriere della Sera*, October 8, 1975.

———. *Marcovaldo, ovvero le Stagioni in città*. Milan: Mondadori, 2002.

———. *Six Memos for the New Millennium: The Charles Eliot Norton Lectures, 1985–86*. Translated by Patrick Creagh. Cambridge, MA: Harvard University Press, 1988.

Canova, Gianni. "La disgregazione del fuoricampo: Gli anni novanta." In Zagarrio, *Trevico-Cinecittà*, 77–87.

———. "Ettore Scola," *Belfagor* 41, no. 3 (1986): 279–96.

———. "Figure di un ordine cannibale." In *Lo sguardo eclettico: Il cinema di Mario Monicelli*, edited by Leonardo De Franceschi, 176–88. Venice: Marsilio, 2001.

Cantatore, Lorenzo and Giuliano Falzone, eds. *La signora Magnani: Antologia di rittrati e conversazioni*. Rome: Edilazio, 2001.

Caprara, Valerio. "Il cattivo Borghese." In *Vittorio Gassman: L'ultimo mattatore*, edited by Fabrizio Deriu, 168–79. Venice: Marsilio, 1999.

———. *Mordi e fuggi: La commedia secondo Dino Risi*. Venice: Marsilio, 1993.

Carpiceci, Stefania. "I labirinti dell'anima nello spazio-tempo familiare." In Zagarrio, *Trevico-Cinecittà*, 174–83.

Castoldi, Alberto. *Il flâneur: Viaggio al cuore della modernità*. Milan-Turin: Mondadori, 2013.

Cattini, Alberto. "Le strutture narrative nei film di Scola." In *Ettore Scola: Il volto amaro della commedia all'italiana*, edited by Giulio Marlia, 30–35. Viareggio: M. Baroni, 1999.

Certeau, Michel de. *The Practice of Everyday Life*. Translated by Steven F. Rendall. Berkeley: University of California Press, 1984.

Ciofalo, Giovanni. "C'eravamo tanto amati: Storia, memoria e industria." In Pierre Sorlin, *Memoria, narrazione, audiovisivo*. Edited by Silvia Leonzi, 35–56. Rome: Armandino, 2013.

Cocciardo, Edoardo. *L'applauso interrotto: Poesia e periferia nell'opera di Massimo Troisi*. Naples: Non solo parole edizioni, 2005.

Comand, Mariapia. *Commedia all'italiana*. Milan: Castoro, 2010.

———, ed. *Sulla carta: Storia e storie della sceneggiatura in Italia*. Turin: Lindau, 2004.

Comuzio, Ermanno. "Monty Python—Brutti, sporchi e cattivi." *Cineforum* 159 (November 1976): 717–19.

Corbett, David. *Art of Character*. New York: Penguin Books, 2013.

Cordelli, Franco. *Vacanze romane. Set, protagonisti, film*. Alessandria: Edizioni Falsopiano, 2008.

Cosulich, Callisto. "Trevico-Torino." *Paese sera*, May 5, 1973.

Crutzen, Paul J. "Geology of Mankind: The Anthropocene." *Nature* 415 (2002): 23.

D'Agostini, Paolo. "Commedia (e comunismo) all'italiana," *Cinecritica* A.16, no. 63 (2011): 32–37.

Dalla, Lucio. "L'anno che verrà." *Lucio Dalla*. PL31424, LP. RCA Italiana, 1978.

D'Amico, Masolino. *La commedia all'italiana*. Milan: Il Saggiatore, 2008.

Danese, Silvio. *Anni fuggenti: Il romanzo del cinema italiano*. Milan: Bompiani, 2003.

Daniele, Antonio Rosario. "Meccanismi iperparodici dalla narrazione al cinema: *La panne* di Dürrenmatt fra Ettore Scola e Alberto Sordi." *Between*, 6, no. 12 (2016). http://ojs.unica.it/index.php/between/article/view/2204.

D'Avino, Mauro, and Lorenzo Rumori. *Roma, si gira! Gli scorci ritrovati del cinema di ieri*. Rome: Gremese, 2012.

De Gaetano, Roberto. *Il corpo e la maschera: Il grottesco nel cinema italiano*. Rome: Bulzoni, 1999.

De Giusti, Luciano. "La lunga durata di *Una giornata particolare*." In Zagarrio, *Trevico- Cinecittà*, 276–83.

Deleuze, Gilles. *Difference and Repetition*. Translated by Paul Patton. New York: Columbia University Press, 1994. First published 1968.

———. *L'image-mouvement*. Paris: Minuit, 1983.
Deleuze, Gilles, and Claire Parnet. *Dialogues*. Translated by Hugh Tomlinson and Barbara Habberrjam. New York: Columbia University Press, 1987. First published 1977.
De Santi, Pier Marco, ed. *Ettore Scola: Immagini per un mondo nuovo*. Pisa: Giardini editori, 1989.
De Santi, Pier Marco, and Rossano Vittori. *I film di Ettore Scola*. Rome: Gremese, 1987.
Detassis, Piera, Emiliano Morreale, and Mario Sesti, eds. *Antonio Pietrangeli: Il regista che amava le donne*. Rome: Edizione Sabinae, 2015.
Di Biagi, Flaminio. *Il cinema a Roma: Guida alla storia e ai luoghi del cinema nella capitale*. Rome: Palombi Editori, 2003.
Di Bianco, Laura. "Women in the Deserted City: Urban Space in Marina Spada's Cinema." In *Italian Women Filmmakers and the Gendered Screen*, edited by Maristella Cantini, 121–48. New York: Palgrave Macmillan, 2013.
Didi-Huberman, Georges. *The Surviving Image: Phantoms of Time and Time of Phantoms. Aby Warburg's History of Art*. Translated by Harvey Mendelsohn. University Park: Pennsylvania State University Press, 2016.
Di Janni, Gisa. "Trevico-Torino." *Politica*, May 27, 1973.
Dionisi, Marco, and Nevio De Pascalis, eds. *Piacere, Ettore Scola*. Rome: Edizioni Sabinae, 2016.
Dominijanni, Ida. *Il trucco: Sessualità e biopolitica nella fine di Berlusconi*. Rome: Ediesse, 2014.
Dostoyevsky, Fyodor. "Bobok," in *White Nights and Other Stories*. Translated by Constance Garnett. New York: Dover Thrift Editions, 2017. First published 1873.
Duggan, Christopher. *The Force of Destiny: A History of Italy Since 1796*. London: Penguin Books, 2007.
Dürrenmatt, Friedrich. *Die Panne*. Verlag der Arche, 1956.
Ebner, Michael. *Ordinary Violence in Mussolini's Italy*. New York: Cambridge University Press, 2011.
Eco, Umberto. *Sulla letteratura*. Milan: Bompiani, 2002.
Ellero, Roberto. *Ettore Scola*. Rome: Il Castoro, 1995.
Esposito, Roberto. *Immunitas: The Protection and Negation of Life*. Translated by Zakiya Hanafi. Cambridge: Polity Press, 2011.
Faccioli, Alessandro. *Leggeri come in una gabbia. L'idea comica nel cinema italiano (1930–1944)*. Turin: Kaplan, 2011.
Fagioli, Alessandra. "Tra Studio e *Kammerspiel*. Tracce di teatro." In Zagarrio, *Trevico-Cinecittà*, 223–32.
Farocki, Harun. "Workers Leaving the Factory." *Senses of Cinema* 21 (July 2002). http://sensesofcinema.com/2002/harun-farocki/farocki_workers/.

Fellini, Federico. *Making a Film*. Translated by Christopher Burton White. New York: Contra Mundum Press, 2015.

Ferrero-Regis, Tiziana. *Recent Italian Cinema: Spaces, Contexts, Experiences*. Leicester: Troubador, 2009.

Field, Syd. *The Screenwriters's Workbook: A Workshop Approach*. New York: Dell, 1984.

Fink, Guido. "Semo tutti cristiani? Ebrei visibili e invisibili nel cinema italiano." In *In nome del cinema*, edited by Vito Zagarrio, 83–102. Milan: Il Ponte, 1999.

Finn, Paolo. "Concorrenza sleale." *Cinemasessanta* 42 (March–April 2001): 21–22.

Fiori, Giuseppe. *Il venditore: Storia di Silvio Berlusconi e della Fininvest*. Milan: Garzanti, 1995.

Foa, Anna. *Ebrei in Europa: Dalla Peste Nera all'emancipazione*. Milan: Mondadori, 2001.

Fofi, Goffredo. *Il cinema italiano servi e padroni*. Milan: Feltrinelli, 1971.

Fofi, Goffredo, Morando Morandini, and Gianni Volpi, eds. *Storia del cinema: Dalle nouvelle vagues ai nostri giorni*. Vol. 3. Milan: Garzanti, 1988.

Forster, Edward Morgan. *Aspects of the Novel*. New York: RosettaBooks, 2010. First published 1927.

Forza Italia. *Una storia italiana*. Milan: Mondadori, 2001.

Foucault, Michel. *L'archéologie du savoir*. Paris: Gallimard, 1969.

———. *Discipline and Punish: The Birth of the Prison*. Translated by Alan Sheridan. New York: Vintage Books, 1995.

———. *Power/Knowledge. Selected Interviews and Other Writings 1972–1977*. Edited by Colin Gordon. Translated by Colin Gordon, Leo Marshall, John Mepham, and Kate Soper. New York: Pantheon Books, 1980.

———. *Society Must Be Defended: Lectures at Collège de France, 1978–1979*. New York: Picador, 2003.

Freud, Sigmund. *The Interpretation of Dreams*. Trans. A. A. Brill. New York: Dover, 2015.

———. *New Introductory Lectures on Psycho-analysis. The Standard Edition of the Complete Psychological Works of Sigmund Freud*. London: The Hogart Press, 1932.

Friedberg, Anne. *Window Shopping: Cinema and the Postmodern*. Berkeley: University of California Press, 1993.

Fullwood, Natalie. *Cinema, Gender, and Everyday Space: Comedy, Italian Style*. New York: Palgrave Macmillan, 2015.

Fusco, Gian-Giacomo. *Ai margini di Roma capitale: Lo sviluppo storico delle periferie San Basilio come caso di studio*. Rome: Edizioni Nuova Cultura, 2013.

Fusco, Maria Pia. "Scola: Uno specchio per i giovani." *La Repubblica*, July 16, 2004, 45.

Galbraith, John Kenneth. *The Affluent Society*. Boston: Houghton Mifflin Harcourt, 1958.

———. *The Age of Uncertainty*. Boston: Houghton Mifflin Harcourt, 1977.

Garofalo, Piero, Elizabeth Leake, and Dana Renga. *Internal Exile in Fascist Italy: History and Representations of Confino*. Manchester: Manchester University Press, 2019.

Ghini, Celso. *Il terremoto del 15 giugno*. Milan: Feltrinelli, 1976.

Giacovelli, Enrico. *Non ci resta che ridere: Una storia del cinema comico italiano*. Turin: Lindau, 1999.

———. *Un secolo di cinema italiano 1900–1999*. Turin: Lindau, 2002.

Gibelli, Antonio. *Berlusconi passato alla storia. L'Italia nell'era della democrazia autoritaria*. Rome: Donzelli, 2010.

Gieri, Manuela. *Contemporary Italian Filmmaking: Strategies of Subversions; Pirandello, Fellini, Scola, and the Directors of the New Generation*. Toronto: University of Toronto Press, 1995.

Gili, Jean. *Arrivano i mostri: I volti della commedia italiana*. Bologna: Cappelli, 1980.

———. *Une pensée graphique*. Enghien Les Bains: Centre des Arts, 2008.

———. "Propos d'Ettore Scola." DVD Bonus, *Gente di Roma*. 2004.

———. "Rome, plateau de cinéma." *Positif—revue mensuelle de cinéma*, no. 664 (June 2016): 94–96.

Ginsborg, Paul. *A History of Contemporary Italy: Society and Politics, 1943–1988*. London: Penguin, 1990.

———. *Italy and Its Discontents: Family, Civil Society, State, 1980–2001*. New York: Palgrave Macmillan, 2003.

Ginsborg, Paul, and Enrica Asquer, eds. *Berlusconismo: Analisi di un sistema di potere*. Bari: Laterza, 2011.

Girlanda, Elio. *Stefania Sandrelli*. Rome: Gremese, 2002.

Giuliani, Francesca. "Al Ghetto per ricordare." *La Repubblica*, August 11, 1997. http://ricerca.repubblica.it/repubblica/archivio/repubblica/1997/08/11/al-ghetto-per-ricordare.html.

Gleber, Anke. *The Art of Taking a Walk. Flânerie, Literature, and Film in Weimar Culture*. Princeton, NJ: Princeton University Press, 1999.

Goel, Vinod. *Sketches of Thought*. Cambridge, MA: MIT Press, 1995.

Gordon, Robert S. C. *The Holocaust in Italian Culture, 1944–2010*. Stanford, CA: Stanford University Press, 2012.

Goretti, Gianfranco, and Tommaso Giartosio. *La città e l'isola: Omosessuali al confine nell'Italia fascista*. Rome: Donzelli Editore, 2006.

Gorfinkel, Elena, and John David Rhodes, eds. *Taking Place: Location and the Moving Image*. Minneapolis: University of Minnesota Press, 2011.

Governi, Giancarlo. *Alberto Sordi, l'italiano*. Rome: Armando Curcio, 2010.

Governi, Giancarlo. *Nannarella: Il romanzo di Anna Magnani*. Rome: Minimum Fax, 2008.

Grande, Maurizio. *Abiti nuziali e biglietti di banca: La società della commedia nel cinema italiano*. Rome: Bulzoni, 1986.

———. *La commedia all'italiana*. Edited by Orio Caldiron. Rome: Bulzoni 2003.

Greco, Michela. "'I nostri ragazzi' di De Matteo, adolescenti pericolosi." *Cinecittà News*, November 12, 2013. http://news.cinecitta.com/IT/it-it/news/55/5410/i-nostri-ragazzi-di-de-matteo-adolescenti-pericolosi.aspx.

Gregg, Melissa. *Work's Intimacy*. New York: John Wiley, 2011.

Gundle, Stephen. *Bellissima: Feminine Beauty and the Idea of Italy*. New Haven, CT: Yale University Press, 2007.

Hansen, Miriam. "The Mass Production of the Senses: Classical Cinema as Vernacular Modernism." *Modernism/Modernity* 6, no. 2 (1999): 59–77.

Hochkofler, Matilde. *Anna Magnani: La biografia*. With the collaboration of Luca Magnani. Milan: Bompiani, 2013.

Horn, David G. *Social Bodies: Science, Reproduction, and Italian Modernity*. Princeton, NJ: Princeton University Press, 1994.

Iaccio, Pasquale. "'Non ti piace la fine del XX secolo?' La storia nei film di Scola." In Zagarrio, *Trevico-Cinecittà*, 133–45.

Iacoboni, Marco. *Mirroring People*. New York: Farrar, Straus, & Giroux, 2008.

Iovino, Serenella. "Sedimenting Stories: Italo Calvino and the Extraordinary Strata of the Anthropocene," *Neohelicon* 44, no. 2 (2017): 315–30.

Jacometti, Alberto. *Ventotene*. Milan: Mondadori, 1946.

Kantrowitz, Andrea. "The Man behind the Curtain: What Cognitive Science Reveals about Drawing." *Journal of Aesthetic Education* 46, no. 1 (2012): 1–14.

Kezich, Tullio. *Federico Fellini: La vita e i film*. Milan: Feltrinelli, 2007.

———. *Il filmsessanta: Il cinema degli anni 1962–1966*. Milan: Il Formichiere, 1969.

Klein, Gabriella. *La politica linguistica del Fascismo*. Bologna: Il Mulino, 1986.

Konnikova, Maria. "What's Lost as Handwriting Fades." *New York Times*, June 3, 2014.

Kracauer, Siegfried. *Theory of Film: The Redemption of Physical Reality*. Princeton, NJ: Princeton University Press, 1997. First published 1960.

La Carrubba, Iolanda. *Fellini il mago, secondo Ettore Scola*. Le reti di Dedalus. November 2013. http://www.retididedalus.it/Archivi/2013/novembre/SPAZIO_LIBERO/5_cineprime/cineprime.pdf.

Landy, Marcia. *Italian Film*. Cambridge: Cambridge University Press, 2000.

———. *Stardom Italian Style*. Bloomington: Indiana University Press, 2008.

Langer, Lawrence. *Holocaust Testimonies: The Ruins of Memory*. New Haven, CT: Yale University Press, 1991.

Lanzoni, Rémi. *Comedy Italian Style: The Golden Age of Italian Film Comedies*. New York: Continuum, 2009.

———. *Rire de plomb: La comédie à l'italienne des années 70*. Paris: Editions L'Harmattan, 2017.
Lefebvre, Henri. *The Production of Space*. Malden: Blackwell, 1991.
Leonzi, Silvia, ed. *Memoria, narrazione, audiovisivo*. Rome: Armandino, 2013.
Levi, Primo. *I sommersi e i salvati*. Turin: Einaudi, 1991.
Levy, Emanuel. *Cinema of Outsiders: The Rise of American Independent Film*. New York: New York University Press, 1999.
Lichtner, Giacomo. "Allegory, Applicability or Alibi? Historicizing Intolerance in Ettore Scola's *Concorrenza sleale*." *Journal of Modern Italian Studies* 17, no. 1 (2012): 95–102.
———. *Fascism in Italian Cinema since 1945: The Politics and Aesthetics of Memory*. New York: Palgrave Macmillan, 2013.
———. "Italian Cinema and the Fascist Past: Tracing Memory Amnesia." *Fascism: Journal of Comparative Fascist Studies* 4 (2015): 25–47.
Lombardi, Giancarlo, and Christian Uva, eds. *Italian Political Cinema: Public Life, Imaginary, and Identity in Contemporary Italian Film*. Oxford: Peter Lang, 2016.
Luijnenburg, Linde. "The Grotesque as a Tool: Deconstructing the Imperial Narrative in Two commedie all'italiana by Ettore Scola." *Incontri: Rivista Europea di Studi Italiani* 29, no. 2 (2014): 43–54.
Lukács, George. "Die Theorie des Romans." *Zeitschrift für Ästhetik und Allgemeine Kunstwissenschaft*. Vol 2. Berlin: P. Cassirer, 1920.
———. *The Theory of the Novel. A Historico-philosophical Essay on the Forms of Great Epic Literature*. London: Merlin Press, 1971.
Lumley, Robert. *Dal '68 agli anni di piombo: Studenti e operai nella crisi italiana*. Florence: Giunti, 1998.
Magi, Giovanni. "Interview—Ettore Scola." Euronews, May 9, 2009. https://www.youtube.com/watch?v=nSTBchUcs00&feature=fvw.
Maraldi, Antonio, ed. *I film e le sceneggiature di Ettore Scola*. Cesena: Quaderni del Centro Cinema, 1982.
Marchesi, Marcello. *Il malloppo*. Milan: Bompiani, 1971.
Marcus, Millicent. "Ettore Scola's *Concorrenza sleale*: The Alter-Biography of the Other-in-Our-Midst." In *Incontri con il cinema italiano*, edited by Antonio Vitti, 79–94. Caltanissetta: Salvatore Sciascia Editore, 2003.
———. *Italian Film in the Light of Neorealism*. Princeton: Princeton University Press, 1986.
———. *Italian Film in the Shadow of Auschwitz*. Toronto: University of Toronto Press, 2007.
———. "Un'ora e mezzo particolare: Teaching Fascism with Ettore Scola." *Italica* 83, no. 1 (2006): 53–61.
———. "Umbilical Scenes: Where Filmmakers Foreground Their Relationships to Literary Sources." *Romance Languages Annual* 10, no. 1 (1998): 19–24.

Marini-Maio, Nicoletta. *A Very Seductive Body Politic: Silvio Berlusconi in Cinema.* Milan: Mimesis, 2015.

Markman, Arthur, and Kristin Wood, eds. *Tools for Innovation.* Oxford: Oxford University Press, 2009.

Marletti, Carlo, and Franca Roncarolo, "Media Influence in the Italian Transition from a Consensual to a Majoritarian Democracy." In *Democracy and the Media: A Comparative Perspective*, edited by Richard Gunther and Anthony Mughan, 195–240. Cambridge: Cambridge University Press, 2000.

Masi, Stefano. *Ettore Scola: Uno sguardo acuto e ironico sull'Italia e gli italiani degli ultimi quarant'anni.* Rome: Gremese, 2006.

———. "I viandanti del teatro di posa. Il viaggio di capitan Luciano e Madame Odette." In Zagarrio, 266–75.

Masoni, Tullio. "La commedia: Primi segnali di decadenza." In *Storia del cinema italiano, 1977–1985*, edited by Vito Zagarrio, 101–15. Venice: Marsilio, 2005.

Miccichè, Lino. *Il cinema del riflusso: Film e cineasti italiani degli anni '70.* Venice: Marsilio, 1997.

———. *Cinema italiano degli anni '70.* Venice: Marsilio, 1980.

———, ed. *Il neorealismo cinematografico italiano.* Venice: Marsilio, 1999.

Micheli, Paola. *Ettore Scola: I film e le parole.* Rome: Bulzoni, 1994.

Minuz, Andrea. *Political Fellini: Journey to the End of Italy.* Translated by Marcus Perryman. New York: Berghahn, 2015.

———. *Viaggio al termine dell'Italia: Fellini politico.* Soveria Mannelli: Rubbettino, 2011.

Mirzoeff, Nicholas. "Visualizing the Anthropocene." *Public Culture* 26, no. 2 (2014): 213–32.

Misiti, Maura Adele, Giuseppe Gesano Menniti, and Marcella Prosperi. "La rivoluzione silenziosa delle donne: Cronologia dei diritti." In *Italia 150 anni: Popolazione, welfare, scienza e società*, edited by Sveva Avveduto, 107–21. Rome: Gangemi, 2005.

Molè, Ilario. "Film," *Città Nuova*, March 1980, 64.

Monicelli, Mario. *Autoritratto.* Florence: Polistampa, 2002.

Monicelli, Mino. *Cinema italiano: Ma cos'è questa crisi?* Bari: Laterza, 1979.

Montini, Franco. "La Roma di Scola." In Zagarrio, *Trevico-Cinecittà*, 218–22.

Morandini, Morando. "Dal 1968 ai giorni nostri: Agonia, morte e resurrezione." In *Commedia all'italiana: Angolazioni controcampi*, edited by Riccardo Napolitano, 87–94. Rome: Gangemi, 1986.

Morando, Paolo. *Dancing Days: 1978–1979. I due anni che hanno cambiato l'Italia.* Milan: Laterza, 2009.

Moravia, Alberto. *Contempt.* Introduction by Tim Parks. Translated by Angus Davidson. New York: New York Review Books, 1999. First published as *Il disprezzo*, 1957.

———. "Ma che cosa aveva in mente?" *L'Espresso*, November 9, 1975.
Morelli, Guglielmina, Giulio Martini, and Giancarlo Zappoli. *Un'invisibile presenza: Il cinema di Antonio Pietrangeli*. Milan: Il Castoro, 1998.
Moretti, Franco, ed. *The Novel*. 4 vols. Princeton, NJ: Princeton University Press, 2006.
———. *Il romanzo*. Vol. 4, *Temi, luoghi, eroi*. Turin: Einaudi, 2003.
Morreale, Emiliano. *L'invenzione della nostalgia: Il vintage nel cinema italiano e dintorno*. Rome: Donzelli, 2009.
Mosca, Umberto. "Che strano chiamarsi Federico." *Panoramiche-panoramiques: Rivista cinematografica quadrimestrale*, no. 56 (2014): 24.
Moscati, Italo. "*Trevico-Torino* di Ettore Scola," *Letture 1973* 27, no.12 (1972): 889–91.
Muscio, Giuliana. "Un mestiere come un altro: Scola sceneggiatore." In Zagarrio, *Trevico-Cinecittà*, 51–58.
Mussolini, Benito. *Opera Omnia*. 35 vols. Florence: La Fenice, 1951–62.
Neutres, Julien. *Rome ville ouverte au cinéma: Entre vision mythologique et géographie sociale*. La Tour-D'Aigues: Éditions de l'Aube, 2010.
Novelli, Diego. "Il caso Trevico-Torino." In Zagarrio, *Trevico-Cinecittà*, 116–19.
Nuvolati, Gian Paolo. *Lo sguardo vagabondo: Il flâneur e la città da Baudelaire ai postmoderni*. Bologna: Il Mulino, 2006.
O'Leary, Alan. "Of Shite and Time." *Italianist* 35, no. 2 (2015): 294–99.
———. *Tragedia all'italiana: Italian Cinema and Italian Terrorism, 1970–2010*. Oxford: Peter Lang, 2011.
Olivieri, Angelo. *L'imperatore in platea: I grandi del cinema dal Marc'Aurelio allo schermo*. Bari: Dedalo, 1986.
Olson, Kirby. *Comedy after Postmodernism: Rereading Comedy from Edward Lear to Charles Willeford*. Lubbock: Texas Tech University Press, 2001.
Orsina, Giovanni. *Il Berlusconismo nella storia d'Italia*. Venice: Marsilio, 2013. Kindle e-book.
Pagani, Malcom, and Fabrizio Corallo. "Fosse stato per me non sarei mai diventato regista: Intervista a Ettore Scola." Traffico di parole, May 16, 2014, http://www.trafficodiparole.com/wordpress/fosse-stato-per-me-non-sarei-mai-diventato-regista-intervista-a-ettore-scola-di-malcom-pagani-e-fabrizio-corallo. First published in *Il fatto quotidiano*.
Panella, Giuseppe. "Dalla farsa della società alla commedia della satira: Ettore Scola 1964/1984." In *Si fa per ridere . . . ma e una cosa seria*, edited by Sandro Bernardi, 89–93. Florence: La Casa Usher, 1985.
Paoli, Enrico "Il maestro rosso." *Libero*, January 20, 2016. http://www.pressreader.com/italy/libero/20160120/282033326204057/TextView.
Parigi, Stefania. *Fisiologia dell'immagine: Il pensiero di Cesare Zavattini*. Turin: Lindau, 2006.

Pasolini, Pier Paolo. *Lettere luterane*. Turin: Einaudi, 1976.

———. "Il mio Accattone in TV dopo il genocidio," in *Lettere luterane*. Turin: Einaudi, 1976, 154. Previously published in *Corriere della Sera*, October 8, 1975.

———. *La nuova gioventù*. Turin: Einaudi, 1996.

———. *Scritti corsari*. Milan: Garzanti, 1975.

Patriarca, Silvana. *Italianità: La costruzione del carattere nazionale*. Rome-Bari: Laterza, 2010.

———. *Italian Vices: Nation and Character from the Risorgimento to the Republic*. Cambridge: Cambridge University Press, 2010.

Pecchioni, Daniela. "Fuori la Storia." *Drammaturgia*, January 1, 2001. http://drammaturgia.fupress.net/recensioni/recensione1.php?id=2558.

Perniola, Ivelise. "Il mestiere di scrittore: Dalla sceneggiatura presunta alla sceneggiatura desunta." In Zagarrio, *Trevico-Cinecittà*, 244–54.

Perra, Emiliano Perra. *Conflicts of Memory: The Reception of Holocaust Films and TV Programmes in Italy, 1945 to the Present*. Oxford: Peter Lang, 2010.

Petrocchi, Policarpo. *Nuovo dizionario universale della lingua italiana*. Milan: Treves Editore, 1912.

Picchietti, Virginia. "A Semiotics of Judaism: Representations of Judaism and the Jewish Experience in Italian Cinema 1992–2004." *Italica* 83, nos. 3 and 4 (2006): 563–82.

Pierangeli, Fabio. *È finita l'età della pietà: Pasolini, Calvino, S. Nievo e "mostri" del Circeo*. Rome: Edizioni Sinestesie, 2015.

Pietrangeli, Antonio. "Ritratti cinematografici della donna italiana." *Bianco e Nero* 28, no. 5 (1967): 35–65.

Pietropaolo, Domenico. "Commedia dell'arte as Grotesque Dance: Decline or Evolution?" In *The Routledge Companion to Commedia Dell'Arte*, edited by Judith Chaffee and Oliver Cric, 338–45. New York: Routledge, 2015.

Pietrzykowski, Szymon. "Gay as a Stranger: Homosexuality during Fascism in Ettore Scola's *Una Giornata Particolare*" ["A Special Day"]. *Maska* 24 (2014): 75–88.

Pistagnesi, Patricia. *Anna Magnani*. Milan: Fabbri Editori, 1988.

Pizzolato, Nicola. "Workers and Revolutionaries at the Twilights of Fordism: The Breakdown of Industrial Relations in the Automobile Plants of Detroit and Turin, 1967–1973." *Labor History* 45, no. 4 (2004), 419–43.

Poerio, Illaria. *A scuola di dissenso: Storie di resistenza al confino di polizia (1925–1943)*. Rome: Carocci, 2016.

Pomella, Andrea. "L'ultimo Scola." Rivista Studio: Attualità Cultura Stili di Vita. January 20, 2016. http://www.rivistastudio.com/standard/lultimo-scola/.

Ponzanesi, Sandra. "Queering European Sexualities through Italy's Fascist Past: Colonialism, Homosexuality, and Masculinities." In *What's Queer about*

Europe? Productive Encounters and Re-enchanting Paradigms, edited by Mireille Rosello and Sudeep Dasgupta, 81–113. New York: Fordham University Press, 2014.

Pravadelli, Veronica. "Voci del maschile, corpi del femminile." In Zagarrio, *Trevico-Cinecittà*, 157–64. Venice: Marsilio, 2002.

Price, Steven. *A History of the Screenplay*. New York: Palgrave Macmillan, 2013.

Reich, Jacqueline. *Beyond the Latin Lover: Marcello Mastroianni, Masculinity, and Italian Cinema*. Bloomington: Indiana University Press, 2004.

Renga, Dana. "Screening *Confino*: Male Melodrama and Exile Cinema." *Journal of Italian Cinema & Media Studies* 5, no. 1 (2017): 23–46.

Rhodes, John David. *Stupendous, Miserable City: Pasolini's Rome*. Minneapolis: University of Minnesota Press, 2007.

Rhodes, John David, and Elena Gorfinkel, eds. *Taking Place: Location and the Moving Image*. Minneapolis: University of Minnesota Press, 2011.

Rigoletto, Sergio. "The Italian Comedy of the Economic Miracle: *L'italiano medio* and Strategies of Gender Exclusion." In *Italy on Screen: National Identity and Italian Imaginary*, edited by Lucy Bolton and Chritina Siggers Manson, 33–47. London: IGRS, 2007.

———. *Masculinity and Italian Cinema: Sexual Politics, Social Conflict and Male Crisis in the 1970s*. Edinburgh: Edinburgh University Press, 2014.

Ritchie, Graeme. "Developing the Incongruity-Resolution Theory." In *Proceedings of the AISB 99 Symposium on Creative Language, Humour and Stories*, 78–85. Edinburgh: University of Edinburgh, 1999.

Rondolino, Gianni. "Le giornate particolari di Ettore Scola: Un profilo critico." In Zagarrio, *Trevico-Cinecittà*, 43–50.

Rosand, David. *Drawing Acts: Studies in Graphic Expression and Representation*. Cambridge: Cambridge University Press, 2002.

Rossi Barilli, Gianni. *Il movimento gay in Italia*. Milan: Feltrinelli, 1999.

Routledge, Clay, Jamie Arndt, Tim Wildschut, Constantine Sedikides, Claire M. Hart, Jacob Juhl, J. J. M. Vingerhoets, and Wolff Schlotz. "The Past Makes the Present Meaningful: Nostalgia as an Existential Resource." *Journal of Personality and Social Psychology* 101 (2011): 638–52.

Russo, Paolo, ed. *Nero su Bianco: Sceneggiatura e sceneggiatori in Italia*. Barcelona: Quaderni del CSCI, 2014.

Salzani, Carlo. *Constellations of Reading: Walter Benjamin in Figures of Actuality*. Bern: Peter Lang, 2009.

Santomassimo, Gianpasquale, ed. *La notte della democrazia italiana: Dal regime fascista al governo Berlusconi*. Milan: Il Saggiatore, 2003.

Sassoon, Donald. *Contemporary Italy: Economy, Society and Politics since 1945*. London: Longman, 1997.

Satta, Gloria. "Carlo Verdone: 'Ettore Scola ha insegnato a tutti noi l'importanza della commedia.'" *Il Mattino*, January 21, 2016. https://www.ilmattino.it/spettacoli/cinema/carlo_verdone_ettore_scola_commedia-1495894.html.

Sbardella, Americo. *Roma nel cinema*. Rome: Semar, 2000.

Schank, Roger. *Tell Me a Story: Narrative and Intelligence*. Evanston, IL: Northwestern University Press, 1990.

Schooler, Jonathan W. and Tonya Y. Engstler-Schooler. "Verbal Overshadowing of Visual Memories: Some Things Are Better Left Unsaid." *Cognitive Psychology* 22, no. 1 (1990): 36–71.

Schopenhauer, Arthur. *The World as Will and Idea*. 6th ed. 2 vols. Translated by Richard B. Haldane and John Kemp. London: Routledge & Kegan Paul, 1907.

Sciarelli, Federica, and Giuseppe Rinaldi. *3 bravi ragazzi. Gli assassini del Circeo. I retroscena di un'inchiesta lunga trent'anni*. Milan: Rizzoli, 2006.

Scola, Ettore. "Attenti al buffone: Testimonianze sparse sulla commedia all'italiana." In *Effetto commedia: Teoria, generi, paesaggi della commedia cinematografica*, edited by Claver Salizzato and Vito Zagarrio, 205–23. Rome: Di Giacomo Editore, 1985.

———. *Concorrenza sleale*. Turin: Lindau, 2001.

———. *Una giornata particolare*. Compagnia Cinematografica Champion, 1977.

———. "I giovani non devono dimenticare Pasolini." Interview by Chiara Ugolini. Repubblica TV. October 30, 2015. http://video.repubblica.it/spettacoli-e-cultura/ettore-scola-i-giovani-non-devono-dimenticare-pasolini/216662/215846.

———. "Ho voluto raccontare la mia generazione." Interview by Piero Spila and Bruno Torri. *Cinecritica* A.16, no. 63 (2011): 7–23.

———. *Parla il cinema italiano*. Vol. 2. Edited by Aldo Tassone. Milan: Il Formichiere, 1980, 298–323.

———. "Il passaporto per il cinema." *Panta Agenda Marchesi* 32 (2015). Kindle ed.

———. "Rome, ville de passage et de saccage." *Cités-cinés*. La Villette: Ramsay et Grande Halle, 1987.

———. "Trevico Torino." *Testo*. 1972. http://image.archivioluce.com/dm_0/IL/luceAamod/allegati/860/000/2014/860.000.2014.0002.pdf.

Scola, Ettore, and Ivo Milazzo. *Un drago a forma di nuvola*. Milan: Bao, 2013.

Shiel, Mark. *Italian Neorealism: Rebuilding the Cinematic City*. London: Wallflower, 2006.

Silvestri, Roberto. "*Concorrenza sleale*." *Il Manifesto*, March 10, 2001.

Snyder, Susan. "Romeo and Juliet: Comedy into Tragedy." *Essays in Criticism: A Quarterly Journal of Literary Criticism* 20, no. 4 (1970): 391–402.

Solomons, Gabriel, ed. *World Film Locations: Rome*. Bristol: Intellect Books, 2014.

Sorlin, Pierre. "Urban Space in European Cinema." In *Revisiting Space: Space and

Place in European Cinema, edited by Wendy Everett and Axel Goodbody, 25–36. New York: Peter Lang, 2005.

Spackman, Barbara. *Fascist Virilities: Rhetoric, Ideology, and Social Fantasy in Italy*. Minneapolis: University of Minnesota Press, 1996.

Spagnoli, Marco. *Alberto Sordi: Storia di un italiano*. Rome: Adnkronos, 2003.

Spinazzola, Vittorio. *Cinema e pubblico: Lo spettacolo filmico in Italia, 1945–1965*. Rome: Bulzoni, 1985.

———, ed. *Pubblico 1981: Produzione letteraria e mercato culturale*. Milan: Libri Milan, 1981.

Stewart-Steinberg, Susan. *L'effetto Pinocchio, Italia 1861–1922: La costruzione di una complessa modernità*. Rome: Elliott, 2011.

———. *The Pinocchio Effect: On Making Italians, 1860–1920*. Chicago: University of Chicago Press, 2007.

Stille, Alexander. *Citizen Berlusconi*. Milan: Garzanti, 2006.

Tassone, Aldo. *Le cinéma italien parle*. Paris: Edilig, 1982.

———. *Parla il cinema italiano*. Vol. 2. Milan: Il Formichiere, 1980.

Tesser, Elisabetta. "Gente di Roma: An Exercise of Dérive by Ettore Scola." *Current Issues in Tourism* 15, no. 6 (2012): 577–90.

Testa, Carlo, ed. *Poet of Civic Courage: The Films of Francesco Rosi*. Westport, CT: Praeger, 1996.

Tester, Keith, ed. *The Flâneur*. London: Routledge. 1994.

Thompson, William. "Freedom and Comedy." *The Tulane Drama Review* 9, no. 3 (1965): 216–30.

Tognolotti, Chiara. "Io la conoscevo bene (Antonio Pietrangeli, 1965)." In Brogi, *La donna visibile*, 59–66.

Tovaglieri, Alberto. *La dirompente illusione: Il cinema italiano e il Sessantotto*. Soveria Mannelli: Rubbettino, 2014.

Tronti, Mario. "Factory and Society." *Operaismo in English*. June 13, 2013. https://operaismoinenglish.wordpress.com/2013/06/13/factory-and-society/.

Turner, Mark. *The Literary Mind: The Origins of Thought and Language*. Oxford: Oxford University Press, 1996.

Tversky, Barbara, and Masaki Suwa. "Thinking with Sketches." In Markman and Wood, *Tools for Innovation*, 75–84.

Ugolini, Chiara. "Che strano chiamarsi Federico!, un ritratto," *La Repubblica*, September 6, 2013.

Uva, Christian. "Un borgo nella metropoli: Ettore Scola a Palazzo Federici." *Italianist* 35, no. 2 (2015): 284–90.

Vargau, Marina. *Romarcord: Flânerie dans la cine-città*. PhD dissertation, Université de Montréal, 2016. https://papyrus.bib.umontreal.ca/xmlui/bitstream/handle/1866/18457/Vargau_Marina_2016_these.pdf?sequence=2.

Verdone, Mario. *Il cinema a Roma*. Rome: Edilazio, 2003.

Veronese, Cosetta. "Paying the Price of Perpetuating Memory: Francesco Rosi's Interpretation of Primo Levi's *The Truce*." *Studies in European Cinema* 5 (January 2008): 55–66.

Vignati, Rinaldo. "Marcello Marchesi, autore di sceneggiature." *L'avventura* 2 (July–December 2016): 231–54.

Villa, Federica. *Botteghe di scrittura per il cinema italiano: Intorno a "Il bandito" di Alberto Lattuada*. Bianco e Nero. Venice: Marsilio, 2002.

———. "Cordoglio ed euforia: La sceneggiatura negli anni '50." In Comand, *Sulla carta*, 143–62.

Wallenstein, Sven-Olov. *Biopolitics and the Emergence of Modern Architecture*. New York: Princeton Architectural, 2009.

Wrigley, Richard, ed. *Cinematic Rome*. Leicester: Troubador, 2008.

———. *The Flâneur Abroad: Historical and International Perspectives*. Newcastle upon Tyne: Cambridge Scholars, 2014.

Zagarrio, Vito. "La sceneggiatura circolare: Strutture narrative in tre film di Ettore Scola." *Italianist* 29 (2009): 265–80.

———, ed. *Trevico-Cinecittà: L'avventuroso viaggio di Ettore Scola*. Venice: Marsilio, 2002.

Zapponi, Bernardino. *"Roma" di Federico Fellini*. Bologna: Cappelli, 1972.

Zavattini, Cesare. "Basta con i soggetti." In *Neorealismo ecc*, ed. Mino Argentieri. Milan: Bompiani, 1979.

Žižek, Slavoj. *For They Know Not What They Do: Enjoyment as a Political Factor*. London: Verso, 2002.

CONTRIBUTORS

Francesca Borrione (Doctorate, University of Perugia) is currently pursuing her PhD in English at the University of Rhode Island, where she studies true crime narratives in Italian American and Italian imaginary. She is the author of four novels and three monographs. Her latest novel, *La stagione arida di Minerva Jones*, was published in 2017. Her works on cinema include *Il cinema specchio della realtà: Modelli culturali a confronto* (2013) and *Il maccartismo e gli anni inquieti del cinema americano* (2007).

Edward Bowen (PhD, Indiana University) is an advanced lecturer of Italian at the University of Kansas. He specializes in Italian film history, exhibition, independent cinema, and urban politics. His dissertation examines the role that cinema reuse has played in urban renewal campaigns in Rome, led by city officials and grassroots movements. He has published in *Studies in Documentary Film*, *Journal of Italian Cinema and Media Studies*, and *Cinema e storia*.

Gian Piero Brunetta (Doctorate, University of Padova) is a professor emeritus of film history at the University of Padova. He directed the *Dizionario dei registi del cinema mondiale* (2005–6) and *La storia del cinema mondiale* (1999–2001). He is the author of numerous books on Italian cinema, including *Guida alla storia del cinema italiano 1903–2003* (*The History of Italian Cinema 1903–2003*, 2009), *Gli intellettuali italiani e il cinema* (2004), *Cent'anni di cinema italiano* (1991), *Buio in sala* (1989), and *Storia del cinema italiano, 1895–1945* (1979). He has curated exhibitions on Italian cinema, including one at Cinecittà in 1995, and he served as historical consultant to Ettore Scola for the film *Splendor* (1988).

Fabrizio Cilento (PhD, University of Washington) is an associate professor of film and digital media at Messiah College. He is the author of *An Investigative*

Cinema: Politics and Modernization in Italian, French, and American Film (2018). He has also published in the journals *Cinema Journal, California Italian Studies,* and *Comedy Studies,* among others, and in numerous edited volumes on Italian cinema. He leads Italian Cityscapes and the Flow of Life, an annual cross-cultural program that explores film locations, and Cinemablography, a collaborative project tracing a cinematic map of the 2000s.

Federica Colleoni (PhD, University of Michigan) has published several essays and articles on contemporary Italian and European cinema and literature, and she coedited the volume *Il cinema di Marco Tullio Giordana: Interventi critici* (2015). Her most recent essays are on the cinema of Marco Tullio Giordana, the Taviani brothers, and Valentino Orsini.

Mariapia Comand (Doctorate, Catholic University of Milan) is a full professor and teaching chair at the University of Udine, Italy, where she teaches film studies, history, and film criticism. Her research focuses on the concept of writing, in both the theoretical sense (*I personaggi dei film*, 2013) and the historiographical (*Sulla carta: Storia e storie della sceneggiatura in Italia*, 2006) and also on Italian cinema (*Commedia all'italiana*, 2011), paying particular attention to cultural and social dynamics in cinema that also involve the whole audiovisual industry. She is the former editor in chief of *Bianco e Nero*.

Emiliano Guaraldo (PhD candidate, University of North Carolina–Chapel Hill) focuses his research on the Anthropocene and the representations of petroleum in Italian visual culture. His interests include film, science and technology studies, cultural studies, and the environmental humanities. He has published essays on ecocriticism and food culture and documentaries on the environment.

Rémi Lanzoni (PhD, University of North Carolina–Chapel Hill) is an associate professor of Romance languages and teaches Italian cinema at Wake Forest University. He specializes in French and Italian film and has published several books on national cinemas: *Rire de plomb: La comédie à l'italienne des années 70* (2017), *French Cinema: From Its Beginnings to the Present* (2015), *French Comedy on Screen: A Cinematic History* (2014), and *Comedy Italian Style: The Golden Age of Italian Film Comedies* (2009).

Dario Marcucci (PhD candidate, CUNY Graduate Center) holds a *laurea magistrale* in Italian Studies from University of Rome 3, with a thesis on the interplay between medieval and twentieth-century poetry in Italy. His main interests include Italian twentieth-century literature, Modernism, and film studies. His doctoral dissertation explores the representation of space in Italian World War I poetry.

Millicent Marcus (PhD, Yale) is a professor of Italian and chair of the Department of Italian Language and Literature at Yale University. Her interdisciplinary research of Italian culture incorporates the study of literature, history, and film. She is author of *Italian Film in the Shadow of Auschwitz* (2007), *After Fellini: National Cinema in the Postmodern Age* (2002), *Filmmaking by the Book: Italian Cinema and Literary Adaptation* (1993), and *Italian Film in the Light of Neorealism* (1986).

Nicoletta Marini-Maio (PhD, University of Pennsylvania) is an associate professor of Italian and Film Studies at Dickinson College. Her research centers on the intersections between politics, cultural discourse, and gender in Italian film and theater. She authored *A Very Seductive Body Politic: Silvio Berlusconi in Cinema* (2015) and coedited several volumes (*Body of State: A Nation Divided*, 2011; *Dramatic Interactions*, 2011; and *Set the Stage*, 2009). She is completing a monograph on the Aldo Moro Affair and working on the collaborative research project Winxology: Grooming the Future Female Consumer. She is the editor of the international journal *Gender/Sexuality/Italy*.

Pierre Sorlin (Doctorate, Paris 1) is a professor emeritus at the University of Sorbonne Nouvelle–Paris 3 and researcher at the Parri Institute of Contemporary History in Bologna. He is the author of books on Italian cinema and the sociology of the cinema, including *Introduzione a una sociologia del cinema* (2017), *Ombre passeggere: Cinema e storia* (2014), *Dreamtelling* (2003), *Italian National Cinema 1896–1996* (1996), *European Cinemas, European Societies: 1939–1990* (1991), and *The Film in History: Restaging the Past* (1980).

Brian Tholl (PhD candidate, Rutgers University) is an instructor of Italian at Duke University. His research examines the ways in which those sent to *confino* under the fascist regime were able to engage in resistance and how they conceptualized Italy in their writing and participated in the reconstruction of the nation, and Europe after World War II.

Christian Uva (Doctorate, Roma Tre University) is an associate professor of film studies at the Roma Tre University. He is the author of *Il sistema Pixar* (2017), *L'immagine politica: Forme del contropotere tra cinema, video e fotografia nell'Italia degli anni settanta* (2015), and *Sergio Leone: Il cinema come favola politica* (2013). He has edited the following volumes: *Italian Political Cinema: Public Life, Imaginary, and Identity in Contemporary Italian Film* (coedited, 2016), *Strane storie: Il cinema e i misteri d'Italia* (2011), and *Schermi di piombo: Il terrorismo nel cinema italiano* (2007). He is also the editor of the book series Cinemaespanso (Bulzoni editore) and Cinema (Rubbettino editore), and codirector of *Cinema e Storia: Rivista di studi interdisciplinari* (Rubbettino editore).

Marina Vargau (PhD, University of Montreal) has taught language, literature, and film at the University of Montreal. Her research has focused on the cinematic poetics of Rome in Federico Fellini's films. She is also the author of several essays on Fellini, including "La figura della flâneuse nel film *Le notti di Cabiria* di Federico Fellini" (2016) and "Freud et Fellini: Une archéologie de la mémoire à Rome" (2016).

Vito Zagarrio (PhD, New York University) is a professor of film analysis at the Roma Tre University, where he teaches Italian and American cinema. He studied filmmaking at the Centro Sperimentale di Cinematografia (Italian National Film School) in Rome, and he has directed three feature films: *Tre giorni di anarchia* (*Three Days of Anarchy*, 2005), *Bonus malus* (1993), and *La donna della luna* (*Woman in the Moon*, 1988). He is also the director of the Audiovisual Production Center of Roma Tre University. He has authored many books on both American and Italian cinema, including an extensive volume in Italian on Scola, *Trevico-Cinecittà: L'avventuroso viaggio di Ettore Scola* (2002).

Luca Zamparini (PhD candidate, CUNY Graduate Center). He primarily works on Italian twentieth-century cinema and intellectual history. His dissertation is titled "From Post-war Auteurs to Global Cinema: Venice Film Festival and Canon-Making."

INDEX

Abatantuono, Diego, 104
Abete, Luigi, 258, 260, 265
Accadde al commissariato (*A Day at the Police Station*, 1954), 27
Accadde al penitenziario (Giorgio Bianchi, 1955), 27
Accattone (1961), 135–37, 143–44, 243
Adua e le compagne (*Adua and Her Friends*, 1960), 2, 25, 28–29
Agamben, Giorgio, 150, 156, 163n27, 164n46
Age (Agenore Incrocci), 11, 86n33, 223n19
Alemanno, Gianni, 254
Altman, Robert, 62
Amarcord (1974), 99n6, 112
Amelio, Gianni, 92, 99n11, 182n3, 261
americano a Roma, Un (*An American in Rome*, 1954), 2, 27, 274, 282
Amici miei (*My Dear Friends*, 1975), 72, 86n34, 237, 241n3
Amidei, Sergio, 40n5, 58, 217, 220, 270
Anderson, Perry, 221, 225n54
Andrejevic, Mark, 149, 154, 163
Andreotti, Giulio, 223n20, 250
Angeletti, Pio, 248
Ángel Exterminator, El (*The Exterminating Angel*, 1962), 231
Annicchiarico, Vito, 98
Anton, Edoardo, 28
Antonioni, Michelangelo, 1, 9, 56, 58, 92, 278, 287n25
Aprà, Adriano, 105, 114n5
arcidiavolo, L' (*The Devil in Love*, 1966), 10, 17, 51, 64n3
Asquer, Enrica, 219, 222n6, 225n44
Astruc, Alexandre, 109, 112, 115n20
avventura, L' (1960), 9

Bakhtin, Mikhail, 70–71, 85n9
Ballando ballando (*Le bal*, 1983), xiii, 6 27, 93, 128, 269, 280, 282–84

bambolona, La (*Baby Doll*, 1968), 76
Barattoni, Luca, 51, 65n13
Barrault, Jean-Louis, 112
Barthes, Roland, 47
Battleship Potemkin (1925), 56, 59, 202n22
Bazin, André, 62, 66n24
Belli, Giuseppe Gioachino, 8, 194
Bellocchio, Marco, 214
Benigni, Roberto, 89, 192
Bentham, Jeremy, 15, 149, 150, 153–54, 163n15
Berlinguer, Enrico, 143, 244, 249
Berlusconi, Silvio, 16, 81, 86, 207–12, 214, 217–25, 246, 251, 253–54
Bertolucci, Bernardo, 58, 264n17
Bertoni, Clotilde, 29
Biancaneve e i sette ladri (*Snow White and the Seven Thieves*, 1949), 47
Bianchi, Giorgio, 27, 48, 64
Bíspuri, Ennio, 3–5, 17–18, 40–41, 106, 114, 171, 183, 185, 188, 202, 212, 223–24, 285–86, 290
Blasetti, Alessandro, 84, 191
Block-notes di un regista (1969), 15, 186, 191, 193, 196, 198
Bloom, Harold, 187, 201
Bondanella, Peter, xxvii, 8, 19, 171, 201
Borelli, Nicola, 259
borghese piccolo piccolo, Un (*An Average Little Man*, 1977), 72, 76, 84, 86
Borghesio, Carlo, 48
Borrione, Francesca, xv, 14, 131–45, 243n14, 305
Bowen, Edward, 16, 245–66, 305
Brasseur, Pierre, 212
Brecht, Bertolt, 274
Brown, Ritza, 140
Brunetta, Gian Piero, xv, xvii, 17, 213–14, 224n26, 227, 242n5, 269–87, 305
Brutti, sporchi e cattivi (*Down and Dirty*, 1976), 4, 14, 26, 40, 68, 72–75, 82, 105, 132,

Brutti, sporchi e cattivi (continued) 144, 188–89, 230, 243, 257, 264, 277–78, 281–82
Buñuel, Luis, 231

Cadel, Francesca, 134, 144
cagna, La (*The Bitch*, 1972), 214
Calvino, Italo, 109–10, 115, 136–37, 144, 178, 185n30, 271
Campanile, Pasquale Festa, 270
Canova, Gianni, 77, 79, 86n26, 103, 113n2, 212, 223
Capra, Frank, 45
Cardinale, Claudia, 99
Carducci, Giosué, 275
Carocci, Valerio, xix, 163, 155, 257–58, 265n46
Cascio, Salvatore, 99
Castellitto, Sergio, 104
Cattini, Alberto, 6, 19n19
cena, La (*The Dinner*, 1998), 7, 27, 102, 130n11, 189, 203n43, 275, 277, 279, 280, 286
C'eravamo tanto amati (*We All Loved Each Other So Much*, 1974), xiii, 6, 8, 10, 12, 14, 16, 27, 29–30, 35, 40, 42, 44, 45–46, 48, 54–63, 79, 90, 93, 106–8, 116–18, 122–25, 128–30, 134, 137, 165, 178, 180–81, 188–93, 202–3, 211, 213, 215–16, 226, 228–32, 236, 240, 242, 264, 270, 272, 275–78, 281–82, 286–87
Cervantes, Miguél de, 274
Chaplin, Charlie, 92, 107, 184
Che ora è? (*What Time Is It?*, 1989), 6, 10, 19n20, 120, 123–24, 129n11, 234n31, 249–50, 280
Che strano chiamarsi Federico (*How Strange to Be Named Federico*, 2013), 3, 8–9, 13, 24, 46–48, 103, 111–12, 115, 190, 210, 246, 258, 278
Chiari, Mario, 28
Chiari, Walter, 47–48
Churchill, Winston, 57
Cilento, Fabrizio, vii, xv, 9, 12, 44–66, 305
Cirillo, Claudio, 46, 64n3
Colasanti, Donatella, 135–36, 138
Colleoni, Federica, viii, xv, 15, 165–85, 306
Collinson, Peter, 175
Comand, Mariapia, vii, xv, xix, 9, 12, 23–43, 306
Comencini, Luigi, 65n18, 74, 84, 223n19, 227

commissario Pepe, Il (*Police Chief Pepe*, 1969), 44, 52, 55, 61, 63n2, 65, 214, 223, 228, 286n17
Concorrenza sleale (*Unfair Competition*, 2001), 5, 10, 13–14, 18n3, 33, 89–91, 93, 95, 100n4, 103–7, 114n6, 272, 279, 286
Confessione di un commissario di polizia al procuratore della Repubblica (*Confession of a Police Captain*, 1971), 214
congiuntura, La (*Hard Time for Princes*, 1964), 17n1, 51, 63n2, 64n3, 275, 281, 287n31
Conrad, Joseph, 241, 274
Corridori, Massimo, 259, 265
Craxi, Bettino, 251

Damiani, Damiano, 214
Dauphin, Claude, 212
Day the Earth Stood Still, The (1951), 26
De Bellis, Vito, 2, 40n2
De Filippo, Edoardo, 274
De Filippo, Peppino, 47
De Gaetano, Roberto, 71–2, 85n13, 86n25
De Giusti, Luciano, 150, 155, 162n4, 163n23
De Gregori, Francesco, 198
Deleuze, Gilles, 14, 186, 187, 200, 201n5, 202n9, 204n52
De Matteo, Ivano, 8
De Pascalis, Nevio, 64n5, 114n4, 247, 264n30, 266n70
De Quevedo, Francisco, 274
De Renzi, Mario, 154
De Santis, Giuseppe, xix, 260–61
Deserto rosso (*Red Desert*, 1964), 56
De Sica, Vittorio, 54, 60, 84n4, 100n3, 102, 108, 110, 139, 169, 171, 202, 270–71, 277–78, 285n1
Di Bianco, Laura, 19n36
Dionisi, Marco, 64n5, 114n4, 247, 264n30, 266n70
dolce vita, La (1960), 9, 59, 108, 188–91, 195, 198, 200, 202n22, 203n24, 224, 232, 235, 277, 278
Dostoevsky, Fyodor, 192–93, 274
Dramma della gelosia—tutti i particolari in cronaca (*The Pizza Triangle*, 1970), 10, 26, 63n2, 64n3, 65n20, 82, 189, 276
Dumas, Alexandre, 54, 275
Dürrenmatt, Friedrich, 79, 212, 217, 218, 224n29, 292

Ecce Bombo (1978), 234
eclisse, L' (1962), 9
Eco, Umberto, 187, 201
Eisenstein, Sergei, 56
Ekberg, Anita, 190
Ellero, Roberto, 18n9, 52, 63n1, 64n11, 65n15, 242n4, 243n12
Esposito, Roberto, 152, 162n10

Fabrizi, Aldo, 46, 98, 229, 236
Fagioli, Alessandra, 7, 19n22
famiglia, La (*The Family*, 1987), 6, 7, 10, 14, 25, 27, 35, 38, 93, 127, 130n11, 189, 203n43, 244n31, 275, 279, 280, 282–83
Fantasmi a Roma (*Phantom Lovers*, 1961), 28
Fears, Rufus, 247, 263n7
Fellini, Federico, viii, xv, 1, 2, 8, 9, 15, 18, 20n37, 24, 32, 43n30, 56, 58, 59, 66n25, 92, 99n6, 108, 109, 111–15, 186–201, 202n12, 203n24, 204n44, 216, 217, 224n32, 232, 251, 264n29, 270, 271, 277–78, 286n17
Fermi tutti arrivo io! (1953), 26, 41, 64n5
Ferreri, Marco, 65n18, 72, 74, 84, 85n19, 214
Ferrero-Regis, Tiziana, 14, 19n36
Fiorentini, Fiorenzo, 195
Fò, Dario, 198
Foà, Anna, 100n5
Foà, Arnoldo, 192
Fofi, Goffredo, 171, 183n14, 185n5, 271
Forte, Enrico, 261
'43–'97 (1997), 13, 18n3, 89–101
Foucault, Michel, 14–15, 138, 140, 145n20, 149, 153–59, 163n20, 164n41, 187, 201n8
Franceschini, Dario, 257, 266n61
Fullwood, Natalie, 14, 19n36, 51, 65n13
Fusillo, Massimo, 29, 42n18

Galbraith, John Kenneth, 135, 144n12
Gassman, Vittorio, 3, 7, 9–10, 38, 45, 46, 48, 51, 61, 63n3, 67, 85n18, 99n4, 117, 126–27, 132, 133, 139, 191, 229, 232, 236, 238, 242n11, 271, 274, 275, 286n16, 287n31
Gattopardo, Il (*The Leopard*, 1963), 99
gaucho, Il (*The Gaucho*, 1964), 25, 26, 41n10
Gauthier, Théophile, 274
Genette, Gérard, 47
Genovese, Paolo, 8
Gente di Roma (*People of Rome*, 2003), viii, 8, 13, 14, 15, 89, 95, 97, 98, 103, 107–13, 114n18, 115n25, 186, 188, 189, 191–200, 201n3, 203n25, 204n44, 209

Gentilomo, Giacomo, 47
Germi, Pietro, 28, 203n24, 239, 241n3, 242n8
Ghira, Andrea, 135, 140
Giacovelli, Enrico, 76, 85n23
Gieri, Manuela, 18n3, 62, 63, 66n25, 202n12, 234, 243n21
Ginsborg, Paul, 219, 222n6, 225n44, 263n11, 264n19
giornata particolare, Una (*A Special Day*, 1977), viii, xiii, xiv, 5, 6, 7, 10–11, 14–16, 19n20, 25, 27, 35, 38, 99, 104, 106–7, 110, 120, 125, 127, 129, 149–50, 161, 162n2, 163n22, 189, 218, 224n27, 230, 243n16, 264n16, 272, 275–76, 285n3
giorno in pretura, Un (*A Day in Court*, 1954), 274
Giraldi, Franco, 76, 264n17
Goldoni, Carlo, 274
Gorfinkel, Elena, 14, 19n36, 151, 162n9
Gozzano, Guido, 275
Gramsci, Antonio, 132, 211
grande abbuffata, La (*The Big Feast*, 1973), 72, 84, 85n19
Grandjacquet, Francesco, 98
Gravina, Carla, 121, 131, 235, 236
Gray, Nadia, 198
Great Dictator, The (1940), 92, 107
Gregoretti, Ugo, xix, 248, 258, 259, 263n13, 264n17, 265n55
Grieco, Sergio, 26, 64n5
Grossi, Marco, xix, 261, 266n67
Guaraldo, Emiliano, viii, xv, 15, 165–85, 306
Guido, Gianni, 135, 140

Hesse, Hermann, 54
Histoire de rire (*Foolish Husbands*, 1941), 26
Horace, 275

Ieracitano, Giuseppe, 99
Io la conoscevo bene (*I Knew Her Well*, 1965), 28–31, 43n27, 44, 51–52, 59–60, 64n3, 239
Io Piaccio (1955), 48
Italian Job, The (1969), 175
It's a Wonderful Life (1946), 45
Izzo, Angelo, 135, 140

Jacometti, Alberto, 152, 162n11
James, William, 275

Kezich, Tullio, 44, 48, 56, 63n2, 64n11, 202n16, 260

Koscina, Sylvia, 49
Kracauer, Siegfried, 197, 204n48

Ladri di biciclette (*Bicycle Thieves*, 1948), 8, 99n2, 171, 202n22, 277, 285n2
ladro di bambini, Il (*Stolen Children*, 1992), 99
Lagostena Bassi, Tina, 137–38
Lancaster, Burt, 99
Landy, Marcia, 10, 19n31, 42n22
Lang, Jack, 251
Lanzoni, Rémi, vii, xv, 40n4, 65n18, 66n22, 67–86, 244n24, 306
Laudadio, Felice, xix, 252, 265n38
Lefebvre, Henri, 14, 15, 172, 173, 184n20
Lemmon, Jack, 124
Leopardi, Giacomo, 275
L'Herbier, Marcel, 26
Lizzani, Carlo, xi, 110, 115n23, 258, 260, 264n17
Lopez, Rosaria, 135–36, 138, 140
Loren, Sophia, xiii, xiv, 6, 9, 10, 11, 38, 84n4, 99, 125, 139, 150, 189, 243n16
Lotta Continua, 168, 182n6
Lotta Continua a Napoli (*Continuous Struggle in Naples*, 1971), 55, 263
Lo Verso, Enrico, 99
Lualdi, Antonella, 49

Maccari, Ruggero, 2, 3, 9, 24, 26, 27, 28, 41n11, 47, 86n33, 223n19, 270
Maccheroni (*Macaroni*, 1985), 124, 129, 280, 282
Maggiorani, Lamberto, 99
Magnani, Anna, 98, 195, 197, 204n44
magnifico cornuto, Il (*The Magnificent Cuckold*, 1964), 28, 76
Manfredi, Nino, 46, 64n3, 67, 73, 85n18, 117, 143n4, 230, 241n2, 243n11, 271
Mangano, Silvana, 191
Manzoni, Alessandro, 25, 40n3, 233
Marc'Aurelio, 2, 9, 12, 24, 27, 29, 40, 44, 46, 48, 52, 57, 58, 63, 112, 188, 262, 270
Marchegiani, Fiorenza, 99
Marchesi, Marcello, 2, 24, 28, 41n11, 44, 47, 48, 58, 64n4, 285
marcia su Roma, La (*March on Rome*, 1962), 242
Marcucci, Dario, viii, xv, 7, 16, 226–44, 307
Marcus, Millicent, vii, xv, xvii, 5, 8, 13, 14, 17n3, 18, 19n28, 20, 43n35, 66n23, 89–101, 105–6, 114, 162, 217, 224, 225n37, 264, 307

Marinelli, Giovanna, 256
Marini-Maio, Nicoletta, viii, xv, 16, 86n32, 207–25, 307
Marino, Ignazio, 256
Marino, Salvatore, 110, 200
Mario, Maria e Mario (*Mario, Maria and Mario*, 1993), 249
Martone, Mario, 261
Maselli, Citto, xi, 259, 264n17
Masi, Stefano, 17, 68, 84n5, 112, 115n21, 130, 248, 263n9
Mastrandea, Valerio, 110
Mastrocinque, Camillo, 48
Mastroianni, Marcello, xiii, 6–9, 10–11, 18n16, 29, 38, 61, 64n3, 84n4, 85n19, 99, 121, 123–25, 131–33, 139, 150, 168, 189, 191, 193, 224n25, 232, 235, 243n16, 244n31, 271
mattatore, Il (*Love and Larceny*, 1960), 25, 63
Mattoli, Mario, 18, 24, 64n9
Medici, Antonio, 253
Metz, Vittorio, 2, 24, 28, 41, 44, 47–48, 58, 64, 285
Miccichè, Lino, xii, xvi, 57, 63n2, 65n19, 66n21, 114n5, 115n23, 238, 244n26, 255
Miracolo a Milano (*Miracle in Milan*, 1951), 102–3, 277
Mirzoeff, Nicholas, 176, 184
mondo nuovo, Il (*That Night in Varennes*, 1982), 6, 10, 105–6, 112, 270, 272, 285, 286n14
Monicelli, Mario, 4, 12, 24, 55, 58, 65n18, 71–72, 74, 77, 82, 84, 85n22, 86n26, 99, 223, 227, 237, 241n3, 242n8, 243n20, 258
Montaldo, Giuliano, xi, 261, 264n17
Monti, Mario, 259
Montini, Franco, 8, 19n25, 202n17, 266n62
Morandini, Morando, 142, 145n24, 241n1, 243n13
Moravia, Alberto, 25, 41n8, 136, 144n16
Mordi e fuggi (*The Dirty Weekend*, 1973), 55, 71, 85n12
Moretti, Linda, 73
Moretti, Nanni, 92, 94, 198–99, 234, 243n20
Morlion, Padre, 26
Moro, Aldo, 65n17, 79
Morricone, Ennio, 137
Mosca, Umberto, 112, 115n31, 270
mostri, I (1963), 2, 4, 46, 58
Mussolini, Benito, 15, 92, 149–50, 152, 157–60, 163n23, 164n37, 193, 258, 272
Muti, Ornella, xiii, 77

Napolitano, Giorgio, 259
Napolitano, Ricardo, 145n24, 241n1
Nata di marzo (*March's Child*, 1958), 25–26, 28–29
Negri, Antonio, 25, 26, 28, 29
Nel nome del padre (*In the Name of the Father*, 1972), 214
Noiret, Philippe, 85n19, 99
nostri ragazzi, I (*The Dinner*, 2014), 8, 19n24
notte, La (1961), 9
notti di Cabiria, Le (*Nights of Cabiria*, 1957), 199, 202n15
Novelli, Diego, 171, 183n14, 184n17, 249
nuovi mostri, I (*Viva Italia!*, 1977), 4, 46, 58, 69, 70, 73, 76–79, 82–83, 86n29, 211, 223, 237
Nuovo Cinema Paradiso (*Cinema Paradiso*, 1988), 92, 99, 108, 184

Occhetto, Achille, 241, 244n32, 249
O'Leary, Alan, 65n18, 71, 85n16
Olson, Kirby, 70, 85n11
O'Neil, Eugene, 48, 59
Orsina, Giovanni, 209, 222n5

Palombella rossa (*Red Wood Pigeon*, 1989), 94, 99
Paolella, Domenico, 26, 28, 41n11, 64n5, 243n18
Paoli, Enrico, 210, 223n12
parmigiana, La (*The Girl from Parma*, 1963), 25, 27–29, 44, 51, 52, 63
Pasolini, Pier Paolo, viii, 1, 14, 58, 131–37, 141, 145n26, 195, 228, 230, 242n9, 243n14, 278, 287n27
Passione d'amore (*Passion of Love*, 1981), 17n1, 231, 240, 244n31, 275, 276, 278, 282
Patriarca, Silvana, 219, 222n4, 225n47
Pellegrini, Glauco, 28
Perego, Gianni, 10, 229, 230, 242n11
Perfetti sconosciuti (*Perfect Strangers*, 2016), 8
Petri, Elio, 171, 184n29, 223n19
Pietrangeli, Antonio, xii, 2, 12, 23, 25–33, 40n5, 42n16, 43n27, 44, 47, 51, 58, 64n3, 65n14, 76, 239, 270
Pirandello, Luigi, 18n3, 66n25, 202n12, 274
più bella serata della mia vita, La (*The Most Wonderful Evening of My Life*, 1972), viii, 4, 10, 16, 27, 69, 79, 81, 83, 86n32, 125, 207–17, 220, 221, 224n34, 281

Pizzolato, Nicola, 169, 182n8
Poe, Edgar Allan, 224n32, 274
Pontecorvo, Gillo, 171, 247, 264n17
Porporati, Andrea, 253
Pravadelli, Veronica, 9, 19
Prodi, Romano, 246
Professione: Reporter (*The Passenger*, 1975), 278

Quinterno, Angiolina, 140

Ralli, Giovanna, 46, 49, 64n3, 236
Ravera, Lidia, 261, 266n65
Recchia, Antonia Pasqua, 259
Reggiani, Serge, 133, 236
règle du jeu, La (*The Rules of the Game*, 1939), 32
Reich, Jacqueline, 5, 18n16, 213, 224n25
Renoir, Jean, 32
Rhodes, John David, 14, 19n36, 151, 162n9
Ricceri, Luciano, xv, 10, 13, 75, 104, 112
Ricomincio da tre (*I'm Starting from Three*, 1981), 99
Ridendo e scherzando (*Laughing and Joking*, 2015), xii, 10, 243n18, 246, 263n5
Rigoletto, Sergio, 10, 19n32, 151, 161, 162n2, 164n45, 220, 222n4, 225n50
Risi, Dino, 2, 4, 6, 10, 25–26, 40, 46, 55, 58, 63, 65n18, 71–74, 76, 77, 85n12, 86n33, 94, 99, 191, 202n23, 223n19, 242n8, 270, 274
Riusciranno i nostri eroi a ritrovare l'amico misteriosamente scomparso in Africa? (*Will Our Heroes Be Able to Find Their Friend Who Has Mysteriously Disappeared in Africa?* 1968), 44, 53, 55, 57, 61, 64n3, 241n2
Rocco e i suoi fratelli (*Rocco and His Brothers*, 1960), 167
Roma (1972), 109
Roma, città aperta (*Rome, Open City*, 1945), 94, 98, 105, 180
Rondolino, Gianni, 7, 19n21
Roosevelt, Franklin, 57
Rosand, David, 34, 43n31
Rosi, Francesco, 20n37, 92, 95, 99, 100n9, 171, 247
Rossellini, Roberto, 28, 58, 86n30, 92, 94, 98, 105, 114n5, 180, 195, 271
Rossetti, Eva, 30
Rousseau, Jean-Jacques, 276

Salò o le 120 giornate di Sodoma (*Salò or the 120 Days of Sodom*, 1975), 28, 228
Sandrelli, Stefania, 9, 43, 45, 46, 51, 59, 61, 64n3, 117, 126, 190, 192, 195, 196, 199, 203n42, 239
Satta-Flores, Stefano, 7, 54, 58, 117, 229, 236, 243n11
Scalici, Valentina, 99
scapolo, Lo (*The Bachelor*, 1955), 2, 26, 28
Scarpelli, Furio, xi, 2, 12, 46, 55, 103, 223n11, 270
Schopenhauer, Arthur, 68, 84n1
Scola, Gigliola, xix, 43n26, 248, 252, 263n10, 264n18
Scola, Paola, xii, 10, 246
Scola, Silvia, xii, xix, 10, 43n26, 223, 246
scopone scientifico, Lo (*The Scientific Cardplayer*, 1972), 84
Senso (1954), 278
Se permettete parliamo di donne (*Let's Talk about Women*, 1964), 3, 10, 30, 44, 48–51, 57, 63, 64, 66, 113, 226
Sessomatto (*How Funny Can Sex Be?*, 1973), 72, 242n3
Signore e signori, buonanotte (*Goodnight, Ladies and Gentlemen*, 1976), 82, 211, 223n19
Simeone, Giuseppe, 261, 266
Simon, Michel, 79, 86n31, 212
Simonelli, Giorgio, 27, 64n9
Snyder, Susan, 69, 78, 84n6, 85n7
sole negli occhi, Il (*Empty Eyes*, 1953), 28, 29
soliti ignoti, I (*Big Deal on Madonna Street*, 1958), 86n34, 99n3
Sordi, Alberto, 8–10, 16, 26, 29, 41n12, 53, 67, 73, 74, 76, 78, 79, 80, 82, 85, 86, 125, 204n44, 208, 212, 218, 220, 224n29, 225n40, 235, 237, 271, 281, 286n18
Sorlin, Pierre, viii, xv, 14, 116–30, 307
sorpasso, Il (*The Easy Life*, 1962), 2, 3, 25, 63, 94, 99, 278, 286n16, 287n31
Souvenir d'Italie (*It Happened in Rome*, 1957), 28
Spaak, Catherine, 51
Spagnoli, Marco, xix, 225n40, 252, 265n39
Splendor (1988), 9, 26, 35, 92, 93, 108, 255, 256, 277, 278, 283, 284, 286, 305
Staiola, Enzo, 60, 99
Stalin, Joseph, 57, 120
Stewart-Steinberg, Suzanne, 113, 115n19
successo, Il (1963), 283

Tarchetti, Iginio Ugo, 231, 275
Taviani, Paolo, xv, 92
Taviani, Vittorio, xv, 92
terrazza, La (*The Terrace*, 1980), viii, 7, 9–16, 26, 41n10, 44, 58, 61, 62, 82, 83, 120–45, 189, 203n43, 211, 226, 231, 233, 236, 238, 240–42, 244n25, 247–49, 279
Tholl, Brian, viii, xv, 10, 14, 15, 149–64, 307
Todorov, Tzvetan, 47
Tognazzi, Ugo, 7, 52, 61, 67, 85n18, 132, 133, 139, 232
Tornatore, Giuseppe, 92, 99, 108
Totò, 2, 18n4, 24, 29, 47, 48, 59, 64, 99, 102, 203, 285n9
Totò, Vittorio e la dottoressa (*The Lady Doctor*, 1957), 48
Totò Tarzan (1950), 18, 24, 285
Tovaglieri, Alberto, 238, 244
Tozzi, Fausto, 72
Trastevere (1971), 72
Travolti da un insolito destino nell'azzurro mare d'agosto (*Swept Away*, 1974), 72, 241n3
tregua, La (*The Truce*, 1997), 92, 99, 100n9
Trevico-Torino: Viaggio nel Fiat-Nam (*Trevico-Torino: Voyage in Fiatnam*, 1973), xvi, 5, 17, 19n21, 40n5, 55, 66n21, 113n2, 114n7, 165–85, 229, 247–48
Trintignant, Jean-Louis, 7, 58, 99, 128, 133, 232, 283, 286n16
Trintignant, Marie, 128
Troisi, Massimo, 6, 9, 99, 123, 144n6, 244
Tronti, Mario, 15, 172, 184n19
Trovajoli, Armando, 10, 46, 64n3, 197, 216

Uccellacci e uccellini (*The Hawks and the Sparrows*, 1966), 278
Unità, L', 3, 114, 183n14, 189, 263n16, 279
Uva, Christian, viii, xii, xv, 13, 14, 20n37, 102–15, 162n5, 213, 214, 224n27, 308

Valentini, Mariella, 99
Vanel, Charles, 212
Vanzina, Stefano, 2
Vargau, Marina, viii, 8, 15, 186–204, 308
Veltroni, Walter, xix, 3, 18n8, 250, 251, 264n23
viaggio di Capitan Fracassa, Il (*The Voyage of Captain Fracassa*, 1990), xiii, 10, 61, 244n31, 279
Vicari, Daniele, xix, 253, 254, 265n41

Vidal, Gore, 109, 194
Villa, Federica, 41n7, 42n15
Visconti, Luchino, 1, 58, 99, 167, 195, 271, 278
visita, La (*The Visit*, 1963), 2, 27–29
vita difficile, Una (1961), 191, 202, 242n8
vita è bella, La (*Life Is Beautiful*, 1997), 89
Vitti, Monica, 9
voce della luna, La (*The Voice of the Moon*, 1990), 193
Vogliamo i colonnelli (*We Want the Colonels*, 1973), 55
Volonté, Gian Maria, 16, 247, 253, 265n43
Vorrei che volo (*I Would Like to Fly*, 1982), 109, 171–72, 248

Wenders, Wim, 245, 263n2
Wertmüller, Lina, 65, 72, 241n3
Wise, Robert, 26

Zagarrio, Vito, xvi, 17n2, 19n 21, 40n5, 42n14, 66n21, 101n10, 113n1, 114n7, 115n32, 130n7, 144n8, 145n23, 162n4, 182n7, 184n17, 201n2, 202n17, 222n1, 265n45, 286n13, 308
Zampa, Luigi, 58, 65n18
Zamparini, Luca, viii, xv, 7, 16, 226–44, 308
Zavattini, Cesare, 9, 58, 110, 115n24, 169, 183n11, 192, 196–97, 200, 204n47, 269–71, 277
Zingaretti, Nicola, 261

www.ingramcontent.com/pod-product-compliance
Lightning Source LLC
Chambersburg PA
CBHW052045220426
43663CB00012B/2446